SUBSTANCE ABUSE IN AMERICA

Recent Titles in
Documentary and Reference Guides

The Patriot Act: A Documentary and Reference Guide
Herbert N. Foerstel

Abortion: A Documentary and Reference Guide
Melody Rose

Immigration: A Documentary and Reference Guide
Thomas Cieslik, David Felsen, Akis Kalaitzidis

Gun Control: A Documentary and Reference Guide
Robert J. Spitzer

Culture Wars in America: A Documentary and Reference Guide
Glenn H. Utter

Civil Liberties and the State: A Documentary and Reference Guide
Christopher Peter Latimer

The Politics of Sexuality: A Documentary and Reference Guide
Raymond A. Smith

U.S. Election Campaigns: A Documentary and Reference Guide
Thomas J. Baldino and Kyle L. Kreider

U.S. Foreign Policy: A Documentary and Reference Guide
Akis Kalaitzidis and Gregory W. Streich

White-Collar and Corporate Crime: A Documentary and Reference Guide
Gilbert Geis

Homelessness: A Documentary and Reference Guide
Neil Larry Shumsky

Victims' Rights: A Documentary and Reference Guide
Douglas E. Beloof

SUBSTANCE ABUSE IN AMERICA

A Documentary and Reference Guide

James A. Swartz

GREENWOOD

AN IMPRINT OF ABC-CLIO, LLC
Santa Barbara, California • Denver, Colorado • Oxford, England

Library of Congress Cataloging-in-Publication Data

Swartz, James, 1955–
Substance abuse in America : a documentary and reference guide / James A. Swartz.
p. cm. — (Documentary and reference guides)
Includes bibliographical references and index.
ISBN 978-0-313-35376-5 (hardcopy : alk. paper) — ISBN 978-0-313-35377-2 (ebook)
1. Substance abuse—United States. I. Title.
HV4999.2.S93 2012
362.290973—dc23 2012006447

ISBN: 978-0-313-35376-5
EISBN: 978-0-313-35377-2

16 15 14 13 12 1 2 3 4 5

This book is also available on the World Wide Web as an eBook.
Visit www.abc-clio.com for details.

Greenwood
An Imprint of ABC-CLIO, LLC

ABC-CLIO, LLC
130 Cremona Drive, P.O. Box 1911
Santa Barbara, California 93116-1911

This book is printed on acid-free paper ∞

Manufactured in the United States of America

To R.C., G.B., and S.S.—thank you
for your patience, love, and support.
Most of all, thank you for
believing in me.
You were always there
when it mattered.
You kept the stars apart.
—JAS

Perhaps history this century, thought Eigenvalue, is rippled with gathers in its fabric such that if we are situated, as Stencil seemed to be, at the bottom of a fold, it's impossible to determine warp, woof, or pattern anywhere else. By virtue, however, of existing in one gather it is assumed there are others, compartmented off into sinuous cycles each of which had come to assume greater importance than the weave itself and destroy any continuity. Thus it is that we are charmed by the funny-looking automobiles of the '30's, the curious fashions of the '20's, the particular moral habits of our grandparents. We produce and attend musical comedies about them and are conned into a false memory, a phony nostalgia about what they were. We are accordingly lost to any sense of continuous tradition. Perhaps if we lived on a crest, things would be different. We could at least see.

—Thomas Pynchon, *V*

CONTENTS

READER'S GUIDE TO RELATED DOCUMENTS AND SIDEBARS

Note: Some documents appear in more than one category.

Drugs and the Media

Anti-Drug Abuse Act of 1986
Drug Epidemics and the Media (sidebar)
Marijuana: Assassin of Youth
Muckraking (sidebar)
Reefer Madness (sidebar)

Drug Treatment and Prevention

Alfred R. Lindesmith (sidebar)
Comprehensive Drug Abuse Control Act of 1970
Drug Addiction, Crime or Disease—ABA-AMA Report
Global Commission on Drug Policy Report on the War on Drugs
Nancy Reagan and "Just Say No" (sidebar)
Porter Narcotic Farm Act

European Approaches to Drug Control Policy

Alfred R. Lindesmith (sidebar)
Drug Addiction, Crime or Disease—ABA-AMA Report
Nightmare in Needle Park

Federal Taxing Authority and Drug Law

Drug Abuse Control Amendments of 1965
The Harrison Narcotics Act
Marijuana Tax Act of 1937

Freud and Cocaine

The Dream of Irma's Injection (sidebar)
"Über Coca"—Sigmund Freud

Harm Reduction Programs and Policy

Nightmare in Needle Park
The Surgeon General's Report on Acquired Immunodeficiency Syndrome
Syringe Exchange Programs in the United States (sidebar)

Harry J. Anslinger and the Federal Bureau of Narcotics

The Boggs Act
Marijuana: Assassin of Youth
Marijuana Tax Act of 1937
Narcotic Control Act of 1956
Reefer Madness (sidebar)

HIV/AIDS and Drug Abuse

HIV/AIDS in the United States 2011 (sidebar)
The Origins of HIV (sidebar)
The Surgeon General's Report on Acquired Immunodeficiency Syndrome

Legalization, Decriminalization, and Depenalization

The Gateway Hypothesis (sidebar)
Global Commission on Drug Policy Report on the War on Drugs
Nightmare in Needle Park
Proposition 215—the Compassionate Use Act of 1996

LSD and Hallucinogenic Drugs

Inside the Hippie Revolution
Psychedelics (sidebar)

Marijuana

The Boggs Act
The Gateway Hypothesis (sidebar)
Hemp for Victory (sidebar)
The La Guardia Report, a Study of the Marijuana Problem
Marijuana: Assassin of Youth
Marijuana Tax Act of 1937
Milton Mesirow (sidebar)
Nancy Reagan and "Just Say No" (sidebar)
Narcotic Control Act of 1956
Proposition 215—the Compassionate Use Act of 1996
Reefer Madness (sidebar)
Robert Mitchum—Hollywood and Bust (sidebar)

Medical Marijuana

The Gateway Hypothesis (sidebar)
Proposition 215—the Compassionate Use Act of 1996

Methamphetamine

Combat Methamphetamine Act of 2005
Dr. Max Jacobson (aka "Dr. Feelgood") (sidebar)
Drug Abuse Control Amendments of 1965
Inside the Hippie Revolution

Mexico, Drug Production, and the Mexican Drug War

Black Tar Heroin—the Xalisco Connection (sidebar)
Texas Heroin Massacre

Morphine, Heroin, Opium, and Other Opioids

Alfred R. Lindesmith (sidebar)
Black Tar Heroin—the Xalisco Connection (sidebar)
The Boggs Act
Comprehensive Drug Abuse Control Act of 1970
The Great American Fraud—*Collier's Weekly*
The Harrison Narcotics Act
Narcotic Control Act of 1956
Negro Cocaine "Fiends" New Southern Menace
Opiates and Opioids (sidebar)
Our Most Dangerous Epidemic—Vietnam Veterans on Heroin
Rush Limbaugh (sidebar)
Texas Heroin Massacre
What Is a Narcotic? (sidebar)

Musicians and Drug Abuse

Amy Winehouse (sidebar)
Charlie Parker (sidebar)
Elvis Presley (sidebar)
Inside the Hippie Revolution
Milton Mesirow (sidebar)
Porter Narcotic Farm Act
This Is the Beat Generation
Texas Heroin Massacre

Organized Crime, Drug Cartels, and Drug Trafficking

Black Tar Heroin—the Xalisco Connection (sidebar)
Bootleggers, Rumrunners, and Speakeasies
Carlos Lehder (sidebar)
Chicago Gangsters Slain by Firing Squad, the Saint Valentine's Day Massacre
The Cocaine Scene
Griselda Blanco (sidebar)
The Kefauver Commission Report on Organized Crime
President Bush's Address to the Nation on Drug Control Strategy

Patent Medicines

The Great American Fraud—*Collier's Weekly*
The Harrison Narcotics Act
Muckraking (sidebar)

Prescription Drug Abuse

Amy Winehouse (sidebar)
Charlie Parker (sidebar)
Comprehensive Drug Abuse Control Act of 1970
Dr. Max Jacobson (sidebar)
Drug Abuse Control Amendments of 1965
Life: Hillbilly Hell
Rush Limbaugh (sidebar)
This Is the Beat Generation

Prohibition

Amendment 18 to the Constitution, the Prohibition Act
Amendment 21 to the Constitution, Repeal of Prohibition
Bootleggers, Rumrunners, and Speakeasies
7 Moran Gangsters Slain, the Saint Valentine's Day Massacre

Racism and Sentencing Disparities in Drug Policy

Anti-Drug Abuse Act of 1986
Negro Cocaine "Fiends" New Southern Menace
Marijuana: Assassin of Youth
Young Black Americans and the Criminal Justice System: Five Years Later

Synthetic and Designer Drugs

Synthetic Cannabis and Bath Salts (sidebar)

Vietnam, Heroin Abuse by Soldiers

Our Most Dangerous Epidemic—Vietnam Veterans on Heroin

World War II Effects on Drug Availability

Hemp for Victory! (sidebar)
The Kefauver Commission Report on Organized Crime
The La Guardia Report, a Study of the Marijuana Problem

FOREWORD

FORGOTTEN BUT NOT GONE: A CENTURY OF THE DRUG WAR

David T. Courtwright

Writers have been assembling documents about drug use and drug policy since 1928, when Charles Terry and Mildred Pellens published *The Opium Problem*, a compendium of knowledge about narcotics. By providing generous excerpts from historical and contemporary sources, Terry and Pellens made it easy for their readers to grasp what James Swartz calls "the unappreciated continuities" of drug history.

This book performs a similar service. Some of Swartz's sources, such as journalist Paul Tough's account of OxyContin abuse, are nothing short of remarkable. To listen to Tough's interviewees describe the seductive high of prescription narcotics and the misery of withdrawal is to hear words that might have been spoken by a heroin addict 50 years ago—or by a morphine addict 100 years ago. The biology of drug use and addiction has little changed.

The sociological continuities are almost as impressive. Many of the users we encounter in these pages—black men on cocaine, jazz musicians on heroin, hippies on everything—were socially marginal, or bohemian, or both. The road to actor Robert Mitchum's sensational 1948 marijuana bust reportedly ran, not through Hollywood, but through Mitchum's vagabond days when he smoked pot to cope with the ardors of hobo life. It is a revealing anecdote, one of several that testify to the enduring importance of social circumstance in explaining who uses which drugs and why.

Harder to explain are the policy continuities that Swartz characterizes as "monotone." For the better part of a century the government has sought to maintain strict control for medical narcotics like morphine and total prohibition of a handful of drugs like heroin or marijuana. "The forgotten war" against these substances has also turned out to be America's longest war, stretching from the gangster-smuggler era centered on New York City to today's high-volume traffic centered on the southwestern border. Readers will meet in these pages the long war's strategists and generals, as well as its casualties and profiteers.

Readers will also discover how much more complex and costly the drug war has become with the passing of time. In 1928, when Terry and Pellens published *The Opium Problem*, opium was, well, the problem, insofar as nonalcoholic drugs were concerned. Cocaine and marijuana use were then uncommon. Synthetic drugs like barbiturates were mostly confined to medical practice. Prohibition-related violence was sporadic. The single worst episode of bootlegger mayhem, the Saint Valentine's Day Massacre, claimed seven lives—small change compared to the drug-related battles in the contested Mexican drug-trafficking zones of our own time.

Americans are not known for tolerating long and expensive wars with disappointing results. Two years seems the limit of their patience–witness the discontent over the Korean situation by 1952, Vietnam by 1967, and Iraq by 2005. Voters punished the politicians associated with those conflicts, which the government proceeded, in one way or another, to wind down. National alcohol prohibition met a similar fate when the noble crusade fell from favor, thanks to gangsterism and corruption, a public-relations push by deep-pocketed wets, and a desperate shortage of revenue triggered by the Depression. Why then, has the American electorate tolerated the continuation and periodic escalation of the drug war, even if local majorities have occasionally mutinied over narrower questions like medical marijuana?

It is a fascinating question, and one to which Swartz's documents offer many hints. Not least of them is recurrent anxiety about the young. When the head of the Bureau of Narcotics, Harry Anslinger, called marijuana an assassin, he said that it was an "assassin of youth." When the Kefauver crime committee declared that the postwar narcotics revival had jolted the nation, it was because "youngsters, especially in larger cities, are using narcotic drugs, many to the point of addiction." President George H. W. Bush rang changes on this theme in a nationally televised 1989 speech. Holding seized crack cocaine in an evidence bag, he denounced the drug (which, he observed, might "as easily have been heroin or PCP") as a poison that was "murdering our children."

Drugs, in short, were an existential threat to the rising generation on which the nation's future depended. Like the Soviet Union during the Cold War or terrorists after 9/11, the drug menace justified far-reaching security measures and a damn-the-costs attitude. That the costs of routinized arrests and prosecutions fell disproportionately on minority communities, while anxious middle-class parents derived most of the psychological benefits, made the drug war palatable, even attractive, to politicians competing for suburban swing voters.

Swartz gives ample space to critics who concede the reality of the threat to the young, yet doubt whether the costly and politicized war has made drugs less available or less dangerous to users. These claims, too, have historical echoes, the debate over prohibition having even deeper roots than the drug war itself. In assembling these documents, Swartz has effectively invited the reader to join the debate—and to appreciate just how long and contentious has been its course.

PREFACE: THE FORGOTTEN WAR

Reviewing the historical and social contexts of drug use and drug policy in America can in no way be characterized as a happy undertaking. Far too often, those who have used drugs, those who have supplied drugs, and those who have sought to control drugs have veered into the darker corners of the human experience and instincts. Unbounded greed drives illicit drug trafficking, at least at the highest levels. Misplaced moralizing, the willful misrepresentation of data and scientific findings, racism, and political self-preservation too often have driven drug policy. Drug use, begun in an effort to enhance pleasure, increase social connectedness, satisfy curiosity, or reduce pain, frequently turns into a persisting, insistent compulsion that instead induces misery and suffering leading to the spread of disease and to a countless number of premature deaths. Still, even with that oft-repeated trajectory, alcohol and other drugs continue to be widely used and misused.

The history of U.S. drug policy is largely about the government's ongoing attempts to tamp down use and the continuing debate about the best way to do that. As different drugs waxed and waned in popularity, reflecting the repeating historical cycles noted in the epigraph by Thomas Pynchon, public perceptions enflamed by exaggerated media accounts have led to legislation that often was a belated overreaction to the latest drug "epidemic." True to the spirit of Pynchon's observations, we failed to see how trends in drug use and policy connect with and repeat past mistakes.

There is no better example of this disconnect than when cocaine reemerged in the 1970s. It was viewed as a harmless, non-addicting drug by the public and by health care professionals alike. The problem of cocaine addiction experienced in the early 1900s was simply ignored as being, perhaps, the relic of a less enlightened, less informed time. Or, perhaps, the past was simply ignored. But of course this misperception was not true and many became addicted to cocaine in the 1970s and 1980s having to learn anew the lessons of the turn of the century firsthand. As Pynchon might observe, we were situated at the bottom of an historical fold. We were there again when heroin returned as a "chic" drug in the 1990s (Snorting heroin is safe, isn't it?) when yet another new generation of users failed to appreciate the lessons of the past. Despite the repeated failure of harshly punitive drug laws to stem either drug availability or use, we continue to pass such laws again and again. "Perhaps if we lived on a crest, things would be different. We could at least see."

An implicit thesis of this book is that there are many such unappreciated continuities in drug use and policy across our history despite the unique social contexts along the way that create the gathers in the historical fabric. We simply need to position ourselves in such a way that we can see the connections. Current events seem to have blurred our perspective on drug policy further. The title of this preface, "The Forgotten War," stems from the observation that the 40-year war on drugs has taken a back seat to the war on terrorism begun with the chain of horrific events now universally known by the date on which they occurred, 9/11. But even as the country has focused on prosecuting that important war, the war on drugs continues, albeit less conspicuously than in the past.

The issues of terrorism and drugs are not unrelated. Growing the poppies that supply morphine and heroin is an important source of income for tribes in Afghanistan. While the Taliban were able to suppress heroin production for a time, it has rebounded sharply since the U.S. invasion of Afghanistan and is again a main source of revenue for that country. In Mexico, the phrase "narco-terrorism" has been used to reference the violent efforts of the powerful and well-financed drug cartels to retain and expand their drug trade and the profits derived there from in the face of growing governmental counter efforts. U.S. concerns about border security and illegal immigration are now linked with concerns about the violence that could spill across the border from Mexico into this country. These events illustrate that drug policy, while perhaps not completely forgotten, is hardly irrelevant as drugs are associated with not only terrorism but also with many other pressing domestic social concerns such as immigration, crime, homelessness, HIV/AIDS, and mental illness.

For most of our history, those who favor a law enforcement approach have won the policy debate in terms of legislation. Recently, signs of small cracks in what has been the lengthy political hegemony of the emphasis on "supply side reduction" or law enforcement and interdiction have occurred. Examples include the growing number of states legalizing marijuana for medical use, lifting the federal ban on funding for needle exchange programs, and reducing the sentencing disparities between powder and crack cocaine. However, the only certainty about the future direction of drug policy is that the sharp political divide between conservatives who favor a law enforcement approach and liberals who favor a public health approach that emphasizes treatment and prevention is that the debate will be divisive and ongoing. Most likely, America's drug policy will continue to be tilted toward law enforcement and interdiction for the near future, at least at the federal level.

Despite the dark edges and the historically monotone policy emphasis, the story of drug policy in the United States is nevertheless an engaging one that does not lack for interest. To review the history of drugs and drug policy in the United States is to embark on a mental journey that visits times, places, and people as rich and diverse as the American people, culture, and landscape permit. And every now and then, there are unintentional moments of black comedy. For instance, there was Elvis Presley visiting President Nixon to get a law enforcement badge as a drug warrior while Elvis was likely stoned on drugs. And then there was the time law enforcement discovered that separate methamphetamine "superlab" operators had so standardized the manufacturing process that they used the same high–thread count Martha Stewart sheets for filtration.

In this book, we begin the journey in the early 1900s in the pharmacies where patent "medicines" that were nothing more than opium, morphine, or cocaine dissolved in liquid (usually one containing alcohol) were peddled as cures for just about every ailment imaginable. The marketing efforts of the patent medicine manufacturers succeeded brilliantly, creating thousands of unwary addicts in the process, and foreshadowed the advertising techniques that are used in the present day in late-night infomercials that sell equally useless products and services to the gullible. From there, we move to the beginnings of the Prohibition Era when church groups in small-town Ohio and the Women's Christian Temperance Union morphed into a potent political force that made alcohol illegal, leading the popular preacher Billy Sunday to proclaim prematurely the end of the "reign of terror" at one of his massive rallies. The journey continues across time and travels to many other places:

- Visiting the speakeasies in New York City where thirsty Americans congregated for a drink or two and sailing with the rumrunners in speedy boats, the forerunners of today's cigarette boats, that ran along the eastern seaboard to supply the alcohol drunk in the speakeasies and in homes.
- Celebrating the beginning of the end of Prohibition by having a beer with President Franklin D. Roosevelt.
- Visiting the first federal treatment programs located in prisons and called narcotics farms in Lexington, Kentucky, and in Fort Worth, Texas, where extensive research on the nature of drug addiction was conducted and where so many jazz musicians were housed that people came to hear weekly concerts by the prison bands.
- Reading the sensationalized distortions characterizing marijuana as the "assassin of youth" penned by Harry J. Anslinger, truly America's first drug czar and, as head of the Federal Bureau of Narcotics, a dominant player in American drug policy for over 30 years.
- Watching the movie *Reefer Madness* in disbelief that at one time, many fully believed it accurately portrayed the effects of marijuana use.
- From a college campus and jazz clubs in New York City and an art gallery in San Francisco converted to a theater for a poetry recital, it's listening to Allen Ginsberg as he captured the angst and anomie of his generation with a new, free-form style of poetry modeled after jazz music while proselytizing for the freedoms from convention afforded by drug use.
- Witnessing a broad social movement that would merge with protests against the Vietnam War and for civil rights all the while proclaiming the use of psychedelic drugs as a means for achieving a new, more equitable, spiritually enlightened social vision.
- Watching the demise of the countercultural movement as it faded into philosophical incoherence, crass commercialism, and rampant drug use driven more by hedonism than by spirituality and idealism all within the span of a few years.
- Witnessing heroin use by American troops in the jungles of Vietnam, fostered by the leaders of the South Vietnamese government, they were there to protect and a subsequent (unrelated) series of heroin epidemics chiefly affecting America's inner cities and minorities.

- Seeing canny Columbian entrepreneurs figure out how to both supply and drive America's appetite for cocaine by importing massive amounts of cocaine through America's porous border and in the process making Miami America's "sun and gun capital."
- Witnessing a mysterious new illness that was first misconstrued as a gay disease spread to and eventually infected large numbers of hemophiliacs and injection drug users while potentially effective harm reduction programs such as needle exchanges are shunned and then subjected to a federal ban on funding.
- Watching the political fallout as the cocaine trade turns violent over gang-related territorial disputes for the rights to sell a cheap, smokable form of cocaine called crack and yet nothing is done until the death of a prominent athlete.
- Seeing America's prisons and jails fill with an unprecedented number of people convicted for drug possession and low-level trafficking as the sentencing disparities in hastily conceived drug laws lead to a disproportionate number of young, undereducated African American men being incarcerated for long periods of time.
- And when it's discovered that the time-release mechanisms that supposedly made it difficult for the latest "wonder drug" to be abused can be overcome by simply chewing or crushing the pills, it's watching the spread of addiction to "hillbilly heroin" in America's rural communities paralleled closely by the spread of methamphetamine, which is cheaply and easily (but not safely) made in home labs from over-the-counter pharmaceuticals.

This book visits all of these times and places to consider these and other events and examines not only their social and historical contexts but also some of the main actors that influenced drug policy. In total, 32 primary documents were selected for inclusion and analysis. Each section includes an excerpt or full reprinting of the document preceded by a brief passage describing its significance. The document is followed by a lengthier analysis (for most documents) of the significance in light of the historical and social context. Within the analysis, issues closely related to those raised by the document are also considered. The primary documents range from constitutional amendments to illustrative stories that appeared in the popular press, to nongovernmental commission reports that critique or defend U.S. drug policy (more the former than the latter), to government commission reports.

The documents were selected after reviewing multiple works that cover the history of drug policy including other reference guides as well as book-length considerations of one or more aspects of drug policy generally or drug policy as it pertains to a specific drug. In the review process, a number of documents or events became apparent as pivotal or important given the degree of coverage across sources. Although quite a few of the documents have been included in other collections or analyzed in other works, there are no other similar document collections of which this author is aware that includes the same set in aggregate. Most prior works have been either document histories with little of the social and cultural context provided or studies of the social and cultural context without the documents provided. This book is an attempt to do both.

Analysis of cultural determinants of changes in the patterns of drug use and of drug epidemics result in abstractions that are prone to speculation and overgeneralization more than analyses of drug trafficking patterns and availability for which at least some hard data exist, however imperfect. For instance, in the analysis of the 1960s and the countercultural movement (see "We Really Thought That Drugs Were Going to Change the World"), it is noted that despite the characterization of the era as a time of protest and growing distrust of government institutions, the majority of American college students did not smoke marijuana or use other illegal drugs. Almost to the very end, the majority of Americans continued to support the Vietnam War. Nevertheless, as long as these speculative limitations and generalizations are recognized, cultural analysis can provide insight into the convergent factors that foster a sudden increase in the popularity of one drug or another for sizeable subpopulations of Americans. Cultural analysis can also reveal the symbolic and social meanings of drugs for those who choose to use them.

Each of the primary documents and its accompanying analysis is intended to represent a starting point for reviewing the many other existing works on U.S. drug policy, including a growing amount of information available on the Internet. At the expense of some redundancy across documents, most sections were constructed so that they might be read independently of one another. The reader can select which documents are of most interest without having to read preceding documents.

Following each document and analysis, a reference list of related documents for further reading is included. Many of the source works that guided the selection of the primary documents appear in the further readings sections. These documents were selected not only to reflect the source works but also to represent a range in terms of the technical sophistication and experience assumed of the reader. The listed readings include articles published in some of the leading scientific journals, such as *Addiction*, that cover substance use and misuse. They also include press accounts and opinion pieces published in the popular media such as the *New York Times*, *Newsweek*, and *Time*. Even in the case of a scientific article, an attempt was made to exclude articles that would require knowledge of advanced statistical techniques and to include articles that summarize or review the current research or which provide commentary by researchers in the field. For the reader willing and able to brave reading articles requiring technical expertise, the included works and books provide many such additional references. The intent here was to provide readings that would be useful to some readers for whom detailed, sometimes technical pieces would be most informative while at the same time providing readings suitable for other readers newer to studying drug policy and history and for whom technical works in scientific journals might be inaccessible as yet.

Where relevant, biographical works that provide more information on one or more of the people discussed are included among the additional readings. Although drug use in America cuts across all social classes and professions, when the famous are arrested, experience an overdose, or die from their drug use, it makes headlines that very often distill and crystallize the social issues and drug-related problems of the time. Their larger-than-life stories shape the popular imagination and frame perceptions of the role(s) drugs play in society, revealing both the appeal as well as the dangers of drug use. Just as significant events in our own lives such as birthdays, weddings, births, and funerals stand in bas-relief among our recollections, celebrity-related news provides an immediately recognizable context for the politics, legislation, and concerns then extant. Thus, the stories of celebrities, the famous, and the infamous are used to highlight historical issues and bring the times into sharper focus. They also illustrate the point that no one is immune to becoming addicted to drugs regardless of their social status, wealth, or fame. Some of those included in the analysis sections or in the sidebars and the issues or drugs they highlight include:

- Sigmund Freud—Perceptions of cocaine at the turn of the century
- Al Capone—Organized crime during Prohibition
- Robert Mitchum—Marijuana policy
- Charlie Parker—Drugs and jazz
- Elvis Presley—Prescription drug abuse
- Griselda Blanco—Cocaine trafficking in the 1970s and 1980s
- Len Bias—High-profile deaths from drug misuse as motivating policy
- Kurt Cobain and Davide Sorrenti—The return of heroin as a "chic" drug
- Rush Limbaugh—How no one is immune to drug addiction
- Amy Winehouse—The continuing problems of alcohol and drug abuse

It is clear that information is increasingly becoming electronic. In the not too distant future, books on home library shelves might soon be nostalgia items akin to vinyl record albums and VHS tapes. Electronic media such as the Internet are increasingly the main sources of information for many. The Internet and other electronic media offer many advantages such as immediate access to information, frequent updates, and the incorporation of multimedia such as videos and "podcasts" to add interest and variety to the information conveyed. Toward that end, the further readings section at the end of each document is followed by an "On the Internet" list of additional, electronic references. Each Internet reference includes a brief description and the URL of the reference work. Reflecting the versatility of information presented on the Internet, these works include videos that can be streamed and watched online such as the original *Reefer Madness*, documentaries on the history of drug policy presented on shows such as *Frontline*, and documents in pdf format such as the full text of excerpted legislation. They also include websites devoted to covering drug policy and related issues and that provide links to additional electronic resources. Every effort was made to insure the links provided were active at the time this book was being prepared. But the Internet is a fluid medium and the location of a document or other resource can change quickly. If this has occurred since publication, the reader should be able to use an Internet search engine such as Google and the document name to find the updated location.

Although the book is intended to be comprehensive, it is simply not possible to tell the entire story of drug policy in America in one book. The references provided at the end of each section remedy this to an extent. But several areas of interest to the student of drug policy could not be covered within the scope of this book. In particular, the history of drug treatment is not discussed in much detail with the exception of the federal narcotics farms in the 1930s, methadone maintenance in the 1960s, and needle exchange programs in the 1980s. Beyond these, however, drug treatment has its own rich history and the interested reader is referred to William White's book *Slaying the Dragon*, which provides an excellent review of this important area. The emphasis on drug policy also did not permit coverage of the clinical and treatment aspects of substance use disorders. There are many good texts and papers on this broad topic. Marc Schuckit's book *Drug and Alcohol Abuse* is a good starting point.

As important emerging trends as they are, the recent rise of drug trafficking on the U.S.-Mexico border and the relevance of the Mexican drug war for U.S. drug policy were deemed to be too expansive and complex to allow coverage through only a few relevant documents. There are, however, an increasing number of texts devoted to this important topic. A good beginning for the interested reader is Sylvia Longmire's recently published book, *Cartel: The Invasion of Mexico's Drug Wars*. Other good sources are Ioan Grillo's *El Narco and* is John Gibler's book, *To Die in Mexico: Dispatches from inside the Drug War*.

Space limitations also led to the demise of additional planned sidebars that covered: the "British system" by which heroin was available to addicts by prescription in that country and a continuing source of debate in the harm reduction argument; Gordon Liddy's colorful take on Operation Intercept as orchestrated by the Nixon administration in 1969 to bend Mexican officials to enact policies more consistent with U.S. drug control strategy; Judy Garland, who exemplified the widespread prescribing and misuse of amphetamines and barbiturates in the 1950s and 1960s; Augustus Owsley Stanley III, the real-life "Kid Charlemagne," the Grateful Dead's master sound technician and purveyor of high-quality LSD in the 1960s; Timothy Leary, whose high-profile, insistent proselytizing for psychedelic drug use led President Nixon to label him the "most dangerous man in America"; the Rockefeller Drug Laws of the 1970s; Janis Joplin, whose untimely death was due to heroin overdose; and Gaëtan Dugas, who was mislabeled as being "Patient Zero" of the HIV/AIDS epidemic in the United States. Although these and a few other sidebars were excised, references for them remain in the relevant document sections and in the bibliography to allow for follow-up and analysis.

Finally, it is important as preface to note the recent passing of two men whose work in the area of drug policy provided considerable input to the present work and to pay brief tribute. David Musto was a physician and drug policy historian *par excellence*, and a true leader and trailblazer in the field. His book *The American Disease* continues to be a recognized classic and is invaluable for the depth of detail surrounding the development of federal drug policy from the beginning of the 20th century to the 1960s. Jim Inciardi, taking a very different approach, made the history of drug policy accessible and entertaining in a way that sometimes masked his considerable erudition and wisdom. Jim was primarily an ethnographer whose interest in drugs took him from the crack houses in Miami, to gay men's bathhouses, to the shantytowns surrounding Rio de Janeiro and to just about anywhere else people congregated to use drugs. When the author of this book was beginning his studies on drug policy back in the early 1990s, Inciardi's book *The War on Drugs II* was invaluable in providing an overview and making sense of the history of drug policy. As this book was being written, the last edition of his book, *The War on Drugs IV*, was always close at hand. Both *The American Disease* and *The War on Drugs IV* are included in the further readings sections for many documents. Any beginning student of drug history and policy in America would do well to read both works cover to cover. The loss to the field of drug policy research of both Dr. Jim Inciardi and Dr. David Musto was considerable indeed.

INTRODUCTION

As the preface describes the way documents were selected for inclusion and how each document section is structured, this introduction will provide a brief overview of the book's overarching structure and the highlights of each chapter. With some arbitrariness, U.S. drug policy has been divided into four historical chapters each covering a roughly similar approximate time frame of 20 to 30 years. Following is a description of the main events covered by the documents included in each chapter.

THE EARLY 20TH CENTURY (CHAPTER 1)

The early history of what would become modern drug policy in the United States begins in the late 1800s when unscrupulous merchants began lacing so-called patent medicines with cocaine and opiates and selling them as cure-alls to a credulous public unprotected by any government regulations. None other than Sigmund Freud got into the act when he wrote an influential article in a scientific journal extolling the benefits of cocaine based on his own self-study. Freud was wrong and he quietly abandoned writing about cocaine and later discontinued his own use. But other journalists and physicians, despite Freud's claims, grew alarmed at the growing number of people addicted to patent medicines began writing about the false claims and the true ingredients of these medicines. Muckrakers such as Uptown Sinclair were writing about similar problems in other industries. Eventually, public pressure resulted in legislative action with the passage of the Pure Food and Drug Act of 1906 and, more importantly from a drug policy perspective, the Harrison Narcotics Act of 1914.

The Pure Food and Drug Act required the products be clearly labeled as to their active ingredients. The Harrison Act used the taxing authority of the federal government to regulate the distribution and sale of any product that contained a narcotic drug. In this case, cocaine was incorrectly included as a narcotic along with opiates such as morphine and heroin. Together, the two pieces of legislation effectively ended the sale of patent medicines but there would be dispute about whether physicians could continue to prescribe narcotics for the sole purpose of providing comfort to an addict. Several important Supreme Court cases would further clarify the law's intent and determine that maintaining an addiction was not within the course of a physician's professional practice.

With the demise of the patent medicine industry, cocaine and opiates would be relegated to niche markets tucked away in the largely forgotten corners of jazz clubs and on the streets of poor, ethnic neighborhoods in America's larger inner cities. The face of addiction changed from that of a white, middle-aged southern woman to that of young men of color living largely in America's inner cities, although Americans of every ethnic persuasion and age used and became addicted to drugs then and now. An ugly side of American politics and society was on blatant display in the times leading up to and after the passage of the Harrison Act. Support for drug-related legislation was garnered by appeals to racial prejudices and xenophobia driven by unscrupulous politicians and the popular media, which linked the use of different drugs to specific ethnic minorities and foreigners amid claims that drug use turned them into wanton, wild-eyed savages. The political appeal of such tripe, however, proved effective.

This was also the era of Prohibition, termed by one President as a "Noble Experiment." The Women's Christian Temperance Union joined with other like-minded groups such as the Anti-Saloon League led by Wayne Wheeler, to become a powerful, single-minded political force. Their efforts led to alcohol being outlawed by a Constitutional Amendment. But alcohol use never went away as the architects of Prohibition had imagined; far from it. While Prohibition resulted in decreased alcohol consumption that did not fully rebound until many years after its repeal, thousands of hale and hearty Americans continued to slake their thirst at local speakeasies. Men like Al Capone made sure there was always an ample supply of liquor on hand as Prohibition provided the economic engine that led to the rise of organized crime. Capone overplayed his hand when, on Valentine's Day, his minions fired a hail of bullets in a beer distribution center run by a rival gang. The violence related to organized crime, the ineffectiveness of law enforcement, and the continuing popularity of alcohol suggested the experiment might not be so noble after all. In the mood for new beginnings following the Great Depression, Americans elected Franklin D. Roosevelt, who celebrated the beginning of the end of Prohibition with a beer, as president.

As this chapter in drug policy comes to a close in the mid-1930s, the Harrison Act was filling federal prisons with addicts. To relieve the burden, Congress passed legislation that created two prisons dedicated to housing, treating, and studying drug addicts. Called "narcotics farms" (the facility in Lexington, Kentucky, included a working farm that was run by inmates as part of their treatment), the two facilities attempted to rehabilitate inmates using the best drug treatment precepts at the time. For a while, the research conducted at the center in Lexington was innovative, leading to advances in our understanding of addiction. But successful rehabilitations were few and far between and the research program breached ethics and was co-opted by larger government interests in testing new drugs and not helping drug addicts. Both facilities would eventually be reestablished as medical prisons, having largely failed at their original missions.

THE 1930s THROUGH THE 1950s (CHAPTER 2)

For almost 30 years, from the early 1930s through the beginning of the 1960s, a single individual dominated American drug policy in a way that had not occurred before and has not occurred since. As head of the Federal Bureau of Narcotics, Harry J. Anslinger became the nation's first drug czar. And in terms of his dominance over drug policy, he truly was a czar in almost every sense of that word. Anslinger was a no-nonsense, single-minded, relentless bureaucrat with finely honed political instincts that allowed him to extend his reign across five presidential administrations, beginning with Herbert Hoover and ending with John F. Kennedy.

Anslinger was a firm believer that marijuana was a stepping-stone drug that inevitably led to harder drug use. As such, his views anticipated the gateway hypothesis that would feature prominently as a rationale for the zero tolerance policy that became an emphasis of the Reagan and George H. W. Bush administrations. Anslinger never let pass an opportunity to demonize marijuana. He maintained a "gore file" of police stories that described heinous crimes and purported without substantiation that the crimes were motivated by marijuana use. Anslinger was also not above using racist imagery to promote his political agenda and, in fact, embraced it. Anslinger was successful in getting his musings widely published. One of his more famous pieces, *Marijuana, Assassin of Youth*, describes several horrid crimes motivated by marijuana and is included in the documents in chapter 2. He was given an able assist by the powerful media magnate, William Randolph Hearst. Hearst had a financial interest in the paper industry, which was in competition with the hemp industry and he stood to lose considerable money if growing marijuana was legalized. He also had an ax to grind against Mexicans, who seized the land he owned in that country. Hearst's publications provided Anslinger with plenty of fodder for his gore files by frequently running lurid, fanciful exposes that also exaggerated the effects of marijuana and linked marijuana use to Mexican immigrants and migrant farm workers.

Anslinger was also extremely effective in getting legislation passed that reflected his views. The Marijuana Stamp Tax Act of 1937 classified marijuana as a narcotic drug (it's not) on par with opiates and cocaine and although a tax act, it basically outlawed marijuana growth, sale, and distribution. Faced with a heroin "epidemic" following World War II after the reestablishment of European supply routes, Anslinger went after marijuana use as a root cause of the heroin epidemic. Legislation passed in the 1950s—the Boggs Act in 1951 and the Narcotic Control Act of 1956—upped the ante by increasing criminal penalties for marijuana and "other narcotic" drugs. Most of these laws were passed with little debate by Congress and with little input from scientists or physician groups. Their opposition to the absurdities on which the laws were premised was instead registered in a report issued by the ABA-AMA and by a report commissioned by New York City mayor Fiorello La Guardia to examine the scientific merits of the claims made against marijuana. Social scientists such as Alfred Lindesmith fought a losing battle to have addiction treated as a public health issue and not a criminal justice problem.

Despite these protestations, Anslinger's drug policy views predominated throughout most of the 1950s. Nevertheless, the seeds that would undo large parts of Anslinger's vision were being sown not in the hallowed halls of Congress but in the dark back rooms of jazz clubs and at poetry readings. A small group of young, talented malcontents began expressing their disdain for the status quo and what they saw as the spiritual hollowness of modern life and its emphasis on materialism. Their poetry and writings railed (howled!) against the prevailing social order and promoted drug use as a way of rebelling. Called the "beat poets" or the "beat generation," they would be derisively dismissed as slothful beatniks. But their message spread and in the next decade, America would experience a period of unparalleled turmoil among its youth fueled in part by disdain for the government and social conventions and in part by a belief that the use of drugs, particularly psychedelic drugs such as LSD, could really "change the world."

THE 1960s THROUGH THE MID-1990s (CHAPTER 3)

As a time of social upheaval, the 1960s and 1970s are best remembered for congregations of hippies openly dropping acid and smoking marijuana at large public celebrations such as took place in 1967 during the "summer of love" in the Haight-Ashbury district of San Francisco and several years later at an outdoor rock music festival called Woodstock as they "turned on, tuned in, and dropped out." Forgotten or never fully appreciated is the fact that many more Americans were quietly (some not so quietly) using and misusing prescription drugs such as amphetamine, barbiturates, and tranquilizers. Heavily marketed by the pharmaceutical companies as miracle drugs for curing all manner of ills—not too unlike what the promoters of patent medicines had done years earlier—doctors were prescribing these drugs by the handfuls as safe and effective. Promoted by celebrities such as comedian Milton "Miltown" Berle, their popularity only grew over time. A gray market arose to divert legally prescribed drugs into the hands of those who did not want to bother obtaining a prescription. As the drugs, addicting properties and side effects became better known, Congress eventually acted to try and curb the abuse but the legislation they passed in the mid-1960s was a case of too little too late and did almost nothing to address the overproduction by the pharmaceutical manufacturers.

In the meantime, proselytizers for drug use as a means to expanding consciousness such as Timothy Leary had their heyday but it would be short lived. The countercultural movement that began with such high ideals would come crashing down as drug use spun out of control and the search for spiritual and personal enlightenment gave way to nothing more than the search for pleasure and escapism. The continued prosecution of the Vietnam War into the 1970s inspired ongoing social divisiveness even though the counterculture movement was fizzling. President Nixon campaigned on restoring law and order and promised to combat drug use as an important cause of crime. Surprisingly, however, he hired a rather progressive minded drug czar, Jerome Jaffe, who implemented a national treatment system that emphasized methadone maintenance and targeted heroin users. Jaffe was also the architect of a successful drug testing campaign in Vietnam that sharply reduced heroin use among the troops through a clever strategy of immediate sanctions (i.e., positive tests resulted in a delay in returns home).

The Controlled Substances Act, which brought all drug policy under one legislative roof by creating a schedule of drugs that would be controlled through the Attorney General's Office, passed in 1970. It remains one of the principal pillars on which current drug policy is based. Cocaine use returned in a big way in the 1970s as American's forgot that it was dangerous to use. It was instead associated with the good times and became the province of the well-to-do and those who wanted to appear well-to-do. They danced and snorted the nights away at Studio 54 and other hot-spot discothèques. Colombian traffickers grew rich supplying Americans with cocaine even as they killed anyone who got in their way; Al Capone would likely have marveled at the brazenness of their executions had he been alive to witness them.

The outbreak of a new, terrifying disease that would soon be identified as HIV/AIDS was first noticed when homosexual men began showing up in 1981 in emergency rooms in Los Angeles with symptoms of infections from diseases like pneumocystis carinii pneumonia that had rarely been seen in their age group and demographic. Even as the disease spread and fears of a true epidemic grew, the Reagan administration was slow to act. Not until Surgeon General C. Everett Koop wrote and distributed a candid report on the causes and consequences of HIV/AIDS and what could be done to prevent infection did the American public come to have a clearer understanding of the disease. Koop's report helped change the public dialogue, allay undue fears, and reduce (to an extent) the stigma associated with HIV/AIDS. Still, effective treatments of the disease remained almost a decade away and many thousands would die from the disease, including injection drug users.

During the 1980s, while there were some political feints made toward controlling cocaine use, it took the cocaine-related death of a popular athlete, Len Bias, and growing violence surrounding trafficking in crack cocaine in the inner cities to spur Congress to action. These events however led to an overreaction. Congress passed legislation in 1986 that provided for lengthy prison sentences for drug possession and trafficking. With little justification, the legislation contained sentencing disparities in the ratio of 100:1 for crack cocaine compared with powder cocaine. As a result, the nation's prisons and jails began to fill with hundreds of thousands of low level drug traffickers, many of whom sold drugs to pay for their own drug use. And because of the sentencing disparities, those sentenced were disproportionately minority. President George H. W. Bush gave his first address to the nation on drug policy. He announced the creation of the Office of National Drug Control Policy. Its new director William Bennett, former secretary of education under President Reagan, would last only two years in the position. But before he left, he crafted a zero-tolerance policy that emphasized going after the "casual user" as the greatest threat to spreading the disease of addiction. Marijuana use was on the political front burner again.

THE MID-1990s TO 2011 (CHAPTER 4)

Nearing the close of the 20th century, the nation began looking toward the new millennium. America was in a time of prosperity driven by the "Internet bubble," high-risk, high-gain hedge funds, and the speculative, unfettered trading of exotic financial instruments called "derivatives" on Wall Street. Fears of the dangers of crack cocaine ebbed and crime rates dropped even as (or as law-and-order proponents would contend because) the prison-building boom and the experiment in mass incarceration continued. The American public's increasingly short attention span was diverted from drugs and crime towards the *crisis du jour,* the possibility of a computer-driven apocalypse called "Y2K" for "year 2000." The fear was that the computer systems that guided everything from planes to elevators would shut down or worse because they would not correctly process dates after midnight December 31, 1999. (Nothing happened.) New developments in HIV treatment—the advent of a new class of drugs called protease inhibitors as part of a drug cocktail for treating HIV/AIDS—meant HIV infection was no longer a certain death sentence. The framework for modern drug policy—the Controlled Substances Act of 1970 and the Anti-Drug Abuse Act of 1986—was in place, would remain largely intact, and would carry into the next century. Subsequent changes to drug-related law at the federal level would amend these existing laws.

The election of the formerly pot-smoking-but-not-inhaling William Jefferson Clinton to the presidency was seen as a transfer of power from the World War II generation of Reagan and Bush to the baby boomers born in the two decades following the war. Somewhat lost during the power shuffle were the children of the baby boomers. Called "Generation X" or "Gen-X," their disillusionment and social disaffection would be reflected in music that originated in Seattle called grunge, the corresponding adoption of a neo-Victorian, morose fashion style called "goth," and the unexpected embrace of an old drug that spawned yet another heroin "epidemic." This time, the epidemic would extend beyond the inner city and minorities (for whom it never ceased being an "epidemic"), reaching small towns and (mostly white) suburban youth like those in Plano, Texas.

In rural America, particularly in southwestern and midwestern states, the evening stillness would be punctuated occasionally with fiery explosions that enveloped resident amateur chemists in toxic miasmas, as methamphetamine was also brewing for a comeback. Californians decided their number one cash crop, marijuana, might be medically useful after all; the federal government's Schedule I classification of it as medically useless be damned. A number of other states soon followed suit. The border between the United States and Mexico became the focus of interdiction (and anti-immigration) efforts as Mexico became a major producer of and source for heroin, methamphetamine, marijuana, and Colombian-produced cocaine.

Throughout it all, America has hewn to a drug policy that emphasizes law enforcement over treatment and prevention. Whereas some European nations such as Portugal, Switzerland, and the Netherlands as well as Canada and Australia have moved toward at least experimenting with harm reduction programs and a public health approach, the United States, despite continually paying lip service to the importance of treatment, continues to staunchly defend its current policy. There have been six directors of the Office of National Drug Control Policy since its creation in 1988. None have come from the drug treatment or prevention fields. Their backgrounds have been in law enforcement or the military, or they have been political conservatives with little experience in drug policy. In the transition leading into the new millennium and in the decade beyond, drug policy–wise at least, many things old were indeed new again.

1

THE EARLY 20TH CENTURY: PATENT MEDICINES, THE RISE AND FALL OF PROHIBITION, THE NARCOTICS FARMS

"The Whole Vast System of Bunco"

- ***Document:*** Samuel Hopkins Adams, "The Great American Fraud," the first of an 11-part series published in *Collier's Weekly*
- ***Date:*** October 7, 1905
- ***Where:*** New York, New York
- ***Significance:*** This article and subsequent ones in the series both captured and incited public concern over the misleading claims and advertising of patent medicines, many of which contained alcohol, opium, and cocaine as their medicinal ingredients. The growing public awareness led to federal legislation that curbed and ultimately ended the false claims and selling of patent medicines.

DOCUMENT

ADVICE TO MOTHERS!—Are you broken in your rest by a sick child suffering with the pain of cutting teeth? Go at once to a chemist and get a bottle of MRS. WINSLOW'S SOOTHING SYRUP. It will relieve the poor sufferer immediately. It is perfectly harmless and pleasant to taste, it produces natural quiet sleep, by relieving the child from pain, and the little cherub awakes "as bright as a button." It soothes the child, it softens the gums, allays all

Exemplary of the deceptive advertising used by the patent medicine industry is this ad for Mrs. Winslow's Soothing Syrup, produced by Meyer, Merkell & Ottmann in New York in 1885. Widely marketed in the United States and the United Kingdom for use by children and adults alike, the main active ingredient was morphine. (National Library of Medicine)

pain, relieves wind, regulates the bowels, and is the best known remedy for dysentery and diarrhea, whether arising from teething or other causes. Mrs. Winslow's Soothing Syrup is sold by Medicine dealers everywhere at 1s. 1½d. per bottle. Manufactured in New York and at 498, Oxford-street, London.

Source: *The Hampshire Telegraph and Sussex Chronicle*, Saturday 9th January 1875. Courtesy of the US National Library of Medicine, here's an 1885 advertising image produced by Meyer, Merkell & Ottmann in New York.

GULLIBLE America will spend this year some seventy-five millions of dollars in the purchase of patent medicines. In consideration of this sum, it will swallow huge quantities of alcohol, an appalling amount of opiates and narcotics, a wide assortment of varied drugs ranging from powerful and dangerous heart depressants to insidious liver stimulants; and, in excess of all other ingredients, undiluted fraud. For fraud, exploited by the skilfulest [*sic*] of advertising bunco men, is the basis of the trade. . . .

When one comes to the internal remedies, the proprietary medicines proper, they all belong to the tribe of Capricorn, under one of two heads, harmless frauds or deleterious drugs. For instance, the laxatives perform what they promise: but taken regularly, as thousands of people take them (and, indeed, as the advertisements urge), they become an increasingly baneful necessity. . . . Cocaine and opium stop pain but the narcotics are not the safest drugs to put into the hands of the ignorant, particularly when their presence is concealed in the "cough remedies," "soothing syrups," and "catarrhal powders" of which they are the basis. Few outside of the rabid temperance advocates will deny a place in the medical practice to alcohol. But alcohol, fed daily and in increasing doses to women and children, makes not for health, but for drunkenness. . . .

The ignorant drug-taker, returning to health from some disease which he has overcome by the natural resistant powers of his body, dips his pen in gratitude and writes his testimonial. The man who dies in spite of the patent medicine—or perhaps because of it—doesn't bear witness to what it did for him. We see recorded only the favorable results: the unfavorable lie silent. How could it be otherwise when the only avenues of publicity are controlled by the heavy advertisers? So while many of the printed testimonials are genuine enough, they represent not the average evidence, but the most glowing opinions which the nostrum vender can obtain, and generally they are the expression of a low order of intelligence. Read in this light, they are unconvincing enough. But the innocent public regards them as the type, not the exception. "If that cured Mrs. Smith of Oshkosh it may cure me," says the woman whose symptoms, real or imagined, are so feelingly described under the picture. . . .

It is impossible, even in a series of articles, to attempt more than an exemplary treatment of the patent medicine frauds. The most degraded and degrading, the "lost vitality" and "blood disease" cures, reeking of terrorization and blackmail, cannot from their very nature be treated of in a lay journal. Many dangerous and health-destroying compounds will escape through sheer inconspicuousness. I can touch upon only a few of those which may be regarded as typical: the alcohol stimulators as represented by Peruna, Paine's Celery Compound, and Duffy's Pure Malt Whiskey (advertised as an exclusively medical preparation); the catarrh powders, which breed cocaine slaves, and the opium-containing soothing syrups, which stunt or kill helpless infants; the consumption cures, perhaps the most devilish of all, in that they destroy hope where hope is struggling against bitter odds for existence; the headache powders, which enslave so insidiously that the victim is ignorant of his own fate; the comparatively harmless fake as typified by that marvelous product of advertising and effrontery, Liquizone; and finally, the system of exploitation and testimonials upon which the whole vast system of bunco rests, as upon a flimsy but cunningly constructed foundation.

SOURCE: Samuel Hopkins Adams, "The Great American Fraud," *Collier's Weekly*, October 7, 1905.

ANALYSIS

For much of the 19th century through the first decade of the 20th century, so-called patent medicines were marketed and sold over the counter without prescription to the American public. Patent medicines originated in England in the 1600s and traveled with British emigrants to the new colony, where they eventually reached their peak in the second half of the 1800s. The term *patent medicines* is something of a misnomer in several respects. First, these products were not patented but trademarked and for good reason; obtaining a patent would have required disclosure of the ingredients, which the makers of patent medicines wanted to keep secret. Trademarking of the product name allowed for exclusivity while at the same time maintaining secrecy. In addition, by keeping the ingredients secret, the manufacturer could change the formula whenever they desired and for whatever reason and continue to sell their concoction under the same trademarked name. The resulting concoctions, or *nostrums* as they have been termed (the word *nostrum* comes from Latin and means "our remedy"), because of their ineffectiveness, were hardly medicinal.

Many patent medicines were nothing more than alcohol-based beverages in which cocaine or opium had been dissolved with additives to enhance the taste and to disguise the bitterness of the cocaine or opium. Exotic ingredients such as snake oil, which were sometimes actually included in the nostrum and sometimes not, were added to increase allure and marketability. Patent medicine marketers often used stories of exotic origins and sources (e.g., the Far East, cures purportedly developed by Native Americans) to give their products a mysterious aura; although, the authenticity of such claims was hard to verify, a primary reason for using them.

One of the covers *Collier's* used in its campaign for the Pure Food and Drugs Act of 1906. The popularity of patent medicines led journalists to investigate the many extravagant but ultimately false marketing claims made by the patent medicine industry resulting in exposés such as the one that appeared in this issue of *Collier's* magazine. The unwelcome publicity led to the passage of laws such as the Pure Food and Drug Act end eventually to the demise of the patent medicine industry. (Library of Congress)

Unchecked by any statutory requirement to demonstrate their effectiveness, patent medicines were aggressively marketed as bringing relief or outright cures for a wide variety of medical ills and symptoms that ranged from cancer to tuberculosis to paralysis to "female complaints." In many instances, the same product was advertized as curing a wide range of medical problems. Tragically, nostrums such as Mrs. Winslow's Soothing Syrup, Kopp's Baby Friend, and Monell's Teething Syrup were marketed for use with infants and children. Mrs. Winslow's Soothing Syrup was marketed as providing relief for infants during teething as well as a cure for diarrhea. Ironically, as Mrs. Winslow's contained opium, and as opium does have antidiarrheal properties, it probably was effective at reducing diarrhea in infants as well as inducing sleep at the expense, of course, of addiction to a potent narcotic (opium) and exposure of the infant to the neurotoxic effects of alcohol. Perhaps most ironically, patent medicines containing opium were marketed as cures for addiction to opiates such as morphine. Using one addictive drug to treat addiction to another addictive drug was common at the time.

By the late 1800s, the growing popularity of the patent medicines brought increased scrutiny as their addicting properties, ineffectiveness, and the falseness of their claims to being cures became apparent to the medical community and a growing number of the general public. As a result, more and more articles warning of the fraud and dangers of patent medicines began appearing in the popular press such as the series of articles by Samuel Hopkins Adams that appeared in *Collier's Weekly*. The *Journal of the American Medical Association* published an entire volume of articles that detailed the fraudulence of the marketing claims underlying patent medicines and other forms of quackery in 1911 with two subsequent volumes published in 1921 and 1936. The push for greater control of the patent medicine market led to the passage of the Pure Food and Drug Act in 1906. This act did not restrict sales of patent medicines but it did require the ingredients be included on the label. Subsequently, the Harrison Stamp Tax Act in 1914 brought narcotics sales and prescriptions under the purview of the federal government. The Harrison Act effectively ended the unrestricted reign of the patent medicine industry and greatly limited the legally prescribed uses of opium and cocaine.

An interesting coda to this episode in American drug policy history is that many of the same advertising techniques used to successfully market patent medicines remain in common use today and constitute a lasting legacy of the turn-of-the-century patent medicine industry. Now amplified by electronic media such as television and the Internet, celebrity pitchmen, personal anecdotes, direct-to-consumer marketing, and compelling images and testimonials from satisfied customers were all first used in patent medicine marketing to the general public. These same techniques are now used to entice and to demonstrate the effectiveness of a wide range of products that includes everything from kitchen gadgets to fad diets, to anti-aging creams, to get-rich real-estate and financial schemes, to arthritis cures, to nutritional supplements and treatments for erectile dysfunction. They are about as effective as were the patent medicines.

FURTHER READING

Barkan, I.D. (1985). Industry invites regulation: The passage of the Pure Food and Drugs Act of 1906. *American Journal of Public Health, 75*, 18–26.

Hodgson, B. (1999). *Opium: A portrait of the heavenly demon.* Vancouver, BC: Greystone Books.

Hodgson, B. (2001). *In the arms of Morpheus: The tragic history of laudanum, morphine, and patent medicines.* Buffalo, NY: Firefly Books Inc.

Inciardi, J. (2007). *The war on drugs IV: The continuing saga of the mysteries and miseries of intoxication, addiction, crime, and public policy, 4th edition.* Boston, MA: Allyn and Bacon.

Kantor, A.F. (1976). Upton Sinclair and the Pure Food and Drugs Act of 1906: "I aimed at the public's heart and by accident I hit it in the stomach." *American Journal of Public Health*, 66, 1202–1205.

Musto, D. (1999). *The American disease: Origins of narcotics control (3rd edition).* New York: Oxford University Press.

Quinones, M.A. (1975). Drug abuse during the Civil War (1861–1865). *International Journal of the Addictions, 10*, 1007–1020.

On the Internet

The toadstool millionaires: A social history of patent medicines in America before federal regulation, a book by James Harvey Young, is available in its entirety at the website Quackwatch at: http://www.quackwatch.org/13Hx/TM/00.html.

The Hagley Museum and Library has an online exhibit on the patent medicine industry that includes image of the advertisements and product labels available at: http://www.hagley.org/library/exhibits/patentmed/index.html.

The full text of the *Collier's Weekly* articles is available through Google books at: http://books.google.com/books?id=oH0xqp0M-U0C&hl=en.

The full text of the *Journal of the American Medical Association's* three issues on *Nostrums and Quackery* can be obtained through Google books at: http://books.google.com/books?id=9gREAAAAIAAJ&hl=en.

MUCKRAKING

The term *muckraking* today can be construed as pejorative referring to someone who likes to stir up trouble for his or her own benefit. However, it did not always have such a negative connotation. The origin of the term into common parlance is attributed to Theodore Roosevelt who, in a 1906 speech that lauded the role of journalism that exposed predatory and unfair business practices, referenced a passage from *Pilgrim's Progress* that described a muckraker as one who could only look down in the direction of the filth he or she was raking on the ground. Muckraking came to be viewed as part of a larger trend in American society known as *Progressivism* in the early late 1800s through the 1920s. The *Progressive Movement* sought to expose not only shoddy working conditions and corrupt business practices, but also to usher in sweeping social changes such as granting women the right to vote as well as, somewhat incongruously, prohibition. The *Collier's Weekly* series on the patent medicine industry is a prime example of muckraking journalism during the progressive era. Another better-known example from the same time is the 1906 novel *The Jungle* by Uptown Sinclair, which described the unsanitary and poor conditions in the meatpacking industry. A more recent example is Rachel Carson's book *Silent Spring,* which described how widespread use of chemical pesticides in agriculture adversely affected the environment. Muckraking journalism marked a turn from reporters and journalists viewing their role as restricted to simply recounting news and events to one whereby they should also investigate the causes and consequences of important social problems. As such, muckraking can be viewed as the direct predecessor of what today would be more commonly referred to as investigative journalism.

"A Big Wild Man Who Has Cocaine in His Body"

- ***Document:*** First published as "Über Coca" (On Cocaine) in *Centralblatt fur die gesammte Therapie, 2,* 289–314. It was the first and most laudatory of three papers written by Freud on the virtues of cocaine as a general tonic for fatigue and depression as well as a cure for morphine addiction and alcoholism.
- ***Date:*** July 1884
- ***Where:*** Vienna, Austria
- ***Significance:*** Freud's prominence as the eventual founder of psychoanalysis generated considerable interest in all of his writings, including those written prior to his psychoanalytic work. Freud's paper, "Über Coca," is a frequently cited example of how there has historically been considerable enthusiasm over what are perceived to be the unalloyed benefits of a newly discovered drug, in this case cocaine. Although Freud had not yet achieved fame at the time the paper was written, it was nevertheless influential in Europe as well as in America. However, in this as in many other instances, the initial enthusiasm over the seeming benefits of the drug gave way to more realistic and pessimistic assessments when the considerable harms associated with cocaine use rapidly became apparent.

DOCUMENT

It seems probable, in the light of reports which I shall refer to later, that coca, if used protractedly but in moderation, is not detrimental to the body. . . . It seems to me noteworthy—and I discovered this in myself and in other observers who were capable of judging such things that a first dose or even repeated doses of coca produce no compulsive desire to use the stimulant further; on the contrary, one feels a certain unmotivated aversion to the substance. . . .

It was inevitable that a plant which had achieved such a reputation for marvelous effects in its country of origin should have been used to treat the most varied disorders and illnesses of the human body. . . . I have tried to collate the recommendations concerning coca, and, in doing so, to distinguish between recommendations based on successful treatment of illnesses and those which relate to the psychological effects of the stimulant. . . .

a) ***Coca as a stimulant.*** The main use of coca will undoubtedly remain that which the Indians have made of it for centuries: it is of value in all cases where the primary aim is to increase the physical capacity of the body for a given short period of time and to hold strength in reserve to meet further demands—especially when outward circumstances exclude the possibility of obtaining the rest and nourishment normally necessary for great exertion. Such situations arise in wartime, on journeys, during mountain climbing and other expeditions, etc.—indeed, they are situations in which the alcoholic stimulants are also generally recognized as being of value. Coca is a far more potent and far less harmful stimulant than alcohol, and its widespread utilization is hindered at present only by its high cost. . . .

b) ***The use of coca for digestive disorders of the stomach.*** This is the oldest and most firmly founded use of coca, and at the same time it is the most comprehensible to us . . . I have experienced personally how the painful symptoms attendant upon large meals—namely, a feeling of pressure and fullness in the stomach, discomfort, and a disinclination to work—disappear with eructation following small doses of cocaine (0.025–0.05). Time and again I have brought such relief to my colleagues; and twice I observed how the nausea resulting from gastronomic excesses responded in a short time to the effects of cocaine, and gave way to a normal desire to eat and a feeling of bodily well-being. I have also learned to spare myself stomach troubles by adding a small amount of cocaine to salicylate of soda. . . .

c) ***Coca in cachexia.*** Long-term use of coca is further strongly recommended—and allegedly has been tried with success—in all diseases which involve degeneration of the tissues, such as severe anemia, phthisis, long-lasting febrile diseases, etc.; and also during recovery from such diseases. . . .

d) ***Coca in the treatment of morphine and alcohol addiction.*** In America the important discovery has recently been made that coca preparations possess the power to suppress the craving for morphine in habitual addicts, and also to reduce to negligible proportions the serious symptoms of collapse which appear while the patient is being weaned away from the morphine habit. . . .

I once had occasion to observe the case of a man who was subjected to the type of cure involving the sudden withdrawal of morphine, assisted by the use of coca; the same patient had suffered severe symptoms as a result of abstinence in the course of a previous cure. This time his condition was tolerable; in particular, there was no sign of depression or nausea as long as the effects of coca lasted; chills and diarrhea were now the only permanent symptoms of his abstinence. The patient was not bedridden, and could function normally. . . .

The treatment of morphine addiction with coca does not, therefore, result merely in the exchange of one kind of addiction for another—it does not turn the morphine addict into a **coquero** [cocaine addict]; the use of coca is only temporary. . . .

e) ***Coca and asthma.*** Tschudi and Markham's report that by chewing coca leaves they were spared the usual symptoms of the so-called mountain sickness while climbing in the Andes; this complex of symptoms includes shortness of breath, pounding of the heart, dizziness, etc. Poizat76 reports that the asthmatic attacks of a patient were arrested in every case by coca. I mention this property of coca because it appears to admit of a physiological explanation. Von Anrep's experiments on animals resulted in early paralysis of certain branches of the vagus; and altitude asthma, as well as the attacks characteristic of chronic bronchitis, may be interpreted in terms of a reflex excitation originating in the pulmonary branches of the vagus. The use of coca should be considered for the treatment of other vagus neuroses.

f) ***Coca as an aphrodisiac.*** The natives of South America, who represented their goddess of love with coca leaves in her hand, did not doubt the stimulative effect of coca on the genitalia. . . . Among the persons to whom I have given coca, three reported violent sexual excitement which they unhesitatingly attributed to the coca. . . .

g) ***Local application of coca.*** Cocaine and its salts have a marked anesthetizing effect when brought in contact with the skin and mucous membrane in concentrated solution; this property suggests its occasional use as a local anesthetic, especially in connection with affections of the mucous membrane. . . . Indeed, the anesthetizing properties of cocaine should make it suitable for a good many further applications.

SOURCE: First published as "Über Coca" [On Cocaine], *Centralblatt fur die gesammte Therapie, 2,* 289–314. By permission of the Marsh Agency Ltd. on behalf of Sigmund Freud Copyrights.

ANALYSIS

At the time he wrote "Über Coca," Freud was still a young neurologist, struggling to make his mark on the world and to find a career path that would allow him to marry and provide for a family. Reading favorable accounts of cocaine's psychological and physical benefits in the European and American medical literature, Freud became interested in testing whether cocaine was useful in alleviating fatigue and depression, both of which he was experiencing at the time. If cocaine proved to be an effective treatment for psychiatric patients suffering from these (and other) problems, Freud would have rightly been given credit and acclaim for the discovery, thereby successfully launching his career.

Experiments for conducting drug tests in the late 19th century were not as rigorously controlled as today and part of Freud's experimentation with cocaine included self-administration of the drug as well as administering it to patients and friends. As cocaine was legal to obtain and distribute at the time, he also occasionally sent some of the drug to his fiancée after corresponding with her about the benefits he had experienced personally. The title quote is excerpted from a passage in one of Freud's letters to his fiancée, Martha Bernays, on cocaine and what she might expect when they were together again should she have the temerity to resist his advances:

> Woe to you, my Princess, when I come. I will kiss you quite red and feed you till you are plump. And if you are froword [oppositional] you shall see who is the

> stronger, a gentle little girl who doesn't eat enough or a big wild man who has cocaine in his body. In my last severe depression I took coca again and a small dose lifted me to the heights in a wonderful fashion. I am just now busy collecting the literature for a song of praise to this magical substance.

Impressed with the results he obtained through self-administration of cocaine—he found it invigorating, that it had indeed alleviated his fatigue, increased his stamina, and allowed him to focus on his work—Freud expanded his experimentation to others. One of the more unfortunate participants in Freud's cocaine studies was his friend and colleague Dr. Ernst von Fleischl-Marxow, who had become severely addicted to the morphine he took to alleviate pain from the amputation of his thumb. Freud prescribed cocaine to Fleishchl to cure his morphine addiction. Although the initial results seemed promising, Fleishchl rapidly became addicted to both cocaine and morphine, injecting the drugs on a daily basis and dying six years later from the steady physical and psychological declines he experienced.

Over the next few years, numerous reports of the risks of cocaine use, its ineffectiveness as a cure for morphine addiction and alcoholism, and the addictive potential of cocaine in its own right began surfacing with increasing frequency in medical reports in both Europe and America, thereby fully discrediting Freud's initial account. One critic of Freud contemptuously proclaimed that through his writings and endorsement, Freud had unleashed "the third scourge of humanity." This is clearly overstatement, however, and there is little evidence that Freud's mistaken impressions of cocaine's benefits led to a "thirty-year cocaine frenzy" in the United States (or anywhere else) as Gugliotta and Leen opine in their book *Kings of Cocaine*. After continuing to defend his original conclusions in a fourth and final paper on cocaine published three years after "Über Coca," Freud abandoned the topic and moved on to the work that would eventually make him famous, more than content to put the entire episode behind him. He would write to Martha in 1885 that his explorations of the uses of cocaine were not serious and simply reflected a "chase after money, position, and reputation."

Some critics contend that Freud knew all along that cocaine was not the wonder drug he wrote about in "Über Coca" and that his misrepresentation of its effects reflected a pattern of lying about and misrepresenting the effectiveness of various interventions—including psychoanalysis—that persisted throughout Freud's career. Possible motivations would have included Freud's intense ambition to be financially successful as well as just plain hubris. It is hard to ignore this criticism given that the poor results of treating Flieschl-Marxow's morphine addiction were readily apparent even before his long decline and death. Yet Freud continued for a time to advocate using cocaine for just this purpose.

Freud's personal foray into using cocaine might have had a more beneficial effect on his career. Medical historian Howard Markel in his recent work *An Anatomy of Addiction* examines at length Freud's cocaine investigations and subsequent 12-year addiction to the drug. Markel speculates that Freud's use of introspection to understand cocaine's psychological effects—at odds with his previous mind-set and work, which was as an objective, detached scientist—set the stage for Freud's later intensely introspective psychological work that led to his development of psychoanalysis.

Ironically, the one legitimate medical use for cocaine, as a topical anesthetic, is mentioned as an aside in the list of potential uses enumerated in "Über Coca." The fame that eluded Freud was ultimately bestowed on his friend and colleague Carl Koller, an ophthalmologist who was working in the same laboratory as Freud. Koller was trying to determine a suitable drug for use as a topical anesthetic during eye surgery. Such surgery requires that the patient be awake during the operation so they may be responsive to the physician's directives while at the same time not flinching or blinking. Freud claims he mentioned almost in passing to Koller that cocaine seemed to have anesthetic properties. In a series of experiments, an intrigued Koller confirmed this was the case, that cocaine indeed was an effective topical anesthetic for eye surgery, and quickly published his findings in the scientific literature. The finding led to Koller, albeit belatedly in his career, receiving acclaim for his important contribution to the field of ophthalmic surgery. Displaying a playful side unfamiliar to most, Freud would later autograph a reprint of "Über Coca" that he dedicated to his friend Coca Koller. (Koller did not especially appreciate the joke and felt it to be dismissive of his discovery.)

The pattern exemplified by Freud's initial enthusiasm for the wondrous effects of cocaine followed by rapid disillusionment when its addictive potential and side effects became more apparent is one that is often repeated in the history of drug discovery and subsequently policy. A very short list of drugs that followed a similar trajectory would include heroin, amphetamine, barbiturates, benzodiazepines (Valium), and LSD. One of the latest examples, OxyContin, a synthetic narcotic manufactured specifically to reduce its potential for abuse, has become nevertheless widely abused, especially in rural areas after it was discovered that crushing the pills defeated the time-release mechanism. The very same mistakes would be made with cocaine again when it reemerged in America in the 1970s as a drug of the rich and famous and as having the same cachet as Dom-Perignon (see "The Cocaine Scene," *Newsweek Magazine*). Forgetting or discounting these earlier experiences of the harms caused by cocaine addiction, many, including prominent scientists who studied addiction as well as physicians, would again proclaim cocaine a harmless drug with few to no ill effects. Inevitably, the considerable harms of cocaine use would become more apparent as a new form of the drug—crack cocaine—became the scourge of inner cities and after several high-profile deaths of professional athletes Len Bias and Don Rogers from cocaine use focused the public's attention on the reemergent drug.

THE DREAM OF IRMA'S INJECTION

Had Freud emphasized cocaine's anesthetic properties rather than its psychoactive properties, he might never have gone on to develop the field of psychoanalysis. He would have gone on, perhaps, to study ophthalmology or anesthesia. There are other examples where Freud demonstrated a propensity for ignoring obvious evidence, and emphasizing instead the obscure; not following his own admonition that sometimes, a "cigar is just a cigar." A famous example is his convoluted interpretation of a dream he called "Irma's injection," recounted and analyzed in his first major psychoanalytic work, *The Interpretation of Dreams*. Irma was in reality, a patient Freud had referred to a friend, Wilhelm Fliess, for nasal surgery to relieve her nosebleeds. According to Fliess's bizarre theory of the "nasal reflex neurosis," the turbinal bones in the nose were directly connected to the sexual organs and removal of the bones would relieve the *neurotic* symptoms.

(continued)

FURTHER READING

Byck, R. (Ed.). (1974). *Cocaine papers: Sigmund Freud*. New York: Stonehill Publishing Co.

Das, G. (1993). Cocaine abuse in North America. *Journal of Clinical Pharmacology, 33*, 296–301.

Dos Reis, A., Jr. (2009). Sigmund Freud (1856–1939) and Karl Koller (1857–1944) and the discovery of local anesthesia. *Revista Brasilear de Anestesiologia, 59*, 244–257.

Freud, S. (1984). Classics revisited: Über coca. *Journal of Substance Abuse Treatment, 1*, 205–217.

Galbis-Reig, D. (2003). Sigmund Freud and Carl Koller: The controversy surrounding the discovery of local anesthesia. *International Congress Series, 1242*, 571–575.

Markel, H. (2011). *An anatomy of addiction: Sigmund Freud, William Halsted, and the miracle drug cocaine*. New York: Pantheon Books.

Musto, D. (1968). A study in cocaine: Sherlock Holmes and Sigmund Freud. *Journal of the American Medical Association, 204*, 27–32.

Musto, D. (1989). America's first cocaine epidemic. *Wilson Quarterly, 13*, 59–64.

On the Internet

Borch-Jacobsen, M. (2000, April 13). How fabrications differ from a lie. (Review of Der Fall Freud: Die Geburt der Psychoanalyse aus der Luge by Han Israels), *London Review of Books*, http://www.lrb.co.uk/v22/n08/borc01_.html.

Brecher, E.M., and the editors of Consumer Reports Magazine (1972). *Chapter 35. Cocaine*, http://www.druglibrary.org/schaffer/library/studies/cu/CU35.html

May, C.D. (1988, July 1) How Coca-Cola obtains its coca. *New York Times*, http://www.nytimes.com/1988/07/01/business/how-coca-cola-obtains-its-coca.html

Peterson, R.C. (1977). History of cocaine. In *Cocaine—NIDA Research Monograph #13* (pp. 17–34). (ADM 77–471). Available at: http://www.drugabuse.gov/pdf/monographs/13.pdf.

A more complete recounting and critique of Freud's interpretation of the Irma's injection dream is at: http://www.why-we-dream.com/freuddream1.htm.

THE DREAM OF IRMA'S INJECTION
(continued)

Fliess botched the unnecessary surgery, leaving a wad of gauze in the patient's nose that subsequently caused bleeding, infection, and permanent disfiguration before a second surgeon was called in, then discovered and removed the putrid gauze. Freud's interpretation of his own dream, in which Freud's psychoanalytic patient Irma experiences discomfort and infection from a contaminated needle, ignored the clear connection to Fliess's surgical ineptitude. Instead, Freud interpreted the dream as meaning he (Freud) wished to exonerate him from a failure to adequately treat Irma through psychoanalysis. Fliess's surgical misadventure is never mentioned. The interpretation might be correct in that Freud wished to exonerate himself. But it totally misses the very obvious point that Freud referred "Irma" to an incompetent surgeon whose ineptness almost cost Irma her life. Not only was the dream a wish fulfillment, so too was the interpretation.

"A Hitherto Inoffensive Negro"

- ***Document:*** Negro Cocaine "Fiends" New Southern Menace
- ***Date:*** February 8, 1914
- ***Where:*** *New York Times*
- ***Significance:*** In the United States, proposed restrictions on the use of one drug or another have often gained support through attributing the harms associated with use to racial or ethnic minorities. This essay exemplifies how such fear mongering was used as a political tactic to gain support for narcotics prohibition. Written by a then prominent physician, the article argues that cocaine use by Southern blacks was associated with almost superhuman acts of criminality. The evidence for such accusations was, at best, suspect and highly exaggerated and reflected social prejudices rather than reality. Nevertheless, such tactics proved to be (and continue to be, albeit stated less directly) politically effective.

DOCUMENT

Murder and Insanity Increasing among Lower Class Because They Have Taken to "Sniffing" since Being Deprived of Whisky by Prohibition

By Edward Huntington Williams, M.D.

FOR some years there have been rumors about the increase in drug taking in the South-vague, but always insistent rumors that the addiction to such drugs as morphine and cocaine was becoming a veritable curse to the colored race in certain regions. Some of these reports read like the wildest flights of a sensational fiction writer. Stories of cocaine orgies and "sniffing parties" followed by wholesale murders seem like lurid journalism of the yellowest variety.

But in point of fact there was nothing "yellow" about many of these reports. Nine men killed in Mississippi on one occasion by crazed cocaine takers, five in North Carolina, three in Tennessee—these are the facts that need no imaginative coloring. And since this gruesome evidence is supported by the printed records of the insane hospitals, courts, jails, and penitentiaries, there is no escaping the conviction drug taking has become a race menace in certain regions south of the line.

In the North drug addiction is prevalent enough, in all conscience. The hospitals for the insane in New York State admitted one insane drug taker to every 380 other patients last year and New York's record is about the same as that of her immediate neighbors. But in Georgia the proportion was one to 42, in North Carolina about 1 to 84, in Tennessee 1 to 74, and in one of the Mississippi hospitals 1 to 23.

Stated otherwise, these Southern States had between them, from five to fifteen times as many insane drug takers as New York State.

But these comparisons, although sufficiently startling, fail to show the extent of drug addiction in the South. For most of these insane drug users, both North and South, were the victims of morphine; whereas the negro drug "fiend" uses cocaine almost exclusively.

This preference is not explained by the difference in the effects of two drugs, but rather in the manner that each may be taken. Morphine, when taken into the stomach acts slowly and tends to upset digestion. If taken hypodermically its effects are produced almost immediately, and gastric functions are less disturbed. But hypodermic medication requires apparatus liquid solution of the drug, and a somewhat complicated process of preparation.

Cocaine, on the other hand, can be taken in the dry form by the simple process of sniffing into the nose like an ordinary pinch of snuff. And the effects are almost instantaneous when so taken. It can indeed, be mixed with, a brown powder that resembles ordinary snuff, and taken without detection under the very eyes of watchful officers.

The drug produces an exhilaration which is usually simply a mild intoxication, although it may produce the wildest form of insane excitation, accompanied by the fantastic hallucinations and delusions that characterize acute mania. But this condition is followed by a state of terrible depression a few hours later, or would be followed by such depression if the drug were not again taken to prevent it. It is for the purpose of averting this depressed state, as well as to produce the exaltation, that the "fiend" continues to use the drug once he has experienced either condition.

Stated thus, the effects of cocaine do not seem very different from these of alcohol. But in point of fact, cocaine exhilaration is much more marked and the depression far more profound and destructive to the nervous system. The victim is much more likely to have peculiar delusions and develop hallucinations of an unpleasant character. He imagines that he hears people taunting and abusing him, and this often incites homicidal attacks upon innocent and unsuspecting victims.

Proof against Bullets

But the drug produces several other conditions which make the "fiend" a peculiarly dangerous criminal. One of these conditions is a temporary immunity to shock—a resistance to the knockdown effects of fatal wounds.

Bullets fired into vital parts, that would drop a sane man in his tracks, fail to check the "fiend"—fail to stop his rush or weaken his attack.

A few weeks ago Dr. Crile's method of preventing shock in anaesthetized patients by use of a cocaine preparation was described in these columns. A similar fortification against this condition seems to be produced in the cocaine-sniffing negro.

A recent experience of Chief of Police Byerly of Asheville, N.C., illustrates this particular phase of cocainism. The Chief was informed that a hitherto inoffensive negro, with whom he was well acquainted, was "running amuck" in a cocaine frenzy, had attempted to stab a storekeeper, and was at the moment engaged in "beating up" various members of his own household. Being fully aware of the respect that the negro has for brass buttons, (and, incidentally, having a record for courage,) the officer went single-handed to the negro's house for the purpose of arresting him.

But when he arrived there the negro had completed the beatings and left the place. A few moments later, however, the man returned, and entered the room where the Chief was waiting for him, concealed behind a door. When the unsuspecting negro reached the middle of the room, the chief closed the door to prevent his escape and informed him quietly that he was under arrest, and asked him to come to the station. In reply the crazed negro drew a long knife, grappled with the officer, and slashed him viciously across the shoulder.

Knowing that he must kill this man or be killed himself, the Chief drew his revolver, placed the muzzle over the negro's heart, and fired-"Intending to kill him right quick," as the officer tells it but the shot did not even stagger the man. And a second shot that pierced the arm and entered the chest had as little effect in stopping his charge or checking his attack. . . .

The list of dangerous effects produced by cocaine just described-hallucinations and delusions, increased courage, homicidal tendencies, resistance to shock is certainly long; enough. But there is still another, and a most important one. This is a temporary steadying of the nervous and muscular system, so as to increase, rather than interfere with, good marksmanship.

Makes Better Marksmen

Many of the wholesale killings in the South may be cited as indicating that accuracy in shooting is not interfered with—is, indeed, probably improved-by cocaine. For a large proportion of such shootings have been the result of drug taking. But I believe the record of the "cocaine nigger" near Asheville who dropped five men dead in their tracks using only one cartridge for each, offers evidence that is sufficiently convincing. I doubt if this shooting record has been equaled in recent years: certainly not by a man under the influence of any other form of intoxicant. For the bad marksmanship of the drunken man is proverbial; while the deadly accuracy of the cocaine user has become axiomatic in Southern police circles . . .

Why Do They Do It?

Many of the negroes, even those who have not yet become addicted, appreciate the frightful penalty of dabbling with the drug. Why, then do so many of them "dabble"?

There are various facts that suggest an answer to this question, and evidence in the form or the opinions of physicians, officers, and the cocaine users themselves, that supports these facts. The "fiend" when questioned, frequently gives his reason in this brief sentence: "Cause I couldn't git nothin' else, boss." That seems to be the crux of the whole matter.

A brief survey of conditions in the South and a bit of recent legislative history make it perfectly evident why the negro "couldn't git nothin' else."

In many States, in the South the negro population constitutes from 30 to 60 per cent of the total population. Most of the negroes are poor, illiterate, and shiftless. If we include in this class the poor whites, who are on a par with the average negro in poverty, ignorance, and general lack of thrift, we may reckon the aggregate number as representing about one person in three in the entire population. Governing, or even keeping in reasonable control, such a host is an onerous task, even when most of the individuals of the host are sober. The inevitable number of alcoholics adds to that task enormously.

The simplest way to remove this added menace—it seems simple, theoretically, at least—would be to keep whisky out of the low-class negro's hands by legislating it out of existence as far as he is concerned. And so Georgia, North Carolina, South Carolina, Mississippi, Tennessee, and West Virginia passed laws intended to abolish the saloon and keep whisky and the negro separated.

These laws do not, and were not intended to prevent the white man or the well-to-do negro getting his accustomed beverages through legitimate channels. They obliged him to forego the pleasure of leaning against a bar and "taking his drink perpendicularly," to be sure; but a large portion of the intelligent whites were ready to make this sacrifice if by doing so they could eliminate the drunken negro. . . .

Should anyone doubt that prohibition is directly responsible for the introduction, and increase, of cocaine-taking in the South, let him consider a few pertinent facts supported by the opinions of competent observers.

Hospital and police records show that during the prohibition period drug habits have increased with alarming rapidity. Physicians, officers, and "fiends," with very few dissenting opinions, attribute the rise of cocainism to the low-class negro's inability to get his accustomed beverages. Of course "fiends" are usually liars, and even officers of the law or practitioners of medicine may be mistaken. But it is entirely improbable that all these men, from such widely different walks of life, should reach the same conclusion without adequate grounds for doing so.

Moreover, in cities where prohibition is strictly enforced, (relatively speaking,) the drug habit is increasing with alarming rapidity; whereas in cities in which little attempt is made to prevent liquor traffic, there is a comparatively slight increase in cocaine taking. Thus the officials of Raleigh, N.C., and Knoxville, Tenn., to mention but two places where the prohibitory statute is enforced, report that cocaine taking has doubled in four years. The Knoxville police arrested seven cocaine-taking women in a single day recently. In Memphis, on the other hand, where half the population is colored, but where no attempt is made to prevent the sale of liquors, the drug habit is increasing slowly, if at all.

From Bad to Worse

In short, the South in attempting to correct a bad condition has created one infinitely worse. For the evils of alcoholism—its effects upon the individual, or even upon the community—are not to be compared with the horrors of cocainism.

What is the South going to do about it.

As far as the thousands who have already formed the habit are concerned there is little choice of remedies. Once the negro has formed the habit he is irreclaimable. The only method to keep him away from taking the drug is by imprisoning him. And this is merely palliative treatment, for he returns inevitably to the drug habit when released.

For the thousands of negroes who have not yet acquired the habit, but who will do so eventually if present conditions continue, the outlook is scarcely more hopeful. The drug traffic puts an irresistible temptation in their way, and this traffic continues to flourish.

The failure to suppress it cannot be attributed to lack of interest or strenuous endeavor on the part of officials. Every one of these is doing his utmost to stop it, not merely from a sense of duty, but because of the much more compelling motive, self-preservation. It is literally a matter of life and death with them. And yet they fail utterly.

The great stumbling block in the way of suppressing the traffic is the fact that the causes that produce it have become entangled with a political issue. The question is not merely—what is best for the negro, or the race? But it is: What is best for the politician? Presently the issue will take some other fantastic political twist, and then they will "call in the surgeons to patch up the wounded."

But meanwhile these politicians have forced a new and terrible form of slavery upon thousands of colored men—a hideous bondage from which they cannot escape by mere proclamation or civil war.

SOURCE: "Negro Cocaine 'Fiends' New Southern Menace," *New York Times*, February 8, 1914.

ANALYSIS

All good people agree,
And all good people say,
All nice people, like Us, are We
And every one else is They. . . .

—Rudyard Kipling

At the time this article was written, a number of states, particularly states in the south, had already passed laws prohibiting alcohol use. The 18th Amendment and the Volstead Act would eventually supersede these state prohibition laws, but while in effect, the state laws were nevertheless effective in reducing alcohol available for consumption on a local basis. They also had the effect of driving up the cost of alcoholic beverages that were still available. Whereas the wealthy could maintain liquor supplies and wine cellars in their homes—the prohibition laws did not make it illegal to possess alcohol for personal use—alcohol was more difficult to get and prohibitively expensive for the poor, who were disproportionately black. To compensate for the lack of alcohol, those who still sought out intoxicants could more easily obtain cocaine and for a relatively cheap price, the "5-cent sniff." The same cost considerations also made marijuana more attractive because of its relative inexpensiveness and easier acquisition.

There is no evidence to suggest these factors caused significant increases in cocaine use or in violent crimes by any particular racial/ethnic group. Although many white

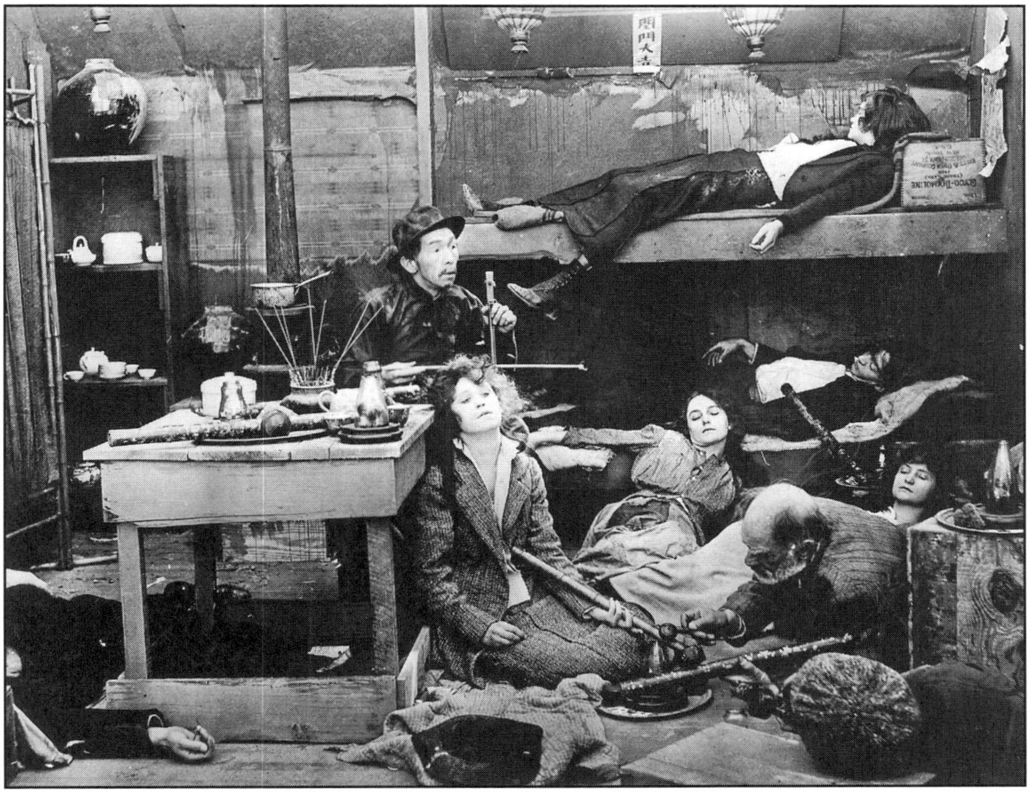

Drug policy has often been motivated by fear mongering fed by racial prejudices and stereotypes. Lurid accounts in the press and images appearing in the popular media reinforced these prejudices. This still from the movie *The Dividend* depicts drugged white women in an opium den being seduced by Chinese men, who were blamed for the problem of opium use in the United States at the time. (Triangle/Photofest)

Americans continued to obtain cocaine (and opiates) from pharmacists and physicians, the perceived increase in cocaine use among blacks was cause for alarm for some but a matter of political expedience for others. Those who sought to prohibit narcotics use on a national level played upon existing racial stereotypes and fears to gain political support among the southern states, which were strongly opposed to ceding any power to the Federal government.

The association of cocaine use and violent crime with African Americans during this time was not the only attempt to use racial stereotypes and fears to bolster support for stronger enforcement of the drug laws and it would not be the last use of such tactics. The history of American drug policy, which after all is about social control, is replete with sometimes coded and sometimes blatant appeals to racist attitudes and fears whether it was the negro "cocaine fiends" of the early 1900s; fears over the violence surrounding the crack cocaine trade attributed to African American gangs and the rise of the largely mythical "super-predators" in the mid-1980s; or concerns about terrorism, illegal immigration, and the violent drug trade in Mexico in the present day. American drug policy has always been (and remains) partially driven by the majority's extant social anxieties and fears of the era.

Nor have black Americans been the only group portrayed as demonic, white-women-and-children-plundering, drug-fueled criminals. Chinese immigrant laborers, known as "coolies," first brought to America to work in the gold mines and transcontinental railroads in the mid-1800s were associated with smoking opiates. Portrayals of Chinese smoking parlors or "opium dens" as they were called, included lurid descriptions of how white women were enticed into licentious behavior through the lure of smoking opium with Chinese men.

> The practice [of smoking opium] spread rapidly and quietly among this class of gamblers and prostitutes until the latter part of 1875, at which time the authorities became cognizant of the fact, and finding, upon investigations, that many women and young girls, as also young men of respectable family, were

> being induced to visit the dens, where they were ruined morally and otherwise. (Terry and Pellens, 1928, p. 73)

Concerned over the corrupting influence of opium smoking Chinamen, but driven more by an even greater desire to insure continued trade with China and be in compliance with following an international conference on opium held in Shanghai, the U.S. government passed the Opiate Exclusion Act of 1909, which banned the importation of opium for smoking (but not for other purposes such as inclusion in pharmaceutical preparations).

Mexican laborers working in agriculture were associated with marijuana use and demonized as becoming criminal and violent when using the drug in much the same way as the blacks and Chinese were portrayed in their use of cocaine and opium. The following excerpt quotes an El Paso police captain describing the connection between violence, marijuana use, and the immigrant Mexican population. Note the similarities in this description and the main document describing the effects of cocaine use on black Americans:

> I have had almost daily experience with the users of [marijuana] for the reason that when they are addicted to the use they become very violent, especially when they become angry and will attack an officer even if a gun is drawn on him, they seem to have no fear, I have also noted that when under the influence of this weed they have abnormal strength and that it will take several men to handle one man where under ordinary circumstances one man could handle him with ease.

As in the case of the Opiate Exclusion Act, political expedience was not the sole motivation behind the desire to prohibit marijuana use; powerful financial interests were also at work. At the time, William Randolph Hearst, owner of a newspaper empire and model for the main protagonist in the movie *Citizen Kane,* had a significant financial stake in the timber industry to supply paper for his newspapers. At the time, paper made from hemp was a competing product. Hearst had also lost 800,000 acres of timberland he owned in Mexico to Pancho Villa during the Mexican Revolution, fueling Hearst's already considerable xenophobia and targeting it toward Mexicans.

To preserve his investment in timber, vent his anger at Mexicans, promulgate widespread fear and anger, and sell more papers, Hearst directed his papers to run stories about the "lazy," "degenerate," "violent," and "marihuana smoking" Mexicans. Hearst publications were already associated with "yellow journalism"—the tendency to create exaggerated, nonfactual stories to gain headlines and promote profits. Illustrative of this bent, lurid titles such as "Marijuana Makes Fiends of Boys in 30 Days" and "Mexican Narcotic, Marihuana Inciting with Lust to Slay, Blamed for Death Cruise" began appearing in Hearst-controlled newspapers such as the *San Francisco Examiner* and in other Hearst publications in the 1920s. Unfortunately, the exaggerated and patently false claims represented in the stories that accompanied these headlines as well as editorials and public testimonials from prominent sources such as law enforcement officials and politicians that were directed against minorities played a significant role in shaping American drug policy for much of the 20th century.

FURTHER READING

Bonnie, R.J. & Whitebread, C.H. (1974). *The marihuana conviction: A history of marihuana prohibition in the United States*. Charlottesville: University Press of Virginia.

Hodgson, B. (1999). *Opium: A portrait of the heavenly demon*. Vancouver, British Columbia, Canada: Greystone Books.

Inciardi, J. (2007). *The war on drugs IV: The continuing saga of the mysteries and miseries of intoxication, addiction, crime, and public policy (4th edition)* . Boston, MA: Allyn and Bacon

Jonnes, J. (1996). *Hep-cats, narcs, and pipe dreams: A history of America's romance with illegal drugs*. New York, NY: Scribner.

Provine, D.M. (2007). *Unequal under the law: Race in the war on drugs* . Chicago, IL: University of Chicago Press.

Terry, C.E., & Pellens, M. (1970). *The opium problem* (Bureau of Social Hygiene, reprint from 1928). Montclair, NJ: Patterson Smith Publishing.

On the Internet

American Chronicle: The Failed Services Economy: Its Link to Illegal Drugs and Illegal Immigration, an essay tracing the history of racism in U.S. drug policy through to the present day and the dispute over immigration policy and Mexican immigrants appears at: https://terrydata.wordpress.com/2010/08/13/american-chronicle-the-failed-services-economy-its-link-to-illegal-drugs-and-illegal-immigration/

The Racial History of U.S. Drug Prohibition: http://www.drugpolicy.org/about/position/race_paper_history.cfm

The Racial Roots of Our Drug Laws: http://www.druglibrary.org/schaffer/LIBRARY/histdrug.htm

The Opium Exclusion Act of 1909. This site has an essay that is highly critical of American international policy as it pertains to drug prohibition: http://www.counterpunch.org/gieringer02062009.html

A history of marijuana-related policies in the United States with additional information on how these policies were shaped by prejudice and financial interests rather than by science and rational discourse: http://www.drugwarrant.com/articles/why-is-marijuana-illegal/

Reprints of the stories that appeared in the *San Francisco Examiner,* a Hearst publication, can be found on the Shaffer Library of Drug Policy website: http://www.druglibrary.org/mags/examiner26.htm http://www.druglibrary.org/mags/examiner23.htm

"In the Course of His Professional Practice Only"

- ***Document:*** The Harrison Narcotics Act
- ***Date:*** December 14, 1914
- ***Where:*** Washington, DC
- ***Significance:*** The Harrison Narcotics Act made the importation, manufacturing, sale, and distribution of narcotics, defined as cocaine, opiates, and opiate derivatives such as heroin, illegal without first registering with the Bureau of Internal Revenue, recording each transaction, and paying an annual tax and licensing fee. The law circumvented the limited policing powers of the Federal government and instead used the Federal powers to tax and control inter-state commerce as the levers for enacting narcotics control. The Harrison Act sharply curtailed the legal availability of narcotic drugs and would remain in effect for over half a century.

DOCUMENT

Chap 1.—

An Act To provide for the registration of, with collectors of internal revenue, and to impose a special tax on all persons who produce, import, manufacture, compound, deal in, dispense, sell, distribute, or give away opium or coca leaves, their salts, derivatives, or preparations, and for other purposes.

Be it enacted by the Senate and House of Representatives of the United States of America in Congress assembled, that on and after the first day of March, nineteen hundred and fifteen, every person who produces, imports, manufactures, compounds, deals in, dispenses, distributes, or gives away opium or coca leaves or any compound, manufacture, salt, derivative, or preparation thereof, shall register with the collector of internal revenue of the district, his name or style, place of business, and place or places where such business is to be carried on. . . .

At the time of such registry and on or before the first of July annually thereafter, every person who produces, imports, manufactures, compounds, deals in, dispenses, distributes, or gives away any of the aforesaid drugs shall pay to the said collector a special tax at the rate of $1 per annum. . . .

It shall be unlawful for any person required to register under the terms of this Act to produce, import, manufacture, compound, deal in, dispense, sell, distribute, any of the aforesaid drugs without having registered and paid the special tax provided for in this section . . .

Sec 2.—

That it shall be unlawful for any person to sell, barter, exchange, or give away any of the aforesaid drugs except in pursuance of a written order of the person to whom such article is sold, bartered, exchanged, or given, on a form to be issued in blank for that purpose by the Commissioner of Internal Revenue. Every person who shall accept any such order, and in pursuance thereof shall sell, barter, exchange, or give away any of the aforesaid drugs shall preserve such order for a period of two years in such a way as to be readily accessible to inspection by any officer, agent, or employee of the Treasury Department duly authorized for that purpose, and the State, Territorial, district, municipal and insular officials named in Section five of this Act. Every person who shall give an order as herein provided to any other person for any of the aforesaid drugs shall, at or before the time of giving of such order, make or cause to be made, a duplicate thereof on a form to be issued in blank for that purpose by the Commissioner of Internal Revenue, and in the case of the acceptance of such order, shall preserve such duplicate for said period of two years in such a way as to be readily accessible to inspection by the officers, agents, employees, and officials herein mentioned. Nothing contained in this section shall apply—

(a) To the dispensing or distribution of any of the aforesaid drugs to a patient by a physician, dentist, or veterinary surgeon registered under this Act in the course of his professional practice only: Provided, That such physician, dentist, or veterinary surgeon shall keep a record of all such drugs dispensed or distributed, showing the amount dispensed or distributed, the date, and the name and address of the person to whom such drugs are dispensed or distributed; except such as may be dispensed or distributed to a patient upon whom such physician, dentist, or veterinary surgeon shall personally attend; and such record shall be kept for a period of two years from the date of dispensing or distributing such drugs, subject to inspection, as provided in this Act.

Sec 6.—

That the provisions of this Act shall not be construed to apply to the sale, distribution, or giving away, dispensing, or possession of preparations and remedies which do not contain more than two grains of opium, or more than one-fourth of a grain of morphine, or more than one-eighth of grain of heroin, or more than one grain of codeine, or any salt or derivative of them in one fluid ounce, or, if a solid or semi-solid preparation, in one avoirdupois ounce, or to liniments, ointments, and other preparations which contain cocaine or any of its salts or alpha or beta eucaine or any of their salts or any synthetic substitute for them: Provided, that such remedies and preparations are sold, distributed, given away, dispensed, or possessed as medicines and not for the purpose of evading the intentions and provisions of this Act. The provisions of this Act shall not apply to decocainized coca leaves or preparations made therefrom, or to other preparations of coca leaves which do not contain cocaine.

Sec 8.—

That it shall be unlawful for any person not registered under the provisions of this Act, and who has not paid the special tax provided for by this Act, to have in his possession or under his control any of the aforesaid drugs; and such possession or control shall be presumptive evidence of a violation of this section, and also a violation of the provisions of section one of this Act: Provided, That this section shall not apply to any employee of a registered person, or to a nurse under the supervision of a physician, dentist, or veterinary surgeon registered under this Act, having such possession or control by virtue of his employment or occupation and not on his own account; or to the possession of any of the aforesaid drugs which has or have been prescribed in good faith by a physician, dentist, or veterinary surgeon registered under this Act. . . .

Sec 9.—

That any person who violates or fails to comply with any of the requirements of this Act shall, on conviction, be fined not more than $2,000 or be imprisoned not more than five years, or both, in the discretion of the court.

SOURCE: Harrison Narcotics Act, Ch. 1, 38 Stat. 785. Public Law No. 223, 63rd Cong.

ANALYSIS

The Harrison Act or Harrison Narcotics Act of 1914 is named after New York Representative Francis Burton Harrison, who sponsored its passage in the U.S. House of Representatives. Reflecting the growing public sentiment at the turn of the century to control drug and alcohol distribution, the Harrison Act predated Prohibition by four years and had both international and national motivations. Internationally, there was general concern over a flourishing Asian opium trade and addiction as significant problems that had festered at least since the time of the first Opium War between Britain and China in 1839. The Asian opium trade became a concern of the United States when it purchased the Philippines from Spain in 1898 at the conclusion of the Spanish-American War. As the convener of the International Opium Conference in 1912 at The Hague, the United States was in the ironic position of signing an international drug control treaty without itself having a national drug control law. Proponents of the Harrison Act argued that it would allow the United States to represent its good faith intention to control narcotic distribution within its own borders. As such, it had the strong backing and support of the State Department in the person of William Jennings Bryan, who was then the U.S. Secretary of State.

Nationally, although the Pure Food and Drug Act of 1906, which required products to label their ingredients, had brought about curbs on the patent medicine industry, it did not proscribe the use of opiates or cocaine, which could still legally be obtained from pharmacists and physicians. Patent medicines could also still be sold over the counter, but the labeling requirement had begun to curtail sales. Those seeking to curb further not only the patent medicine industry but also the legal sale and distribution of opiates and cocaine sought a stronger, more direct measure; the Harrison Act would fill that need.

The Harrison Act in many respects reflected compromises with powerful special interests such as pharmaceutical manufacturers, druggists, and the American Medical Association who were concerned that the legislation would curtail income and impose onerous record-keeping requirements. The act did not prohibit the sale or distribution of narcotics but "merely" required those who did so to register with the Treasury Department, keep records of their transactions, and pay taxes and fees. Transactions between physicians, pharmacists, and patients were not taxed but did have to be recorded. The act did not prohibit narcotics use or sale as prohibition did with alcohol; manufacturers could still make narcotics, physicians could still prescribe them, pharmacists could still dispense them, and patients could still take them. The law was initially, however, vague with respect to what circumstances constituted valid prescribing practices and the extent to which sanctions would be imposed and violators prosecuted.

The main question concerning the extent of the law was the phrase in §2 that dispensation and distribution should be carried out *in the course of professional practice only*. In particular, it was unclear whether the course of professional practice included the provision of narcotics to maintain an addiction or whether that would constitute a violation of the law. A number of cases involving the Harrison Act reached the Supreme Court subsequent to its passage. The court rulings in these cases ultimately decided the issue, prohibiting the prescription of narcotics solely for the purpose of maintaining an addiction.

In *Webb et al. v. United States* (1919), the court considered whether a physician and pharmacist in Tennessee could prescribe large amounts of morphine on a regular basis to "habitual" morphine users with no intent of weaning them from the drug. The court decided prescribing and selling narcotics under such circumstances violated the intent of the law and, moreover, enforcement of the Harrison Act under such circumstances did not unconstitutionally circumvent states' rights. With respect to providing a user with morphine sufficient to keep him comfortable, the majority opinion noted, "To call such an order for the use of morphine a physician's prescription would be so plain a perversion of the use of meaning that no discussion of the subject is required."

The court upheld this position in *Jin Fuey Moy v. United States* (1920). In this instance, the court examined whether the defendant, a practicing physician in Pittsburgh, could write prescriptions for opiates without conducting thorough (or any) physical examinations of patients for the primary purpose of generating income through the sheer volume of prescriptions written. Fuey Moy charged each patient by the amount prescribed. The case highlights a problem caused by the *Webb* decision whereby many physicians curtailed prescribing narcotics, even when it would have been legal, simply because they did not want to risk arrest and prosecution. With fewer and fewer legitimate sources for obtaining drugs, the addict community

WHAT IS A NARCOTIC?

The Harrison Narcotics Act profoundly changed drug policy in the United States by statutorily controlling the production, sale, distribution, and prescribing of opium, cocaine, and their derivatives. In so doing, the act included both cocaine and opium in the definition of narcotic drugs. However, from a pharmacological standpoint, only opium, its derivatives (morphine and codeine), and semi-synthetic (heroin, hydromorphone [Dilaudid]) or synthetic (methadone, meperidine [Demerol]) substitutes that have a similar chemical structure and effect are technically narcotics. As a class, narcotics are characterized as having analgesic (i.e., pain-killing) and sedating effects. Cocaine (and its derivatives) has neither analgesic nor sedating properties when ingested, although it can be used as a topical anesthetic, and is classified as a central nervous system stimulant. In blurring this important distinction between two very different drug classes, the Harrison Act set precedent for subsequent legislation (e.g., Controlled Substances Act of 1970) that continued to misuse the term narcotic as referring to virtually any drug deemed to be harmful, and thereby warranting restricted access. As a result, drugs such as marijuana, PCP, and amphetamines among others have been included in anti-narcotics legislation even though, like cocaine, none are pharmacologically narcotics.

was funneled toward unscrupulous "dope doctors" who would write prescriptions purely for financial gain and outside the bounds of what could even broadly be construed as professional practice. Not surprisingly, the Supreme Court found that Fuey Moy's prescribing patterns were not within the boundaries of "professional practice" and were in clear violation of the Harrison Act.

In *United States v. Behrman* (1922), the court again considered whether prescribing large amounts of narcotics, in this case, heroin, morphine, and cocaine, to a single patient solely for the purpose of maintaining the patient's addiction could also be construed as a violation of the Harrison Act. The distinction here is that Behrman was prescribing the drugs in good faith to a patient with whom he was well acquainted and the motivation was not so obviously profiteering. The case more clearly honed in on defining what were and what were not legal prescribing practices. The court affirmed its prior rulings by a 6 to 3 margin, indicating with clarity that prescribing narcotics for the purpose of maintaining an addiction was illegal. This would remain the case over the next 40 years until methadone, a synthetic narcotic, was studied by researchers Vincent Dole and Marie Nyswander and shown to be an effective substitute therapy for narcotic addicts.

FURTHER READING

Acker, C. J. (2002). *Creating the American junkie: Addiction research in the classic era*. Baltimore, MD: Johns Hopkins University Press.

Courtwright, D. T. (2001). *Dark paradise: A history of opiate addiction in America*. Cambridge, MA: Harvard University Press.

Feiling, T. (2009). *Cocaine nation: How the white trade took over the world*. New York, NY: Pegasus Books.

Jonnes, J. (1996). *Hep-cats, narcs, and pipe dreams: A history of America's romance with illegal drugs*. New York: Scribner.

Musto, D. (1999). *The American disease: Origins of narcotics control (3rd edition)*. New York: Oxford University Press.

On the Internet

A critique of the Harrison Narcotics Act from the perspective of a physician writing shortly after its passage is available at the Schaffer Library of Drug Policy website: http://druglibrary.net/schaffer/History/e1910/drugaddictionandharrison.htm.

"The Great Social and Economic Experiment, Noble in Motive and Far Reaching in Purpose"

- ***Document:*** Amendment 18 to the Constitution
- ***Dates:*** December 18, 1917, passed by Congress
  January 16, 1919, ratified by 36 states
  January 16, 1920, effective as law
- ***Where:*** U.S. Congress, Washington, DC
- ***Significance:*** Amended the U.S. Constitution by making the sale, manufacturing, and distribution of alcohol illegal thereby marking the beginning of prohibition, a social experiment on a national scale that would last for 13 years before being repealed by the 21st Amendment in 1933. The effects of prohibition continue to be debated through the present day, resurfacing most prominently in the current debate on drug policy and the merit of harm reduction approaches versus outright prohibition of drugs.

DOCUMENT

Amendment XVIII

Section 1

After one year from the ratification of this article the manufacture, sale, or transportation of intoxicating liquors within, the importation thereof into, or the exportation thereof from the United States and all territory subject to the jurisdiction thereof for beverage purposes is hereby prohibited.

Section 2

The Congress and the several States shall have concurrent power to enforce this article by appropriate legislation.

Section 3

This article shall be inoperative unless it shall have been ratified as an amendment to the Constitution by the legislatures of the several States, as provided in the Constitution, within seven years from the date of the submission hereof to the States by the Congress.

SOURCE: National Archives.

ANALYSIS

Because the 18th Amendment to the Constitution and the National Prohibition Act are so closely tied together, they are analyzed as such following the presentation of the National Prohibition Act document.

"No One but a Physician"

- ***Document:*** The National Prohibition Act (also known as the Volstead Act)
- ***Dates:*** January 17, 1920
- ***Where:*** Washington, DC, and the nation
- ***Significance:*** The Volstead Act provided the legal means and definitions for enforcing prohibition. Provisions in the law that allowed for private consumption, manufacturing of alcoholic beverages for "sacramental purposes," by prescription, and in "preserved sweet cider," allowed sufficient latitude for widespread production and consumption of alcohol in spite of the law's other rather stringent provisions such as restricting the legal alcohol content of any beverage to less than one half of one percent. Lack of funding for enforcement and the laxity with which the Volstead Act was enforced together with these loopholes allowed for widespread distribution of alcohol after its enactment, ultimately leading to a growing sense of the futility of prohibition and its eventual repeal.

DOCUMENT

An Act to prohibit intoxicating beverages, and to regulate the manufacture, production, use, and sale of high-proof spirits for other than beverage purposes, and to insure an ample supply of alcohol and promote its use in scientific research and in the development of fuel, dye, and other lawful industries.

Be it enacted by the Senate and House of Representatives of the United States of America in Congress assembles, That the short title of this Act shall be the "National Prohibition Act." . . .

Title I.
To Provide for the Enforcement of War Prohibition

The term "War Prohibition Act" used in this Act shall mean the provisions of any Act or Acts prohibiting the sale and manufacture of intoxicating liquors until the conclusion of the present war and thereafter until the termination of demobilization, the date of which shall be determined and proclaimed by the President of the United States. The words "beer, wine, or other intoxicating malt or vinous liquors" in the War Prohibition Act shall be hereafter construed to mean any such beverages which contain one-half of 1 per centum or more of alcoholic beverages by volume.

SEC. 2. The Commissioner of, Internal Revenue, his assistants, agents, and inspectors, shall investigate and report violations of the War Prohibition Act to the United States attorney for the district in which committed, who shall be charged with the duty of prosecuting, subject to the direction of the Attorney General, the offenders as in the case of other offenses against laws of the United States; and such Commissioner of Internal Revenue, his assistants, agents, and inspectors may swear out warrants before United States commissioners or other officers or courts authorized to issue the same for the apprehension of such offenders, and may, subject to the control of the said United States attorney, conduct the prosecution at the committing trial for the purpose of having the offenders held for the action of a grand jury. . . .

Title II
Prohibition of Intoxicating Beverages

SEC. 3. No person shall on or after the date when the eighteenth amendment to the Constitution of the United States goes into effect, manufacture, sell, barter, transport, import, export, deliver, furnish or possess any intoxicating liquor except as authorized in this Act, and all the provisions of this shall be liberally construed to the end that the use of intoxicating liquor as a beverage may be prevented.

Liquor for nonbeverage purposes and wine for sacramental purposes may be manufactured, purchased, sold, bartered, transported, imported, exported, delivered furnished and possessed, but only as herein provided, and the commissioner may, upon application, issue permits therefore. . . . Provided, That nothing in this Act shall prohibit the purchase and sale of warehouse receipts covering distilled spirits on deposit in Government bonded warehouses, and no special tax liability shall attach to the business of purchasing and selling such warehouse receipts.

SEC. 4. The articles enumerated in this section shall not, after having been manufactured and prepared for the market, be subject to the provisions of this Act if they correspond with the following descriptions and limitations, namely:

(a) Denatured alcohol or denatured rum produced and used as provided by laws and regulations now or hereafter in force.

(b) Medicinal preparations manufactured in accordance with formulas prescribed by the United States Pharmacopoeia, National Formulary of the American Institute of Homeopathy that are unfit for beverage purposes.

(c) Patented, patent, and proprietary medicines that are unfit for use for beverage purposes.

(d) Flavoring extracts and syrups that are unfit for use as a beverage, or for intoxicating beverage purposes.
(e) Flavoring extracts and syrups that are unfit for use as a beverage, or for intoxicating beverage purposes.
(f) Vinegar and preserved sweet cider. . . .

SEC. 6. No one shall manufacture, sell, purchase, transport, or prescribe any liquor without first obtaining a permit from the commissioner so to do, except that a person may, without a permit, purchase and use liquor for medicinal purposes when prescribed by a physician as herein provided, and except that any person who in the opinion of the commissioner is conducting a bona fide hospital or sanatorium engaged in the treatment of persons suffering from alcoholism, may, under such rules, regulations, and conditions as the commissioner shall prescribe, purchase and use, in accordance with the methods in use in such institution, liquor, to be administered to the patients of such institution under the direction of a duly qualified physician employed by such institution.

Nothing in this title shall be held to apply to the manufacture, sale, transportation, importation, possession, or distribution of wine for sacramental purposes, or like religious rites, except section 6 (save as the same requires a permit to purchase) and section 10 hereof, and the provisions of this Act prescribing penalties for the violation of either of said sections. No person to whom a permit may be issued to manufacture, transport, import, or sell wines for sacramental purposes or like religious rites shall sell, barter, exchange, or furnish any such to any person not a rabbi, minister of the gospel, priest, or an officer duly authorized for the purpose by any church or congregation, nor to any such except upon an application duly subscribed by him, which application, authenticated as regulations may prescribe, shall be filed and preserved by the seller. The head of any conference or diocese or other ecclesiastical jurisdiction may designate any rabbi, minister, or priest to supervise the manufacture of wine to be used for the purposes and rites in this section mentioned, and the person so designated may, in the discretion of the commissioner, be granted a permit to supervise such manufacture.

SEC. 7. No one but a physician holding a permit to prescribe liquor shall issue any prescription for liquor. And no physician shall prescribe liquor unless after careful physical examination of the person for whose use such prescription is sought, or if such examination is found impracticable, then upon the best information obtainable, he in good faith believes that the use of such liquor as a medicine by such person is necessary and will afford relief to him from some known ailment. Not more than a pint of spirituous liquor to be taken internally shall be prescribed for use by the same person within any period of ten days and no prescription shall be filled more than once. . . .

SEC. 17. It shall be unlawful to advertise anywhere, or by any means or method, liquor, or the manufacture, sale, keeping for sale or furnishing of the same, or where, how, from whom or at what price the same may be obtained. No one shall permit any sign or billboard containing such advertisement to remain upon one's premises. But nothing herein shall prohibit manufacturers and wholesale druggists holding permits to sell liquor from furnishing price lists; with descriptions of liquor for sale, to persons permitted to purchase liquor, or from advertising alcohol in business publications or trade journals circulating generally among manufacturers of lawful alcoholic perfumes, toilet preparations, flavoring extracts, medicinal preparations, and like articles. . . .

SEC. 18. It shall be unlawful to advertise, manufacture, sell, or possess for sale any utensil, contrivance, machine, preparation, compound, tablet, substance, formula direction, recipe advertised, designed, or intended for use in the unlawful manufacture of intoxicating liquor.

SEC. 21. Any room, house, building, boat, vehicle, structure, or place where intoxicating liquor is manufactured, sold, kept, or bartered in violation of this title, and all intoxicating liquor and property kept and used in maintaining the same, is hereby declared to be a common nuisance, and any person who maintains such a common nuisance shall be guilty of a misdemeanor and upon conviction thereof shall be fined not more than $1,000 or be imprisoned for not more than one year, or both. . . .

SEC. 25. It shall be unlawful to have or possess any liquor or property designed for the manufacture of liquor intended for use in violating this title or which has been so used, and no property rights shall exist in any such liquor or property. . . . No search warrant shall issue to search any private dwelling occupied as such unless it is being used for the unlawful sale of intoxicating liquor, or unless it is in part used for some business purposes such as a store, shop, saloon, restaurant, hotel, or boarding house. . . .

SEC. 29. Any person who manufactures or sells liquor in-violation of this title shall for a first offense be fined not more than $1,000, or imprisoned not exceeding six months, and for a second or subsequent offense shall be fined not less than $200 nor more than $2,000 and be imprisoned not less than one month nor more than five years.

Any person violating the provisions of any permit, or who makes any false record, report, or affidavit required by this title, or violates any of the provisions of this title, for which offense a special penalty is not prescribed, shall be fined for a first offense not more than $500; for a second offense not less than $100 nor more than $1,000, or be imprisoned not more than ninety days; for any subsequent offense he shall be fined not less than $500 and be imprisoned not less than three months nor more than two years. . . .

SEC. 33. After February 1, 1920, the possession of liquors by any person not legally permitted under this title to possess liquor shall be prima facie evidence that such liquor is kept for the purpose of being sold, bartered, exchanged, given away, furnished, or otherwise disposed of in violation of the Provisions of this title. . . . But it shall not be unlawful to possess liquors in one's private dwelling while the same is occupied and used by him as his dwelling only and such liquor need not be reported, provided such liquors are for use only for the personal consumption of the owner thereof and his family residing in such dwelling and of his bona fide guests when entertained by him therein; and the burden, of proof shall be upon the possessor in any action concerning the same to prove that such liquor was law fully acquired, possessed, and used. . . .

SOURCE: Statutes at Large, vol. 41, pp. 305–323 (41 Stat. 305).

ANALYSIS

The title quote describing Prohibition as a "great social and economic experiment, noble in purpose" is from Herbert Hoover's nomination acceptance speech at the

1928 Republican Convention. In time, Hoover's description would be shortened. As the years passed, and with more than a little irony, Prohibition would come simply to be known as the "noble experiment." By 1928, national Prohibition had been in effect for eight years. Hoover was already late to the party. Despite the rhetoric, his personal support for Prohibition was only lukewarm, and his public stance reflected the continuing social and political influence of the Prohibition movement. However, in four years, the Democratic presidential candidate, Franklin D. Roosevelt, would be running on a platform that openly supported the repeal of Prohibition. Support for Prohibition was also clearly waning in the Republican Party. By 1933, the noble experiment would be over, assessed according to most but not all measures as having been a massive policy failure.

The relatively short time national Prohibition was in effect in the United States (other countries such as Canada, Sweden, Mexico, and—most incongruously—Russia, also experimented with forms of prohibition that were equally unsuccessful and lasted for equally short periods) belies the long period of growing support for Prohibition, manifested collectively as the temperance movement. One of the earliest influences on the temperance movement was Dr. Benjamin Rush, a signer of the Declaration of Independence and a prominent physician who became the forefather of modern psychiatry. Rush wrote with force and eloquence of the dire consequences of drinking and alcoholism as early as 1785. For example, in summing up these consequences, Rush noted, "Thus we see poverty and misery, crimes and infamy, diseases and death, are all the natural and usual consequences of the intemperate use of ardent spirits."

Influenced by the work of Rush and other, even fierier orators such as the Reverend Lyman Beecher, the first temperance group, the American Temperance Society, formed in 1826. At the time, it is estimated that per capita consumption of alcohol, mostly whisky, was three times what it is today, giving those in the temperance movement plenty of impetus to correct what they perceived as the cause of numerous social problems such as those enumerated by Rush. Gaining in influence over the next few decades, the influence of the temperance movement waned during the Civil War as the country necessarily turned its attentions elsewhere.

Following the war, the temperance movement was reinvigorated, increasing in popularity within Protestant and other religious groups throughout the Northeast and Midwest. The temperance movement was highlighted prominently through the actions of Carrie (sometimes Carry) Nation, who gained fame and publicity for the cause as an ardent supporter of the Kansas state law prohibiting alcohol. Famous for using an ax to damage saloons violating the state law, she capitalized on her fame by making replica axes, which she sold along with publicity photos of herself holding an ax to raise funds.

Billy Sunday is another famous and colorful public figure associated with the rise of Prohibition. Sunday became the most popular evangelical minister at the time and was a strong supporter of Prohibition. Large crowds came to hear his theatrical, animated, impassioned sermons wherein he railed against behaviors he considered vices including card playing, attending the theater, and drinking alcoholic beverages. Lyrics from the song "Chicago (That Toddlin' Town)" contain a succinct nod to Sunday's popularity and political agenda as well as to the limits of his influence: Chicago was "the town that Billy Sunday could not shut down." An excerpt from a sermon Sunday delivered before 10,000 congregants in Norfolk, Virginia, that celebrated the onset of Prohibition illustrates his dramatic flare and soaring expectations for the outcome:

> The reign of tears is over. The slums will soon be only a memory. We will turn our prisons into factories and our jails into storehouses and corncribs. Men will walk upright now, women will smile, and the children will laugh. Hell will be forever for rent.

The crucial support for temperance that would provide the political backbone and social will for passage and ratification of the 18th Amendment came about with the formation and subsequent persuasive advocacy and politicking of two organizations that grew increasingly powerful over time: the Women's Christian Temperance Union (WCTU), founded in Cleveland, Ohio, in 1874 and the Anti-Saloon League (ASL), founded in Oberlin, Ohio, in 1893.

Both organizations favored complete abstinence from alcohol as opposed to, for instance, moderate drinking. However, they differed in the extent to which they focused on Prohibition as their primary issue. For the WCTU, under the leadership of its second and most famous president, Frances Wheeler, Prohibition was but one of a number of important social and moral issues that they sought to address such as suffrage, prison reform, labor laws, and prostitution. A woman's right to vote was seen by the WCTU as the means by which women could finally voice a progressive political agenda to help rid society of the numerous social ills they attributed to alcohol use. In contrast, the ASL was singular in focus to the extent they would support any political candidate regardless of party affiliation, stance on other issues, or even personal consumption of alcohol, as long as that candidate staunchly supported Prohibition. Under the direction of its general counsel, Wayne B. Wheeler, the ASL became a potent political force able to swing elections to their favored candidate, gradually stocking the Senate and House with members outwardly, if not in personal practice, favorable to their sole cause.

In part owing to their grass roots origins and their emphasis on local elections and candidates, the ASL and WCTU were effective at the state as well as at the national level. By the time the 18th Amendment was passed, 28 states had already passed their own Prohibition laws demonstrating the movement's gathering momentum and political strength. The two groups also successfully leveraged other social factors at the time. For instance, the ASL was able to tap into anti-German sentiment fomented by the start of World War I as most of the prominent brewery owners and beer distributers were German Americans (e.g., Anheuser-Busch, Coors, Pabst, Schlitz). Prohibition supporters, not just those in the WCTU or ASL, exploited anti-immigrant sentiment against Germans and Italians, who were seen as especially prone to making and drinking alcoholic beverages and the cause of many social ills. In the South, where many states were dry, lingering resentments over Reconstruction was used as political leverage with a vote for Prohibition seen as a vote against the wet and former union states in the north. As earlier, with the fomenting of racial hysteria that helped lead to the passage of the Harrison Narcotics Act, sentiment in support of prohibition was bolstered by the portrayal of blacks as dangerous, criminal, and out of control when under the influence of drugs, in this case alcohol.

As part of the larger Progressive Movement that championed using the powers of government to solve social problems, the ASL and WCTU were able to couple these extant social prejudices and animosities with a fervid moral belief in the correctness of their cause to form a potent and, for a time, extremely powerful political force. The power of their influence is reflected in the lopsided vote in both houses of Congress by which the resolution to present the 18th Amendment to the states for ratification passed. In the House of Representatives, the vote was 282 to 128 and in the Senate, the vote was 65 to 20. In a little over a year, 36 of 48 state legislatures, the three-quarters necessary, voted to ratify the 18th Amendment with 46 of 48 states ultimately voting to ratify the amendment, Connecticut and Rhode Island being the two hold-outs.

The National Prohibition Act or Volstead Act as it was commonly known, is named after the Minnesota congressman and chair of the Judiciary Committee, Andrew Volstead, who introduced the legislation in 1919. The Volstead Act defined terms and provided the legal means by which the 18th Amendment would be enforced. Although introduced by Volstead, the ASL's Wayne Wheeler is thought to have been the primary author. The act was strict in many respects, including its definition of an alcoholic beverage as anything containing over one half of 1 percent alcohol. The law had several important loopholes, however. It did not make consumption of alcohol within one's legal residence illegal. Hence, those with the means to afford it could stockpile and consume alcohol purchased prior to Prohibition in their homes, such as in wine cellars. Alcohol could also be made legally for sacramental purposes, leading to a large jump in the amount of alcohol that was (ostensively) consumed in churches, temples, and other houses of worship. In a nod to the power of the rural vote, the law made an exception for preserved sweet cider. This opened the door to people fermenting grapes for producing wine for personal consumption in their homes. Anyone with access to a physician willing to write a prescription could also legally obtain alcohol for whatever qualifying medical ailment they might have had.

These loopholes were perhaps larger than the drafters of the Volstead Act might have imagined and they eventually lead to the perception of widespread disregard for the law. More importantly, however, there was a provision in the law that the states and federal government would concurrently enforce provisions of the act with the federal government consigning enforcement to the Treasury Department and a small policing unit, the 1,500-member Prohibition Bureau. In practice, however, the states varied widely in their enthusiasm for enforcement and the degree to which they committed resources for doing so. In states such as New York, where enforcement was lax, illegal saloons called speakeasies quickly sprung up to slake the continuing thirst for alcohol. Over time, the volume of offenses attributable to the Volstead Act overwhelmed both state and federal enforcement efforts. The widespread disregard for the Volstead Act led to concern that it would foster a more general contempt and disregard for the rule of law. The beginning of the end of Prohibition was well in sight as Hoover took to the podium to deliver his nominating acceptance speech.

FURTHER READING

Burns, E. (2004). *Spirits of America: A Social history of alcohol*. Philadelphia, PA: Temple University Press.

Grace, F. (2001). *Carry A. Nation: Retelling the life*. Religion in North America. Bloomington: Indiana University Press.

BOOTLEGGERS, RUMRUNNERS, AND SPEAKEASIES

In addition to the seemingly endless cast of colorful characters associated with Prohibition, a number of terms entered the English language or became popular during this time. *Bootlegging,* which referred to illegally selling or transporting alcohol, is a prime example. The term originated in the 19th century with the practice of using high boots to conceal any illegal item, including alcohol. Today, bootlegging refers more generally to the practice of producing and distributing something illegally such as music and video CDs. *Rum-running,* was another term used to describe the illegal transport of alcohol but over water instead of land. Among the most famous rum-runners, Bill McCoy transported liquor from the island of Bimini just off the coast of Florida to destinations along the eastern seaboard. Although not originating with him, McCoy's guarantee of the quality of his product led to the popularization of the phrase, *the real McCoy. Speakeasy* was the term used to describe the many illegal bars that arose during Prohibition, so-named because customers were asked to *speak easy* to avoid attracting attention.

Okrent, D. (2010). *Last call: The rise and fall of Prohibition*. New York: Scribner.

Okrent, D. (2010, May). Wayne B. Wheeler: The Man Who Turned Off the Taps. *Smithsonian Magazine*.

Pegram, T.R. (1999). *Battling demon rum: The struggle for a dry America, 1800–1933*. The American Ways Series. Landham, MD: Ivan R. Dee.

Rush, B. (1972). An Inquiry into the Effects of Ardent Spirits upon the Human Body and Mind, with an Account of the Means of Preventing, and of the Remedies for Curing Them (1785). Reprinted in *Medical inquiries and observations*. New York: Arno.

Steuart, J. (1971). *Wayne Wheeler, dry boss: An uncensored biography of Wayne B. Wheeler*. Santa Barbara, CA: Greenwood Press.

On the Internet

The full text of Amendments 11 through 17 to the U.S. Constitution are available at: http://www.archives.gov/exhibits/charters/constitution_amendments_11–27.html#18

The full text of the Volstead Act is available at: http://www.archives.gov/education/lessons/volstead-act/

"Nobody Shot Me"

- ***Document:*** "7 Chicago Gangsters Slain by Firing Squad of Rivals, Some in Police Uniforms" (*Chicago Daily News*)
- ***Date:*** February 14, 1929
- ***Where:*** 2122 N. Clark Street (SMC Carthage Company), Chicago, IL
- ***Significance:*** The Saint Valentine's Day Massacre as it came to be known was only one in a long series of violent incidents surrounding the illegal liquor distribution network that arose after Prohibition. Descriptions and photographs of the incident that appeared the next day on the front pages of newspapers such as the *Chicago Daily News* highlighted the brazenness and brutality of the crime, signifying for many that enforcement of Prohibition was having unintended consequences and that the policy had, in fact, fostered the rapid growth of organized crime.

DOCUMENT

7 Moran Gangsters Slain Victims Are Lined against Wall; One Volley Kills All

Assassins Pose as Policemen; Flee in "Squad Car" after Fusillade; Capone Revenge for Murder of Lombardo, Officers Believe

Seven Moran-O'Banion gangsters were lined up against the wall of a beer-distributing point at 2122 North Clark street at 10:30 o'clock today. Four men, two of them in police uniforms, stood before them, armed with machine guns and sawed-off shotguns. The leader of the execution squad barked an order and the seven fell, six dying at once, the seventh three hours later.

The execution, carried out with the precision of a Mexican firing squad, is charged by the police to the Capone-Lombardo interests. Greatest in point of numbers, it was the most cold-blooded in the history of Chicago's gangland slaughters.

The dead as identified by police were:

GUSENBERG. PETER, notorious gunman for the O'Bannion-Weiss-Drucci-Moran mob.
GUSENBERG, FRANK, brother of Peter. He died after the others were killed, but refused to talk, though conscious.
WEINSHANK, AL, north side "alky" peddler
MAY, JOHN; 1249 West Madison street, a $50-a-week mechanic apparently killed to silence him.
CLARK, JOHN, brother-in-law of George ("Bugs") Moran, leader of the gang.
DAVIS, ARTHUR, west side racketeer
FOSTER, FRANK, hoodlum

A second theory, advanced by federal prohibition agents was that the massacre was perpetrated by a band of rum runners from Detroit to pay off the Moran gang for hi-jacking two truckloads of Chicago-bound Canadian whiskey two weeks ago. This, the police agreed, would account for the boldness with which the killers operated.

Two other theories under consideration by the police are that the Moran gang and the Atello clan, who have been working in harmony on the north side may have had some connection with the government conviction of Ald. Titus A. Haffa, in whose territory they operated. But little credence was given by the police to these theories.

The building at 2122 North Clark street, scene of the wholesale slaughter, is a one-story brick garage, its windows bearing the sign, "The S.M.C. Cartage company."

Scene Before Tragedy

The scene, as reconstructed by a police racketeer expert who viewed the shambles after the shooting was over, was about as follows:

This morning about 10' o'clock, as mail men heavily laden with the missives of St. Valentine's day went their rounds, seven men sat about the garage, two in the front, five others behind a wooden partition in the garage proper. The men munched away [on breakfast], in between telephone calls.

Perhaps they said:

"Two barrels of beer for Joe."

"A can of 'alky' for Mike over on Broadway."

The fifth man, John May, the mechanic, possibly was puttering about the trucks one of which was loaded with a new wooden beer vat. May worked alone, thinking to himself, perhaps, that was a good job. These fellows might be tough, but they paid him and all he did was repair trucks, no chance for him being "bumped off" in this gang war.

Looks Like a "Pinch"

There was a noise outside that rose above the clatter of Clark street traffic, sounding like a police gong. The front door of the garage opened. In marched two men, wearing the uniforms of policemen, their stars gleaming against the blue of the cloth. Two men in civilian attire followed them. All were armed, the first two with submachine guns, the last two with shotguns, sawed off for short-range sure-fire murder.

The two men in the front office throw up their hands.

"A pinch," they thought. "Well, that can be fixed."

Hands in the air they marched to the rear. There was a scramble among the men about the improvised breakfast table. They saw the police uniforms.

"No gun play," they thought, "it isn't a bumpoff. We can fix this."

One of the men in police uniforms barked an order.

Forced to Face Wall

"Get up against the wall, hands up, face to the wall."

One of the four gunmen spotted May.

"Come here, you. Line up with these guys."

The seven stood there, face to the north wall, their eyes staring at its whitewashed surface. Hands flashed up and down their clothes. Their guns were taken.

Offers a Protest

Peter Gusenberg, not cowed by the police—the police were an old story to him—turned around to growl.

"What is this —a—"

He never finished. A hoarse voice interrupted him.

"Give it to him," it said.

Buzz went the machine guns. The roar of the shotguns followed, interspersed with a clatter like that of a gigantic typewriter.

May, incredulous that he, an ordinary mechanic, should be in on this made a mad leap. He got within a half foot of a man wielding a shotgun. He body dropped to the floor headless.

The four men looked a moment at the writhing heap on the floor. The machine gunners sprayed the heap and the writhing lessened. Then coolly they turned from the acrid smoke that swirled about the garage. One of the men in police uniform took three of the guns. The men in civilian attire raised their hands above their heads.

"Arrest" Covers Flight

All of this probably happened, the police expert thinks. Anyway, the men were killed and then to resume the known facts—

Out marched the four. A tailor glanced up from his pressing from next door—a woman living nearby ran down—

They saw what appeared to be two men under arrest, their hands in the air, followed by two policemen. The four climbed into what looked like a squad car. A fifth man sat at the wheel of the car, the motor humming. In got the four and the car roared south in Clark street, sweeping around the wrong side of a street car and was lost in traffic.

Death Scene Rum Depot

Police said they believed the garage area was a distributing point, a depot for the beer and alcohol that the Moran gang peddled to north side speakeasies. In one of the trucks was a new wooden vat, of the kind used for beer; in another, an apparatus for making mash.

In the pockets of one of the dean men was found a book, Capt. Thomas of Hudson avenue station refused to reveal what it contained but it was said to be a list of the various "spots" in which Moran beer and alcohol were sold.

The seven bodies were first removed to an undertaker's, later taken to the county morgue. The inquest will be hold (sic) tomorrow morning in the county morgue with Coroner Herman N. Bundesen in charge.

Russell Inspects Scene

Police Commissioner William F. Russell went to the scene of the massacre, conferred there—after paling slightly at the sight of the bodies—with Assistant State's Attorney David D. Stansbury, Deputy Commissioner Thomas Wolfe, Chief of Detectives John Egan and Capt. Thomas of Hudson avenue.

The headquarters for the investigation was shifted from the Hudson avenue station to the Criminal court building, where State's Attorney Swanson took personal charge. A veil of secrecy such as has never been known in the history of the prosecutor's office, was thrown about his activities as policemen and witnesses arrived at the building.

Question Moran Gangster

Among the witnesses brought in was Paddy Kane, a north side hoodlum. Tense and whitefaced, Kane was hustled in the prosecutor's office. Kane is a Moran gangster and police believe he may be able to furnish a clew (sic) to the identity of the killers. Henry Gusenberg, a brother of the slain Gusenberg, was reported to have been seized in a north side hotel and he too was taken to the prosecutor's office.

Another witness was Sam Schneider, a tailor at 2124 North Clark street next door to the garage, who looked up from his pressing iron to see the men—in the supposed arrest formation—march from the garage.

"I thought they were prisoners and police who had just made an arrest—and because this is Chicago," he added—"and thought no more of it."

Two others taken to the prosecutor's office were Mrs. Julius Landesman, who lives at 2120 North Clark street, and Mrs. Joseph Morrin, 2125 North Clark street, who witnessed the killers leave from the third floor window of her home across the street.

Find Abandoned Cap

The police also brought to the prosecutor's office a gold-braided uniform cap. It is not a police cap, but at first glance it might be taken for one. It is believed to have been dropped by one of the slayers.

Present at the questioning of the witnesses were Mrs. Swanson, Detective Chief Egan, Assistant State's Attorneys Stansbury and Harry S. Ditchburne, and Capt. William Schoemaker, veteran fighter against gangland.

Hayes had $1,135 in his pockets, Weinshank had $900 and a bank book drawn on the Hamilton State bank, Peter Gusenberg, $500, and May carried $18 in currency, which was perforated by slugs.

. . .

One of the men in the plain clothes, she said, had on a brown suit. Moran has been known to have been wearing a brown suit of lat and the rest of the description furnished by Mrs. Moran tallied with that of Moran.

Reading When She Heard Shots

"I was just sitting there reading," Mrs. Moran said, as she tried to readjust herself to the events that had taken place in such rapid succession. "I heard a car pull up close by with a gong sounding, but I didn't pay much attention, as we're on a street car line and got used to that sort of thing.

"Then—! Mustn't have been more than a couple of minutes—I heard a round of shots that almost deafened me, even though I learned later the firing was near the alley in the rear of the building."

Gang Auto Like Police Car

"I ran to the window and saw a big car like a police-squad car parked in front. Then the four men came out and the pair in uniform forced two into the automobile. It was plainly evident that the men in uniforms were keeping the others covered and were serious about it.

The possibility of a kidnapping of those gangsters allowed to live for a time, police theorized, might mean that whoever was responsible for the murders was anxious to glean some information from the gang leaders before sending them too, to their deaths.

SOURCE: "7 Chicago Gangsters Slain by Firing Squad of Rivals, Some in Police Uniforms," *Chicago Daily News*, February 14, 1929.

ANALYSIS

Perhaps no other incident dramatically illustrates the shortcomings of Prohibition than what became known as the Saint Valentine's Day Massacre, so named because it occurred on February 14, 1929. On that day, members of Al Capone's gang and hired hit men from outside Chicago (so they would not be identifiable to the rival gang if there were survivors) confronted seven members of another Chicago-based organized crime gang at their liquor distribution warehouse. Dressed as policemen and arriving in stolen police cars complete with gongs, Capone's gang members tricked the rival gang into believing the encounter was simply a Prohibition era police raid. Offering no resistance, the rival gang members lined up against the wall for what they expected would be a weapons pat down and arrest. Instead, they were shot in the back by a hail of Thompson submachine gun (i.e., "tommy gun") and shotgun bullets that instantly killed six of them, with the seventh dying several hours later in a local hospital. Photographs taken at the time and published in the local press captured and memorialized the bloodiness and brutality of the crime and shocked the public.

Although the most famous incident, the Saint Valentine's Day Massacre was but one in a long series of continual shootings and killings over control of alcohol distribution in major American cities. The killings in Chicago were motivated by a long-running, violent feud between Bugs Moran's North Side gang and Al Capone's South Side gang over control of beer and liquor distribution in the city and a recent failed assassination attempt on Jack McGurn by Malone's associates. McGurn, one of Capone's lieutenants, is thought to have masterminded the revengeful attack after receiving Capone's blessings to carry it out. Ironically, Bugs Moran, the main target of the raid, was not on the premises at the time. It is believed that one of Capone's lookout men mistook a Moran gang member who physically resembled Moran as being the targeted leader. Moran had simply overslept that morning. Arriving late, he fled the scene when he saw the police cars. In this respect, McGurn's otherwise clever plot backfired. The sole survivor of the attack, Moran enforcer Frank Gusenberg, was questioned about the incident by police as he lay dying in the hospital. Riddled with 22 bullet wounds but ever the good soldier, Gusenberg refused to say who the attackers were and proclaimed to the incredulous interrogating police sergeant who asked who shot him: "No one—Nobody shot me."

Despite the fact that Capone was long-suspected of involvement, there was not sufficient evidence to arrest and charge him; Capone made sure he was "vacationing" in his Florida villa at the time of the incident. McGurn did not take part in the shootings either and spent the entire day with his girlfriend, providing him with what became known as the "blonde alibi." In fact, no one was ever convicted of the crimes committed as part of the Saint Valentine's Day Massacre. However, the incident embarrassed and angered law enforcement, which began to come down harder on organized crime and political corruption in Chicago. These efforts led to Capone's eventual arrest, conviction, and sentencing on tax-evasion charges in 1931.

Capone was the John Gotti of his day, characterized by flamboyance in demeanor and dress, a dandy who favored flashy suits, ties, and fedoras. In private (and sometimes very publicly), he was violent, foul-mouthed, bullying, and ill-tempered, whereas in public, he sought the spotlight as a charitable bon vivant and "man of the people." Capone once commented, "When I sell liquor, it's called bootlegging. When my patrons serve it on silver trays on Lake Shore Drive, it's called hospitality." Like Gotti, early successes in avoiding prosecution led to hubris and a sense of impunity that resulted in increasingly brazen misdeeds such as the Saint Valentine's Day Massacre. Also like Gotti, Capone died a broken man. After serving 7 years of an 11-year sentence, with 4 1/2 of those years in Alcatraz, Capone reemerged from prison much diminished, ravaged by the effects of neurosyphilis, which he likely contracted from a prostitute. He died quietly in 1947 in his Palm Island, Florida, home of complications from the disease. During his last years, he continued to be haunted by fears that Bugs Moran was still plotting against him from prison.

The Saint Valentine's Day Massacre had broader immediate and lasting repercussions aside from leading to Capone's demise. The audacious killings made headlines across the country and cemented a lasting reputation for Chicago as a haven for political corruption and organized crime. It also highlighted the manner in which organized crime had grown during Prohibition, funded by the vast amount of money that could be made through bootlegging. During Prohibition, famous mobsters such as Lucky Luciano and Meyer Lansky, in addition to Capone, made fortunes and in the process transformed organized crime from a collection of loosely organized street gangs into a powerful national syndicate. The recognition that Prohibition provided financial resources to support organized crime contributed to the public's sense that Prohibition, on balance, was a failed policy, and led to growing support for repeal of the 18th Amendment.

In a lengthy report that detailed problems with enforcing Prohibition, the Wickersham Commission, appointed by President Hoover in 1931 to review and make recommendations for improving enforcement of the law, noted the following when describing the unprecedented amount of corruption attributable to Prohibition:

> As to corruption it is sufficient to refer to the reported decisions of the courts during the past decade in all parts of the country, which reveal a succession of prosecutions for conspiracies, sometimes involving the police, prosecuting and administrative organizations of whole communities; to the flagrant corruption disclosed in connection with diversions of industrial alcohol and unlawful production of beer; to the record of Federal prohibition administration as to which cases of corruption have been continuous and corruption has appeared in services which in the past had been above suspicion; to the records of state police organizations; to the revelations as to police corruption in every type of municipality, large and small, throughout the decade; to the conditions as to prosecution revealed in surveys of criminal justice in many parts of the land; to the evidence of connection between corrupt local politics and gangs and the organized unlawful liquor traffic, and of systematic collection of tribute from that traffic for corrupt political purposes. There have been other eras of corruption. Indeed, such eras are likely to follow wars. Also there was much corruption in connection with the regulation of the liquor traffic before prohibition. But the present regime of corruption in connection with the liquor traffic is operating in a new and larger field and is more extensive.

The Saint Valentine's Day Massacre continues to inform the debate on current drug policy. It provides a ready illustration that punitive restrictions on drug manufacturing and distribution can create more harm than good, corrupt public officials, and encourage the growth of illegal manufacturing and distribution networks. Violent crime often follows suit owing to the enormous profits to be made and the criminal propensities of those inclined to get involved in selling illegal drugs. Historically, the Saint Valentine's Day Massacre serves as a modest preamble to more recent episodes of much more violent and pervasive drug-related crime. In each case, the motivation for the violence is the same as it was for the Saint Valentine's Day Massacre: control of a lucrative illegal drug market. For example, in the late 1970s and early 1980s, Colombian cocaine dealers routinely killed Cuban competitors and each other while vying for control of national distribution channels for which Miami was the hub. In the mid- to late 1980s, drug related violence spread rapidly to other American cities when rival gangs used guns to settle disputes over the distribution of crack cocaine, sometimes literally fighting over specific street corners and neighborhoods. Drug-related violence in Mexico over the territorial distribution rights for selling cocaine, heroin, marijuana, and methamphetamine escalated in 2006 when the Mexican government declared their own "war on drugs." Since then, competing Mexican drug cartels have vied with each other to maintain and expand their markets through intimidation and, if necessary, elimination of any opposition including governmental. In light of the intensifying lethality, body counts and brazenness exhibited during these more recent conflicts, the Capone-engineered massacre of a few rival gang members, as shocking and as violent as it was at the time, seems very small-scale by comparison.

FURTHER READING

Asbridge, M., & Weerasignhe, S. (2009). Homicide in Chicago from 1890 to 1930: Prohibition and its impact on alcohol and non-alcohol-related homicides. *Addiction, 104*, 355–364.

Bergreen, L. (1994). *Capone: The man and the era*. New York: Simon & Schuster.

Howell, J.C., & Decker, S.H. (1999, January). *The youth gangs, drugs, and violence connection*. U.S. Department of Justice, Office of Justice Programs, Office of Juvenile Justice and Delinquency Prevention (NCJ 171152). Washington DC: Author.

Johnson, N. (2010). *Boardwalk empire: The birth, high times, and corruption of Atlantic City*. Medford, NJ: Plexus Publishing.

Miron, J.A. (1999). Violence and the U.S. prohibitions of drug and alcohol. *American Law and Economics Review, 1*, 78–114.

"38 slain in four years of inter-gang warfare." *Chicago Daily Tribune*, February 15, 1929, 2.

Werb, D., Rowell, G., Guyatt, G., Kerr, T., Montaner, J., & Wood, E. (2011). Effect of drug law enforcement on drug market violence: A systematic review. *International Journal of Drug Policy, 22*, 87–94.

On the Internet

Report on the Enforcement of the Prohibition Laws of the United States by the National Commission on Law Observance and Enforcement. Wickersham Commission Report on Alcohol Prohibition. 1931 (Available from the Shaffer Library on Drug Policy at http://druglibrary.org/schaffer/Library/studies/wick/index.html)

A fairly extensive profile of Al Capone's life and criminal exploits is available at the TruTV Crime Library at: http://www.trutv.com/library/crime/gangsters_outlaws/mob_bosses/capone/index_1.html

The website, My Al Capone Museum, has photos and drawings related to the Saint Valentine's Day Massacre at: http://www.myalcaponemuseum.com/id27.htm

An excerpt from the book *Get Capone* by Jonathan Eig that deals with the massacre was reprinted in *Chicago Magazine* and is available at: http://www.chicagomag.com/Chicago-Magazine/May-2010/Get-Capone-St-Valentines-Day-Massacre-Jonathan-Eig/

"I Believe This Would Be a Good Time for a Beer"

- ***Document:*** Amendment 21 to the Constitution
- ***Dates:*** February 20, 1933, passed by Congress
  December 5, 1933, ratified by 36 states
- ***Where:*** U.S. Congress, Washington, DC
- ***Significance:*** Repealed the 18th Amendment to the U.S. Constitution ending federal prohibition of alcohol, returning control of alcohol manufacturing and distribution to the states.

DOCUMENT

Amendment XXI

Section 1

The eighteenth article of amendment to the Constitution of the United States is hereby repealed.

Section 2

The transportation or importation into any State, Territory, or Possession of the United States for delivery or use therein of intoxicating liquors, in violation of the laws thereof, is hereby prohibited.

Section 3

This article shall be inoperative unless it shall have been ratified as an amendment to the Constitution by conventions in the several States, as provided in the

Constitution, within seven years from the date of the submission hereof to the States by the Congress.

SOURCE: National Archives.

ANALYSIS

It is not unreasonable to suppose that the decade of the 1920s, bracketed as it was by the beginning and end of national Prohibition, would have been a time of sobriety, austerity, respect for public institutions and the law, and personal and public piety. It was everything but. Labeled the "Roaring 20s" and the "Jazz Age" the 1920s were a time of social upheaval, increasing urbanization, economic prosperity (following a recession at the end of World War I), and rapid changes in technology, industry, entertainment, and fashion. It was the decade that saw the advent of the radio and the beginning popularization of mass media, the widespread production of automobiles, and movies that "talked." In 1920, with the ratification of the 19th Amendment, women were granted the right to vote. Younger women, called "flappers," took off their corsets and donned shorter dresses that scandalously revealed their knees and calves, bobbed their hair, wore makeup, and danced the Charleston and Lindy Hop to the strains of live jazz music at the more fashionable speakeasies. Much of the nation's modern infrastructure such as roads, bridges, phone lines, and the electrical grid were begun or significantly expanded during this time. America's economic prosperity allowed it to become a world power.

But there was also a dark side, evidenced most visibly by the rise of organized crime, widespread corruption, and violence such as the Saint Valentine's Day Massacre. The stock market crash at the end of the decade that led to the Great Depression caused unprecedented social decimation and the financial ruin of many. The decade that began as one of hope for a more advantaged and peaceful future and a seemingly nonstop celebration of change and prosperity ended in disillusion, rampant unemployment, and soup kitchen lines. The rapid growth in personal wealth (for some), decadence, and ultimate decline at the era's end were perhaps best captured in F. Scott Fitzgerald's cautionary tale, *The Great Gatsby*. Gatsby, the eponymous and doomed protagonist who had acquired his wealth bootlegging by supplying alcohol to "drug stores," represents the corruptness, shallowness, and demise of the nouveau riche of the time.

Throughout the decade, despite Prohibition and the earnest efforts in some states to enforce the Volstead Act, alcohol continued to flow throughout the country, traveling by rail, truck, speedboat, and any other means that could be conjured by enterprising bootleggers, who showed the same creativity then that drug traffickers transporting cocaine and heroin from South America through Mexico into the United States do in the present day. Over time, the continued flow of alcohol and the crime that sprang up to support alcohol distribution added to a growing disillusionment among the public. Perhaps of equal if not more importance, however, is that with alcohol production and manufacturing illegal during Prohibition, the government had lost a source of considerable revenue. To an extent, the loss of revenue from taxing alcohol production and consumption had been offset by the federal income tax, which was instituted in 1913 with the passage of the 16th Amendment. Wayne Wheeler and his associates in the Anti-Saloon League (ASL) had argued that the passage of Prohibition and the loss of revenue from making alcohol illegal would be offset by the new income tax.

Still, particularly when the Great Depression hit in 1929, the government needed an additional revenue source because of plunging taxes. Repeal of the 18th Amendment and the restoration of a federal tax on alcohol production and sales became a compelling idea, especially to wealthy Americans such as Pierre du Pont, who also stood to benefit personally from repeal of the federal tax. Du Pont had been an early supporter of Prohibition, thinking that the ban on alcohol would, among other benefits, increase worker productivity; he was a director of General Motors at the time. Like many others, du Pont had become disillusioned by the crime spawned by Prohibition, and he feared that Prohibition would lead to a general disregard for all law. But the libertarian du Pont also saw reinstitution of an alcohol tax as an opportunity for repealing the personal income tax and lessening what he believed was an undue intrusion by the federal government. Eventually, du Pont became head of the increasingly influential organization called the Association against the Prohibition Amendment (AAPA); a political counterweight to the ASL, whose influence was beginning to wane after the death of Wheeler in 1927. In speeches and writing, du Pont argued forcefully for the repeal of Prohibition.

Joined by other wealthy and influential individuals such as Pauline Sabine, who founded the Women's Organization for National Prohibition Reform, du Pont and others set the stage for the repeal of the 18th Amendment, making it politically safe to do so. Running on a platform that called for ending Prohibition, Franklin D. Roosevelt was elected in a landslide and took office in the winter of 1933. One of his first acts was to successfully urge Congress to redefine the term intoxicating as being 0.5 percent to 3.2 percent with passage of the Cullen-Harrison Act in March 1933, after which Roosevelt is said to have proclaimed with no small sense of irony, "I believe this would be a good time for a beer." Amid crumbling public support, and with its most politically adept champion deceased, Prohibition was repealed shortly thereafter with the passage and rapid ratification by the states of the 21st Amendment. The vote in Congress for repeal was as substantial and lopsided as it had been for Prohibition, passing by a margin of 63 to 23 in the Senate and 289 to 121 in the House. To this date, the 18th Amendment remains the only constitutional amendment to be repealed. Ratification of the 21st Amendment in 1933 meant that the power to prohibit liquor consumption was returned to the states. Some held on for a while. The last state to repeal Prohibition was Mississippi, which did so in 1966. Return of control of alcohol distribution and consumption to the state level explains the patchwork of varying state rules and regulations that continue through the present day.

From a policy standpoint, what are we to make of the short-lived attempt to prohibit alcohol distribution in the United States? Current historians suggest that it was not the abject failure that it has been portrayed as being. For instance, J. S. Blocker's recent analysis of the effects of Prohibition note that alcohol consumption was sharply down while the law was in effect as were death rates from cirrhosis and alcoholism, alcohol psychosis hospital admissions, and arrests for drunkenness. Moreover, the relative decline in per capita alcohol consumption persisted until the 1970s. Despite the attempts to circumvent the law then, Prohibition successfully reduced alcohol consumption and its attendant ills. To some extent, the problems with Prohibition and its ultimate demise are attributable to the rigidity of the law, which prohibited virtually all alcohol production as well as to the promise by its proponents that it would lead to greater economic prosperity through increased worker productivity. The Great Depression and the loss of tax revenues to the federal government, which cast these latter claims in doubt, probably had as much to do with wavering public support as the widespread attempts to circumvent the law and highly publicized reports of violent crime. This does not mean that Prohibition need be viewed as an example of a successful policy, only that perceptions of its effects should be more nuanced than has generally been the case.

FURTHER READING

Allen, F.L. (2000). *Only yesterday: An informal history of the 1920s*. New York: Harper Collins.
Blocker, J.S. (2006). Did prohibition really work? Alcohol prohibition as a public health innovation. *American Journal of Public Health*, 96, 233–243.
Fitzgerald, F.S. (2004). *The great Gatsby* (reissue edition). New York, NY: Scribner.
Hall, W. (2010). What are the policy lessons of national alcohol prohibition in the United States, 1920–1933? *Addiction*, *105*, 1164–1173.
Kahn, G. & Hirschfield, A. (2005). *The Speakeasies of 1932:* Over 400 Drawings, Paintings, and Photos: Glenn Young Books/Applause: New York, NY.
Kleiman, M. (1992). Neither prohibition nor legalization: Grudging toleration in drug control policy. *Daedalus*, *121*, 53–83.
Kyvig, D.E. (2000). *Repealing National Prohibition*. Kent, OH: Kent State University Press.
Levine, H.G., & Reinarman, C. (1991). From Prohibition to regulation: Lessons from alcohol policy for drug policy. *The Milbank Quarterly*, 69, 461–494.
Peck, G. (2009). *The Prohibition hangover: Alcohol in America from demon rum to cult cabernet*. New Brunswick, NJ: Rutgers University Press.
Van de Water, F. (2007). *The real* McCoy. Mystic, CT: Flat Hammock Press.

"The Sick and Afflicted Shall Be Set in the Way of Strength and Hope"

- ***Document:*** Porter Narcotic Farm Act (P.L. 70–672, 45 Stat. 1085)
- ***Date:*** January 19, 1929
- ***Where:*** Washington, DC
- ***Significance:*** In response to federal prison overcrowding due to drug addicts incarcerated for violating provisions of the Harrison Act, this law established two prison-based hospitals for drug treatment and research. Called "narcotic farms," the first facility opened in 1935 in Lexington, Kentucky; the second opened in 1938 in Fort Worth, Texas. Federal prison inmates addicted to drugs could be assigned or transferred to one of these two facilities to serve out their prison sentences while receiving drug treatment; however, success rates were not impressive. Important research on the nature of addiction and the psychopharmacology of drugs was also carried out at the facilities, but substantial ethical questions surrounding the conduct of the research arose over time. The facilities eventually reverted back to prisons in 1975.

DOCUMENT

An Act to establish two United States narcotic farms for the confinement and treatment of persons addicted to the use of habit-forming narcotic drugs who have been convicted of offenses against the United States, and for other purposes.

Be it enacted by the Senate and House of Representatives of the United States of America in Congress assembled, That when used in this Act—

(a) The term "habit-forming narcotic drug "or "narcotic "means opium and coca leaves and the innumerable alkaloids derived there-from, the best known of these alkaloids being morphia, heroin, and codeine, obtained from opium, and cocaine derived from the coca plant; all compounds, salts, preparations, or other derivatives obtained either from the raw material or from the various alkaloids;

Indian hemp and its various derivatives, compounds, and preparations, and peyote in its various forms.

(b) The term "addict" means any person who habitually uses any habit-forming narcotic drug as defined in this Act so as to endanger the public morals, health, safety, or welfare, or who is or has been so far addicted to the use of such habit-forming narcotic drugs as to have lost the power of self-control with reference to his addiction.

SEC. 2. That the Attorney General, the Secretary of the Treasury, and the Secretary of War be. and are hereby, authorized and directed to select sites for two institutions for the confinement and treatment of persons who have been or shall be convicted of offenses against the United States, including persons convicted by general courts-martial and consular courts, and who are addicted to the use of habit-forming narcotic drugs, and for the confinement and treatment of addicts who voluntarily submit themselves for treatment.

SEC. 5. That the control and management of the United States narcotic farms shall be vested in the Secretary of the Treasury, who shall have power to appoint competent superintendents, assistant superintendents, physicians, pharmacists, psychologists, nurses, and all other officers and employees necessary or the safe keeping, care, protection, treatment, and discipline of the inmates. There is hereby created in the office of the Surgeon General of the Bureau of the Public Health Service, in the Department of the Treasury, a division to be known as the Narcotics Division, which shall be in charge of a physician trained in the treatment and care of narcotic addicts, and which division shall have charge of the management, discipline, and methods of treatment of said United States narcotic farms under the rules and regulations promulgated by the Secretary of the Treasury.

SEC. 6. That the care, discipline, and treatment of the persons admitted to or confined in a United States narcotic farm shall be designed to rehabilitate them, restore them to health, and where necessary train them to be self-supporting and self-reliant. . . .

SEC. 7. That the authority vested with the power to designate the place of confinement of a prisoner is hereby authorized and directed to transfer to the United States narcotic farms, as accommodations become available, all addicts, as herein defined, who are now or shall hereafter be sentenced to confinement in or be confined in any penal, correctional, disciplinary, or reformatory institution of the United States, including those addicts convicted of offenses against the United States who are confined in State and Territorial prisons, penitentiaries, and reformatories: *Provided,* That no addict shall be transferred to a United States narcotic farm who, in the opinion of the officer authorized to direct the transfer, is not a proper subject for confinement in such an institution either because of the nature of the crime he has committed, or his apparent incorrigibility. . . .

SEC. 11. That not later than one month prior to the expiration of the sentence of any addict confined in a United States narcotic farm, he shall be examined by the Surgeon General of the Bureau of the Public Health Service, or his authorized representative. If he believes the person to be discharged is still an addict within the meaning of this Act and that he may by further treatment in a United States narcotic farm be cured of his addiction. The addict shall be informed, under such rules and regulations as the Secretary of the Treasury may promulgate, of the advisability of his submitting himself to further treatment. The addict may then apply in writing to the Secretary of the Treasury for further treatment in a United States narcotic farm for a period not exceeding the maximum length of time considered necessary by the Surgeon General of the Bureau of the Public Health Service. Upon approval of the application by the Secretary of the Treasury or his authorized agent, the addict may be given such further treatment as is necessary to cure him of his addiction.

SEC. 12. That any person, except an unconvicted alien, addicted to the use of habit-forming narcotic drugs, whether or not he shall have been convicted of an offense against the United States, may apply to the Secretary of the Treasury, or his authorized representative, for admission to a United States narcotic farm. Any such addict shall be examined by the Surgeon General of the Bureau of the Public Health Service or his authorized agent, who shall report to the Secretary of the Treasury whether the applicant is an addict within the meaning of this Act; whether he believes he may by treatment in a United States narcotic farm be cured of his addiction and the estimated length of time necessary to effect a cure, and any further pertinent information bearing on the addiction, habits, or character of the applicant. The Secretary of the Treasury may, in his discretion, admit the applicant to a United States narcotic farm. No such addict shall be admitted unless he voluntarily submits to treatment for the maximum amount of time estimated by the Surgeon General of the Bureau of the Public Health Service as necessary to effect a cure, and unless suitable accommodations are available after all eligible addicts convicted of offenses against the United States have been admitted.

SOURCE: Porter Narcotic Farm Act (P.L. 70–672, 45 Stat. 1085).

ANALYSIS

An eventual but virtually inevitable consequence of passing criminal laws that include among their sanctions the incarceration of people who abuse drugs is a large increase in the size and percentage of prisoners addicted to drugs (see Anti-Drug Abuse Act of 1986). The cost, administrative complexities, and management issues attending the increases are rarely appreciated prospectively when the legislation is being crafted. The primary motivation for such laws has always been to use the criminal justice system as a means of social control to discourage use in the first place and to punish those who use drugs in disregard of the law. This, in essence, is what "criminalizing" drug use means: management of whatever drug is perceived as the current social menace through enactment of tough criminal sanctions.

Following passage of the Harrison Act, mainly intended to curb the use of opiates but with cocaine thrown in for good measure, a predictable course of events ensued, one that would continue to be repeated over the next half century and beyond: violators of the law's provisions were arrested, convicted, and incarcerated in federal (and state) prisons. As the number of prisoners arrested for violations increased, the prisons became overcrowded, causing management problems and an increased financial burden on the prison system. Drug policy historian David Musto has provided numerical perspective on the magnitude of these problems as of 1928. Writing about the conditions in the federal penitentiaries in Atlanta, Leavenworth, and McNeil Island, he notes,

> The three Federal penitentiaries had a cell capacity of 3,738 while on the first of April 1928 they had a population of 7,598. Of the prisoners, about 2,300 were narcotic law violators of whom 1,600 were addicted. The wardens did not like to care for addicts—prisons were not equipped to handle them, they smuggled drugs into the prison, and the associations with other prisoners was bad for both groups. (1999, p. 204)

To put these figures in further perspective, 2,300 Harrison Act violators represented almost two-thirds (61%) of the three penitentiaries' original collective operating capacity in 1928. The 1,600 inmates addicted to drugs represented one-fifth (21%) of the over-capacity census of 7,598. Clearly, none of the crafters of the Harrison Act had envisioned that their tax law would engender these kinds of effects on the federal prison system. Nor would they be the last legislators to fail to take into account how such laws affect not only the criminal justice system but also the lives of individuals and their families who are incarcerated and the fabric of the communities in which they live.

Thus, one motivation for the construction of separate, dedicated prisons for housing drug-addicted federal prisoners was simply to reduce overcrowding. Another motivation was to relieve other federal penitentiaries of the administrative and management complexities of housing large numbers of addicts. The two institutions built as a result of the Porter Narcotic Farm Act—one in Lexington, Kentucky, which opened in 1935, and one in Fort Worth, Texas, which opened in 1938—embodied larger ambitions as well. The quote that titles this document is from the dedication of the Lexington facility delivered by Dr. Hugh S. Cumming, who was the Surgeon General of the Public Health Service. His speech reflected the hope that by providing facilities dedicated to drug treatment and research, those who received treatment could be cured of their addictions while incarcerated and return to society as productive citizens and that through an active program of research, further advances in the understanding of addiction and treatment could be attained.

The U.S. Public Health Service and the Federal Bureau of Prisons jointly handled operation of the prison-based hospitals (or hospital-based prisons as some thought of them). The Lexington "farm," referred to as "Narco" by its residents and staff, was situated on 1,050 acres of land in rural Kentucky and was a 1,500-bed facility. The surrounding grounds included an actual working farm complete with dairy cows, food crops, and animals raised for slaughter. Inmates participated in operating the farm and carrying out other work-related activities within the institution as part of their rehabilitation.

Voluntary patients could be admitted to the narcotics farms as well as prisoners and probationers, resulting in a diverse and sometimes literally entertaining mix. For instance, heroin use was an extensive problem among jazz musicians. It was viewed almost as a right-of-passage to qualify as a "hep cat." As a result, famous or soon-to-be-famous jazz musicians such as trumpet player Chet Baker, saxophonist Sonny Rollins, and pianist Ray Charles were admitted to the narcotics farms either voluntarily or as the end result of an arrest and conviction. While there, they formed bands that practiced and performed concerts on the lawn for other inmates and staff. The notoriety of prison jazz bands led none other than the Commissioner of the Federal Bureau of Narcotics, Harry Anslinger, to quip, "We had more jazz bands in jail in the 1930s than I can count." Famous actors such as Peter Lorre and Sammy Davis Jr. also spent time on the narcotics farms. William S. Burroughs, beat writer and lifelong heroin addict, chronicled his experiences at Narco in the book *Junkie*. He noted that the food was "excellent."

The man selected to be the first medical director at Lexington, Dr. Lawrence Kolb, was a leading researcher and expert on drug addiction at the time. He designed a three-phase program that, with only a few adjustments, could be applied as a framework for current prison-based programs: a short phase to address physical withdrawal; a middle phase of rehabilitation and therapy that lasted the majority of the inmate's prison tenure; and a final phase to prepare for release. In practice, however, recidivism rates were high: over 70 percent and as high as 90 percent by some estimates. Despite the progressive three-phase design, treatment of addiction, now better understood as being a chronic condition where relapse is common (in part, owing to the research done at the narcotics farms), was at a very early stage then. Additionally, the same social-contextual issues that adversely affect prisoners with addiction problems returning to society today were in operation back then and never well addressed: poor family and social support networks, lack of employment opportunities, and a return to environments where alcohol and drugs were readily available and widely used.

The Lexington prison included a research facility that eventually became known after 1948 as the Addiction Research Center (ARC). Staffed with some of the brightest researchers culled from the ranks of the Public Health Service, the ARC sought initially to investigate basic questions about the nature of drug addiction: Why are some people more susceptible to addiction than others? Why do some relapse and others not? What are the psychological and physiological changes that occur during withdrawal to different drugs? The prison provided a continual source of research subjects and in a time prior to strict human subject oversight, the experimenters were able to conduct investigations that would never be approved today. For instance, some studies provided subjects with drugs over extended periods followed by a sudden withdrawal of the drugs so their physiological response during the withdrawal period could be measured.

Research on the nature of addiction eventually gave way to serving as a testing ground for new drugs to determine their relative analgesic versus addicting properties. Such compounds were of interest to the pharmaceutical industry, which wanted to find drugs useful for reducing pain but which were not habit-forming. They wanted to avoid making the same mistake as when heroin was synthesized. Initially believed to be non-addicting, heroin was first used as a cough suppressant and a "safer" alternative to morphine and codeine, both of which were used for that same purpose. Addicts who had been clean for some time were reintroduced to drug use again for the purposes of such studies, the justification being there was time enough before their release date for them to go through withdrawal (again) and get clean. ARC researchers also involved unwitting subjects in CIA-sponsored studies as part of a project named MK-ULTRA to gauge the usefulness of experimental drugs such as LSD in interrogations.

In 1967, as the facilities in Lexington and Forth Worth neared the end of their existence as "narcotics farms," a visiting British researcher made the following observations about the lack of ethical standards at the Lexington facility:

> I believe that there is a nightmarish quality to the use of inmates for experimental purposes. One experimenter referred to this category of patients as "old dopeys," and said that whatever the future of the Lexington operation there would be a need to obtain a "stock" of such human subjects. A free drug experience, better ward conditions, remission of sentence, that together constituted quite an inducement. (Edwards, 2010, p. 985)

By the 1950s, the initial hopes that accompanied the construction of the narcotics farms had given way to cynicism and disenchantment over the poor treatment results and research that was increasingly deflected from the original goal of understanding addiction to less noble, ethically questionable pursuits. ARC was moved out of Lexington to the medical campus of Johns Hopkins University in Baltimore and eventually became the intramural research program of the National Institute on Drug Abuse. The narcotics farm in Lexington closed its doors to drug treatment in 1975 and became a federal prison, time having simply passed it by with local, less expensive, and more advanced treatment programs becoming more common across the country. It is presently used as a facility to provide medical care to inmates in the federal prison system.

Until a recent documentary movie and book, the narcotics farms were slowly becoming historical arcana. But they mark an important aspect of American drug policy, that being the continued tension between treating drug abuse as a criminal justice problem versus treating it as a public health issue. Located exactly at that intersection, the narcotics farms were the forerunners of the therapeutic community treatment programs that now operate in America's prisons and the dedicated drug treatment prisons such as the one now in operation at the Sheridan Correctional Center in Illinois. To a large extent, they were harbingers of other efforts such as drug courts, boot camps, and diversion programs that began to spring up in the 1980s to handle yet another large influx of drug-addicted individuals swept into the criminal justice system by yet another round of laws that provided ever more severe criminal sanctions for drug use and possession.

FURTHER READING

Acker, C. J. (1997). The early years of the PHS narcotic hospital at Lexington, Kentucky. *Public Health Reports, 112,* 245–247.

Ball, J. C., Thompson, W. O., Allen, D. M. (1970). Readmission rates at Lexington Hospital for 43,215 narcotic drug addicts. *Public Health Reports, 85,* 610–616.

Burroughs, W. S. (2003). *Junky: The definitive text of "junk" (50th Anniversary Edition).* New York, NY: Penguin Books.

Campbell, N. D. (2006). A "new deal" for the drug addict: The addiction research center, Lexington, Kentucky. *Journal of the History of Behavioral Sciences, 42,* 135–157.

Campbell, N. D., Olsen, J. P., & Walden, L. (2008). *The narcotic farm: The rise and fall of America's first prison for drug addicts.* New York, NY: Abrams.

Edwards, G. (2010). Seeing America—diary of a drug-focused study tour made in 1967. *Addiction, 105,* 984–990.

Kolb, L., & Ossenfort, W.F. (1938). The treatment of addicts at the Lexington Hospital. *Southern Medical Journal, 31*, 914–920.

Musto, D. (1999). *The American disease: Origins of narcotics control, 3rd edition* (pp. 204–206). New York, NY: Oxford University Press.

On the Internet

Interviews with the filmmaker and author behind the movie and book *The Narcotic Farm* are available at: http://www.wheelmeout.com/6_2.php.

The Narcotic Farm project has its own website that updates when the documentary will be shown on PBS stations at: http://www.narcoticfarm.com/ and a video interview of Nancy Campbell, one of the principal authors of *The Narcotic Farm* is on YouTube at: http://www.youtube.com/watch?v=U90SFs1JyC8.

2

THE 1930s THROUGH THE 1950s: HARRY J. ANSLINGER AND THE FEDERAL BUREAU OF NARCOTICS, *REEFER MADNESS*, THE KEFAUVER COMMITTEE, THE BEAT GENERATION

"As Dangerous as a Coiled Snake"

- ***Document:*** Marijuana: Assassin of Youth
- ***Date:*** July 1937
- ***Where:*** *American Magazine*
- ***Significance:*** This article is typical of the public relations campaign waged to foster support for stricter laws that specifically targeted marijuana use and distribution. Co-authored by the first commissioner of the Federal Bureau of Narcotics, Harry J. Anslinger, the article grossly exaggerates the effects of marijuana use, citing anecdotal evidence from multiple unsubstantiated sources. Relying on similar evidence and rhetoric, Anslinger frequently testified on the dangers of drug use before Congress. His efforts were successful and ultimately led to the passage of a succession of increasingly stringent laws based on the premise that marijuana use was as dangerous as the use of cocaine and opiates such as heroin. Despite their dubious origins, these characterizations persist, albeit in less exaggerated form, and continue to influence the current debate on the decriminalization and use of marijuana for medical purposes.

Narcotics Commissioner Harry J. Anslinger announces a series of raids in the nation's big cities aimed at crippling the narcotics traffic in New York on January 4, 1958. More than 500 suspected peddlers were bagged. Despite Anslinger's bluster and single-minded focus on law enforcement and criminalizing drug use, such efforts did little to decrease either the availability or use of drugs throughout Anslinger's 32-year tenure as Narcotics Commissioner. (AP/Wide World Photos)

DOCUMENT

Marijuana: Assassin of Youth

Harry J. Anslinger with Courtney Ryley Cooper

THE sprawled body of a young girl lay crushed on the sidewalk the other day after a plunge from the fifth story of a Chicago apartment house. Everyone called it suicide, but actually it was murder. The killer was a narcotic known to America as marijuana, and to history as hashish. It is a narcotic used in the form of cigarettes, comparatively new to the United States and as dangerous as a coiled rattlesnake.

How many murders, suicides, robberies, criminal assaults, holdups, burglaries, and deeds of maniacal insanity it causes each year, especially among the young, can be only conjectured. The sweeping march of its addiction has been so insidious that, in numerous communities, it thrives almost unmolested, largely because of official ignorance of its effects.

Here indeed is the unknown quantity among narcotics. No one can predict its effect. No one knows, when he places a marijuana cigarette to his lips, whether he will become a philosopher, a joyous reveler in a musical heaven, a mad insensate, a calm philosopher, or a murderer.

That youth has been selected by the peddlers of this poison as an especially fertile field makes it a problem of serious concern to every man and woman in America.

THERE was the young girl, for instance, who leaped to her death. Her story is typical. Some time before, this girl, like others of her age who attend our high schools, had heard the whispering of a secret, which has gone the rounds of American youth. It promised a new thrill, the smoking of a type of cigarette, which contained a "real kick." According to the whispers, this cigarette could accomplish wonderful reactions and with no harmful aftereffects. So the adventurous girl and a group of her friends gathered in an apartment, thrilled with the idea of doing "something different" in which there was "no harm." Then a friend produced a few cigarettes of the loosely rolled "homemade" type. They were passed from one to another of the young people, each taking a few puffs.

The results were weird. Some of the party went into paroxysms of laughter; every remark, no matter how silly, seemed excruciatingly funny. Others of mediocre musical ability became almost expert; the piano dinned constantly. Still others found themselves discussing weighty problems of youth with remarkable clarity. As one youngster expressed it, he "could see through stone walls." The girl danced without fatigue, and the night of unexplainable exhilaration seemed to stretch out as though it were a year long. Time, conscience, or consequences became too trivial for consideration.

Other parties followed, in which inhibitions vanished, conventional barriers departed, all at the command of this strange cigarette with its ropy, resinous odor. Finally there came a gathering at a time when the girl was behind in her studies and greatly worried. With every puff of the smoke the feeling of despondency lessened. Everything was going to be all right—at last. The girl was "floating" now, a term given to marijuana intoxication. Suddenly, in the midst of laughter and dancing she thought of her school problems. Instantly they were solved. Without hesitancy she walked to a window and leaped to her death. Thus can marijuana "solve" one's difficulties.

The cigarettes may have been sold by a hot tamale vendor or by a street peddler, or in a dance hall or over a lunch counter, or even from sources much nearer to the customer. The police of a Midwestern city recently accused a school janitor of having conspired with four other men, not only to peddle cigarettes to children, but even to furnish apartments where smoking parties might be held.

A Chicago mother, watching her daughter die as an indirect result of marijuana addiction, told officers that at least fifty of the girl's young friends were slaves to the narcotic. This means fifty unpredictables. They may cease its use; that is not so difficult as with some narcotics. They may continue addiction until they deteriorate mentally and become insane. Or they may turn to violent forms of crime, to suicide or to murder. Marijuana gives few warnings of what it intends to do to the human brain.

THE menace of marijuana addiction is comparatively new to America. In 1931, the marijuana file of the United States Narcotic Bureau was less than two inches thick, while today the reports crowd many large cabinets. Marijuana is a weed of the Indian hemp family, known in Asia as Cannabis Indica and in America as Cannabis Sativa. Almost everyone who has spent much time in rural communities has seen it, for it is cultivated in practically every state. Growing plants by the thousands were destroyed by law-enforcement officers last year in Texas, New York, New Jersey, Mississippi, Michigan, Maryland, Louisiana, Illinois, and the attack on the weed is only beginning.

It was an unprovoked crime some years ago which brought the first realization that the age-old drug had gained a foothold in America. An entire family was murdered by a youthful addict in Florida. When officers arrived at the home they found the youth staggering about in a human, slaughterhouse. With an ax he had killed his father, his mother, two brothers, and a sister. He seemed to be in a daze.

"I've had a terrible dream," he said. "People tried to hack off my arms!"

"Who were they?" an officer asked.

"I don't know. Maybe one was my uncle. They slashed me with knives and I saw blood dripping from an ax."

He had no recollection of having committed the multiple crime. The officers knew him ordinarily as a sane, rather quiet young man; now he was pitifully crazed.

They sought the reason. The boy said he had been in the habit of smoking something which youthful friends called "muggles," a childish name for marijuana.

Since that tragedy there has been a race between the spread of marijuana and its suppression. Unhappily, so far, marijuana has won by many lengths. The years 1935 and 1936 saw its most rapid growth in traffic. But at least we now know what we are facing. We know its history, its effects, and its potential victims. Perhaps with the spread of this knowledge the public may be aroused sufficiently to conquer the menace. Every parent owes it to his children to tell them of the terrible effects of marijuana to offset the enticing "private information" which these youths may have received. There must be constant enforcement and equally constant education against this enemy, which has a record of murder and terror running through the centuries.

THE weed was known to the ancient Greeks and it is mentioned in Homer's Odyssey. Homer wrote that it made men forget their homes and turned them into swine. Ancient Egyptians used it. In the year 1090, there was founded in Persia the religious and military order of the Assassins whose history is one of cruelty, barbarity, and murder, and for good reason. The members were confirmed users of hashish, or marijuana, and it is from the Arabic "hashshashin" that we have the English word "assassin." Even the term "running amok" relates to the drug, for the expression has been used to describe natives of the Malay Peninsula who, under the influence of hashish, engage in violent and bloody deeds.

Marijuana was introduced into the United States from Mexico, and swept across America with incredible speed.

It began with the whispering of vendors in the Southwest that marijuana would perform miracles for those who smoked it, giving them a feeling of physical strength and mental power, stimulation of the imagination, the ability to be "the life of the party." The peddlers preached also of the weed's capabilities as a "love potion." Youth, always adventurous, began to look into these claims and found some of them true, not knowing that this was only half the story. They were not told that addicts may often develop a delirious rage during which they are temporarily and violently insane; that this insanity may take the form of a desire for self-destruction or a persecution complex to be satisfied only by the commission of some heinous crime.

IT would be well for law-enforcement officers everywhere to search for marijuana behind cases of criminal and sex assault. During the last year a young male addict was hanged in Baltimore for criminal assault on a ten-year-old girl. His defense was that he was temporarily insane from smoking marijuana. In Alamosa, Colo., a degenerate brutally attacked a young girl while under the influence of the drug. In Chicago, two marijuana smoking boys murdered a policeman.

In at least two dozen other comparatively recent cases of murder or degenerate sex attacks, many of them committed by youths, marijuana proved to be a contributing cause. Perhaps you remember the young desperado in Michigan who, a few months ago, caused a reign of terror by his career of burglaries and holdups, finally to be sent to prison for life after kidnapping a Michigan state policeman, killing him, then handcuffing him to the post of a rural mailbox. This young bandit was a marijuana fiend.

A sixteen-year-old boy was arrested in California for burglary. Under the influence of marijuana he had stolen a revolver and was on the way to stage a holdup when apprehended. Then there was the nineteen-year-old addict in Columbus,

Ohio, who, when police responded to a disturbance complaint, opened fire upon an officer, wounding him three times, and was himself killed by the returning fire of the police. In Ohio a gang of seven young men, all less than twenty years old, had been caught after a series of 38 holdups. An officer asked them where they got their incentive.

"We only work when we're high on 'tea,'" one explained.

"On what?"

"On tea. Oh, there are lots of names for it. Some people call it 'mu' or 'muggles' or 'Mary Weaver' or 'moocah' or 'weed' or 'reefers'—there's a million names for it."

"All of which mean marijuana?"

"Sure. Us kids got on to it in high school three or four years ago; there must have been twenty-five or thirty of us who started smoking it. The stuff was cheaper then; you could buy a whole tobacco tin of it for fifty cents. Now these peddlers will charge you all they can get, depending on how shaky you are. Usually though, it's two cigarettes for a quarter."

This boy's casual story of procurement of the drug was typical of conditions in many cities in America. He told of buying the cigarettes in dance halls, from the owners of small hamburger joints, from peddlers who appeared near high schools at dismissal time. Then there were the "booth joints" or Bar-B-Q stands, where one might obtain a cigarette and a sandwich for a quarter, and there were the shabby apartments of women who provided not only the cigarettes but rooms in which girls and boys might smoke them.

"But after you get the habit," the boy added, "you don't bother much about finding a place to smoke. I've seen as many as three or four high-school kids jam into a telephone booth and take a few drags."

The officer questioned him about the gang's crimes: "Remember that filling-station attendant you robbed—how you threatened to beat his brains out?"

The youth thought hard. "I've got a sort of hazy recollection," he answered. "I'm not trying to say I wasn't there, you understand. The trouble is, with all my gang, we can't remember exactly what we've done or said. When you get to 'floating,' it's hard to keep track of things."

From the other youthful members of the gang the officer could get little information. They confessed the robberies as one would vaguely remember bad dreams.

"If I had killed somebody on one of those jobs, I'd never have known it," explained one youth. "Sometimes it was over before I realized that I'd even been out of my room."

THEREIN lies much of the cruelty of marijuana, especially in its attack upon youth. The young, immature brain is a thing of impulses, upon which the "unknown quantity" of the drug acts as an almost overpowering stimulant. There are numerous cases on record like that of an Atlanta boy who robbed his father's safe of thousands of dollars in jewelry and cash. Of high-school age, this boy apparently had been headed for an honest, successful career. Gradually, however, his father noticed a change in him. Spells of shakiness and nervousness would be succeeded by periods when the boy would assume a grandiose manner and engage in excessive, senseless laughter, extravagant conversation, and wildly impulsive actions. When these actions finally resulted in robbery the father went at his son's problem in earnest—and found the cause of it a marijuana peddler who catered to school children. The peddler was arrested.

It is this useless destruction of youth which is so heartbreaking to all of us who labor in the field of narcotic suppression. No one can predict what may happen after the smoking of the weed. I am reminded of a Los Angeles case in which a boy of seventeen killed a policeman. They had been great friends. Patrolling his beat, the officer often stopped to talk to the young fellow, to advise him. But one day the boy surged toward the patrolman with a gun in his hand; there was a blaze of yellowish flame, and the officer fell dead.

"Why did you kill him?" the youth was asked.

"I don't know," he sobbed. "He was good to me. I was high on reefers. Suddenly I decided to shoot him."

In a small Ohio town, a few months ago, a fifteen-year-old boy was found wandering the streets, mentally deranged by marijuana. Officers learned that he had obtained the dope at a garage.

"Are any other school kids getting cigarettes there?" he was asked.

"Sure. I know fifteen or twenty, maybe more. I'm only counting my friends."

The garage was raided. Three men were arrested and 18 pounds of marijuana seized.

"We'd been figuring on quitting the racket," one of the dopesters told the arresting officer. "These kids had us scared. After we'd gotten 'em on the weed, it looked like easy money for a while. Then they kept wanting more and more of it, and if we didn't have it for 'em, they'd get tough. Along toward the last, we were scared that one of 'em would get high and kill us all. There wasn't any fun in it."

Not long ago a fifteen-year-old girl ran away from her home in Muskegon, Mich., to be arrested later in company with five young men in a Detroit marijuana den. A man and his wife ran the place. How many children had smoked there will never be known. There were 60 cigarettes on hand, enough fodder for 60 murders.

A newspaper in St. Louis reported after an investigation this year that it had discovered marijuana "dens," all frequented by children of high-school age. The same sort of story came from Missouri, Ohio, Louisiana, Colorado—in fact, from coast to coast.

In Birmingham, Ala., a hot-tamale salesman had pushed his cart about town for five years, and for a large part of that time he had been peddling marijuana cigarettes to students of a downtown high school. His stock of the weed, he said, came from Texas and consisted, when he was captured, of enough marijuana to manufacture hundreds of cigarettes.

In New Orleans, of 437 persons of varying ages arrested for a wide range of crimes, 125 were addicts. Of 37 murderers, 17 used marijuana, and of 193 convicted thieves, 34 were "on the weed."

ONE of the first places in which marijuana found a ready welcome was in a closely congested section of New York. Among those who first introduced it there were musicians, who had brought the habit northward with the surge of "hot" music demanding players of exceptional ability, especially in improvisation. Along the Mexican border and in seaport cities it had been known for some time that the musician who desired to get the "hottest" effects from his playing often turned to marijuana for aid.

One reason was that marijuana has a strangely exhilarating effect upon the musical sensibilities (Indian hemp has long been used as a component of "singing seed" for canary birds). Another reason was that strange quality of marijuana which makes a rubber band out of time, stretching it to unbelievable lengths. The musician who uses "reefers" finds that the musical beat seemingly comes to him quite slowly, thus allowing him to interpolate any number of improvised notes with comparative ease. While under the influence of marijuana, he does not realize that he is tapping the keys, with a furious speed impossible for one in a normal state of mind; marijuana has stretched out the time of the music until a dozen notes may be crowded into the space normally occupied by one. Or, to quote a young musician arrested by Kansas City officers as a "muggles smoker":

"Of course I use it—I've got to. I can't play any more without it, and I know a hundred other musicians who are in the same fix. You see, when I'm 'floating,' I own my saxophone. I mean I can do anything with it. The notes seem to dance out of it—no effort at all. I don't have to worry about reading the music—I'm music-crazy. Where do I get the stuff? In almost any low-class dance hall or night spot in the United States."

Soon a song was written about the drug. Perhaps you remember:

"Have you seen
That funny reefer man?
He says he swam to China;
Any time he takes a notion
He can walk across the ocean."

It sounded funny. Dancing girls and boys pondered about "reefers" and learned through the whispers of other boys and girls that these cigarettes could make one accomplish the impossible. Sadly enough, they can—in the imagination. The boy who plans a holdup, the youth who seizes a gun and prepares for a murder, the girl who decides suddenly to elope with a boy she did not even know a few hours ago, does so with the confident belief that this is a thoroughly logical action without the slightest possibility of disastrous consequences. Command a person "high" on "mu" or "muggles" or "Mary Jane" to crawl on the floor and bark like a dog, and he will do it without a thought of the idiocy of the action. Everything, no matter how insane, becomes plausible. The underworld calls marijuana "that stuff that makes you able to jump off the tops of skyscrapers."

REPORTS from various sections of the country indicate that the control and sale of marijuana has not yet passed into the hands of the big gangster syndicates. The supply is so vast and grows in so many places that gangsters perhaps have found it difficult to dominate the source. A big, hardy weed, with serrated, swordlike leaves topped by bunchy small blooms supported upon a thick, stringy stalk, marijuana has been discovered in almost every state. New York police uprooted hundreds of plants growing in a vacant lot in Brooklyn. In New York State alone last year 200 tons of the growing weed were destroyed. Acres of it have been found in various communities. Patches have been revealed in back yards, behind signboards, in gardens. In many places in the West it grows wild. Wandering dopesters gather the tops from along the right of way of railroads.

An evidence of how large the traffic may be came to light last year near La Fitte, La. Neighbors of an Italian family had become amazed by wild stories told by the children of the family. They, it seemed, had suddenly become millionaires. They talked of owning inconceivable amounts of money, of automobiles they did not possess, of living in a palatial home. At last their absurd lies were reported to the police, who discovered that their parents were allowing them to smoke something that came from the tops of tall plants which their father grew on his farm. There was a raid, in which more than 500,000 marijuana plants were destroyed. This discovery led next day to another raid on a farm at Bourg, La. Here a crop of some 2,000 plants was found to be growing between rows of vegetables. The eight persons arrested confessed that their main source of income from this crop was in sales to boys and girls of high-school age.

With possibilities for such tremendous crops, grown secretly, gangdom has been hampered in its efforts to corner the profits of what has now become an enormous business. It is to be hoped that the menace of marijuana can be wiped out before it falls into the vicious protectorate of powerful members of the underworld.

BUT to crush this traffic we must first squarely face the facts. Unfortunately, while every state except one has laws to cope with the traffic, the powerful right arm which could support these states has been all but impotent. I refer to the United States government. There has been no national law against the growing, sale, or possession of marijuana.

As this is written a bill to give the Federal government control over marijuana has been introduced in Congress by Representative Robert L. Doughton of North Carolina, Chairman of the House Ways and Means Committee. It has the backing of Secretary of the Treasury Morgenthau, who has under his supervision the various agencies of the United States Treasury Department, including the Bureau of Narcotics, through which Uncle Sam fights the dope evil. It is a revenue bill, modeled after other narcotic laws which make use of the taxing power to bring about regulation and control.

The passage of such a law, however, should not be the signal for the public to lean back, fold its hands, and decide that all danger is over. America now faces a condition in which a new, although ancient, narcotic has come to live next door to us, a narcotic that does not have to be smuggled into the country. This means a job of unceasing watchfulness by every police department and by every public-spirited civic organization. It calls for campaigns of education in every school, so that children will not be deceived by the wiles of peddlers, but will know of the insanity, the disgrace, the horror which marijuana can bring to its victim. And, above all, every citizen should keep constantly before him the real picture of the "reefer man"—not some funny fellow who, should he take the notion, could walk across the ocean, but—

In Los Angeles, Calif., a youth was walking along a downtown street after inhaling a marijuana cigarette. For many addicts, merely a portion of a "reefer" is enough to induce intoxication. Suddenly, for no reason, he decided that someone had threatened to kill him and that his life at that very moment was in danger. Wildly he looked about him. The only person in sight was an aged bootblack. Drug-crazed nerve centers conjured the innocent old shoe-shiner into a destroying monster. Mad with fright, the addict hurried to his room and got a gun. He killed the old man, and then, later, babbled his grief over what had been wanton, uncontrolled murder.

"I thought someone was after me," he said. "That's the only reason I did it. I had never seen the old fellow before. Something just told me to kill him!"

That's marijuana!

SOURCE: Harry J. Aslinger and Ryley Cooper, "Marijuana: Assassin of Youth," *American Magazine* 124, no. 1 (July 1937).

ANALYSIS

It would be hard to overstate the influence that Harry J. Anslinger had and continues to have on public perceptions and, ultimately, federal and state drug laws in the United States, particularly with respect to marijuana. Anslinger was more or less a lifelong federal bureaucrat. The son of immigrant parents, Anslinger first worked for the Pennsylvania Railroad where he rose through the ranks to become an inspector for arson-related cases. During World War I, he applied for and was given an appointment to the State Department where he worked overseas, in large part because of his fluency in German that he later parlayed into becoming fluent in Dutch. Following his time in Europe, Anslinger was promoted and transferred to Latin America where he came to witness firsthand the extensiveness of rum-running during Prohibition. While on assignment in the Caribbean, he successfully persuaded Britain to maintain records of ship movements, aiding to a small extent the effort to track and prosecute rum-running entrepreneurs.

Because of this success, Anslinger was promoted to assistant and then deputy commissioner in the Bureau of Prohibition in the Treasury Department. Owing to his time in the State Department and overseas experience, he was given responsibility for overseeing the international unit. At the time, the Treasury Department had purview for enforcing federal law with respect to both alcohol and narcotics. The prohibition unit within the Bureau of Prohibition, however, was rife with corruption. Staffing was determined by cronyism and political patronage rather than merit and experience. The unit was widely viewed as ineffective and, in retrospect, its corruption and ineffectiveness were seen as contributing to public disregard for the law and to Prohibition's demise.

While the Narcotic Division was less a patronage dumping ground, operating under the protection of civil service laws, there was a growing sense that the job of policing both alcohol and narcotics distribution was too large for a single governmental entity. This consideration, as well as a political scandal involving Levi Nutt, head of the Narcotics Division, whereby arrest statistics were being padded and collusion with organized crime suspected, led the Hoover administration to create a separate Bureau of Narcotics in 1930. The Bureau had broad statutory responsibility for domestic enforcement of the narcotics laws as well as coordinating the nation's international and diplomatic efforts to reduce drug trafficking.

Given his successful career trajectories within the State Department and Bureau of Prohibition, his international experience, and his small but noteworthy success in aiding the effort to combat rum-running, Harry Anslinger was well placed to become the first Acting Commissioner of the Bureau of Narcotics. Nor were his chances diminished by the fact that he was recently married to the niece of the Treasury Secretary to whom he would be reporting, Andrew Mellon. Anslinger's appointment was also supported by wealthy and influential power brokers such as William Randolph Hearst, who had a vested interest in seeing tougher laws against marijuana and hemp. Several months after his initial appointment, the provisional title was removed and Anslinger became the first Bureau of Narcotics Commissioner. In his new role, Anslinger was savvy, energetic, passionate for the cause, and, above all, a political survivor. He would remain Commissioner for 32 years, working under five presidential administrations until he finally retired in 1962. For the next few years after his retirement, ever the good civil servant, Anslinger served as the U.S.

Representative to the United Nations Narcotics Commission after which he fully retired from public life.

The Bureau of Narcotics had a relatively small staff and budget with which to work making extensive and expensive field operations cost prohibitive. Instead, Anslinger relied on a well-orchestrated public relations campaign aimed at the popular press and Congress to support his efforts to strictly control domestic and international narcotics distribution and enhance legal efforts at the state level. (Here, and throughout we use the legal convention of including cocaine, opiates, opiate derivatives, and marijuana as narcotic drugs even though pharmacologically, only opiates and their derivatives meet the technical definition of a narcotic. See sidebar *What Is a Narcotic*, page 24). As cocaine and opiate distribution had largely been addressed and relatively well controlled by the provisions of the Pure Food and Drug Act in 1906 and in 1914 by the Harrison Act and subsequent Supreme Court interpretations, Anslinger targeted marijuana.

On the domestic side, articles such as "Assassin of Youth" were published in popular media outlets of the time such as *American Magazine* and *Reader's Digest*. Anslinger was also frequently called upon to testify before Congress about his Bureau's domestic and international efforts. His testimony included the same fantastical and often unsubstantiated claims to move Congress to enact tougher antidrug legislation. By exaggerating the drug menace faced by the country, Anslinger not only made the case for tougher legislative action, he also underscored the need for the continued existence of and budgetary support for the Narcotics Bureau.

His articles and testimony were shrewdly tailored to stoke existing fears in the general public about the dangers of drug use and the selected stories often played on racial prejudices and stereotypes to achieve that end. The notion from the article above that marijuana was introduced into the United States by Mexicans is patently false and Anslinger knew it. Marijuana, or cannabis as it was better known at the time, grew natively as a weed throughout the United States and had been cultivated to make hemp, birdseed, and industrial products for many years prior to any concerns about its abuse as a drug. While it is true that Mexican immigrants helped spread the use of marijuana as an intoxicant, providing a new name for the plant in the process ("marihuana"), in no way did they introduce the plant into the United States.

Anecdotal evidence for his stories and testimony were drawn from a compilation of police accounts of "drug-related" arrests and sensationalistic stories that Anslinger maintained called the Gore File. The anecdotes in the "Assassin of Youth" article reproduced above were drawn from cases included in the Gore File. They exemplify Anslinger's predilection for using lurid accounts to drive home policy points with visceral, racially charged imagery. Several other anecdotes drawn from the Gore File as cited by Jim Inciardi, illustrate the use of racial stereotyping to fear monger:

> Colored students at the Univ. of Minn. Partying with female students (white), smoking [marijuana] and getting their sympathy with stories of racial persecution. Result pregnancy.
>
> Two Negroes took a girl fourteen years old and kept her for two days under the influence of marihuana. Upon recovery she was found to be suffering from syphilis.

Many of the stories collected by Anslinger had first appeared in publications owned by Hearst. In this regard, Anslinger's campaign of distortions and exaggerations about the effects of marijuana use has been regarded as providing a bully pulpit in support of Hearst's economic (i.e., eliminate hemp as a competing source for paper products) and retributory (i.e., the appropriation of timberland Hearst owned in Mexico by Mexican nationals) interests. Another suspected (but never directly demonstrated) impetus for Anslinger's single-mindedness about marijuana is the fact that his step-uncle and boss, Treasury Secretary Andrew Mellon, was a heavy investor in DuPont Industries. DuPont had recently patented a process for producing synthetic nylon from oil and coal as well as a process to make paper from wood pulp. The ability to cheaply create paper products from the more environmentally friendly hemp plant could have damaged DuPont's profitability.

Anslinger was equally shrewd in using fear to maintain support for the Bureau's efforts internationally, tying worldwide opiate distribution channels to the rise of communism and the beginnings of the Cold War in the post–World War II era. In his worldview, international drug smuggling and importation into the United States were politically subversive acts supported by communist nations acting on multiple fronts to destabilize the United States. He well understood that he could solidify support for his agency's international efforts by (again) tying drug distribution and use to the extant fears of the threat represented by communism.

In an ironic side note, Anslinger, the tough-on-drugs crusader who believed severe penalties and prison sentences were the best way to handle substance abuse, protected the secret of the infamous anticommunist crusader, Senator Joseph McCarthy, who was addicted to morphine. As detailed by Anslinger, biographer McWilliams in a largely sympathetic portrait of the country's first *drug czar*, upon learning of McCarthy's addiction, Anslinger attempted to persuade the senator to seek treatment and threatened to cut off his supply of drugs. When Senator McCarthy refused treatment and threatened to go directly to the drug sellers, Anslinger retreated, fearful of the political fallout if the Senator's secret was betrayed. Anslinger would keep McCarthy's addiction a secret (and help supply him with drugs) until the Senator's death in 1957.

There is no doubt Harry Anslinger sincerely believed drug use (including alcohol use) was a dire social problem and that strict law enforcement and international cooperation on all levels were necessary to control the problem. Regardless of whether or not one supports these ends, the means by which he attempted to achieve them bring into strong question his scrupulousness and integrity. His willingness to cherry-pick information, to use unsubstantiated, sensationalistic

REEFER MADNESS

If one could select from among the more heinous acts attributed to smoking marijuana in Anslinger's "Gore Files," condense them into a script for a movie designed to be a morality tale, and then film the script with bad directing, bad acting, and low production values, the result would be the infamous 1936 movie now known as *Reefer Madness.* Although, there were other more direct attempts to capture Anslinger's fantastical stories on film, most notably, *Assassin of Youth,* none ever achieved the same level of infamy as *Reefer Madness.* Originally titled *Tell Your Children* the movie was produced by a church organization. Their intent was to distribute the movie at church and school functions such as PTA meetings to warn parents and students of the extreme dangers of marijuana use.

The film tells the story of a couple that sells marijuana to, among their main clients, high school and college students. Over the course of the short 68 minutes running time, as direct results of smoking marijuana at a party or two at the couple's apartment, there ensues in rapid succession among the partygoers: vehicular homicide, sexual assault, murder with a handgun, a frame-up for the handgun murder, murder with a fireplace poker, a suicidal leap out of a high-rise window, and confinement to a mental hospital for life. The story is told from the perspective of and with occasional narration by a high school principal talking to a gathering of parents. At the conclusion of the film, the principal turns and points directly into the camera at the viewer cautioning that it could be "your children" ending with the words "tell your children" on screen before the final credits roll.

(continued)

REEFER MADNESS
(continued)

The movie *Reefer Madness* was originally titled "Tell Your Children." It was produced to be distributed to parents as an accurate representation of and warning about the ill effects of marijuana use by children. In reality it was a gross distortion based on the deliberate misperceptions and exaggerations of Harry Anslinger and his acolytes. *Reefer Madness* continues to live on as a comical camp classic. (George A. Hirliman Productions Inc./Photofest)

Shortly after its release, the film was bought by an independent producer and given the more dramatic title of *Reefer Madness* by which it is now known. The intent was to show it on what was called the exploitation film circuit that featured similar melodramatic, low budget fare designed mainly to shock and titillate. But the movie was a flop even by those marginal standards and so with little fanfare, it was stored away and largely forgotten for over 30 years.

Keith Stroup, the President of the National Organization for the Reform of Marijuana Laws (NORML), which advocates for the removal of criminal penalties for marijuana use, rediscovered the movie in the Library of Congress in the 1970s. As the movie had been allowed to fall into the public domain (it can be freely downloaded from the Internet or viewed in its entirety online), he was able to show it on college campuses as a piece of reverse propaganda, arguing that the movie illustrated the absurd characterizations of marijuana used to justify past and current laws. Beyond its intended use as a political prop by both sides of the legalization debate, the film's poor production values, bad acting, and over-the-top script made it a camp classic, suitable for midnight showings on weekends in much the same way the *Rocky Horror Picture Show* achieved lasting fame (infamy) following its theatrical release.

anecdotes, to vigorously suppress contradictory evidence and to smear those who would question policies he supported (e.g., most notably, Alfred R. Lindesmith, who wrote extensively in opposition of American drug policy during Anslinger's reign at the Federal Bureau) and pandering to racial prejudices will forever tarnish his legacy. Moreover, disentangling his concerns over drug use as a social ill from his desire to solidify power, authority, and his own bureaucratic longevity by any means seems impossible. His lasting imprint on drug policy, the long-standing perception and legal standing of marijuana as a drug that causes social and medical consequences on par with cocaine and opiates despite considerable scientific evidence to the contrary and an abiding belief in the use of tough criminal sanctions to deter drug use, remain his other dubious legacies.

FURTHER READING

Anslinger, H.J., & Ousler, W. (1963). *The murderers: The shocking story of the narcotics gangs*. New York: Farrar, Strauss, and Dudahy.

Earlywine, M. (2005). *Understanding marijuana: A new look at the scientific evidence*. New York: Oxford University Press.

Inciardi, J. (2007). *The war on drugs IV: The continuing saga of the mysteries and miseries of intoxication, addiction, crime, and public policy, 4th edition* . Boston, MA: Allyn and Bacon.

Kinder, D.C., & Walker, W.O. (1986). Stable force in a storm: Harry J. Anslinger and United States narcotic foreign policy, 1930–1962. *Journal of American History, 72*(4), 908–927.

McWilliams, J.C. (1989a). *The protectors: Harry J. Anslinger and the Federal Bureau of Narcotics*. Newark: University of Delaware Press.

McWilliams, J.C. (1989b). Unsung partner against crime: Harry J. Anslinger and the Federal Bureau of Narcotics, 1930–1962. *Pennsylvania Magazine of History and Biography, 113*, 207–236.

Musto, D. (1999). *The American disease: Origins of narcotics control, 3rd edition* . New York: Oxford University Press.

Sloman, L. (1998). *Reefer madness: A history of marijuana*. New York: Bobbs-Merrill.

On the Internet

General references related to Harry Anslinger as well as transcripts of congressional testimony are available at the Shaffer Drug Policy Library at: http://www.druglibrary.org/Schaffer/people/anslinger/index.htm.

A copy of the movie *Reefer Madness*, which is in the public domain, can be downloaded or viewed online free from Google videos at: http://video.google.com/videoplay?docid=-6696582420128930236#

"It Has Something to Do with Something That Is Called Marihuana"

- ***Document:*** Marihuana Tax Act of 1937
- ***Date:*** August 2, 1937
- ***Where:*** Washington, DC
- ***Significance:*** Passed with virtually no deliberation by the Congress, the Marihuana Tax Act required that transactions involving marijuana or, technically, any parts of the plant *Cannabis sativa* L. save the stalk and sterilized seeds, be taxed and accompanied by a stamp and records kept indicating compliance with the law. Because the government issued few such stamps, however, the law effectively prohibited growing, using or distributing marijuana in the United States placing the substance on prohibition.

DOCUMENT

Be it enacted by the Senate and House of Representatives of the United States of America in Congress assembled, That when used in this Act —

(a) The term "person" means an individual, a partnership, trust, association, company, or corporation and includes an officer or employee of a trust, association, company, or corporation, or a member or employee of a partnership, who, as such officer, employee, or member, is under a duty to perform any act in respect of which any violation of this Act occurs.

(b) The term "marihuana" means all parts of the plant Cannabis sativa L., whether growing or not; the seeds thereof; the resin extracted from any part of such plant; and every compound, manufacture, salt, derivative, mixture, or preparation of such plant, its seeds, or resin- but shall not include the mature stalks of such plant, fiber produced from such stalks, oil or cake made from the seeds of such plant, any other compound, manufacture, salt, derivative, mixture, or preparation of such mature stalks (except the resin extracted therefrom), fiber, oil, or cake, or the sterilized seed of such plant which is incapable of germination.

(c) The term "producer" means any person who (1) plants, cultivates, or in any way facilitates the natural growth of marihuana; or (2) harvests and transfers or makes use of marihuana.

(d) The term "Secretary" means the Secretary of the Treasury and the term "collector means collector of internal revenue.

(e) The term "transfer" or "transferred" means any type of disposition resulting in a change of possession but shall not include a transfer to a common carrier for the purpose of transporting marihuana.

SEC. 2. (a) Every person who imports, manufactures, produces, compounds, sells, deals in, dispenses, prescribes, administers, or gives away marihuana shall (1) within fifteen days after the effective date of this Act, or (2) before engaging after the expiration of such fifteen-day period in any of the above mentioned activities, and (3) thereafter, on or before July 1 of each year, pay the following special taxes respectively:

(1) Importers, manufacturers, and compounders of marihuana, $24 per year.

(2) Producers of marihuana (except those included within subdivision (4) of this subsection), $1 per year, or fraction thereof, during which they engage in such activity.

(3) Physicians, dentists, veterinary surgeons, and other practitioners who distribute, dispense, give away, administer, or prescribe marihuana to patients upon whom they in the course of their professional practice are in attendance, $1 per year or fraction thereof during which they engage in any of such activities.

(4) Any person not registered as an importer, manufacturer, producer, or compounder who obtains and uses marihuana in a laboratory for the purpose of research, instruction, or analysis, or who produces marihuana for any such purpose, $1 per year, or fraction thereof, during which he engages in such activities.

(5) Any person who is not a physician, dentist, veterinary surgeon, or other practitioner and who deals in, dispenses, or gives away marihuana, $3 per year: Provided, That any person who has registered and paid the special tax as an importer, manufacturer, compounder, or producer, as required by subdivisions (1) and (2) of this subsection, may deal in, dispense, or give away marihuana imported, manufactured, compounded, or produced by him without further payment of the tax imposed by this section. . . .

SEC. 4. (a) It shall be unlawful for any person required to register and pay the special tax under the provisions of section 2 to import, manufacture, produce, compound, sell, deal in, dispense, distribute, prescribe, administer, or give away marihuana without having so registered and paid such tax.

(b) In any suit or proceeding to enforce the liability imposed by this section or section 2, if proof is made that marihuana was at any time growing upon land under the control of the defendant, such proof shall be presumptive evidence that at such time the defendant was a producer and liable under this section as well as under section 2.

SEC. 5. It shall be unlawful for any person who shall not have paid the special tax and registered, as required by section 2, to send, ship, carry, transport, or deliver any marihuana within any Territory, the District of Columbia, or any insular possession, or from any State, Territory, the District of Columbia, any insular possession of the United States, or the Canal Zone, into any other State, Territory, the District of

Columbia, or insular possession of the United States: Provided, That nothing contained in this section shall apply to any common carrier engaged in transporting marihuana; or to any employee of any person who shall have registered and paid the special tax as required by section 2 while acting within the scope of his employment; or to any person who shall deliver marihuana which has been prescribed or dispensed by a physician, dentist, veterinary surgeon, or other practitioner registered under section 2, who has been employed to prescribe for the particular patient receiving such marihuana; or to any United States, State, county, municipal, District, Territorial, or insular officer or official acting within the scope of his official duties.

SEC. 6. (a) It shall be unlawful for any person, whether or not required to pay a special tax and register under section 2, to transfer marihuana, except in pursuance of a written order of the person to whom such marihuana is transferred, on a form to be issued in blank for that purpose by the Secretary.

(b) Subject to such regulations as the Secretary may prescribe, nothing contained in this section shall apply:

(1) To a transfer of marihuana to a patient by a physician, dentist, veterinary surgeon, or other practitioner registered under section 2, in the course of his professional practice only: Provided, That such physician, dentist, veterinary surgeon, or other practitioner shall keep a record of all such marihuana transferred, showing the amount transferred and the name and address of the patient to whom such marihuana is transferred, and such record shall be kept for a period of two years from the date of the transfer of such marihuana, and subject to inspection as provided in section 11.

(2) To a transfer of marihuana, made in good faith by a dealer to a consumer under and in pursuance of a written prescription issued by a physician, dentist, veterinary surgeon, or other practitioner registered under section 2: Provided, That such prescription shall be dated as of the day on which signed and shall be signed by the physician, dentist, veterinary surgeon, or other practitioner who issues the same; Provided further, That such dealer shall preserve such prescription for a period of two years from the day on which such prescription is filled so as to be readily accessible for inspection by the officers, agents, employees, and officials mentioned in section 11.

(3) To the sale, exportation, shipment, or delivery of marihuana by any person within the United States, any Territory, the District of Columbia, or any of the insular possessions of the United States, to any person in any foreign country regulating the entry of marihuana, if such sale, shipment, or delivery of marihuana is made in accordance with such regulations for importation into such foreign country as are prescribed by such foreign country, such regulations to be promulgated from time to time by the Secretary of State of the United States.

(4) To a transfer of marihuana to any officer or employee of the United States Government or of any State, Territorial, District, county, or municipal or insular government lawfully engaged in making purchases thereof for the various departments of the Army and Navy, the Public Health Service, and for Government, State, Territorial, District, county, or municipal or insular hospitals or prisons

(S) To a transfer of any seeds of the plant *Cannabis sativa* L. to any person registered under section 2.

(c) The Secretary shall cause suitable forms to be prepared for the purposes before mentioned and shall cause them to be distributed to collectors for sale. The price at which such forms shall be sold by said collectors shall be fixed by the Secretary but shall not exceed 2 cents each. Whenever any collector shall sell any of such forms he shall cause the date of sale, the name and address of the proposed vendor, the name and address of the purchaser, and the amount of marihuana ordered to be plainly written or stamped thereon before delivering the same.

(d) Each such order form sold by a collector shall be prepared by him and shall include an original and two copies, any one of which shall be admissible in evidence as an original. The original and one copy shall be given by the collector to the purchaser thereof. The original shall in turn be given by the purchaser thereof to any person who shall, in pursuance thereof, transfer marihuana to him and shall be preserved by such person for a period of two years so as to be readily accessible for inspection by any officer, agent, or employee mentioned in section 11. The copy given to the purchaser by the collector shall be retained by the purchaser and preserved for a period of two years so as to be readily accessible to inspection by any officer, agent, or employee mentioned in section 11. The second copy shall be preserved in the records of the collector.

SEC. 7. (a) There shall be levied, collected, and paid upon all transfers of marihuana which are required by section 6 to be carried out in pursuance of written order forms taxes at the following rates:

(1) Upon each transfer to any person who has paid the special tax and registered under section 2 of this Act, $1 per ounce of marihuana or fraction thereof

(2) Upon each transfer to any person who has not paid the special tax and registered under section 2 of this Act, $100 per ounce of marihuana or fraction thereof.

(b) Such tax shall be paid by the transferee at the time of securing each order form and shall be in addition to the price of such form. Such transferee shall be liable for the tax imposed by this section but in the event that the transfer is made in violation of section 6 without an order form and without payment of the transfer tax imposed by this section, the transferor shall also be liable for such tax.

(c) Payment of the tax herein provided shall be represented by appropriate stamps to be provided by the Secretary and said stamps shall be affixed by the collector or his representative to the original order form. . . .

SEC. 8. (a) It shall be unlawful for any person who is a transferee required to pay the transfer tax imposed by section 7 to acquire or otherwise obtain any marihuana without having paid such tax; and proof that any person shall have had in his possession any marihuana and shall have failed, after reasonable notice and demand by the collector, to produce the order form required by section 6 to be retained by him, shall be presumptive evidence of guilt under this section and of liability for the tax imposed by section 7.

(b) No liability shall be imposed by virtue of this section upon any duly authorized officer of the Treasury Department engaged in the enforcement of this Act or upon any duly authorized officer of any State, or Territory, or of any political subdivision thereof, or the District of Columbia, or of any insular possession of the United States, who shall be engaged in the enforcement of any law or municipal ordinance dealing with the production, sale, prescribing, dispensing, dealing in, or distributing of marihuana.

SEC. 9. (a) Any marihuana which has been imported, manufactured, compounded, transferred, or produced in violation of any of the provisions of this Act shall be subject to seizure and forfeiture and, except as inconsistent with the provisions of this

Act, all the provisions of internal-revenue laws relating to searches, seizures, and forfeitures are extended to include marihuana.

(b) Any marihuana which may be seized by the United States Government from any person or persons charged with any violation of this Act shall upon conviction of the person or persons from whom seized be confiscated by and forfeited to the United States.

(c) Any marihuana seized or coming into the possession of the United States in the enforcement of this Act, the owner or owners of which are unknown, shall be confiscated by and forfeited to the United States.

(d) The Secretary is hereby directed to destroy any marihuana confiscated by and forfeited to the United States under this section or to deliver such marihuana to any department, bureau, or other agency of the United States Government, upon proper application therefore under such regulations as may be prescribed by the Secretary.

SEC. 10. (a) Every person liable to any tax imposed by this act shall keep such books and records, render under oath such statements, make such returns, and comply with such rules and regulations as the Secretary may from time to time prescribe.

(b) Any person who shall be registered under the provisions of section 2 in any internal- revenue district shall, whenever required so to do by the collector of the district, render to the collector a true and correct statement or return, verified by affidavits, setting forth the quantity of marihuana received or harvested by him during such period immediately preceding the demand of the collector, not exceeding three months, as the said collector may fix and determine. If such person is not solely a producer, he shall set forth in such statement or return the names of the persons from which said marihuana was received, the quantity in each instance received from such persons, and the date when received.

SEC. 12. Any person who is convicted of a violation of any provision of this Act shall be fined not more than $2,000 or imprisoned not more than five years, or both, in the discretion of the court.

SOURCE: Marihuana Tax Act of 1937, Pub. 238, 75th Congress, 50 Stat. 551, August 2, 1937.

ANALYSIS

The events surrounding the passage of legislation that effectively made the distribution, sale, and use of marijuana illegal would be comical, if the consequences had been short-lived and minimal and the lives affected had been few; neither was the case. The Marihuana Tax Act would have repercussions that lasted for decades, adversely affecting the lives of many for generations whose marijuana use became a serious federal crime overnight.

As with many things related to U.S. drug policy history, however, the story is not quite that simple. Prior to the passage of the federal law that once again, similar to the Harrison Act, used the taxing powers of the federal government to criminalize drug use, many states had already adopted laws restricting marijuana use and distribution to medicinal purposes only. The legislation was adopted by the large majority of states in the absence of any real evidence that marijuana was addicting, medically harmful, or associated with unpredictable (or predictable for that matter) criminal acts, and violence. It's the story of a passionately motivated few, forcefully acting to pass legislation that would affect the ill-informed many.

In their detailed legal analysis of how federal legislation that essentially prohibited the use and distribution of a drug that was not in widespread use nor particularly dangerous from either a medical or legal standpoint, was passed with almost no opposition, Bonnie and Whitebread note,

> The middle class had successfully frustrated alcohol prohibition because the public opinion process came to reflect its view that the law should not condemn intoxication. Yet because marijuana use was primarily a lower class phenomenon, the middle class was generally unaware of the proposed legislation. The public opinion process did not operate, and decisionmakers remained uninformed about the drug. Quickly and with neither consideration nor dissent, the laws were enacted, thus establishing a deliberative format followed often in the succeeding decades. (pp. 1027–1028)

Although marijuana, or cannabis as it was more commonly known in the early part of the 20th century, had been grown in the United States for some time for various purposes such as veterinary medicine, birdseed, and hemp, its use as an intoxicant was generally rare. Introduction of the practice of smoking marijuana for its intoxicating effects in the United States is generally attributed to Mexican immigrants in the southwestern and western states who came to America in the early part of the 20th century to farm American fields. For a time, little was made of their smoking marijuana to relax and escape the boredom of lives of hard labor in much the same way others used alcohol or the Chinese coolies smoked opium. But when the economy declined rapidly during the Great Depression, the continued presence and immigration of Mexican laborers was seen as an economic threat to American workers scrambling for fewer and fewer available jobs. It was then that fear began to grow about the perceived social menace posed by marijuana use and its attendant criminal behavior. Stories about loco weed and the effects it had on "drug-crazed Mexicans" who committed violent crimes while using marijuana began to appear more often in the press and in police reports, particularly in the same western and southwestern states with the largest Mexican immigrant populations.

Louisiana was another state affected by an influx of marijuana. In this case, marijuana arrived from the Caribbean through Louisiana's port city of New Orleans. It soon spread throughout the black community, becoming an integral part of the jazz scene that began in and flourished there. The New Orleans press ran sensationalized stories about marijuana use by the jazz bands that played for clients of the city's red-light district bordellos. In the 1930s, Louis Armstrong would write and record a song in tribute to marijuana, of which he was fond. The song was titled "Muggles," the slang word used by jazz musicians to refer to marijuana cigarettes or *reefers* and no relation to the same word referencing those without magic powers that would, much later, be made famous in the *Harry Potter* novels of J.K. Rowling. Other jazz artists paid similar tribute in songs such as "Reefer Man," "A Viper's Drag," "When I Get Low, I Get High," and "Texas Tea Party."

Jazz musicians and southern blacks that migrated north, in particular to New York, brought marijuana with them where its use flourished in Harlem nightclubs and other spots throughout the city dedicated to smoking marijuana known as *tea pads*. The use of marijuana was by no means constrained to the black community, however, as white patrons mingled and indulged at the very same fashionable nightclubs and tea pads. Outside of these enclaves, however, marijuana use was uncommon and remained largely invisible to most of the population save for the occasional story of a sensational crime in the press. Nevertheless, concern arose about the still-legal use of marijuana spreading outward, owing to alcohol prohibition (weakly enforced as it was in New York) and the sharply reduced availability of opiates and cocaine. The fear was that marijuana would become a cheap and readily available alternative for opportunistic addicts unable to get their preferred drug and, from there, be spread to the vulnerable in need of protection (i.e., white women and children).

Photo of jazz artist Mezz Mezzrow, 1940. The unlikely purveyor of the finest marijuana available in New York City, Milton "Mezz" Mesirow, a jazz musician and dealer par excellence, inspired songs by other jazz musicians about the "Mighty Mezz" that celebrated the high quality of his marijuana. (Redferns/Getty Images)

Prior to passage of the Federal Marihuana Tax Act in 1937, a majority of states (35) had adopted passage of laws modeled after the Uniform Narcotics Drug Act. The Uniform Narcotics Drug Act was crafted by an organization called the National Commissioners on Uniform State Laws. Every state had two governor-appointed representatives on the Commission. The Commission's role was to develop blueprints to guide states in enacting uniform laws in areas where interstate cooperation and coordination was deemed essential; in this instance, the area was the use and distribution of drugs (narcotics).

Whereas the Harrison Act levied a tax on transactions involving opiates and cocaine, constitutionally, it could not use police powers beyond those provided in the tax code to go after violators or to penalize non-tax-related activities such as simple possession. Hence the federal government was dependent on the states to craft laws that would allow criminal enforcement supporting the intent of the Harrison Act, which was to prohibit distribution, use, and possession of narcotic drugs (cocaine and opiates).

The push for uniform narcotics legislation was led by the western and southwestern states, which had the strongest concerns about marijuana. Many of these states had already enacted laws making marijuana use illegal. They were supported by the American Medical Association, which wanted consistency in the laws across states to make it easier to guide its physician members on legal practice and by Anslinger's Federal Bureau of Narcotics, which had a small staff and enforcement budget and hence was reliant on the states to carry out the bulk of enforcement activities. Over successive drafts of the model law, marijuana was first included and then excluded from the definition of a narcotic drug along with cocaine and opiates even though it was not covered in the Harrison Act. In the final draft that was adopted as the model, marijuana continued to be excluded from the drafted definition as a narcotic drug but supplemental text was provided that, at the discretion of the state, could be used to include marijuana as one of the prohibited narcotics. This was the option adopted by most states and by 1937, 35 states had enacted some version of the Uniform Narcotics Drug Act that included prohibition of marijuana along with cocaine and opiates.

Following the widespread adoption of the Uniform Narcotics Drug Act, Commissioner Anslinger continued to push for a federal law to close loopholes in the state laws and make marijuana use and distribution federal offenses. His lobbying of Congress about the urgent need for such legislation was so successful, that the three days of hearings prior to passage of the legislation were something of a charade. Commissioner Anslinger testified of the growing menace of marijuana use (without providing any statistics), of its ties to Mexican laborers, and that American youth in particular were susceptible targets for this new threat.

Marijuana was portrayed as the root of three evils: insanity, criminality, and death. The evidence supporting these contentions during the hearings came from horror stories based on unsubstantiated newspaper accounts; a nonscientific study by the New Orleans District Attorney on marijuana use by jail detainees in that city; and a scientific study on the physiological effects of marijuana based on experiments with dogs. No scientific evidence based on human studies or observations of humans was presented. The absurdity of the proceedings is nicely captured by this excerpt (cited in Bonnie and Whitebread, 1970) of the testimony of the scientist (Dr. Munch) who experimented with dogs and how he concluded it led to degeneration of the brain as underlying the effects seen in humans:

Mr. McCormack: Have you experimented upon any animals whose reaction to this drug would be similar to that of human beings?

Dr. Munch: The reason we use dogs is because the reaction of dogs to this drug closely resembles the reaction of human beings.

Mr. McCormack: And the continued use of it, as you have observed the reaction on dogs, has resulted in the disintegration of the personality?

Dr. Munch: Yes. So far as I can tell, not being a dog psychologist.

The sole witness representing the AMA testified against passage but was accused of obstructionism and summarily dismissed with no consideration of his arguments. The majority of the hearings were devoted to how the law should be amended so as not to harm the interests of businesses such as birdseed manufacturers, who used the processed seeds from the marijuana plant.

When the final bill first came to the House floor for passage late in the day on June 10, 1937, there was little discussion save the appropriateness of voting at such a late hour on a bill that members knew little about in terms of its substance or necessity. The Congressional Record of discussion of the bill is very brief, several pages, and indicates that passage of the bill occurred in the absence of any serious debate or discussion. The following passage from the Congressional Record (again as cited in Bonnie and Whitebread, 1970) between Congressman Sam Rayburn of Texas and Congressman Bertrand Snell of New York reveals quite clearly the depth and intensity of the discussion:

Mr. RAYBURN: Mr. Speaker if the gentleman will yield, I may say that the gentleman from North Carolina has stated to me that this bill has a unanimous report from the committee and that there is no controversy about it.
Mr. SNELL: What is the bill?
Mr. RAYBURN: It has something to do with something that is called marihuana. I believe it is a narcotic of some kind.

And without much more discussion or debate than that (literally), the Marihuana Tax Act was passed, classifying marijuana as a narcotic along with cocaine and opiates and making it illegal to possess, grow, or distribute the drug without first registering with the federal authorities and paying a stamp tax. Since few stamps were ever issued, except for a brief period when there was a shortage of hemp during World War II, marijuana essentially became a prohibited substance in America. The ban on marijuana also prevented research into potential medical uses.

It did not take long for the new law to generate an arrest. The law went into effect October 1, 1937. The first arrests under the laws provisions occurred on October 4 and 5 in Denver, Colorado. Moses Baca, a 23-year-old Mexican American was arrested and charged with possession of one-fourth of an ounce of marijuana, while 57-year-old Samuel Caldwell, an unemployed white American who supported himself selling marijuana cigarettes, was arrested for attempting to sell three such cigarettes. Punishment was swift and severe. Within a week, Baca received an 18-month sentence and Caldwell a 4-month sentence, both to be served in Leavenworth. The sentencing judge, J. Foster Symes, gave the following short speech summarizing his thoughts on both cases and the new law:

> I consider marijuana the worst of all narcotics—far worse than the use of morphine or cocaine. Under its influence men become beasts, just as was the case with Baca. Marijuana destroys life itself. I have no sympathy with those who sell this weed. In [the] future I will impose the heaviest penalties. The government is going to enforce this new law to the letter.

Needless to say, Anslinger was delighted with the trial's outcome. In a statement to the press he said, "These men have shown the way to other district attorneys throughout the nation." Subsequent legislation in the 1950s, always with the enthusiastic approval and lobbying of Commissioner Anslinger, would increase the sanctions fourfold and remove judicial sentencing discretion for good measure.

MILTON MESIROW—"THE MAN THAT HIPPED THE WORLD"

One of the more interesting and improbable characters associated with both the jazz and marijuana scenes in 1930s Harlem was Milton Mesirow who would become better known as Mezz Mezzrow or simply Mezz. Born into a white, middle-class Jewish family in 1899 in Chicago and coming of age during Prohibition, Mezzrow played jazz clarinet and saxophone in Chicago speakeasies; among them, ones owned by Al Capone. When the great depression hit in 1929, leaving Mezzrow penniless and down on his luck, he decided to follow the migration of many jazz musicians from the north to the growing scene in New York. Prior to heading off, Mezzrow was introduced to using marijuana in the restroom of one of the nightclubs in which he performed. Believing it made him a better musician, he became an instant convert and ambassador for marijuana, extolling its virtues to other musicians and club patrons to whom he began selling and distributing the drug.

Using his midwestern-based Mexican connections to obtain an especially potent form of the drug, Mezz became something of a minor celebrity during his time in Harlem. There, he fully embraced black jazz culture to the extent he considered himself an "honorary negro". Although, never known as one of the better jazz musicians, Mezzrow became very well known for the quality of the marijuana he provided. His fame was to the extent that the word Mezz came to stand for a superior grade marijuana cigarette as exemplified by lyrics from the song "If You're a Viper," one of many jazz songs to pay tribute to marijuana use. The slang term viper was used to designate a marijuana smoker and references the hissing sound made during the deep inhalation phase of smoking. Written by Stuff Smith but more famous as a Fats Waller recording, the beginning lyrics of "If You're a Viper" are:

Dreamed about a reefer five foot long
The mighty mezz, but not too strong . . .

Mezzrow's career as a drug connoisseur and purveyor came to a sudden halt in 1940 when he was arrested on Long Island in possession of several handfuls of marijuana cigarettes. He served his time on Riker's Island where he requested and received a transfer to the section that held black inmates because he felt more comfortable being among them. In 1946, Mezz co-authored a book, *Really the Blues,* which chronicled his experiences as a hepster. Mezzrow later joined a second migration of jazz musicians, this time as expatriates to Paris, where he died in 1972.

FURTHER READING

Berger, M. (1938, March 12). Tea for a viper, *New Yorker,* 36–48.

Bonnie, R.J., & Whitebread, C.H. (1970). The forbidden fruit and the tree of knowledge: An inquiry into the legal history of American marijuana prohibition. *Virginia Law Review, 56,* 971–1201.

Galliher, J.F., & Walker, A. (1977). The puzzle of the social origins of the Marihuana Tax Act of 1937. *Journal of Social Problems, 24,* 374.

Jonnes, J. (1996). *Hep-cats, narcs, and pipe dreams: A history of America's romance with illegal drugs.* New York: Scribner.

Mezzerow, M., & Wolfe, B. (1946). *Really the blues.* New York: Citadel Press.

Sloman, L.R. (1998). *Reefer madness: A history of marijuana.* New York: St. Martins Griffin Edition.

Taxation of Marijuana, Hearings before the Committee on Ways and Means, U.S. House of Representative, 75th Cong., 1st Sess., on H.R. 6385, April 27–30 and May 4, 1937 (Washington DC: U.S, Government Printing Office, 1937).

On the Internet

The PBS program *Frontline* produced a documentary on the history of drug policy in the United States as it relates to marijuana. A website with information about the documentary that includes an excerpt of the show as well as an interview with David Musto, who has chronicled the history of U.S. drug policy in several books and articles and who knew and interviewed Harry Anslinger is available at: http://www.pbs.org/wgbh/pages/frontline/shows/dope/.

A more accessible and very amusing recounting of the events surrounding marijuana prohibition is contained in a 1995 speech given by Charles Whitebread to the California Judges Association. A transcript of the speech is available at: http://www.druglibrary.org/schaffer/history/whiteb1.htm.

A recording of Louis Armstrong and his band playing "Muggles" is available on YouTube at: http://www.youtube.com/watch?v=qY6Yo6lE-Jg.

A detailed description of the New York tea pads in Harlem and the relationship between jazz and marijuana is at: http://www.druglibrary.org/Schaffer/hemp/history/first12000/12.htm.

Current information on marijuana, its psychoactive and physiological effects, and trends in current use are available at the National Institute on Drug Abuse website at: http://drugabuse.gov/ResearchReport/Marijuana/marijuana2.html.

"It Is Concluded That Marihuana Is Not a Drug of Addiction, Comparable to Morphine"

- ***Document:*** The Marijuana Problem in the City of New York: Sociological Medical, Psychological and Pharmacological Studies, by the Mayor's Committee on Marijuana ("The La Guardia Report")
- ***Date:*** 1944
- ***Where:*** New York, New York
- ***Significance:*** The steady stream of stories in the press and testimony before government subcommittees about the presumed role of marijuana in violent crime and the seduction of youth into drug use by marijuana peddlers raised considerable public concern. The Mayor of New York City, Fiorello La Guardia, requested the New York Academy of Medicine conduct a study of the extent of marijuana use and its physiological and psychological effects. New York City was viewed as something of an epicenter of illegal drug use at the time. The findings of the study were published in a 1944 report that contradicted many of the claims about marijuana use that underlay public and political support for the Marihuana Tax Act and related state policies. The report did not receive much publicity in the media, however. Not surprisingly, Commissioner Anslinger and the Federal Bureau of Narcotics were deeply upset with the report's conclusions and roundly attacked the study's methods and findings. The report ultimately had little influence on public policy and perceptions and laws providing for even stricter sanctions against marijuana production and use were enacted in the next decade. The section represented here is an excerpt from the report's conclusions.

DOCUMENT

The widespread publicity describing the dangerous effects of marihuana usage in New Orleans and other southern cities, especially among school children, had its repercussion in the city of New York, and some anxiety was experienced as to the possibility that similar conditions were present or might develop here. Because of this, Mayor La Guardia asked The New York Academy of Medicine for an opinion as to the advisability of studying the whole marijuana problem. The Academy recommended that such a study be made and outlined its scope in general terms. Following this, the Mayor appointed a committee empowered to make the study. This committee consisted of two internists, three psychiatrists, two pharmacologists, and one public health expert, and the Commissioners of Psychiatry of the Department of Hospitals, *ex officio*.

The Committee formulated a plan for the study, and the expenses were arranged for through grants by the New York Foundation, the Friedsam Foundation and the Commonwealth Fund. The study was begun in April 1940.

The first phase of the study concerned the extent of marihuana smoking in New York City, its incidence among school children, its relation to crime, and its effects on individuals using it. For obtaining this information, the Commissioner of Police assigned to the Committee six police officers, four men and two women, who served as "plain clothes" investigators. Those investigators circulated in the districts in which marihuana appeared to be most widely used, particularly Harlem, associated with marihuana users, and found out as much as possible about sources of supply, means of distribution, and effects of marihuana on users. Included in this survey were a careful watch on school children in both grade and high schools and interviews with school principals.

As a result of this investigation the Committee came to the conclusion that marihuana distribution and usage is found mainly in Harlem, the population of which is predominantly Negro and Latin-American, and to a less extent in the Broadway area extending from 42nd to 59th Streets. The local supply comes from individual peddlers and from "tea-pads," which are establishments for marihuana users in New York City, but a conservative estimate is that there are some 500 peddlers and 500 "tea-pads" in Harlem.

The marihuana users with whom contact was made in this study were persons without steady employment. The majority fall in the age group of 20 to 30 years. Idle and lacking initiative, they suffer boredom and seek distraction. Smoking is indulged in for the sake of conviviality and sociability and because it affords a temporary feeling of adequacy in meeting disturbing situations.

The confirmed user smokes from 6 to 10 cigarettes a day. The effects are easily recognized by the smoker, the desirable stage being what is known as "high." When this is reached, the smoking is stopped. If a "too high" state is reached, the taking of beverages such as beer or sweet pop, or a cold bath are considered effective countermeasures.

In most instances, the behavior of the smoker is of a friendly, sociable character. Aggressiveness and belligerency are not commonly seen, and those showing such traits are not allowed to remain in "tea-pads."

The marihuana user does not come from the hardened criminal class and there was found no direct relationship between the commission of crimes of violence and marihuana. "Tea-pads" have no direct associations with houses of prostitution, and marihuana itself has no specific stimulant effect in regard to sexual desires.

There is no organized traffic in marihuana among New York City school children, and any smoking that occurs in this group is limited to isolated instances.

Smoking marihuana can be stopped abruptly with no resulting mental or physical distress comparable to that of morphine withdrawal in morphine addicts.

The second division of the study was the clinical one, the purpose of which was to ascertain the effects of marihuana on the individual user. There were two phases of this work, the general medical study and the psychological study. Wards in the municipal hospital on Welfare Island (now known as Goldwater Memorial Hospital) were made available by the Commissioner of Hospitals. The subjects for the study were drawn from the prison population at the Penitentiary on Riker's Island, as arranged by the Commissioner of Correction. They were under sentence for terms varying from three months to three years, most of them for what would be called minor criminal offenses. They volunteered for the study, the purpose and procedure of which had been fully explained to them. They were kept in the hospital in groups of 6 to 10, for a period of study of approximately a month. The subjects afforded the sample especially desired, for over half of them were marihuana smokers and the others of the class from which marihuana smokers come. The personnel conducting the study consisted of a physician in charge, with an assistant physician, three psychologists, and a secretary. The subjects were under the constant supervision of the medical staff, nurses and attendants.

In studying the effects of marihuana on the 77 subjects selected for the study, the drug was given either in the form of an extract taken by mouth, or was smoked in cigarettes. The dose given to produce definite systemic reactions ranged from a minimal one of 1 cc. to a maximum of 22 cc. of the extract, and from 1 to 10 cigarettes. The effects of smoking appeared immediately and usually passed off in from one to three or four hours. Those from the extract came on more gradually and persisted for a longer time, in some instances for twenty-four hours or more. As the dose for any individual was increased, the effects usually were more marked and of longer duration, but the effect of any given dose varied with the individual subjects.

Although some of the subjects became restless and talkative under marihuana influence, a mental state characterized by a sense of well-being, relaxation and unawareness of surroundings, followed by drowsiness, was present in most instances when the subject was left undisturbed. Generally, there was observed a difficulty in focusing and sustaining mental attention. In company, the subjects were lively and given to talkativeness, fits of laughter and good-natured joking. The pleasurable effects, classed as euphoric, were frequently interrupted or replaced by a state of apprehension of varying degree.

In a limited number of the subjects there were alterations in behavior giving rise to antisocial expression. This was shown by unconventional acts not permitted in public, anxiety reactions, opposition and antagonism, and eroticism. Effects such as these would be considered conducive to acts of violence. However, any tendency toward violence was expressed verbally and not by physical actions, and in no case was restraint by force needed.

In addition to its effect on mental states, physical symptoms resulting from the administration of marihuana were recorded. Of these, tremor, ataxia, dizziness, a sensation of floating in space, dilation of the pupils, dryness of the throat, nausea and vomiting, an urge to urinate, hunger, and a desire for sweets were the most striking. Tremor and ataxia and dizziness were of the greatest frequency. These symptoms may be disturbing to the subject, and if marked enough, cause anxiety and interrupt the euphoric state.

On some occasions, instead of the marihuana concentrate, preparations supplied by Dr. Roger Adams were given. These were tetrahydrocannabinol, made from cannabadiol, corresponding to a principle found in the plant, a synthetic tetrahydrocannabinol, an isomer of the natural one, and a synthetic hexyl-hydro-cannabinol. They all produced effects similar in character to those from the concentrate. Their relative potency could be determined only approximately. The rough estimate was that 1 cc. of the concentrate had as its equivalent 15 mg. of the natural tetrahydrocannabinol, 60 mg. of the hexyl-hydro-cannabinol, and 120 mg. of the synthetic tetrahydrocannabinol.

In the total group studied, what are known as psychotic episodes occurred in 9 of the subjects. In 6 instances, they were of short duration, persisting for from three to ten hours, and were characterized by mental confusion and excitement of a delirious nature with periods of laughter and of anxiety. These effects correspond to those often reported in marihuana literature and are examples of acute marihuana intoxication which in many ways is similar to acute alcoholic intoxication. In the other 3 cases, one subject had a mild psychotic reaction after smoking one cigarette. Later, a typical psychotic state came on four hours after the subject had taken tetrahydrocannabinol and persisted for six days. This subject was subsequently found to have a history of epileptic attacks so that the psychotic episode was probably related to epilepsy. The second subject had previously been a drug addict. She was given marihuana on several occasions, at times showing only euphoric effects and other times confusion and worriment. She left the hospital with the diagnosis of psychosis. After six months, she was discharged as cured. The third subject showed no unusual effects of marihuana which was given on several occasions during his stay at the hospital. Some days after his return to the penitentiary he developed a psychotic state diagnosed "Psychosis with psychopathic personality." This was considered an example of what is known as "prison psychosis," a condition which has been noted in persons emotionally unstable subjected to the depressing atmosphere of prison incarceration. The precise role of marihuana in the psychotic states in the three unstable subjects is not clear. In the case of the second and third subject, the fact that they were sent back to prison to complete their sentences must be considered an important if not the main factor in bringing on the psychosis.

In the clinical study of the effect of marihuana on functions of various organs off the body, there was found an increase in pulse rate and blood pressure and an increase in blood sugar and metabolic rate. No changes were found in the circulation rate and vital capacity. Tests on renal and liver function were negative. No changes were found in blood counts and hemoglobin, or blood nitrogen, calcium, and phosphorous concentrations. The electrocardiogram showed no abnormalities which could be attributed to direct action on the heart, and from a few observations made, marihuana appeared to be without effect on gastric motility and secretion. The positive results found, as well as the occurrence of nausea and vomiting, an increase in the frequency of urination, and the sensation of hunger and an increase in appetite, may be considered results of central nervous excitation, producing peripheral effects through the autonomic nervous system.

The psychological study, planned and carried out by experienced psychologists, was concomitant with the general medical one and was devoted to determining the effects of marihuana on psychomotor responses and certain special abilities on intellectual functioning, and on emotional reactions and personality structure.

For psychomotor effects, procedures were followed which gave records affording quantitative measurement. Static equilibrium and body steadiness were the functions most strongly affected by marihuana. The body swaying was general in the direction and not greater on one axis than in others. These effects came on during the first hour after the extract was given, reached a peak in about four hours, and persisted for some eight hours. After smoking, the effects came on much sooner—within a few minutes—and were of shorter duration, about three hours. Complex hand and foot reactions showed impairment, but simple reaction time, the strength of grip, speed of tapping, auditory acuity and musical ability, and estimation of short time intervals and small linear distances were unchanged. The findings in the women corresponded to those in the male subjects. In both groups there was marked individual variability, irrespective of dosage.

It was found that marihuana in an effective dose impairs intellectual functioning in general. Included under this heading are adverse effects on speed and accuracy in performance, on the application of acquired knowledge, on carrying out routine tasks, on memory, and on capacity for learning.

Marihuana does not change the basic personality structure of the individual. It lessens inhibition and this brings out what is latent in his thoughts and emotions but it does not evoke responses which would otherwise be totally alien to him. It induces a feeling of self-confidence, but this is expressed in thought rather than in performance. There is, in fact, evidence of a diminution in physical activity. While suggestibility may be increased by small doses, larger ones tend to induce a negativistic attitude.

From the study as a whole, it is concluded that marihuana is not a drug of addiction, comparable to morphine, and that if tolerance is acquired, this is of a very limited degree. Furthermore those who have been smoking marihuana for a period of years showed no mental or physical deterioration which may be attributed to the drug.

The lessening of inhibitions and repression, the euphoric state, the feeling of adequacy, the freer expression of thoughts and ideas, and the increase in appetite for food brought about by marihuana suggest therapeutic possibilities. From limited observation on addicts undergoing morphine withdrawal and on certain types of psychopathic disturbances, the impression was gained that marihuana had beneficial effects, but much more extensive and controlled study is required for definite conclusions to be drawn concerning therapeutic usage. It should be borne in mind that the effects of marihuana, more than in the case of other drugs, are quite variable in different individuals and in the same one at different times.

SOURCE: The La Guardia Committee Report: The Marihuana Problem in the City of New York. Mayor's Committee on Marihuana (New York: New York Academy of Medicine City of New York, 1944).

ANALYSIS

The passage of the Marihuana Tax Act in 1937 followed a steady series of reports in the press on the dangers of marijuana use that tied the drug to the commission of all manner of violent crimes, including stabbings, fratricide, cannibalistic acts, and beheadings. Local law enforcement officials played a role in propagating these stories during public hearings held prior to consideration of passage of laws that criminalized marijuana use at the state level. Federal Bureau of Narcotics Commissioner Anslinger did his part by orchestrating a successful parallel campaign at the federal level, penning pieces that appeared in popular magazines and which repeated many of the more lurid stories.

Lost or completely absent from the accounts that appeared in the media and testimony at committee hearings was a more dispassionate consideration of the available scientific evidence. Although there was not the wealth of scientific data that are available today, existing studies were ignored, presumably because their findings contradicted the desired portrayal of marijuana as an extremely dangerous drug.

An example of a study of the effects of marijuana available but ignored at the time was conducted by Bromberg and published in the *American Journal of Psychiatry* in 1934, three years prior to passage of the Marihuana Tax Act. Bromberg reviewed data on 2,216 inmates convicted of felony offenses. Among the report's conclusions:

> A study of the relation between violent crime (murder, assault, rape, etc.) with marihuana showed no direct correlation. It is clear from this study, that in this region the drug is a "breeder of crime" only when used by psychopathic types in whom the drug allows the emergence of aggressive, sexual, or anti-social tendencies. The addiction to marihuana is not on the same deep physiological or psychologic (sic) level that morphine addiction is. (p. 303)

An earlier study of soldiers stationed in the Panama Canal Zone is another example of evidence that was never presented or considered during congressional testimony. The Panama Canal Zone Governor's Committee report concluded, albeit based on limited longitudinal data, that the habitual use of marijuana was detrimental to health but noted that marijuana was not habit forming in the same way as opiates and cocaine based on there being no withdrawal symptoms. The report also noted that marijuana use was unrelated to acts of violence and that "delinquencies due to mariajuana [*sic*] smoking, which result in trial by military court, are negligible in number when compared with delinquencies resulting from the use of alcoholic drinks." Using language common in psychiatry at the time, the report indicated that most habitual users of marijuana were "psychopaths and morons."

Because New York City had been identified as an urban center where marijuana use was a particular problem (along with New Orleans), Mayor Fiorello La Guardia, a strong opponent of the Marihuana Tax Act, wanted a study of the extent of the problem in New York. In September 1938, Mayor La Guardia asked the New York Academy of Medicine to conduct the study. Supported by foundation money, the Academy divided the research into two areas: (1) a sociological study that examined the extent of marijuana use, how the drug is obtained, in which geographical locations the drug is used most often, the profile of the typical user in terms of age, race/ethnicity, and social class, whether marijuana use was a factor in juvenile delinquency and violent crime, and the extent to which the drug was being peddled to school children; and (2) controlled experiments to determine the physiological, pharmacological, and psychological effects of marijuana use.

The sociological study was conducted as field research using a small cadre of specially trained, undercover male and female police officers who identified and then frequented areas of the city where marijuana trafficking and use were either already known or suspected by the police. The medical/psychological study was conducted as a controlled experiment by medical staff in which volunteers culled from the ranks of prisoners were given varying dosages of marijuana followed by direct observation and measurement of the drug's effects. After providing details of the methodology used and a narrative description of the main findings, each of the two main sections of the report enumerated a succinct list of the study conclusions. The lists are clearly and simply worded and present the finding unambiguously. Following are the conclusions from each section.

Conclusions from the sociological study were as follows:

1. Marihuana is used extensively in the Borough of Manhattan but the problem is not as acute as it is reported to be in other sections of the United States.
2. The introduction of marihuana into this area is recent as compared to other localities.
3. The cost of marihuana is low and therefore within the purchasing power of most persons.
4. The distribution and use of marihuana is centered in Harlem.
5. The majority of marihuana smokers are Negroes and Latin-Americans.
6. The consensus among marihuana smokers is that the use of the drug creates a definite feeling of adequacy.
7. The practice of smoking marihuana does not lead to addiction in the medical sense of the word.
8. The sale and distribution of marihuana is not under the control of any single organized group.
9. The use of marihuana does not lead to morphine or heroin or cocaine addiction and no effort is made to create a market for these narcotics by stimulating the practice of marihuana smoking.
10. Marihuana is not the determining factor in the commission of major crimes.
11. Marihuana smoking is not widespread among school children.
12. Juvenile delinquency is not associated with the practice of smoking marihuana.
13. The publicity concerning the catastrophic effects of marihuana smoking in New York City is unfounded.

Conclusions from the medical/psychological study were as follows:

1. Under the influence of marihuana the basic personality structure of the individual does not change but some of the more superficial aspects of his behavior show alteration.
2. With the use of marihuana the individual experiences increased feelings of relaxation, disinhibition and self-confidence.
3. The new feeling of self-confidence induced by the drug expresses itself primarily through oral rather than through physical activity. There is some indication of a diminution in physical activity.
4. The disinhibition which results from the use of marihuana releases what is latent in the individual's thoughts and emotions but does not evoke responses which would be totally alien to him in his undrugged state.

5. Marihuana not only releases pleasant reactions but also feelings of anxiety.
6. Individuals with a limited capacity for effective experience and who have difficulty in making social contacts are more likely to resort to marihuana than those more capable of outgoing responses.

Commissioner Anslinger was extremely unhappy with the report's findings. He immediately went on the counteroffensive. Ironically, the same person who uncritically accepted newspaper accounts of heinous crimes committed by persons while purportedly under the influence of marijuana and who presented little scientific data to back his much-publicized and repeated claims about the many deleterious effects of marijuana became a stickler for methodological rigor. It is also interesting to note, that in the excerpt below, Anslinger refers to an editorial piece that appeared in the *Journal of the American Medical Association* without attribution of authorship. The piece has been assessed as similar in style to the writings of Anslinger and possibly written by or heavily influenced by him. This means he possibly used the publication of his own opinions in an editorial in a well-respected medical journal to give his critique of the La Guardia Report an air of scientific respectability:

> "For many years medical scientists have considered Cannabis a dangerous drug," the Journal's editorial of April 26, 1945 stated. "Nevertheless . . . the Mayor's Committee on Marijuana submits an analysis by seventeen doctors of tests on 77 prisoners and, on this narrow and thoroughly unscientific foundation, draws sweeping and inadequate conclusions which minimize the harmlessness of marijuana. Already the book has done harm. One investigator has described some tearful parents who brought their 16-year-old boy to a physician after he had been detected in the act of smoking marijuana. . . . The boy said he had read an account of the La Guardia committee report and this was his justification for using marijuana."

Ultimately, Commissioner Anslinger's opinions held sway over the next decade and well beyond and the La Guardia Report had little effect on either public opinion or in lessening the penalties for marijuana. In fact, just the opposite occurred. Following an interruption of the flow of opiates into the country during World War II, the drug began to flow again into the United States and opiate addiction began to rise to pre-war levels and beyond. In the 1950s, this provided the impetus for passing even tougher legislation to increase the penalties for narcotics use and possession and, for the

ROBERT MITCHUM—HOLLYWOOD AND BUSTED

With state and Federal laws in the books providing criminal penalties for marihuana use, it was only a matter of time before a major celebrity was swept up in the police dragnet that followed passage of the new laws; that celebrity would be Robert Mitchum and the year was 1948.

After Robert Mitchum was jailed for conspiracy to possess marijuana in 1947, the press was granted free access to document the event with photos of Mitchum performing daily activities such as mopping the floor or drinking coffee from a jail-issue mug. In the end, the arrest and surrounding publicity only served to benefit Mitchum's film career by fostering his image as a Hollywood "bad boy." (Getty Images)

(continued)

first time, equating marijuana with cocaine and opiates as a narcotic drug. The main justification would be the novel (at the time) hypothesis that marijuana use was a stepping stone to heroin and cocaine addiction, an idea that today is known as the gateway hypothesis. This idea is flatly rejected in the conclusions of the La Guardia Report but like the rest of the report's conclusions, it was ignored. Marijuana would continue to be equated with cocaine and opiates in terms of its potential for addiction when the first schedule of dangerous drugs was created by 1970s legislation. In fact, marijuana would be scheduled as an even worse drug than either cocaine or heroin because it was perceived as having no legitimate medical uses.

ROBERT MITCHUM—HOLLYWOOD AND BUSTED

(continued)

Mitchum was not the first nor would he by any means be the last from among the famous in the television, movie, sports, broadcasting, and music industries to be arrested for drug use; Rush Limbaugh, Lindsay Lohan, Robert Downey, Jr., Lawrence Taylor, and Charlie Sheen are among only some of the more recent examples. Before Mitchum's high profile arrest, Gene Krupa, a famous jazz drummer and swing-band leader, was arrested in 1943 for allegedly sending a 17-year-old to his hotel room to fetch some marihuana cigarettes.

Mitchum was already a major celebrity and still on the rise in 1948, having made his way to Hollywood as a vagrant. Through his movie roles and public persona, he became the heartthrob of "bobby-soxers" who swooned over his droopy-eyed on-screen sensuality. According to at least one biographer, Mitchum's marihuana smoking started during his teens as he made his way across the country by hitching free rides on trains, hobo-style. Marihuana made the long rides and cold nights bearable. He continued using the drug after his rise to fame, bringing him to the attention of L.A. narcotics detectives investigating the local drug scene. The detectives shadowed Mitchum for months before staking out a rented home in Laurel Canyon suspected of being used for smoking marihuana. Observing what they presumed to be the lighting of marihuana cigarettes, the police quickly moved in to make their high-publicity arrest. Mitchum was busted for possession along with two minor starlets and a real estate agent. When asked his occupation on arrest, Mitchum famously quipped, "former actor."

If law enforcement authorities thought the arrest of celebrities such as Mitchum would discourage drug use among the general public and widen support for stricter enforcement, they were likely disappointed. The arrest enhanced Mitchum's celebrity and marketability. Although Mitchum and studio executives were initially concerned that his legal troubles would ruin his reputation and movie career, it only added to his allure by underscoring his film persona as a badboy. He would go on to have a long and successful acting career that spanned the next four decades.

FURTHER READING

Bonnie, R.J., & Whitebread, C.H. (1970). The forbidden fruit and the tree of knowledge: An inquiry into the legal history of American marijuana prohibition. *Virginia Law Review*, 56(6), 1052–1063.

Bromberg, W. (1934). Marihuana intoxication: A clinical study of Cannabis Sativa intoxication. *American Journal of Psychiatry*, 303–330.

Editorial. (1945). "Marijuana Problems." *Journal of the American Medical Association*, *127*, 1129.

Hall, W., & Lynskey, M. (2009). The challenges in developing a rational cannabis policy. *Current Opinion in Psychiatry*, *22*, 258–262.

Macleod, J., & Hickman, M. (2010). How ideology shapes the evidence and the policy: What do we know about cannabis use and what should we do? *Addiction*, *105*, 1326–1330.

Mayor's Committee on Marihuana. (1973). The Marihuana Problem in the City of New York: Sociological, Medical, Psychological and Pharmacological Studies. Metuchen, NJ: Scarecrow Reprint Co.

Server, L. (2001). *Robert Mitchum: Baby, I don't care*. New York: St. Martin's Press.

Sloman, L. (1998). *Reefer madness: A history of marijuana*. New York: Bobbs-Merrill.

On the Internet

The full text of the La Guardia Report is available at: http://www.druglibrary.net/schaffer/Library/studies/lag/lagmenu.htm.

A copy of 1933 Panama Canal Zone report on the extent of and effects of marijuana use among American soldiers is available at: http://www.drugtext.org/Table/Panama-Zone-Report/.

An excerpt from the book *Hemp around Their Necks* gives Harry Anslinger's response to the La Guardia Report wherein he vehemently and in characteristically florid terms rejects the methods and conclusions of the study on which the La Guardia Report was based: http://www.druglibrary.net/schaffer/History/murd3.htm.

"They Go from Sneaky Pete to Pot to Horse to Banging"

- ***Document:*** Organized Crime in Interstate Commerce—Final Report
- ***Date:*** April 17, 1951
- ***Where:*** Washington, DC
- ***Significance:*** Concerns about the perceived growing role of organized crime in relation to gambling, racketeering, and narcotics distribution across international and state borders led to the formation of a special Senate Committee to study the problem. Known informally as the "Kefauver Committee" for Senator Estes Kefauver of Tennessee who was the chair, the committee traveled the country interviewing hundreds of witnesses in televised proceedings. Although focused on organized crime and its role in drug distribution, the report also described an alarming increase in narcotics use. The increase was attributed to a new and younger generation of users in the post–World War II era who had become addicted to narcotics—mainly heroin—after first using alcohol and then marijuana. The idea that marijuana use directly leads to heroin use and addiction would later become known as the "gateway hypothesis." It became a primary rationale for subsequent legislation in the 1950s that significantly increased federal criminal sanctions for marijuana use and trafficking. The gateway hypothesis would again be invoked to justify a zero-tolerance policy and the return of mandatory minimum sentences in the 1980s. State laws followed suit and possession and sale of marijuana would be treated, from a legal standpoint, as equivalent to the possession and sale of heroin and cocaine. The excerpts from the report presented here focus on the panel's findings on illegal narcotic drug use and its recommendations for a federal and state level response to the problem.

DOCUMENT

Final Report of the Special Senate Committee to Investigate Organized Crime in Interstate Commerce

I. General Observations

This committee has served as a powerful searchlight, exposing widespread national and local crime conditions to public gaze. Its activities have had a tremendous effect upon the whole field of law enforcement. Everywhere throughout the country citizens, made suddenly aware of the character and ramifications of organized crime, have risen up to demand greater vigilance in stamping out crime and corruption. . . .

In the field of narcotics, the committee's searchlight has created a Nation-wide awareness of the seriousness of this great evil. As a result, investigations have been started, court procedures have been modified, remedial laws have been passed, educational programs have been undertaken and the despicable drug peddler has run for cover. The President of the United States only recently has been prompted to call for increased penalties in narcotics cases. . . .

VII. The Findings of the Committee

B. Illegal Narcotic Drugs

Introduction

The illegal traffic in narcotic drugs exemplifies organized crime at its devastating worst. It represents one of the great tragedies of our times, especially when it preys upon young people who are ignorant of drug addiction not only upon themselves as individuals but also upon the family and society as a whole.

Addiction resulting from an ignorant or depraved attempt to obtain temporary pleasure is an inexcusable tragedy. Drug addiction is a form of contagious disease with a high recurrence. Anyone who starts abusing a drug for whatever reason is immediately exposed to a serious danger of becoming addicted. Addiction occurs in a very short time and once it occurs there is no going back. The addict's whole life changes from one of usefulness and normalcy to one of suffering and degradation and in many cases, eventually to crime. One of the great contributions that could be made to the welfare of the young people of today would be to bring home to them the cold fact that narcotic drugs are to be avoided like the plague.

Against this backdrop of tragedy, the picture of the dope peddler promoting drug addiction in order to create new customers is nothing short of revolting.

A parade of witnesses representing every sector of the narcotics problem came before the committee. Physicians explained the properties of drugs, the course of addiction, the clinical processes of its treatment, and the psychological after-effects. Citizens of aroused communities described alarming local situations and told of efforts to stem the evil of narcotics abuse. Heartbroken parents described the tragedies that had befallen their children through drug addiction. Enforcement agents bared the workings of the international network through which illegal drugs move and the fabulous amounts of money involved in the traffic.

The committee traveled to the Maryland House of Correction, the Woman's Prison of Maryland near Baltimore, and to the United States Public Health Service

Hospital, Lexington, Ky., to hear the story first-hand from prisoners serving time for narcotics violations and from patients under treatment for addiction. The professional nonaddict peddlers told of giving "for free" enough heroin to get new customers "hooked," i.e., dependent on drugs; and of employing addicts as "testers" to judge the quality of the merchandise at the wholesale level. Nervous teen-agers, still jittery following withdrawal of narcotics, spoke haltingly of the confusion and the futile misery of the drug habit. Some had suffered enough for a dozen lives, yet they were not old enough to vote.

From the testimony of these witnesses and from other data submitted for study, the committee formulated the observations that comprise the body of this report on the illegal narcotics market and the extensive many-sided problems it presents.

(a) The drugs of addiction

The drugs usually abused to the point of addiction are grouped as stimulants and depressants, according to the effects they produce on the behavior of the user.

Of the stimulants, the most common and most dangerous is cocaine, derived from the leaves of the coca plant growing in South America and Java. In large doses, cocaine incites a transient reaction, followed by extreme nervous discomfort, irritability, and paranoid delusions that make the user a menace to those around him. Among the other stimulant drugs are benzedrine, dexedrine, and mescaline, a drug used by the Indians in the southwestern United States to "help them see God."

The depressants, on the other hand, relieve tension and nervous disturbance, producing a false and temporary feeling of well-being. They are used medically as pain relievers (called "analgesics") and many of them are necessary and extremely valuable for this purpose. They include opium and its derivatives such as morphine, heroin, dilaudid, codein [*sic*], and metapon, to mention a few. They also include synthetic pain relievers such as demerol, methadon [*sic*], and the new levo-iso-methadon. The depressants also include alcohol and marijuana. The bromides and barbiturates are classed as hypnotic drugs.

Frequently addicts take a depressant and a stimulant simultaneously, the depressant serving as an antidote for the dangerous and unpleasant effects of the stimulant. Known as a "speedball," one of these concoctions is a mixture of heroin and cocaine. The former relieves tension and anxiety; the latter furnishes the concurrent feeling of well-being and subdues fatigue. Some addicts engage in the viciously dangerous practice of spending long hours balancing the exciting effects of the cocaine with the restful euphoria of the heroin.

According to Federal law, the habit-forming drugs, those for which the Government provides addiction treatment facilities, are cocaine, coca leaves, codein [*sic*], dicodid, hycodan, dilaudid, heroin, marijuana, laudanum, demerol, isonipecaine, methadon, metapon, morphine, opium, pantopon, paregoric, mescaline, and other drugs that may be designated by the President. These statutes do not encompass alcohol, the barbiturates, or the bromides.

(b) Laws relating to narcotic drugs

Recognizing the profound seriousness of the rapidly growing drug-addiction problem, Congress passed in 1914 the first comprehensive Federal narcotics law—the Harrison Act. Under the provisions of this law, commerce in medicinal and other legitimate narcotics was legalized and controlled under the Federal taxing power. By the same mechanism, illicit traffic in opium and its derivatives and in the coca leaf and its derivatives (cocaine) was outlawed.

The Miller-Jones Act, passed in 1922, established a system of import and export permits and restricted the import of raw narcotic material to medical needs. By an amendment adopted in 1924 the dangerous and currently popular heroin was forbidden entrance to this country as was also opium for use in manufacturing heroin.

The Opium Poppy Act of 1942 insures against the growing of opium poppies in the United States.

Controls on the traffic in marijuana were imposed by the Marijuana Tax Act of August 2, 1937. It provides an occupational tax on all persons legally permitted to produce, sell or deal in marijuana. There is also a heavy transfer levy when unauthorized individuals are involved in a marijuana transaction.

On the state and municipal levels, uniform laws and ordinances help to control the traffic in narcotics within their jurisdictions. Forty-two states have enacted the Uniform Narcotic Drug Act and two others have the equivalent. The only states which do not have restrictive legislation are Kansas, Massachusetts, New Hampshire and Washington. Recent enactments in Illinois and New York have stiffened the penalties for sales to minors.

(c) Cause and nature of addiction

The crux of the narcotics problem lies not in the drugs themselves but in the persons who abuse them. Addiction involves taking drugs in excessive quantities.

Some individuals by reason of their physical and psychological make-up can become addicted to drugs more easily than others. Persons easily addicted are referred to as "addiction prone." There are some individuals who are relatively immune to addiction. The difficulty is that no one knows for certain whether he is addiction prone until after he has become addicted and then it is too late.

The most a victim can expect from treatment is to be taken off the drug and furnished psychological aid to remain off it. Medicines given during treatment do no more than relieve the tortures of withdrawal. No one, however strong his psychological framework, should run the risk of ruining his life and the lives of his friends and family by using any narcotic drug except under the strictest medical control. Prescribed in proper amounts, narcotic drugs are important aid in the practice of medicine and serve the humanitarian purpose of helping to alleviate the pain of the suffering. They should not be denied those who need them merely because of their addicting qualities. Until a nonaddicting pain reliever is discovered, physicians must use narcotics. Those who divert the stream of legitimate narcotics for their own selfish gain, actually rob the sick and the injured.

Although the therapeutic use of opium traces back some 6,000 years, nonmedical addiction dates only to the latter part of the nineteenth century when the "social use" of opium for its euphoric effect became known in India and China. Many of the cure-all patent medicines so popular in the United States at the turn of the century had opium as their principal ingredient. These preparations were later banned from public sale by the Federal narcotics control legislation.

Most habitual users of narcotics have psychoneuroses and personality disorders of varying degree, ranging from those of the criminal psychopath to the immature thrill seeker who craves extraordinary excitement. Addiction prones experience difficulty adapting themselves to the ordinary pressures and tensions of living. They may be extremely dependent or unusually hostile, incapable of entering into normal human relationships. In their discomfort, they frequently suffer obscure symptoms of indeterminable origin.

The average human being has normal defenses with which to cope with life's disappointments, frustrations, and conflict. But the potential addict lacks this natural ability to battle successfully against emotional problems and the anxieties they engender. If he looks to narcotics to ease his pain, subdue his disturbance, and escape his problems, he may find in drugs the substitute for his weak defenses. The feeling that "all is well" gives him a paper crutch of power and security and he is on the way to a heavy drug habit that only a life of crime can maintain. This is the weak, irresponsible creature on whom the parasitic illicit narcotic trader feeds and grows rich.

(d) Use of drugs by young people

In the past 24 months, America has been jolted to its foundations by the discovery that youngsters, especially in the larger cities, are using narcotic drugs, many to the point of addiction. New York, Chicago, Baltimore, and Washington, D.C., saw big increases in the number of under-age drug users coming to the attention of the police. In a large number of cases, these young people were engaging in crime for the sole purpose of supporting their drug habit.

The United States Public Health Service Hospital at Lexington, Ky., the larger of the two Federal hospitals devoted chiefly to treating addicts, compared the year 1946 when patients below the age of 21 represented 3 percent of the patients in the hospital, with the early part of 1951 when, with a higher total patient count, the proportion of young patients had climbed to 18 percent. Nearly three-quarters of these youngsters had no record of criminality or delinquency prior to addiction. Testimony from an experienced social worker on the situation in New York City revealed that the narcotics problem cuts across all social and economic lines. A young negro addict from Chicago said, "There is no segregation in the use of dope."

The committee interviewed many of these youngsters, among them a 19-year-old boy who quit school, throwing away a full scholarship in an eastern university, because of narcotics. To support his habit, he stole Government pension checks. A midwestern college freshman said he dropped out in the middle of his first semester and shortly thereafter was arrested for stealing money from the mails, all because of dope. Another collegian revealed that he and his friends grew marijuana in a yard and dried it in the oven of their apartment before rolling it into cigarettes. Girls in their late teens with narcotic addiction lasting several years, admitted that they had resorted to prostitution rather than endure the horror of going without drugs.

While many of these boys and girls do not evidence the character and personality disorders of the veteran addict, they have proven themselves susceptible to drugs, at least enough to continue taking narcotics to the point of becoming "hooked." Representing the carefree, thrill-seeking youth, they told the committee that they started on narcotics or "junk" as they sometimes call it, out of curiosity, because their friends were doing it and because they didn't want to be considered "square" or unsophisticated.

Youngsters place great value on "belonging" in their group. They resent the rejection that would go with being labeled "chicken" by their associates in the playground, ice-cream parlor, or on the street corner. So they tend to follow the leader who unfortunately turns out to be a hoodlum or emotionally twisted "bebopper," bent on introducing them to the pseudo pleasures of smoking marijuana and shooting heroin.

Mr. James R. Dumpson, consultant on correction and delinquency of New York's welfare council, described the situation in east Harlem as follows:

Social workers dealing with gangs all report that the rate of marijuana usage is at least 50 percent with this being a very conservative figure in their estimation. These include youths 13 years of age, and you have many indications that the age of this type of addiction is lowering steadily. In fact, one minister reported that several 9-year-old boys had been approached by peddlers attempting to have them take the drug.

In a social athletic club in one of the blocks with a membership of about 50 boys, at least 18 to 20 were known to be regular heroin users.

Dr. Lois Higgins, director of the crime prevention bureau in Chicago, cited statistics on the growth of the narcotic problem in her home city. In 1948, 136 out of 738 arrests were under 21. The following year, under-age persons accounted for 203 of 2,230 narcotic arrests. Of the total of 4,437 narcotic arrests in 1950, 1,107 were under 21. And for the period January 1 to late June 1951, Dr. Higgins gave a figure of 989 under-age narcotic arrests.

The path to addiction ran practically the same throughout the testimony taken from young addicts. In their own vernacular, Mr. Dumpson put it this way: "They say they go from sneaky Pete to pot to horse to banging." In ordinary language this describes the popular sequence—drinking wine, smoking "reefers" or marijuana cigarettes (sometimes starting at the age of 13 or 14) then sniffing or "snorting" heroin, finally injecting it directly into the vein.

The committee believes that drug addiction should be treated as a contagious disease and that its sufferers should be treated as patients, not as criminals. It also believes that like any disease it can be attacked with greater vigor if brought out in the open and discussed in a forthright manner. If by education the young people of the Nation can be made aware of the true character of narcotic drugs and the dangers of addiction, they will become strong fighters in the campaign against the evil.

(e) Methods of illegal importation and sale

The narcotic drugs lend themselves conveniently to illicit traffic. A fortune in narcotics can be carried in one pocket. Easy to handle, transport, and conceal, drugs slip quickly through the underworld's serpentine labyrinth, making it extremely difficult for enforcement officers to track down the carriers.

Narcotics have a ready market of insatiable consumers who keep coming back for more, often several times a day. The amount an addict will use depends solely on the amount he can get. He will "shoot" all he has available.

Narcotics move in a seller's market where the customer is always wrong. Dope peddlers charge all the money in the buyer's pocket, keeping him financially, as well as physically, enslaved. Witnesses told the committee how in Baltimore the identical quality and quantity of heroin sold for three times the amount charged in Washington. Drug sellers swindle their customers, adulterating the merchandise to almost nothing, heedless of the suffering they inflict on their victims. An addict who "squeals" to the authorities is likely to get a "hot shot" (a highly concentrated or poisoned dosage) the next time he comes to the peddler for his drug. The helpless addict struggles along from day to day a captive of the greedy criminals who have him hopelessly trapped.

Most American addicts, including practically all of the younger group, use heroin, the drug banned by law from the United States since 1924. Since heroin is the drug peddled on street corners through organized crime syndicates, its traffic presents the most serious aspect of the narcotic problem. Morphine and the opiate synthetics are more commonly diverted from legitimate channels, often by forging prescriptions and stealing from drugstores. The committee heard several addicted nurses and pharmacists tell how they obtained medicinal drugs in this manner.

Heroin is a fine white powder legitimately manufactured for medical use in several countries including Italy, Turkey, and China. However, through illegal dealings, a substantial part of this legal output, after it leaves the factory, finds its way to the United States, concealed on the persons and in the luggage of crewmen and passengers coming in from abroad.

Experienced enforcement officers believe that the present influx of heroin from abroad is managed by the Mafia with Charles "Lucky" Luciano, notorious gangster, vice king, and racketeer deported convict, now resident in Italy, as the operating head. . . .

World-wide in scope, the Mafia is believed to derive the major source of its income from the distribution and smuggling of narcotics. An undercover agent of the Treasury Department's Bureau of Narcotics testified at length before the committee just after his return from an extended assignment in Italy. Asked whether Luciano is the kingpin of the Mafia, the agent responded that if "Lucky" isn't the kingpin, "he is one of the royal family," that he receives large sums of money from American gangsters and that he certainly wields influence in Mafia policy matters. To the question "Is Lucky Luciano the kingpin of the narcotics traffic in the United States?" he answered, "The United States and Italy." The agent further revealed that in Mafia circles, Luciano enjoys the honorable title "Don," a symbol of the respect and esteem the membership holds for him.

(f) Possible remedies

The committee has come to the conclusion that illegal narcotic drugs constitute an evil of great magnitude. The problem calls for vigorous and effective action at all levels of our social and governmental system.

The problem should be attacked from many different angles with the hope that the combined effect will be to stop the spread of illegal drug use and perhaps eventually reduce it to controllable proportions. The committee suggests the following approaches:

(i) Sociological approach.—The deep-seated sense of personal insecurity which causes an individual to be addiction-prone may be the result of any one or more of a number of complex forces. Personal tragedy, unidentified childhood frustrations, family discord, poverty, loss of employment, and similar factors contribute to this. Perhaps the congenital character of the individual's nervous system is as important a factor as any. The addict seldom feels that he is to blame for his predicament and in large measure he is right. His affliction is caused by forces he cannot understand or control. He is sick and should be treated as such.

Obviously any action which has the effect of improving living conditions, strengthening the home environment and generally contributing to the security of the individual will help eliminate the causes of drug addiction.

(ii) Education.—The committee does not subscribe to the theory that public discussion of drug addiction should be avoided to protect nonaddicts from being tempted to try drugs. As in the case of venereal diseases, the attack upon which has been greatly enhanced by public knowledge, the committee believes that much will be gained by a carefully devised program of education designed to make the people of the Nation aware of the true facts regarding the excessive use of narcotic drugs.

Most of the objection to public discussion is based upon a danger which the committee believes can be avoided in a well-conceived educational program. There is no doubt that a drug user before he is actually "hooked" experiences a temporary pleasurable sensation and it is this sensation that might tempt others to try it. Improved emphasis on this sensation should be avoided and the true facts with regard to it should be brought out.

Actually, the sensation is extremely short-lived and is ordinarily followed by addiction within a period of from 10 days to 3 weeks of repeated use. Once addiction sets in, the victim cannot go back and from then on he takes the drug not for pleasure but for the sole purpose of avoiding the dread sickness caused by his physical need for the drug.

The committee believes that education should start in the schools and social organizations of the country and should be carried from there to the home. The basic responsibility for such a program rests on the shoulders of the country's educational leaders who should carry it forward at the local level.

(iii) Treatment facilities.—Medical science has not yet found a specific for the cure for drug addiction. Much has been accomplished in this direction at the United States Public Health Service Hospitals at Lexington, Ky., and Fort Worth, Tex., but the only available treatment is to take the addict gradually off the drug and thereafter, through psychiatric treatment, to attempt to help him overcome the deep-seated weaknesses that contributed to his illness.

The Lexington and Fort Worth hospitals are minimum-secured institution with modern hospital facilities to treat narcotic addiction and any other chronic or addict condition from which the patients may be suffering. Although these hospitals were established to receive Federal prisoners who are also addicted to drugs, they also admit nonprisoner addicts as voluntary patients. There are no separate accommodations for prisoner and nonprisoner patients. These hospitals are excellently managed under the supervision of Dr. Victor H. Vogel and Dr. Richard B. Holt, medical officer in charge at Lexington and Fort Worth, respectively.

Facilities for the treatment of addiction at State and community levels are extremely limited. The establishment of local clinical resources, at least for putting new drug users under immediate treatment, may preclude the tragedy of addiction in many cases.

Perhaps the greatest weakness in the field of treatment lies in the lack of facilities for following up patients after they leave the hospital.

Actual rehabilitation of the addict covers a span of years, not merely the 4 to 6 months spent in the controlled hospital environment. Supervision of the patient is necessary for a long period beyond the direct treatment phase. It is wasteful to spend millions of dollars each year caring for these addicts if they are to go back among people who are abusing drugs and thus be exposed to the temptation of starting again.

The United States Public Health Service has prepared and is hoping to undertake a program of local follow-up on a trial basis in New York or Chicago or both. The plan is to send teams of social workers and psychiatrists to those cities to maintain contact with former patients and assist them in using community facilities to help them rebuild their lives.

Local communities over the Nation can make real contributions toward insuring the rehabilitation of addicts by providing adequate mental health services where they may seek and receive understanding and intelligent advice. Too often the former addict will seek the answer to his dilemma in narcotics, lacking a secure source of counsel. One worthwhile utilization of community funds might consist of providing transportation for addicts to proper treatment centers.

(iv) Increased penalties.—Bills are now pending in Congress, two sponsored by members of this committee, proposing sharp increases in the fines and prison sentences that may be imposed for violation of the Federal narcotics laws. Efforts should be made to enact legislation along these lines.

The committee believes that casting the shadow of steep penalties over the path of the dope peddler will do much to deter him. A criminal bent upon performing an illegal act always weighs the risks against the rewards. At present the financial reward to the peddler seems to outbalance the fear of a 1- or 2-year prison term with a fair chance of having his sentence suspended.

In this connection, much can be accomplished by making judges aware of the seriousness of the crime of drug peddling. A judge passing upon an individual case is often tempted to be lenient, but if he appreciates the true relationship between the case before him and the over-all aspects of the drug evil, he will be more likely to mete out the punishment that is deserved.

(v) Increased enforcement.—Old-time addicts who have spent their lives struggling to escape from the drug habit say that the best solution to the problem is to kill the source of supply. They say that as long as the drug is available to them, they are not able to resist it.

The Narcotics Bureau of the Treasury Department has a staff of 180 skillful agents serving long hours in what is probably the most hazardous type of enforcement work. Under present conditions this number of men is discouragingly small. Mr. Harry J. Anslinger, head of the Bureau, is convinced that with twice the force he could stamp out the peddling of narcotic drugs. The committee believes he is right.

(vi) Port and border control.—The committee was impressed with the futility of attempting to stop the flow of heroin through customs search at the borders. The drug is so easy to conceal that finding it on the person of a passenger or sailor or in the many hiding places aboard ship is virtually impossible. The type of search that is required to find hidden drugs is often obnoxious to the person being searched and, even when done on a sampling basis, it gives rise to some resentment.

However, the committee feels that the present procedures of the Customs Bureau in this regard should be continued as a deterrent to drug smuggling.

(vii) Revised court procedures.—Early in April of 1951, Chicago's chief justice of the municipal court, Edward S. Scheffler, issued an order designating a specific courtroom for the special purpose of hearing all cases in which narcotics are in any way involved. Special prosecutors were assigned to the narcotics court, the first of its kind to be created, by the State's attorney for Cook County and the corporation counsel of the city of Chicago. In addition, the Chicago Board of Health appointed a full-time psychiatrist to serve this court. There are also present a social worker and representatives of the Crime Prevention Bureau. This appears to be an experiment worth watching and studying with a view to putting similar arrangements into effect in other jurisdictions. It is a step in the direction of treating the addict, as a patient rather than a criminal.

(viii) Mexican border.—Information has reached the committee to the effect that in towns across the Mexican border where Americans may come and go without restriction, a dangerous situation has arisen involving narcotic drugs. Many youngsters are visiting these towns for the sole purpose of obtaining drugs, including marijuana and heroin, which can be purchased on the street. Restrictions on narcotic drugs under our law are of little benefit to the citizens of border communities if their children are able and perhaps encouraged to cross freely into Mexico where the drugs are readily available.

The Committee believes that the appropriate agencies of the Federal Government should study this problem with a view to finding a solution. The answer may lie in prohibiting minors to cross the border when not accompanied by their parents.

(ix) World-wide prohibition of opium poppy growing.—Opium, which is the raw material from which heroin, morphine, and similar drugs are manufactured, is produced in China, India, Iran, and Turkey. Experience has shown that neither the United Nations nor the nations themselves are able to control the amount of opium poppy plants grown. They grow about 40 times the amount required to satisfy medical needs of the world.

Most of the countries have been wholly cooperative, although there is some doubt as to the attitude of Communist China. When the United States representative on the Commission on Narcotic Drugs of the United Nations called attention to the large heroin manufacture in Communist China, the Russian delegate tried unsuccessfully to have his remarks stricken from the record.

Nevertheless, experience has shown that the manufacture of opiates, as distinguished from the growing of opium poppy plants, can be controlled within reasonable limits. Accordingly, a great step forward would be accomplished if the growing of these plants could be completely prohibited.

This, of course, is feasible only if there arc adequate synthetic substitutes for the medicinal opiates. In this connection, the committee heard the testimony of Dr. Henry K. Beecher, of Harvard University, head of the department of anaesthesia of Massachusetts General Hospital. He told the committee that methadon and levoisomethadon, newly developed products, are not only adequate substitutes, but in many ways superior to morphine as pain-relieving drugs. He said, "I shouldn't be worried at all if there were no morphine." Dr. Beecher said that adequate synthetic substitutes for codeine have not yet been developed but he considers codeine to be a minor problem compared with morphine.

The committee is satisfied that these synthetic substitutes make the manufacture of morphine entirely unnecessary and that nothing of importance would be lost to the medical profession or to the people of the world if the growing of opium poppy plants were wholly prohibited in every country.

The very existence of opium appears to be the root of one of the greatest evils known to man and the committee strongly urges the Department of State and the United States delegates to the Commission on Narcotics of the United Nations to make strenuous efforts to bring about a world-wide prohibition against the growing of the plant from which opium is extracted.

SOURCE: Organized crime in interstate commerce. *Final report of the special committee to investigate organized crime in interstate commerce*, United States Senate pursuant to S. Res. 202 (81st Cong.) as amended by S. Res. 60 and S. Res. 129 (82d Cong.) Washington, DC: Government Printing Office, 1951.

ANALYSIS

As a means of reducing the use of heroin and other opiates, no policy, law, treatment, interdiction, or enforcement strategy has ever been as effective as World War II. During the war years, the number of opiate addicts in America plunged from an estimated pre-war level of 500,000 to as few as 20,000 by the war's end. The Federal Bureau of Narcotics was a primary source for these estimates and political motivations for bending the numbers to demonstrate the Bureau's effectiveness can't be discounted. However, multiple other accounts suggest the decrease in the number of opiate addicts was real and substantial during the war years.

World War II disrupted long-standing opiate distribution channels that stretched from southeastern Asian countries such as Burma and Laos or Middle Eastern countries such as Turkey and Iran where the poppies were grown and morphine extracted; to Europe where the drug was further refined and packaged; to America where it was cut with fillers, repackaged, and sold to consumers. Moreover, the relatively small number of poppies grown domestically had been further curtailed owing to the Opium Poppy Control Act passed in 1942, which placed the domestic growing of poppies under strict federal control. The combined effect was that there was very little morphine, heroin, or other forms of opiates available to U.S. opiate addicts during World War II.

In an especially prescient move, Commissioner Anslinger, who well understood opiate production and international trade routes, foresaw the likely shortage that would be caused by the war. Recognizing that their legitimate medical use as analgesics could be especially important for the treatment of injured soldiers should the United States enter the war, he stockpiled 300 tons of opiates in the U.S. Treasury vaults prior to 1940. This proved to be a more than adequate supply for both domestic and military needs over the course of the war.

But the end of World War II led quickly to the resumption of the international production and distribution of opiates, albeit with a slightly altered trajectory as new players moved in to control the market. Distribution points linking Europe to the United States came increasingly under the control of gangsters who added narcotics trafficking to other lucrative illegal activities they were suspected of controlling such as gambling. The FBI, under its prominent and long-serving Director J. Edgar Hoover had been puzzlingly slow to investigate or to even acknowledge the existence of organized crime in the United States. But perceptions of the growing influence of a criminal enterprise that was potentially national (and international) in scope and its role in distributing drugs to a new generation of young addicts (among other criminal activities) led to a sense there should be a more forceful and coordinated federal response. The Special Senate Committee to investigate Organized Crime, led by an ambitious first-term Democratic Senator from Tennessee, Estes Kefauver, represented an attempt to fill that void. Over time, the committee would come to be known by the name of its Chair as simply the Kefauver Committee.

Established in May 1950, the Kefauver Committee held hearings in 14 major cities across the United States before issuing a final report in April 1951. Over the course of the hearings, the Committee interviewed over 600 witnesses. The witness list included a rogue's gallery of reputed mobsters as both those who would become infamous such as Tony "Big Tuna" Accardo, Frank Costello and Meyer Lansky and those who remained obscure such as Jake "Greasy Thumb" Guzik were called to testify. Many of the proceedings were televised making for great political theater as a rapt American public watched, many in front of the first television set they ever owned.

The Committee was not persuasive in making the case for a vast, single criminal enterprise that was organized at a national level. Instead, it found that multiple, criminal groups of varying sizes and degrees of organization composed of members of varying nationalities and ethnicities were engaged in the distribution of narcotics. However, as the excerpts from the final report make clear, the Committee emphasized the role of Italian gangsters as comprising a particularly large and powerful criminal entity. In the process, they introduced the American public to the Mafia, the colorful names of its members, its secretive induction rituals, and its rules of conduct. In particular, the committee connected Mafia boss Charles "Lucky" Luciano with controlling much of the international and national trafficking in narcotics, as well as being deeply involved in gambling, loan-sharking, and corruption in the labor unions. This set the stage for increased attention and law enforcement efforts within the FBI to address organized crime, in effect forcing Hoover's hand, as he could no longer ignore the issue given the high profile nature of the hearings.

With respect to narcotics use, and keeping in mind that the term *narcotics* was used to refer to virtually any illegal drug, the report emphasized heroin and morphine and the increasing numbers of recent and young opiate addicts post–World War II as major concerns. However, the report also connected marijuana use to opiate use. The testimony cited in the report that is the title of this document describes the pathway from marijuana to opiates using the street jargon of the time: Sneaky Pete refers to fortified wines with names such as MD 2020 and Thunderbird favored by youthful drinkers and the skid row alcoholic alike because they were (and still are) inexpensive but had (and still do) a relatively high alcohol content. The presumed inevitable path to addiction following use of Sneaky Pete was pot (marijuana), then smack (smoking or taking opiates in pill form), and then banging (injecting opiates) with the last stage indicative of a life characterized by chronic addiction and crime.

The idea that use of softer drugs such as marijuana inevitably leads to or increases the chances of using harder drugs that are more addictive has become known as the gateway hypothesis. This hypothesis continues to be the source of ongoing debate and research and also continues to drive current policy, particularly at the federal level. Within the historical context of the 1950s, the significance of the gateway hypothesis as described in the Kefauver Committee final report is that it would provide justification for including marijuana in legislation passed in 1951 (the Boggs

Amendment to the Harrison Narcotics Act) and 1956 (the Narcotics Control Act) that greatly increased the criminal penalties for the sale and possession of all narcotic drugs.

Some points made in the report regarding the problem of narcotics use and addiction and proposed remedies are remarkable in their anticipation of developments and thinking about drug addiction that would become prominent decades later. In some respects, the report has the feel and language of a modern document describing the problems caused by drug use and recommended remedies. For instance, the report mentions the opening of a narcotics court in Chicago to handle drug-related cases and that was to include medical professionals as part of a court team that would work toward rehabilitating arrested and charged addicts brought before the court. Although the narcotics court in Chicago did not function anywhere close to this ideal and ultimately operated in an almost opposite way to quickly clear drug cases off the dockets, the idea of using the legal power of the criminal courts to encourage treatment participation and rehabilitation under the watchful eye of an informed and specialized judiciary (therapeutic jurisprudence) would resurface again in the late 1980s with the establishment of the first drug courts in Broward County, Florida. The movement to establish additional drug courts gained considerable momentum over time. At present, there is at least one specialized drug court in every state and over 2,000 such courts across the country.

Other observations and recommendations in the report that continue to echo through the present day:

- How the effectiveness of drug treatment programs is compromised by the lack of resources for extended follow-up and monitoring following treatment discharge. The report attributes the high relapse rates seen with addiction to this treatment gap. This analysis anticipates the emphasis on addiction as a chronic relapsing disease that today guides thinking on treatment structure and provision. Unfortunately, the same lack in long-term follow-up care, driven largely by a paucity of resources, continues to exist now as it did then.
- The potential use of synthetic opiates as replacements for opiates derived from the poppy plant. The report incorrectly projected that synthetic opiate such as methadone could eventually replace natural opiates. But the idea that a drug such as methadone could provide a medically manageable substitute for another drug such as heroin foreshadows the development of methadone maintenance as a (still controversial) treatment for heroin addiction by Dole and Nyswander in the 1960s.
- The recommendation that transportation be provided to drug addicts to assist and encourage them to keep treatment appointments. Transportation issues continue to be highlighted as barriers to participation in outpatient drug treatment programs.
- A continuing emphasis on interdiction of drugs at the border despite the fact that such efforts curtail only a small fraction of the drugs entering the country. The report findings were honest in this regard, acknowledging the ease with which drugs can be hidden for illegal importation into the country. However, the report emphasized that interdiction is nevertheless important for its deterrent effects. Interdiction of drugs at the borders

continues to be a centerpiece of U.S. drug policy, consuming a large portion of the federal budget allocated to reducing drug use and its attendant problems.

- On a non-policy level, important perhaps only as a point of historical interest, the report mentions the particularly dangerous practice of mixing depressants and stimulants into a drug cocktail called a speedball. Using both drugs together is a way of counterbalancing the effects of each drug thereby enhancing the overall experience. The term was not widely familiar to the American public and the extent of the practice was largely unknown, when in 1982, at the age of 33, comedian John Belushi died from the effects of injecting a heroin and cocaine speedball. The publicity after his death introduced the term to a new generation.

In terms of serving as a platform for having its policy recommendations transformed into legislation, the report was something of a failure. Few of the recommendations were ever adopted by statute. However, the report's contention that marijuana use led to opiate addiction—fostered in part by the testimony of Anslinger before the Committee—would provide justification for two pieces of 1950s legislation that would substantially increase the penalties for narcotics use and sales and in the process remove judicial sentencing discretion. The legislation would also provide for expanded interdictory powers for the Federal Bureau of Narcotics. The new laws represented the apotheosis of Commissioner Anslinger's emphasis on increasingly punitive measures as important deterrents to drug use as his long tenure as the nation's first "drug czar" neared its conclusion in 1962.

Even as this legislation was being crafted and enacted into law, the stirrings of a countercultural movement that came to embrace drug use as a way of expanding consciousness, promoting peace, and gaining greater insight into the human condition had already begun. The counterweight to the legislative excesses of the 1950s would not be political in origin or the result of careful consideration of scientific and medical evidence although the American Medical and Bar Associations would make such an attempt. It would arise instead in the poetry and literature crafted by a generation that was growing increasingly disillusioned with the social strictures, conservative policies, conformity, and materialism of 1950s America. It would begin not in the halls of Congress but in places like a small San Francisco art gallery at a poetry reading by an obscure group of writers. Before devolving into directionless hedonism and its own excesses only a decade later, this nascent movement would forever change the arc of American culture and its views on drug use and policy.

FURTHER READING

Courtwright, D. T. (2002). The roads to H: The emergence of the American heroin complex, 1898–1956. In D. F. Musto (Ed.), *One hundred years of heroin* (pp. 43–54). Westport, CT: Greenwood Press.

Dole, V. P., & Nyswander, M. E. (1967). Heroin addiction—a metabolic disease. *Archives of Internal Medicine, 120,* 19–24.

Kefauver, E. (1969). *Crime in America.* Westport, CT: Greenwood Press.

Moore, William H. (1974). *The Kefauver Committee and the politics of crime.* Columbia: University of Missouri Press.

HEMP FOR VICTORY!

Opiate distribution routes were not the only drug supply routes affected by World War II. Domestic production of hemp for industrial and commercial use was sharply curtailed after passage of the Marijuana Tax Act of 1937. Although the same plant produces both marijuana and hemp, varieties cultivated for optimal hemp production have relatively low concentrations of the psychoactive ingredients optimal for marijuana production and vice versa. Regardless the law made no such distinction, effectively limiting domestic production of the *Cannabis sativa L.* plant for either hemp or marijuana because the varieties are indistinguishable to the eye and can only be distinguished by testing samples for the concentration of the psychoactive compounds.

World War II cut off the supply of hemp from the Philippines and sisal from the Dutch East Indies. Given the shortage of hemp, and its necessity for making products vital to the military such as rope and twine, the United States Department of Agriculture (USDA) launched a campaign to promote domestic hemp production as a patriotic act supporting the war effort. With the Federal Bureau of Narcotics blessing and issuance of tax stamps to participating farmers, the campaign included a movie produced by the USDA titled *Hemp for Victory* that explained the uses of hemp and why the war necessitated renewed domestic production. The 14-minute film also explained optimal growing conditions and when and how to harvest but cautioned that growing the plant is restricted and should only be used for the express purpose of providing hemp. The movie neglects to mention the role of Federal law in decreasing domestic production of hemp, instead making the dubious claim that production declined because economically cheaper alternatives were available for import.

The promotional campaign was effective. With seeds provided by the USDA, and closely guarded in warehouses in Kentucky and neighboring states, domestic production of hemp fiber and seed reached a peak of more than 150 million pounds. This was in comparison to a prewar level of one million pounds and was followed by a return to a lower level of about three million pounds immediately following the war per USDA estimates and after trade routes were reopened.

Musto, D. (1999). *The American disease: Origins of narcotics control, 3rd edition*. New York: Oxford University Press.

Public Law 78–797 (Opium Poppy Control Act), December 11, 1942.

Schneider, E.C. (2008). *Smack: Heroin and the American city*. Philadelphia: University of Pennsylvania Press.

Special to the *New York Times* (1982, March 10). Belushi's death attributed to heroin and cocaine, *New York Times*, A22.

On the Internet

Full text copies of the interim and final reports of the Special Committee are available for viewing and downloading at: http://www.onewal.com/maf-kef.html.

The National Association of Drug Court Professionals (NADCP) provides the history and information on the development of drug courts since the 1980s at: http://www.nadcp.org/nadcp-home/.

A description of narcotics offenders in courts and prisons including a very critical analysis of the function of the 1950s era narcotics court in Cook County is available as part of the free full text of Alfred R. Lindesmith's book *The Addict and the Law* at the Drug Policy Foundation website. Lindesmith was a staunch and early critic of drug policy, evoking the considerable ire of Commissioner Anslinger. Lindesmith's book chapter on courts and prisons is at: http://www.drugtext.org/library/books/adlaw/chapter03.htm.

The 14-minute USDA video, *Hemp for Victory*, can be viewed at: http://video.google.com/videoplay?docid=-117344919147932597#.

"They Took the Needle When the Thrill of Marijuana Was Gone"

- ***Document:*** The Boggs Act (P.L. 82–255)
- ***Date:*** November 2, 1951
- ***Where:*** Washington, DC
- ***Significance:*** Sponsored by Representative Hale Boggs of Louisiana, the Boggs Act increased the penalties for narcotic drugs reflecting a continuing policy trend toward ever more punitive measures as a way of deterring drug use and trafficking. The law was in response to the growing number of heroin users in the period immediately following World War II and the idea that marijuana use was a dangerous stepping-stone drug that led to heroin use and addiction. The title quote exemplifies that concern and is from testimony given by Federal Bureau of Narcotics Commissioner Anslinger before the House subcommittee considering the bill. The Act provided for uniform penalties for violators of either the Narcotic Drugs Import and Export Act or the Marijuana Tax Act and in so doing, penalized marijuana use and trafficking to the same extent as cocaine and heroin use and trafficking. For repeat offenses, judicial discretion was abolished with the law's provisions requiring mandatory sentencing. By 1956, 28 states had passed "little Boggs Acts" by following suit and increasing criminal sanctions for drug-related crimes.

DOCUMENT

An Act to amend the penalty provisions applicable to persons convicted of violating certain narcotic laws, and for other purposes.

Be it enacted by the Senate and House of Representatives of the United States of America in Congress assembled, That section 2(c) of the Narcotic Drugs Import and Export Act as amended (U.S.C., title 21, sec 174), is amended to read as follows:

"(c) Whoever fraudulently or knowingly imports of brings any narcotic drug into the United States or any territory under its control or jurisdiction, contrary to law, or receives, conceals, buys, sells, or in any manner facilitates the transportation, concealment, or sale of any such narcotic drug after being imported or brought in, knowing the same to have been imported contrary to law, or conspires to commit any of such acts in violation of the laws of the United States, shall be fined not more than $2,000 and imprisoned not less than two or more than five years. For a second offense, the offender shall be fined not more than $2,000 and imprisoned not less than five or more than ten years. For a third or subsequent offense, the offender shall be fined not more than $2,000 and imprisoned not less than ten or more than twenty years. Upon conviction for a second or subsequent offense, the imposition or execution of sentence shall not be suspended and probation shall not be granted. . . .

"Whenever on trial for a violation of this subdivision the defendant is shown to have or to have had possession of the narcotic drug, such possession shall be deemed sufficient evidence to authorize conviction unless the defendant explains the possession to the satisfaction of the jury."

SOURCE: Boggs Act, Pub. L. No. 82–255, ch. 666, 65 Stat. 767 (1951) [codified in 21 U.S.C. § 174 (1964)].

ANALYSIS

The passage of the Boggs Act in 1951 was the first of several important federal legislative acts that steadily increased the penalties for narcotics production, distribution, and possession. The decade and legislation were the apotheosis of the 30-year career of Harry Anslinger, who saw his vision for drug control fully codified into federal and state statutes. Despite his and Congress's efforts, change was in the air fostered by a cultural upheaval that would last beyond the 1950s through the end of the 1960s. Moreover, despite the harshness of the penalties, the laws did little to stem the larger cultural shifts that led to large increases in drug use, particularly marijuana use, even as the Boggs Act and the Narcotic Control Act were in effect.

Despite the ineffectiveness of these laws, legislators in New York led by Governor Nelson Rockefeller would pass even tougher (but still ineffective) state drug laws in the 1970s and again at the federal level in the 1980s with the passage of the Anti-Drug Abuse Act of 1986, which sharply increased the penalties for crack cocaine. Hence, the Boggs Act was the beginning of a long period in drug policy that has yet to abate save for a brief time in the late 1960s, whereby tough criminal sanctions have been the preferred policy method for dealing with drug use.

FURTHER READING

Boggs Act Hearings. "Hearings on H.R. 3490 before the Subcommittee on Narcotics of the House Committee on Ways and Means," 82nd Cong., 1st Sess., 147–148 (1951).

Bonnie, R.J., & Whitebread, C.H. (1970). The forbidden fruit and the tree of knowledge: An inquiry into the legal history of American marijuana prohibition. *Virginia Law Review, 56*, 1063–1076.

Musto, D. (1999). *The American disease: Origins of narcotics control, 3rd edition*. New York: Oxford University Press.
Reuter, P. (1992). Hawks ascendant: The punitive trend of American drug policy. *Daedalus, 121*, 15–52.
Reuter, P. (1997). Why can't we make prohibition work better? Some consequences of ignoring the unattractive. *Proceedings of the American Philosophical Society, 141*, 262–275.

On the Internet

Detail on Anslinger's role in passage of the 1951 Boggs Act, in particular his thesis that marijuana use led to harder drug use, an idea that became known as the "gateway hypothesis" (see sidebar on the gateway hypothesis) is available at: http://herbgrinders.onsugar.com/Boggs-Act-12633013.

The Schaffer Drug Policy Library discusses the history leading up to the Boggs Act and the Narcotic Control Act of 1956 including the relevance of the Kefauver Commission hearings at: http://www.druglibrary.org/schaffer/library/studies/nc/nc2_7.htm.

"To Provide a More Effective Control of Narcotic Drugs and Marihuana"

- ***Document:*** Narcotic Control Act of 1956 (P.L. 84–728)
- ***Date:*** July 18, 1956
- ***Where:*** Washington, DC
- ***Significance:*** Despite or perhaps because of indications that drug use was decreasing or had at least plateaued by the mid-1950s, Congress enacted legislation that further increased the penalties for drug possession and trafficking. The Narcotic Control Act of 1956 amended the Internal Revenue Code of 1954 and the Narcotic Drug Import and Export Act. No distinction was made in the law's provisions between marijuana and cocaine or heroin nor did the law make a distinction between simple possession and trafficking. The act was the legislative capstone to the long, controversial, and contentious, but politically influential career of Federal Bureau of Narcotics Commissioner Harry Anslinger. It reflected his primary drug control strategy premised on deterrence through law enforcement and increasingly severe sanctions. The Narcotic Control Act stipulated a mandatory minimum of two to ten years in prison for a first conviction for possession of marijuana. The law also provided for the death penalty for offenders convicted of selling heroin to minors. Those convicted of a drug offense were required to register with customs on entering and leaving the country as a means of detecting and controlling drug smuggling.

DOCUMENT

An Act to amend the Internal Revenue Code of 1954 and the Narcotic Drugs Import and Export Act to provide a more effective control of narcotic drugs and marihuana, and for other related purposes.

Be it enacted by the Senate and House of Representatives of the United States of America in Congress assembled. That this Act may be cited as the "Narcotic Control Act of 1956."

Sec. 103. Violations of Narcotic Drug and Marihuana Laws.

Secton 7237 of the Internal Revenue Code of 1954 (violations of laws relating to narcotic drugs and marihuana) is amended to read as follows:

Sec. 7237. Violation of Laws Relating to Narcotic Drugs and to Marihuana

"(a) WHERE NO SPECIFIC PENALTY IS OTHERWISE PROVIDED.—Whoever commits an offense, or conspires to commit an offense, described in part I and part II of subchapter A of chapter 30 for which no specific penalty is otherwise provided, shall be imprisoned not less than 2 or more than 10 years and, in addition, may be fined not more than $20,000. For a second offense, the offender shall be imprisoned not less than 5 or more than 20 years and, in addition, may be fined not more than $20,000. For a third or subsequent offense, the offender shall be imprisoned not less than 10 or more than 40 years and, in addition, may be fined not more than $20,000.

"(b) SALE OR OTHER TRANSFER WITHOUT WRITTEN ORDER.—Whoever commits an offense, or conspires to commit an offense, described in section 4705 (a) or section 4742 (a) shall be imprisoned not less than 10 or more than 40 years and, in addition, may be fined not more than $20,000. If the offender attained the age of 18 before the offense and—

"(1) the offense consisted of the sale, barter, exchange, giving away, or transfer of any narcotic drug or marihuana to a person who had not attained the age of 18 at the time of such offense, or

"(2) the offense consisted of a conspiracy to commit an offense described in paragraph (1), the offender shall be imprisoned not less than 10 or more than 40 years and, in addition, may be fined not more than $20,000. . . .

"(d) NO SUSPENSION OF SENTENCE; NO PROBATION; ETC.—Upon conviction—

"(1) of any offense the penalty for which is provided in subsection (b) of this section, subsection (c), (h), or (i) of section 2 of the Narcotics Drug Import and Export Act, as amended, or such Act of July 11, 1941, as amended or

"(2) of any offense the penalty for which is provided in subsection (a) of this section, if it is the offender's second or subsequent offense.

Sec. 7607. Additional Authority for Bureau of Narcotics and Bureau of Customs

The Commissioner, Deputy Commissioner, Assistant to the Commissioner, and agents, of the Bureau of Narcotics of the Department of the Treasury, and officers of the customs . . . may—

"(1) carry firearms, execute and serve search warrants and arrest warrants, and serve subpoenas and summonses issued under the authority of the United States, and

"(2) make arrests without warrant for violations of any law of the United States relating to narcotics drugs . . . or marihuana . . . where the violation is committed in the presence of the person making the arrest or where such person has reasonable grounds to believe that the person to be arrested has committed or is committing such violation.

Sec. 107. Sale of Drugs to Juveniles—Penalties

Section 2 of the Narcotic Drugs Import and Export Act, as amended, is further amended by adding at the end thereof the following:

"(1) Not withstanding any other provision of law, whoever, having attained the age of eighteen years, knowingly sells, gives away, furnishes, or dispenses, facilitates the sale, giving, furnishing, or dispensing, or conspires to sell, give away, furnish, or dispense, and heroin unlawfully imported or otherwise brought into the United States, to any person who has not attained the age of eighteen years, may be fined not more than $20,000, shall be imprisoned for life, or for not less than ten years, except that the offender shall suffer death if the jury in its discretion shall so direct.

Sec. 1407. Border Crossings—Narcotic Addicts and Violators

"(a) In order further to give effect to the obligations of the United States pursuant to the Hague convention of 1912, proclaimed as a treaty on March 3, 1915, and the limitation convention of 1931, proclaimed as a treaty on July 10, 1933, and in order to facilitate more effective control of the international traffic in narcotic drugs, and to prevent the spread of drug addiction, no citizen of the United States who is addicted to or uses narcotic drugs . . . (except a person using such narcotic drugs as a result of sickness or accident or injury and to whom such narcotic drug is being furnished, prescribed, or administered in good faith by a duly licensed physician in attendance upon such person, in the course of his professional practice) or who has been convicted of a violation of any of the narcotic or marihuana laws of the United States, or of any State thereof, the penalty for which is imprisonment for more than one year, shall depart from or enter into or attempt to depart from or enter into the United States, unless such person registers, under such rules and regulations as may be prescribed by the Secretary of the Treasury with a customs official, agent or employee shall issue a certificate to any such person departing from the United States; and such person shall, upon returning to the United States, surrender such certificate to the customs official, agent, or employee present at the port of entry or border customs station.

"(b) Whoever violates any of the provisions of this section shall be punished for each violation by a fine of not more than $1,000 or imprisonment for not less than one nor more than three years, or both.

SOURCE: Narcotic Control Act of 1956, ch. 629, 70 Stat. 567.

ANALYSIS

See analysis under the Boggs Act of 1951.

FURTHER READING

Bonnie, R.J., & Whitebread, C.H. (1970). The forbidden fruit and the tree of knowledge: An inquiry into the legal history of American marijuana prohibition. *Virginia Law Review, 56*, 1076–1083.

Musto, D. (1999). *The American disease: Origins of narcotics control, 3rd edition*. New York: Oxford University Press.

Reuter, P. (1992). Hawks ascendant: The punitive trend of American drug policy. *Daedalus, 121*, 15–52.

Reuter, P. (1997). Why can't we make prohibition work better? Some consequences of ignoring the unattractive. *Proceedings of the American Philosophical Society, 141*, 262–275.

On the Internet

The Schaffer Drug Policy Library discusses the history leading up to the Boggs Act and the Narcotic Control Act of 1956 including the relevance of the Kefauver Commission hearings at: http://www.druglibrary.org/schaffer/library/studies/nc/nc2_7.htm.

"I Saw the Best Minds of My Generation Destroyed by Madness"

- ***Document:*** "This Is the Beat Generation," *New York Times Magazine*
- ***Date:*** November 16, 1952
- ***Where:*** Columbia University and Greenwich Village, New York
- ***Significance:*** The following essay was written by one of the lesser-known members of a group of writers that became known as the "beat writers" or the "beat generation." The essay discusses the concerns of the generation for whom the beat writers' work and message had particular resonance. The growing popularity of the beat writers toward the end of the 1950s portended what would become a much larger countercultural movement in the 1960s. Perceiving the prevailing social order as stultifying, hypocritical, and hollow, the movement would eventually lead to a surge in drug use as an integral part of the rebellion against that order.

DOCUMENT

This Is the Beat Generation

by John Clellon Holmes

Several months ago, a national magazine ran a story under the heading "Youth" and the subhead "Mother Is Bugged At Me." It concerned an eighteen-year-old California girl who had been picked up for smoking marijuana and wanted to talk about it. While a reporter took down her ideas in the uptempo language of "tea," someone snapped a picture. In view of her contention that she was part of a whole new culture where one out of every five people you meet is a user, it was an arresting photograph. In the pale, attentive face, with its soft eyes and intelligent mouth, there was no hint of corruption. It was a face which could only be deemed criminal through an enormous effort of righteousness. Its only complaint seemed to be: "Why don't people leave us alone?" It was the face of a beat generation.

That clean young face has been making the newspapers steadily since the war. Standing before a judge in a Bronx courthouse, being arraigned for stealing a car, it looked up into the camera with curious laughter and no guilt. The same face, with a more serious bent, stared from the pages of *Life* magazine, representing a graduating class of ex-GI's, and said that as it believed small business to be dead, it intended to become a comfortable cog in the largest corporation it could find. A little younger, a little more bewildered, it was this same face that the photographers caught in Illinois when the first non-virgin club was uncovered. The young copywriter, leaning down the bar on Third Avenue, quietly drinking himself into relaxation, and the energetic hotrod driver of Los Angeles, who plays Russian Roulette with a jalopy, are separated only by a continent and a few years. They are the extremes. In between them fall the secretaries wondering whether to sleep with their boyfriends now or wait; the mechanic berring up with the guys and driving off to Detroit on a whim; the models studiously name-dropping at a cocktail party. But the face is the same. Bright, level, realistic, challenging.

Any attempt to label an entire generation is unrewarding, and yet the generation which went through the last war, or at least could get a drink easily once it was over, seems to possess a uniform, general quality which demands an adjective. . . . The origins of the word "beat" are obscure, but the meaning is only too clear to most Americans. More than mere weariness, it implies the feeling of having been used, of being raw. It involves a sort of nakedness of mind, and, ultimately, of soul; a feeling of being reduced to the bedrock of consciousness. In short, it means being undramatically pushed up against the wall of oneself. A man is beat whenever he goes for broke and wagers the sum of his resources on a single number; and the young generation has done that continually from early youth.

Its members have an instinctive individuality, needing no bohemianism or imposed eccentricity to express it. Brought up during the collective bad circumstances of a dreary depression, weaned during the collective uprooting of a global war, they distrust collectivity. But they have never been able to keep the world out of their dreams. The fancies of their childhood inhabited the half-light of Munich, the Nazi-Soviet pact, and the eventual blackout. Their adolescence was spent in a topsy-turvy world of war bonds, swing shifts, and troop movements. They grew to independent mind on beachheads, in gin mills and USO's, in past-midnight arrivals and pre-dawn departures. Their brothers, husbands, fathers or boy friends turned up dead one day at the other end of a telegram. At the four trembling corners of the world, or in the hometown invaded by factories or lonely servicemen, they had intimate experience with the nadir and the zenith of human conduct, and little time for much that came between. The peace they inherited was only as secure as the next headline. It was a cold peace. Their own lust for freedom, and the ability to live at a pace that kills (to which the war had adjusted them), led to black markets, bebop, narcotics, sexual promiscuity, hucksterism, and Jean-Paul Sartre. The beatness set in later.

It is a postwar generation, and, in a world which seems to mark its cycles by its wars, it is already being compared to that other postwar generation, which dubbed itself "lost". The Roaring Twenties, and the generation that made them roar, are going through a sentimental revival, and the comparison is valuable. The Lost Generation was discovered in a roadster, laughing hysterically because nothing meant anything anymore. It migrated to Europe, unsure whether it was looking for the "orgiastic future" or escaping from the "puritanical past." Its symbols were the flapper, the flask of bootleg whiskey, and an attitude of desperate frivolity best expressed by the line: "Tennis, anyone?" It was caught up in the romance of disillusionment, until even that became an illusion. Every act in its drama of lostness was a tragic or ironic third act, and T.S. Eliot's *The Waste Land* was more than the dead-end statement of a perceptive poet. The pervading atmosphere of that poem was an almost objectless sense of loss, through which the reader felt immediately that the cohesion of things had disappeared. It was, for an entire generation, an image which expressed, with dreadful accuracy, its own spiritual condition.

But the wild boys of today are not lost. Their flushed, often scoffing, always intent faces elude the word, and it would sound phony to them. For this generation lacks that eloquent air of bereavement which made so many of the exploits of the Lost Generation symbolic actions. Furthermore, the repeated inventory of shattered ideals, and the laments about the mud in moral currents, which so obsessed the Lost Generation, do not concern young people today. They take these things frighteningly for granted. They were brought up in these ruins and no longer notice them. They drink to "come down" or to "get high," not to illustrate anything. Their excursions into drugs or promiscuity come out of curiosity, not disillusionment.

Only the most bitter among them would call their reality a nightmare and protest that they have indeed lost something, the future. Forever since they were old enough to imagine one, that has been in jeopardy anyway. The absence of personal and social values is to them, not a revelation shaking the ground beneath them, but a problem demanding a day-to-day solution. *How* to live seems to them much more crucial than *why*. And it is precisely at this point that the copywriter and the hotrod driver meet and their identical beatness becomes significant, for, unlike the Lost Generation, which was occupied with the loss of faith, the Beat Generation is becoming more and more occupied with the need for it. As such, it is a disturbing illustration of Voltaire's reliable old joke: "If there were no God, it would be necessary to invent him." Not content to bemoan his absence, they are busily and haphazardly inventing totems for him on all sides.

For the giggling nihilist, eating up the highway at ninety miles an hour and steering with his feet, is no Harry Crosby, the poet of the Lost Generation who planned to fly his plane into the sun one day because he could no longer accept the modern world. On the contrary, the hotrod driver invites death only to outwit it. He is affirming the life within him in the only way he knows how, at the extreme. The eager-faced girl, picked up on a dope charge, is not one of those "women and girls carried screaming with drink or drugs from public places," of whom Fitzgerald wrote. Instead, with persuasive seriousness, she describes the sense of community she has found in marijuana, which society never gave her. The copywriter, just as drunk by midnight as his Lost Generation counterpart, probably reads *God and Man at Yale* during his Sunday afternoon hangover. The difference is this almost exaggerated will to believe in something, if only in themselves. It is a *will* to believe, even in the face of an inability to do so in conventional terms. And that is bound to lead to excesses in one direction or another.

The shock that older people feel at the sight of this Beat Generation is, at its deepest level, not so much repugnance at the facts, as it is distress at the attitudes which move it. Though worried by this distress, they most often argue or legislate in terms of the facts rather than the attitudes. The newspaper reader, studying the eyes of young dope addicts, can only find an outlet for his horror and bewilderment in demands that passers be given the electric chair. Sociologists, with a more academic concern, are just as troubled by the legions of young men whose topmost ambition seems to be to find a secure birth in a monolithic corporation. Contemporary historians express mild surprise at the lack of organized movements, political, religious, or otherwise, among the young. The articles they write remind us that being one's own boss and being a natural joiner are two of our most cherished national traits. Everywhere people with tidy moralities shake their heads and wonder what is happening to the younger generation.

Perhaps they have not noticed that, behind the excess on the one hand, and the conformity on the other, lies that wait-and-see detachment that results from having to fall back for support more on one's capacity for human endurance than on one's philosophy of life. Not that the Beat Generation is immune to ideas; they fascinate it. Its wars, both past and future, were and will be wars of ideas. It knows, however, that in the final, private moment of conflict a man is really fighting another man, and not an idea. And that the same goes for love. So it is a generation with a greater facility for entertaining ideas than for believing in them. But it is also the first generation in several centuries for which the act of faith has been an obsessive problem, quite aside from the reasons for having a particular faith or not having it. It exhibits on every side, and in a bewildering number of facets, a perfect craving to believe.

Though it is certainly a generation of extremes, including both the hipster and the radical young Republican in its ranks, it renders unto Caesar (i.e., society) what is Caesar's and unto God what is God's. For the wildest hipster, making a mystique of bop, drugs and the nightlife, there is no desire to shatter the "square" society in which he lives, only to elude it. To get on a soapbox or write a manifesto would seem to him absurd. Looking at the normal world, where most everything is a "drag" for him, he nevertheless says: "Well, that's the Forest of Arden after all. And even *it* jumps if you look at it right." Equally, the young Republican, though often seeming to hold up Babbitt as his culture hero, is neither vulgar nor materialistic, as Babbitt was. He conforms because he believes it is socially practical, not necessarily virtuous. Both positions, however, are the result of more or less the same conviction—namely that the valueless abyss of modern life is unbearable.

For beneath the excess and the conformity, there is something other than detachment. There are the stirrings of a quest. What the hipster is looking for in his "coolness" (withdrawal) or "flipness" (ecstasy) is, after all, a feeling on somewhereness, not just another diversion. The young Republican feels that there is a point beyond which change becomes chaos, and what he wants is not simply privilege or wealth, but a stable position from which to operate. Both have had enough of homelessness, valuelessness, faithlessness.

The variety and the extremity of their solutions are only a final indication that for today's young people there is not as yet a single external pivot around which they can, as a generation, group their observations and their aspirations. There is no single philosophy, no single party, no single attitude. The failure of most orthodox moral and social concepts to reflect fully the life they have known is probably the reason for this, but because of it each person becomes a walking, self-contained unit, compelled to meet, or at least endure, the problem of being young in a seemingly helpless world in his own way.

More than anything else, this is what is responsible for this generation's reluctance to name itself, its reluctance to discuss itself as a group, sometimes its reluctance to be itself. For invented gods invariably disappoint those who worship them. Only the need for them goes on, and it is this need, exhausting one object after another, which projects the Beat Generation forward into the future and will one day deprive it of its beatness.

Dostoyevski wrote in the early 1880s that "Young Russia is talking of nothing but the eternal questions now." With appropriate changes, something very like this is beginning to happen in America, in an American way; a re-evaluation of which the exploits and attitudes of this generation are only symptoms. No single comparison of one generation against another can accurately measure effects, but it seems obvious that a lost generation, occupied with disillusionment and trying to keep busy among the broken stones, is poetically moving, but not very dangerous. But a beat generation, driven by a desperate craving for belief and as yet unable to accept the moderations which are offered it, is quite another matter. Thirty years later, after all, the generation of which Dostoyevski wrote was meeting in cellars and making bombs.

This generation may make no bombs; it will probably be asked to drop some, and have some dropped on it, however, and this fact is never far from its mind. It is one of the pressures which created it and will play a large part in what will happen to it. There are those who believe that in generations such as this there is always the constant possibility of a great new moral idea, conceived in desperation, coming to life. Others note the self-indulgence, the waste, the apparent social irresponsibility, and disagree.

But its ability to keep its eyes open, and yet avoid cynicism; its ever-increasing conviction that the problem of modern life is essentially a spiritual problem; and that capacity for sudden wisdom which people who live hard and go far possess, are assets and bear watching. And, anyway, the clear, challenging faces are worth it.

SOURCE: John Clellon Holmes, "This Is the Beat Generation," *New York Times Magazine*, November 16, 1952.

ANALYSIS

Looking at pictures of the overflow crowds that attended the Woodstock music festival in 1969, it is hard to imagine that this iconic event wherein those present flaunted their drug use in open defiance of the strict laws put in place only a decade earlier, owed a cultural and philosophical debt to a small group of writers who met in the 1940s while attending Columbia University in New York. Like many young writers, they struggled at first to find their unique voices as authors. In the process, they adopted the improvisational musical conventions of bebop jazz to create their writing styles. They also adopted the culture of drug use that surrounded the jazz scene at the time. They rebelled in their writing styles and lifestyles against the accepted academic norms for structuring prose and poetry and against the norms for what constituted acceptable social behavior; testing those limits to find meaning and to revel in the sensate.

A number of members of the original group would become famous countercultural figures in their own right, most notably, Jack Kerouac, William Burroughs, and Alan Ginsberg. They became the leaders of the "beat generation" so designated by Kerouac because they felt they had been beaten down by life but also because they were living to a beat as in a musical beat. Their writings gave voice to a generation looking for, as the above essay opines, "something to believe in." The willingness to test limits, to experiment with drugs, and social and sexual boundaries was, however, as the essay also notes, "bound to lead to excesses in one direction or another." Kerouac would struggle with alcoholism and eventually die from it at the age of 47. Burroughs would alternately indulge in and then struggle with his heroin and morphine addictions his whole life. Ginsberg would find his way to the home of Timothy Leary and together they would become leading proponents of psychedelic drug use as a way of expanding consciousness. But Ginsberg's protestations remained diffuse and never produced a clear direction or purpose other than protestation for its own sake.

The beat writers drew inspiration from the jazz scene in the New York nightclubs they frequented. At the time, bebop jazz was popular. Bebop is characterized by a frenetic, intricate, highly improvisational style that emphasizes musical virtuosity and complex syncopation. The free form style of bebop was a clear departure from the danceable, easily identifiable melodies of the big band swing era that preceded it. In practice and metaphorically, it reflected a change of emphasis from the collective (the big band) to the individual (the improvisational player). It was a highly personal musical style played in small rooms by small groups of musicians; intimate, spontaneous, unpredictable, and at times inscrutable. Bebop was created and played by the likes of brilliant musicians such as Dizzy Gillespie, Charlie Parker, John Coltrane, and Thelonious Monk.

In their prose and poetry, the beat writers attempted to emulate the bebop style, producing prose that, for example, was more like a spontaneous stream-of-consciousness than a clearly structured set of sentences grouped into paragraphs that moved logically from one idea to the next. Like bebop music, their writing was personal and of the moment. In days well prior to televised talk show tell-alls such as Dr. Phil, their writing was also intimate and confessional. Ginsberg's first and most famous poem, *Howl,* was constructed to be read aloud with the phrasing determined by how many words he could read before needing to take a breath. This kind of phrasing emulates the way a jazz musician might blow a long series of notes on a saxophone during an improvisational passage before taking a breath and then blowing the next series of notes. The poem also described sexual acts in frank language that was shocking for the time. Jack Kerouac took spontaneity to a new level when, working from notebooks in which he had recorded his thoughts on cross-country car trips, he typed *On the Road* on one continuous 120-foot scroll of paper during a three-week, Benzedrine-fueled burst of creativity. At the time, Benzedrine, an amphetamine, was widely available for relief of decongestion in the form of inhalers. Breaking open the inhaler and ingesting the contents or dissolving them in coffee provided an immediate, large dose of amphetamine, 50 times the equivalent of the five-milligram standard dose when taken in pill form.

Drug use was an integral part of the jazz scene. It provided, in the eyes of those who used drugs, an enhanced sensory experience. Using drugs was also a symbolic badge of honor, signifying "hipness" and belonging to a marginalized but enlightened social group that did not accept the prevailing social norms. Marijuana, amphetamines, cocaine, and heroin use were common in jazz clubs among both patrons and musicians. Along with the musical conventions of bebop jazz, the beat writers adopted the larger ethos that surrounded it, including drug use. Describing the experience of using drugs and their experiences while using drugs became an integral if not central topic in their writings. Burroughs' most famous works, *Junky* and *Naked Lunch*, center thematically on his adventures and (more often) misadventures as a lifelong heroin addict. Kerouac's *On the Road* includes many references to drinking and drug use. Following the first line of Ginsberg's *Howl*, which is the title for this document analysis, subsequent lines frequently mention drugs:

> Who got busted in their public beards returning through Laredo with a belt of marihuana for New York,
>
> . . . with chained themselves to subways for the endless ride from Battery to holy Bronx on Benzedrine until the noise of wheels and children brought them down shuddering mouth-wracked and battered bleak of brain all drained of brilliance in the drear light of Zoo.

Beyond the style of writing they developed and their openly defiant proselytizing for the benefits of drug use, both of which were at sharp angles to 1950s' mainstream culture, the beat writers gave voice to the sense of alienation felt by many. The sense that something is not quite right would lead to a broader questioning of the social order and cultural values in post–World War II America. The themes that appeared in the prose and poetry of the beat writers espousing personal freedom, individuality, and sensual experiences to enhance spirituality appealed to the generation that came of age in the late 1950s and 1960s, the baby boomers.

This was a time of unparalleled prosperity and expansion in America's history. A new interstate highway system connected the country from coast to coast. Large suburban communities where many Americans could afford their first homes sprang up around urban centers. Manufacturing abetted by technological advances provided factory jobs with good pay for the new suburbanites and fostered the rise of a growing middle class. Television shows such as *Father Knows Best*, *Leave It to Beaver*, and *Ozzie and Harriet* provided a gauzy, idealized view of family life during this time where the worst problems were portrayed as small tensions and misunderstandings that were easily resolvable through Dad's gentle wisdom and a little discussion around the dinner table or fireplace.

Not depicted in the sunny scenarios depicted in these shows, however, were the darker and larger concerns that were also extant. These were also the times of a growing sense of anxiety about the Cold War prompted by concerns over Soviet expansionism. The times saw the beginnings of a nuclear arms race. These were also the times when Senator Joe McCarthy held hearings to ferret out Communists he was convinced had secretly insinuated themselves into virtually every aspect of American society for the purpose of subversion. Senator Estes Kefauver held hearings to determine the extent to which organized crime had infiltrated and corrupted legitimate businesses, fostered trafficking in narcotics, and promoted vice for profit (see Organized Crime in Interstate Commerce—Final Report).

Nor did television reflect the ennui and purposelessness felt most keenly by (some) youth, a spiritual void, and a sense that while the material gains made over the last decade made life more comfortable, continued pursuit of material goods and the life they provided gave little ultimate satisfaction. Photographs that show the vast stretches of identical tract houses that were built to quickly construct suburbia perhaps best symbolize the conformity and boredom engendered by 1950s culture. Tract housing developments would be satirized in a 1962 song written by Malvina Reynolds and titled "Little Boxes" in which the repeated phrase "boxes made of ticky tacky" referenced the cheap, prefabricated construction materials used to build the tract house developments.

A planned prefabricated housing development in Levittown, Pennsylvania, circa 1950. Inexpensive tract housing afforded many Americans the possibility of owning their own homes for the first time. But tract housing communities such as the one in Levittown came to symbolize social conformity and banality against which the beat poets and disaffected youth rebelled in the 1950s. Openly flaunting and proselytizing drug use became a symbol of their rebellion and led to the much larger countercultural movement of the 1960s. (Library of Congress)

The concerns of 1950s youth were memorably captured in *Rebel without a Cause*. Its posthumous star, James Dean, personified adolescent angst, disillusionment, and rebellion and he became a lasting American icon who reflected the times and those sentiments. The beat writers provided a voice for the alienated young and, for a time, by their lifestyles, provided an example of the means by which to rebel; a means centered on individual expression, music, and open experimentation with drugs and sex.

It is coincidental that the first public reading of *Howl* by Ginsberg was in 1955, and that one year later, Congress would pass the most stringent antidrug laws ever enacted. It was the proverbial two ships passing in the night. Ginsberg was one of five poets to give a reading before 150 people in a small San Francisco art gallery. Those in attendance responded to Ginsberg's performance with enthusiasm and immediately recognized the significance of his poetry. As a result, Ginsberg would achieve instant and lasting fame and the beat movement would begin to reach a larger public. When *Howl* was published in 1956 and *On the Road* was published the year after that, the beat writers gained a much wider audience and the seeds for cultural change and upheaval that would follow in the 1960s had been sown.

Acceptance of the style and message of the beat writers was far from universal. Herb Caen, a columnist who wrote about the social scene for the *San Francisco Chronicle* coined the derisive term *beatnik*, a portmanteau of the words *beat* and *Sputnik*, the recently launched Soviet satellite. His perception was that the beat generation was simply a bunch of lazy bohemians. From Caen's original column: "*Look* magazine, preparing a picture spread on S.F.'s Beat Generation (oh, no, not AGAIN!), hosted a party in a No. Beach house for 50 Beatniks, and by the time word got around the sour grapevine, over 250 bearded cats and kits were on hand, slopping up Mike Cowles' free booze. They're only Beat, y'know, when it comes to work."

Caen's neologism and characterization stuck. The term *beatnik* came to stand for a caricature of the beat writers and their followers. Labeled as beatniks, they were portrayed as bongo-playing, self-absorbed, goateed, and aimless slouches. More serious criticism came from conservative thinkers, the young Republicans mentioned in Holmes's column. For example, Norman Podhoretz, who would become a leading thinker and writer for the neoconservative movement that provided the intellectual underpinnings of Ronald Reagan's political ascendance, wrote a scathing critique of the beat writers. In his 1958 essay titled "The Know-Nothing Bohemians," published in the *Partisan Review*, Podhoretz took unsparing aim: "I think it is legitimate to say, then, that the Beat Generation's worship of primitivism and spontaneity is more than a cover for hostility to intelligence; it arises from a pathetic poverty of feeling as well. The hipsters and hipster-lovers of the Beat Generation are rebels all right, but not against anything so sociological and historical as the middle class of capitalism or even respectability. This is the revolt of the spiritually underprivileged and the cripples of soul—young men who can't think straight and so hate anyone who can; young men who can't get outside the morass of self."

Despite such criticisms, the beat writers remained influential. Their writings and increasingly public lifestyles owing to their growing notoriety provided the tinder for a countercultural movement that would enflame America over the next decade. Rock and roll would supplant jazz as musical accompaniment but drug use would remain a central part of that movement. Musicians as diverse as Bob Dylan and Jim Morrison would acknowledge the beat writers' influence. Drug use would reach unprecedented levels as larger social forces exposed the ineffectiveness of the Boggs Act and Narcotic Control Act as deterrents. The strategy of controlling drug use primarily with criminal justice sanctions would be rethought, making way for the rise of a treatment system that was focused on helping people overcome addiction and, for at least a short time, legislation would be passed that lessened sanctions in support of a more balanced approach that recognized drug use as a public health issue and not simply a criminal justice problem.

CHARLIE PARKER—"BIRD"

There are no good estimates of the extent to which drugs were used by jazz musicians and those who patronized their performances in the 1940s and 1950s. However, the long list of jazz musicians whose lives were either cut short by drug addiction or who struggled throughout their lives to overcome addiction and alcoholism suggests that drug-related problems were extensive. An especially poignant and tragic example of the toll that addiction to heroin and alcoholism took on the jazz world is the life and death of Charlie Parker. His death in 1955 at the age of 34 and his reflections on drug use also serve as a cautionary tale but one that was likely not fully appreciated at the time.

Jazz saxophonist Charlie Parker is seen performing backstage at Carnegie Hall, New York, circa 1947. Parker was but one of many jazz musicians who became addicted to heroin and other drugs and whose life was cut short because of it. Later, numerous rock musicians and singers from Jim Morrison to Whitney Houston would follow the same sad path. (William P. Gottlieb/Ira and Leonore S. Gershwin Fund Collection, Music Division, Library of Congress)

(Continued)

FURTHER READING

Burroughs, W. (1990). *Naked Lunch*. New York: Grove Press.
Charters, A. (2001). *Beat down to your soul: What was the beat generation?* New York: Penguin Group.
Ginsberg, A. (2001). *Howl, and other poems*. San Francisco, CA: City Light Pocket Poets.
Gitler, I. (1987). *Swing to bop: An oral history of the transition in jazz in the 1940s*. New York: Oxford University Press.
Halberstam, D. (1994). *The fifties*. New York: Ballentine Books.
Jonnes, J. (1996). *Hep-cats, narcs, and pipe dreams: A history of America's romance with illegal drugs*. New York: Scribner.
Kerouac, J. (1976). *On the road*. New York: Penguin Books.
McAdams, L. (2001). *Birth of the cool: Beat, bebop, and the American avant-garde*. New York: Free Press.
McNally, D. (2003). *Desolate angel: Jack Kerouac, the Beat Generation and America*. Cambridge, MA: DeCapo Press.
Oshinsky, D. M. (2005). *A conspiracy so immense: The world of Joe McCarthy*. New York: Oxford University Press.
Podhoretz, N. (2004). The know-nothing bohemians. Reprinted in *The Norman Podhoretz reader: A selection of his writings from the 1950s through the 1990s* (pp. 29–40). New York: Simon & Schuster.
Russell, R. (1973). *Bird lives! The high life and hard times of Charlie (Yardbird) Parker*. New York: Charterhouse.

On the Internet

A 1994 essay by Levi Asher on the history of what came to be called the beat generation with accompanying photos is at: http://www.litkicks.com/BeatGen.

An essay on associations among bebop jazz, the beat poets, and drug use is available at: http://www.litkicks.com/Topics/Jazz.html.

A description of the evening's events during the first public reading of *Howl* and other poems at Six Gallery is available at: http://www.litkicks.com/Places/SixGallery.html.

A reprint of Herb Caen's 1958 *San Francisco Chronicle* column in which he coined the derogatory term *beatnik* is available at: http://www.sfgate.com/cgi-bin/article.cgi?f=/c/a/1997/02/06/MN18715.DTL.

A discussion of the beat writers and the importance of their writings as literary contributions is at: http://www.poets.org/viewmedia.php/prmMID/20201.

Biographical information on the life of Charlie "Bird" Parker is available at: http://www.jazzine.com jazzstuff/biographies / /charlie_parker.phtml.

CHARLIE PARKER—"BIRD"

(continued)

Parker was an influential and brilliant saxophonist. Along with Dizzy Gillespie he is credited as one of the originators of what would become known as bebop jazz that artistically inspired the Beat Writers. He was nicknamed Yardbird because, according to the most frequently recounted story, a car he was riding in while on tour with a band hit a chicken. Parker insisted on salvaging and cooking the dead yardbird rather than abandoning it to the street as road kill. Later, the nickname would be shortened to simply bird. Parker's addiction to narcotics began before he performed professionally as a jazz musician. His introduction to narcotics occurred when he was a teenager. During a hospitalization for injuries from an automobile accident, doctors gave him morphine to treat his pain per standard medical practice. At the time, he was likely already into heavy use of amphetamines.

It is not clear if Parker became addicted shortly after that initial incident or if his narcotics use gradually escalated into an addiction some time later. It is clear, however, that as he became immersed in performing jazz professionally he was addicted to heroin, amphetamines, and alcohol. He struggled with these addictions for the rest of his short life. Periods of relative sobriety (he continuously used beer and amphetamines), sometimes after treatment and hospitalization, would be punctuated by a return to heroin use. Based on his experiences, Parker tried to dissuade other musicians of the notion that using drugs improved their performances. In a *Downbeat Magazine* interview he is quoted as saying: "Any musician who says he's playing better either on tea, the needle, or when he is juiced is a plain, straight liar. When I get too much to drink, I can't even finger well, let alone play decent ideas. In the days when I was on the stuff, I may have thought I was playing better. Listening to some of the records now, I know I wasn't. Some of these smart kids who think you have to be completely knocked out to be a good hornman are just plain crazy. It isn't true. I know, believe me."

"Current Treatment of Addiction Is Unsatisfactory"

- ***Document:*** Drug Addiction, Crime or Disease? Interim and Final Reports of the Joint Committee of the American Bar Association and the American Medical Association on Narcotic Drugs
- ***Date:*** 1961
- ***Where:*** Washington, DC/Bloomington, Indiana
- ***Significance:*** Concerned about the procession of federal (and state) laws that increased already stringent criminal penalties for drug offenses as well as inaccurate, politically motivated portrayals of the consequences of drug addiction and of those addicted to drugs, the American Bar and Medical Associations (ABA-AMA) convened a joint commission to review the available medical and scientific evidence on drug addiction and to consider alternative policy models. The resulting report called for taking more of a public health and less of a criminal justice approach toward drug addiction and for further research to provide policy direction.

Ultimately, the report had limited impact although many of its conclusions and recommendations continue to resonate for those advocating a public health approach to drug use and addiction. Ignored by the federal government, the report was published by Indiana University Professor Alfred R. Lindesmith, a leading critic of federal drug policy at the time. The reprinted excerpts include Dr. Lindesmith's introduction; the report's concluding recommendations; and an appendix to the report written by commission member Rufus King, which discusses an alternative treatment model for managing drug addiction based on the "British system."

DOCUMENT

Drug Addiction, Crime or Disease? Interim and Final Reports of the Joint Committee of the American Bar Association and the American Medical Association on Narcotic Drugs

Introduction

by Alfred R. Lindesmith

The work of the Joint Committee of the American Bar Association and the American Medical Association on Narcotic Drugs may well be a landmark in the history of the drug problem in this country. It marks the first cooperative undertaking between these two important professions in this area in which both are vitally involved and in which both have important practical responsibilities. It is safe to say that if and when basic changes are made in present methods of handling the drug problem these two professions will play an important role in bringing them about.

On the question of how to deal with drug addiction there are two opposing schools of thought. The Federal Bureau of Narcotics and its supporters regard addiction to narcotic drugs as an activity that is properly subject to police control. With the growth of addiction in the United States since World War II, increasingly severe penalties have been incorporated into both Federal and state laws, and the distinction between the peddler of drugs and the user of them has grown smaller and smaller. The advocates of this punitive approach argue that crimes committed by addicts are a direct result of the drug; they also contend that most addicts were criminals before they became addicted.

Critics of this view regard addiction as a disease, or something akin to it, for which punishment is inappropriate. They argue that many addicts become criminals in order to get money to buy drugs, since there is no way in which they can obtain them legally and the cost of illegal procurement is high. This state of affairs, they contend, encourages the spread of addiction among criminals and juvenile delinquents who have easy access to drug peddlers. From this point of view, drug addiction is primarily a problem for the physician rather than for the policeman, and it should not be necessary for anyone to violate the criminal law solely because he is addicted to drugs. This necessity might be avoided by a system of clinics for treating addicts, or by adopting the British practice of permitting physicians to prescribe legal drugs in cases of addiction. Such measures, it is argued, would also remove the stigma of criminality from addiction, and, at the same time, would aid materially in undermining the illicit traffic.

It is understandable that legislators and officials should be reluctant to introduce drastic changes in present laws and practices without long and careful consideration in the light of available factual evidence. The problem deserves careful study. It is of concern to both the legal and the medical profession.

In 1955–56 the American Bar Association and the American Medical Association appointed a Joint Committee on Narcotic Drugs to explore the problem.

The Joint Committee gave relatively little attention to the role of the medical profession in relation to addiction and to the evolution of national policy on this subject. This was because the Council on Mental Health of the American Medical Association had covered these phases of the subject in a comprehensive report issued in 1956. The summary and recommendations of this report are included in the present volume. The Council's recommendations resemble those of the Joint Committee in that they also reflect dissatisfaction with the operation of existing laws, that they emphasize the medical rather than the punitive approach, that they indicate a positive but cautious attitude toward the possibility of adopting British practices, and that they stress above all the need for more investigation and for more reliable information.

The Bureau of Narcotics was established in 1930. The Harrison Anti-Narcotic Act was passed in 1914 and by 1925 the crucial legal questions raised by the Act had been dealt with in the Supreme Court decisions reviewed by Judge Ploscowe. The present pattern of enforcement was thus established before the Bureau was in existence. Even the regulations issued by the Treasury Department for the guidance of enforcement agents had been formulated in substantially their present form before 1930. Certainly the Bureau of Narcotics cannot be held accountable for these early developments, nor does criticism of statutes or of court decisions have any derogatory implications for the police. The police themselves are often among the most vigorous critics of laws which they are called upon to enforce and of court decisions affecting enforcement of such laws. . . .

Before the 1950s very few Americans knew anything about how the drug problem was handled in Britain or in any other European country. During the last ten years interest in British practices and knowledge of what they are have increased greatly, but profound ignorance is still the rule with respect to the drug control policies of other European nations. For example, with the exception of a few United Nations technical documents, there are no publications which describe the policies, laws, and practices of any of these countries. With respect to Britain the descriptive literature is very sparse, consisting largely of a handful of articles tucked away in professional journals, special reports, and Congressional hearings. One of the reasons for the lack of information is that the drug problem is a very minor one in virtually all European countries, receives little public attention, and is hardly ever mentioned in connection with crime. Discussions of it are usually found in medical journals and these ordinarily deal with various technical medical matters rather than with the broad questions of social policy which are debated in the United States.

The debate in the United States during the last ten years or so concerning British practices is a strange one indeed, since it is a debate over what is essentially a simple, easily ascertainable factual matter. While, as Mr. King indicates, there is a difference of opinion between American authorities as to what British practices are, there is no such difference of opinion among the British authorities.

The British government has made no secret of its program, the essentials of which are regularly set forth in its annual report to the United Nations and republished by that organization. Nevertheless, for reasons which are indicated in Mr. King's statement, there is still considerable confusion in this country concerning both the nature of the British system and the extent of the drug problem in that country.

For several years most Americans, assuming that American methods of handling addicts were standard practice, have regarded suggestions that addicts be given access to legal drugs as a startling, radical, or dangerous idea. At the same time it has apparently seemed quite normal and acceptable to them that alcohol and barbiturate addicts obtain their supplies legally without police interference, despite the fact that the alcohol and barbiturate habits are probably at least as harmful and more prevalent than is addiction to heroin or morphine. During the years after the war the increased prevalence of addiction stimulated an interest in foreign practices and there has been a growing realization, to which Mr. King's statement should make a substantial contribution, that in reality it is the European practices which are standard rather than the American. The significance of this is enhanced by the fact that even if one accepts the lowest estimates of the number of addicts in this country there would still be more here than in all the countries of Europe combined. Chicago and New York City, with a combined population of about 11 million or one-fifth that of Britain, are ordinarily estimated to have about 30,000 addicts, which is from thirty to fifty times as many as there are said to be in Britain.

The proposals of the Joint Committee are formulated with commendable modesty and caution. Since they call primarily for the collection of more information and for more study of possible alternative programs, they present no inherent obstacles to a joint enterprise involving not only the cooperation of the legal and medical professions but also that of the police and of all other interested groups and individuals. The two basic needs in such an enterprise are full and free investigation and full and free discussion.

Summary and Recommendations of Report on Narcotic Addiction by the Council on Mental Health of the American Medical Association

Summary

1. Study of the operations of clinics which dispensed drugs to addicts between 1919–1923 shows that data available on these clinics are not sufficiently objective to be of any value. The clinics were set up hastily as emergency measures, did not have well defined objectives, were inadequately staffed, and made little effort to rehabilitate addicts. There is no doubt that there was some abuse of the clinics, but the extent of the abuse is undeterminable.
2. The medical profession played a major role in formulating a policy which led to closing the clinics.
3. The best evidence indicates that the incidence of addiction in the United States has declined since passage of the Federal Narcotics laws. During World War II, the number of addicts reached an all-time low, probably because of the decline in illicit traffic, due to war-time conditions.
4. Addiction in persons under 21 years of age has also increased since World War II. The extent of adolescent addiction, however, does not justify the degree of public alarm which has arisen. Adolescent addiction is not a new phenomenon.
5. The greatest incidence of addiction occurs in minority groups residing in the slums of certain large cities. Such areas have the highest rates of delinquency, alcoholism, crime, and mental disease, as well as of addiction.
6. Deliberate proselytizing by drug peddlers in order to expand their market plays only a minor role in spreading addiction; rather, addiction spreads from person to person. Initial doses are usually supplied to the neophyte by a friend, and as a friendly gesture.
7. The most common psychiatric entities associated with addiction are personality disturbances and character disorders.
8. Opiates do not directly incite persons to commit violent crimes. Crimes committed by addicts are usually crimes against property. A proportion of

addicts—various sources give figures ranging from 25 to 80%—have records of delinquent activity prior to addiction.

9. Current treatment of addiction is unsatisfactory. The relapse rate, though not known exactly, is high. One possible reason for such poor results is the lack of post-institutional treatment.
10. The advisability of establishing clinics or some equivalent system to dispense opiates to addicts cannot be settled on the basis of objective facts. Any position taken is necessarily based in part on opinion, and opinions on this question are divided.

Recommendations

1. Improvement of the care of addicts.
   It is recommended that the American Medical Association continue to study and to support reasonable proposals designed to improve the treatment and prevention of drug addiction. Such measures might include:
   (a) Development of institutional care programs in cities and states with significant problems.
   (b) Study of various means to obtain institutional care in states with small addiction loads. One such proposal is for several states to set up an institution which could be operated jointly.
   (c) Development of programs for intensive post-institutional treatment of addicts. Such measures would include supplying of various social services, vocational rehabilitation and, where possible, psychotherapy to addicts for adequate periods following discharge from institutions. In many instances, available facilities in other programs might be utilized. States with serious problems should develop special programs for addiction.
   (d) Development of methods for commitment of addicts to institutions by civil action rather than through actions in the criminal courts. In this connection the Council further recommends that where civil commitment procedures can be used criminal sentences for addicts who are guilty only of illegally possessing and obtaining opiates, marihuana, and cocaine should be abolished. Criminal sentences for illegal sale of narcotics should be retained but persons who are addicts and who are sentenced for such offenses should have the same opportunity for probation and parole as is afforded offenders against other laws. Mandatory minimum sentences for addict violators would interfere with the possible treatment and rehabilitation of addicts and therefore should be abolished.
   (e) The Council strongly recommends that the policy of voluntary admissions for the treatment of addiction should be continued, extended and encouraged.
   (f) Continue support and expansion of mental health programs. Because of the importance of psychiatric factors in addiction, such programs should eventually have an effect in reducing addiction even though not specifically aimed at that problem.

2. It is recommended that the American Medical Association support proposals for increased research on the problems of addiction. One of the current difficulties in formulating adequate programs is lack of knowledge which can be gained only through research. Support should be given not only to "basic" laboratory investigations but also to continuation of sociological studies, and to an intensive program of clinical research based on adequate facilities for following addicts after institutional discharge. Such research might yield results that would be valuable in areas other than addiction.
3. Clinic Plans. In view of all of the available evidence at the present time it does not seem feasible to recommend the establishment of clinics for the supply of drugs to addicts. This is true for the Eggston resolution and the plan of the New York Academy of Medicine even though there are many aspects of these plans that could be looked upon with favor. This opinion should be subject to frequent review in accordance with new scientific knowledge that may become available.
4. It is recommended that the American Medical Association continue to study the narcotic laws with the view of further clarification of the rights and duties of physicians and allied professional persons in the handling of addicts.

The phrases in the current law ". . . in the course of professional practice only" and "prescription," remain vague and confusing, despite Supreme Court decisions. Regulations on dispensing drugs to addicts should be eased so that the patients can have a reasonable time to arrange their affairs prior to entering a hospital for treatment. The 1924 Resolution of the House of Delegates should be revised.

Consideration should be given to broadening the Resolution to include a plan endorsing regulations somewhat similar to those currently in force in England.

Appendix B

An Appraisal of International, British and Selected European Narcotic Drug Laws, Regulations and Policies

by RUFUS KING

In canvassing existing sources and planning its own studies, the Joint Committee of the American Bar Association and the American Medical Association on Narcotic Drugs had necessarily to inquire about the workings of comparable narcotic drug control systems in other parts of the world.

It quickly developed that American authorities are in conflict about other systems; especially with respect to the situation in Great Britain there is disagreement even as to whether a so-called narcotics problem exists on any significant scale.

The conclusions which follow are thus supported by direct study and interviews with public officials and others in the United Nations headquarters in New York and Geneva, and in England, Scotland, Denmark, Norway, Sweden, Belgium and Italy. No effort has been made to appraise conditions in areas other than the United Kingdom and Western Europe because analogies with nations which produce drugs domestically on an extensive scale, or whose political and cultural patterns differ widely from our own, seem sharply limited in value as guidance for the Joint Committee.

The conclusions reached in this study are two: first, efforts to control drugs by international prohibition measures, though desirable and successful in part, are unlikely to be a major factor in solving our domestic addiction problem within the United States; and second, the experience of comparable national communities in Europe in recent years has been startlingly different from our own with respect to the drug addiction problem, owing largely to a difference in their attitudes and enforcement policies regarding addicted persons and the medical profession.

Great Britain

The British experience in controlling drug addiction has become a subject of controversy in the United States. The Federal Bureau of Narcotics insists that the English have an illicit drug traffic of the same magnitude and viciousness as our own, and that the enforcement policies of the two countries are identical." Since 1954 the Bureau has been circulating a document entitled, "British Narcotic System" which asserts: "Several years ago a professor of sociology at an American university . . . wrote an article in which he advocated that the United States adopt the British system of handling drug addicts by having doctors write prescriptions for addicts. He reported that this system had abolished the black market in narcotics and that consequently there were only 326 drug addicts in the United Kingdom . . . .

Nothing could be further from the truth. The British system is the same as the United States system. The following is an excerpt of a letter dated July 18, 1953, from the British Home Office, concerning the prescribing of narcotic drugs by the medical profession: "A doctor may not have or use the drugs for any other purpose than that of ministering to the strictly medical needs of his patients. The continued supply of drugs to a patient either direct or by prescription, solely for the gratification of addiction is not regarded as a medical need. . . ."

"The British Government is a party to all of the international narcotic conventions to which the United States is a party. They enforce treaties in the same manner as the United States. The British and United States systems for enforcing narcotic laws are exactly the same." Giving full weight to such disparity of views, it is nonetheless stated here without hesitation that England (and the U.K. countries which follow her pattern) has no significant drug-addiction problem, no organized illicit trafficking, and no drug-law enforcement activities that could be regarded as comparable to those which preoccupy our own authorities.

The key to this difference appears to be that the British medical profession is in full and virtually unchallenged control of the distribution of drugs, and this includes distribution, by prescription or administration, to addicts when necessary. The police function is to aid and protect medical control, rather than to substitute for it.

Some of the distinctions are subtle. Discrepancies between British form and British substance, in the endearing tradition of "muddling through," make it possible to focus upon statements, like that quoted from the Home Office letter in the document referred to above, which are true and yet misleading apart from their qualifying context—i.e., in the instant case, doctors include the imminence of withdrawal symptoms among the "strictly medical needs" of their patients, and ministering to an addict under the conditions which will be discussed below is not regarded by either the profession or the authorities as "solely for the gratification of addiction." The controlling fact is that the medical profession accepts and treats addicts as patients so that virtually none are driven to support a black market; the prime corollary is that if all curative efforts fail the incurable addict may still be provided for on a medically-supervised regime; and the remarkable consequence is that the number of persons in the incurable or extended-regime category—out of Britain's population of over fifty millions—remains year after year in the range between three and four hundred. At the end of 1956 the figure was 333.

It is of interest that around one hundred of these chronic cases are from the ranks of the medical profession itself (75,000 doctors, plus nurses, hospital staffs, technicians, and persons in related careers). British authorities concede that some persons—scores, perhaps—may be obtaining and using narcotics by some personal arrangement which makes it unnecessary for them to appear on the Home Office list. But the list is inclusive, with only this minimal degree of probable error. It does not include persons whose addiction has been medically induced, i.e., terminal cancer patients and other chronic sufferers; another list of addicted persons in this category averages about the same length, remaining at less than four hundred.

The British first imposed controls on narcotic drugs in the same period (1920) when our enforcement policies were being developed under the Harrison Act. Their regulatory pattern is very similar to ours: everyone who has occasion to handle "dangerous drugs" must register, obtain a license, and keep accurate records. With respect to distribution, pharmacists must preserve prescriptions and record all sales, and pharmacists' records are inspected periodically by local police officers (who also keep an eye on the distribution of other substances in the dangerous drug and poison categories). Pharmacists are thus watched with some care. The requirement that doctors keep records, however, is not vigorously enforced, but if a doctor's practice in the matter is questioned, or if the prescription records show him to be prescribing unusual amounts, he may be approached by a medical inspector from the Ministry of Health, though he would never be called to account by the police agencies. The Act now provides maximum penalties of one thousand pounds' fine and ten years' imprisonment, though such penalties are not meted out in practice. The usual kinds of offense are petty defections like the forgery of personal prescriptions, or the practice of deception by an addict's representing himself to be in need of treatment simultaneously to more than one doctor. It is of interest that the latter offense is cast by the regulations solely in terms of the deception practiced on the second prescriber, so the doctors themselves cannot become implicated. The offense of unauthorized possession is qualified as follows:

"Provided that a person supplied with a drug or preparation by, or upon a prescription given by, a medical practitioner shall not be deemed to be a person generally authorized to be in possession of the drug or preparation if he was then being supplied with a drug or preparation by, or on a prescription given by, another medical practitioner in the course of treatment, and did not disclose the fact to the first-mentioned medical practitioner before the supply by him or on his prescription."

In 1956, sentences for offenses involving opium ranged from 2 months to 6 months and fines from 5 pounds to 100 pounds; for marihuana offenses, from 6 weeks to 5 years and from 5 pounds to 250 pounds; and for manufactured drug offenses (heroin, morphine, etc.), from 1 day to 6 months and 10s. to 100 pounds. Addiction among doctors is a comparatively serious problem, as has been noted, but the sanction applied in such cases is loss of authority to prescribe narcotic drugs under the

Dangerous Drugs Act, and not loss of authority to practice medicine. If an addicted doctor puts himself under the care of another doctor, he is not likely to encounter any sanctions or difficulties.

The first regulations under the Dangerous Drug Act of 1920 actually left unsettled the same ambiguity which has given so much trouble in interpreting the Harrison Act: whether the treatment of addicted persons is bona fide medical practice or not. They merely exempted classes of persons from the ban on possession in the following general language: "Subject to the provisions of these Regulations a person who is a member of any of the following classes, that is to say:

(a) duly qualified medical practitioners;
(b) Shall be authorised, so far as may be necessary for the practice or exercise of his said profession, function or employment, and in his capacity as a member of his said class, to be in possession of and to supply drugs."

Paralleling the course of development in the United States even further, the Home Office early took a narrow view of this exemption. Its ruling—still set forth as a guide for practitioners and hence still properly cited as in the letter referred to by the Narcotics Bureau was as follows:

"7. The authority granted to a doctor or dentist to possess and supply dangerous drugs is limited by the words so far as may be necessary for the practice or exercise of his profession. In no circumstances may dangerous drugs be used for any other purpose than that of ministering to the strictly medical or dental needs of his patients. The continued supply of dangerous drugs to a patient solely for the gratification of addiction is not regarded as 'medical need.' In a number of cases doctors and dentists who have obtained drugs ostensibly for the needs of their practices and have subsequently diverted them to the gratification of their own addiction have been convicted of offenses under the Dangerous Drugs Act."

Here, however, the parallel ended, for after several years of confusion, while the Home Office refrained from prosecutions based on bona fide ministrations to addicts in view of the ambiguity of the law and regulations, the British medical profession took matters into its own hands.

In 1926 the Rolleston Committee, a committee of eminent doctors appointed by the Government to advise on the point, concluded that providing addicted drug users with drugs under suitable controls was distinguishable from supplying "solely for the gratification of addiction," and set forth the following guiding precepts:

Precautions to be Observed in the Administration of Morphine or Heroin.

The position of a practitioner when using morphine or heroin in the treatment of persons who suffer from addiction to either of these drugs obviously differs in several important respects from that in which he is placed when using the drug in the ordinary course of his medical practice for the treatment of persons not so affected. Not only will the objects of treatment usually differ but also the dangers to be avoided, and the precautions that are therefore necessary. It is thus convenient to discuss these precautions separately as regards:

(i) The administration of the drugs to persons who are already victims of addiction, and
(ii) The ordinary use of the drugs in medical and surgical practice.

In the preceding section, the conclusion has been stated that morphine or heroin may properly be administered to addicts in the following circumstances, namely, (a) where patients are under treatment by the gradual withdrawal method with a view to cure, (b) where it has been demonstrated, after a prolonged attempt at cure, that the use of the drug cannot be safely discontinued entirely on account of the severity of the withdrawal symptoms produced, (c) where it has been similarly demonstrated that the patient, while capable of leading a useful and relatively normal life when a certain minimum dose is regularly administered, becomes incapable of this when the drug is entirely discontinued.

Precautions in the Treatment of Addicts by the Gradual Withdrawal Method.

In these cases the primary object of the treatment is the cure of the addiction, if practicable. The best hope of cure being afforded by treatment in a suitable institution or nursing home, the patient should, if possible, be induced to enter such an institution or home. If he is unable, or refuses to adopt this course, the practitioner must attempt to cure his condition by steady, judicious reduction of the dose. The general lines of the treatment, as carried out by the practitioners of special experience, have already been described.

For success it is necessary that the patient should be seen frequently, be under sufficient control, and be in the care of a capable and reliable nurse. The practitioner should endeavour to gain his patient's confidence, and to induce him to adhere strictly to the course of treatment prescribed, especially as regards the amount of the drug of addiction which is taken. This last condition is particularly difficult to secure, as such patients are essentially unreliable and will not infrequently endeavour to obtain supplementary supplies of the drug. If, however, the practitioner finds that he cannot maintain the necessary control of the patient, he must consider whether he can properly continue indefinitely to bear the sole responsibility for the treatment.

When the practitioner finds that he has lost control of the patient, or when the course of the case forces him to doubt whether the administration of the drug can, in the best interests of the patient, be completely discontinued, it will become necessary to consider whether he ought to remain in charge of the case, and accept the responsibility of supplying or ordering indefinitely the drug of addiction in the minimum doses which seem necessary. The responsibility of making such a decision is obviously onerous, and both on this ground, and also for his own protection, in view of the possible inquiries by the Home Office which such continuous administration may occasion, the practitioner will be well advised to obtain a second opinion on the case.

Precautions in Treatment of Apparently Incurable Cases.

These will include both the cases in which the severity of withdrawal symptoms, observed on complete discontinuance after prolonged attempted cure, and the cases in which the inability of the patient to lead, without a minimum dose, a relatively normal life appear to justify continuous administration of the drug indefinitely. They may be either cases of persons whom the practitioner has himself already treated with a view to cure, or cases of persons as to whom he is satisfied, by information received from those by whom they have been previously treated, that they must be regarded as incurable. In all such cases the main object must be to keep the supply of the drug within the limits of what is strictly necessary. The practitioner must, therefore, see the patient sufficiently often to maintain such observation of his condition as is necessary for justifying the treatment. The opinion expressed by witnesses was to the effect that such patients should ordinarily be seen not less frequently than once a week.

The amount of the drug supplied or ordered on one occasion should not be more than is sufficient to last until the next time the patient is to be seen. A larger supply would only be justified in exceptional cases, for example (on a sea voyage), when the patient was going away in circumstances in which he would not be able to obtain medical advice. In all other cases he should be advised to place himself under the care of another practitioner, who should be placed in communication with his previous medical adviser in order that he might be informed as to the nature of the case and the course of treatment which was being pursued.

"A practitioner when consulted by a patient not previously under his care, who asks that morphine or heroin may be administered or ordered for him for the relief of pain or other symptoms alleged to be urgent, should not supply or order the drug unless satisfied as to the urgency, and should not administer or order more than is immediately necessary. If further administration is desired, in a case in which there is no organic disease justifying such administration, the request should not be acceded to until after the practitioner has obtained from the previous medical attendant an account of the nature of the case. Requests from one practitioner to another for such information should obviously receive immediate attention."

Thus it came to be recognized and established many years ago that the addict in British society remained the addict-patient; he never became, as in ours, the addict-criminal. The precepts just quoted, from the Rolleston Report, have been printed ever since as an appendix to the Home Office Instructions on the Duties, etc. of doctors under the Act.

The official attitude is well summarized in the Government's current report to the U.N. Commission:

"There is no compulsory treatment of drug addicts in the United Kingdom. . . . In the United Kingdom the treatment of a patient is considered to be a matter for the doctor concerned. The nature of the treatment given varies with the circumstances of each case."

Nor is it as illogical as might appear at first blush to leave the Home Office statement and Sir Humphrey Rolleston's in juxtaposition in the current regulatory instructions. Lurking behind all regulatory efforts in the 'twenties was the spectre of the "script doctor," the truly unethical practitioner who abused his license to fill the role, in effect, of our detested dope peddler. If he appeared in England, and did not yield to the gentle suasions of his professional confreres and the civil authorities, it is safe to surmise that he might have been—and could still be—vigorously prosecuted as a grave offender against the Act and Regulations.

The British medical profession has remained, with the inevitable occasional exception, very responsible in the application of the foregoing principles. The primary aim of treatment is to cure the patient by freeing him from his affliction if possible, precisely as in other branches of therapy. Consultation and the concurrence of a second medical opinion are sought as a matter of course before an addicted person is put on any kind of permanent regime.

Great care is ordinarily taken to examine and probe into the condition and history of any new patient who claims a history of addiction. And doctors cooperate informally with the Home Office by reporting addicts under treatment to the Dangerous Drugs Division.

The last mentioned cooperation by the medical profession is, of course, supplemented by the reports of the police inspectors who check pharmacists' registers from time to time. Addicts who are receiving a steady supply of narcotic drugs will be revealed by this check, as well as those who falsify prescriptions or are receiving double dosages by practising fraud—the offense at which police activities are primarily aimed. The number of addicts presently known to the authorities by virtue of this double check, less than 400 in the non-medical category, as has been noted, hence seems quite likely to be a reliable measure.

Enforcement officials in the Home Office say that there is simply no illicit trafficking in the opiates; that no drugs of British manufacture have ever been identified in seizures in the illicit markets of other countries; and that new addicts usually become known to the authorities within six months. The possibility of some epidemic-like change in the pattern is recognized (as has been observed, on a minute scale, in the use of marihuana); but the situation has remained stable for many years and there are no present indications to suggest any significant growth in the addict population.

In 1956 the Minister of Health, allegedly responding to pressure from the United States, announced that he proposed to ban the use of heroin in Great Britain for medical purposes. Following this announcement medical practitioners began to buy up supplies, prices rose, and it is believed that a small black market may have made its appearance. Some prominent doctors thereupon organized a campaign to oppose the ban, prevailing upon the Minister, after a much-publicized controversy, to prohibit only the exportation of the drug. Thus the Minister "saved face" while leaving the profession free in the matter. There is still mild resentment over the fact that because heroin was removed from the British Pharmacopeia in 1956 when the ban was proposed, American authorities hailed this as a prohibition and still make statements to the effect that England has joined the United States in outlawing the drug.

Home Office officials believe that even if they stopped all lawful importation of opiates for all purposes, the problem of addiction would remain because addicted persons would be compelled to sustain their condition by the development of a black market. They complain that most of the publicity and press comments about drug problems in the United Kingdom are not authoritative. It was suggested that some of the addicts who have run afoul of the law (or who may be importing their own drugs) are simply unaware of the true state of affairs and of the fact that they can obtain relief and assistance from the medical profession merely by application to a doctor.

The foregoing general and statistical observations were confirmed in a study of local conditions in Glasgow and Edinburgh. In Glasgow, with a population of 1.45 million, four officers of the police department are assigned to enforcement of the regulatory provisions of the Dangerous Drug Act, devoting their full time to inspecting pharmacies, checking records, and investigating alleged violations and abuse. These men are wholly unaware of any serious problem of addiction, and state that there is no black market, with the possible exception that hemp and smoking opium may sometimes get past the customs authorities and into the waterfront district to Chinese and West Indian consumers. There are approximately 350 pharmacies in the city, less than a score of known addicts, and two doctors (out of a total of 40 in the United Kingdom) whose authority to prescribe drugs is currently under suspension.

One of the two doctors has succeeded in curing himself of his addiction, and it is expected that his authority to prescribe drugs will be restored if he makes application.

The officers reflected an attitude of great respect for the medical profession, and stated that they are "not encouraged" to approach the doctors in matters within their jurisdiction; if a questionable or unusual practice comes to their attention, they are expected to report through channels to the Home Office and the matter may then be taken up through the Ministry of Health and the local medical boards.

It was also stated that although the pharmacists are universally cooperative, some doctors, especially the older practitioners, would probably refuse to cooperate with the police concerning their patients under any circumstances, and the suspicion was voiced that 90% of the doctors up here don't keep any records at all. There was no identification between addicted persons and persons engaging in criminal activity.

In Edinburgh, with a population of half a million, two men are assigned to policing the Dangerous Drugs Act, and one investigation conducted by them within the last eighteen months has resulted in the preferring of charges.

This was the case of an addict who had made application simultaneously to more than one doctor for care, with a long record of similar activities in the past. Because his wife cooperated with the police in reporting on his activities, he was let off without a sentence as a result of their recommendation to the prosecutor. The officers speculated that he might receive a short prison sentence if he were caught and charged again. They also recalled one case in the preceding year involving a doctor-addict who appeared to have violated the Act by making personal use of drugs purchased by him for administration to his patients. This case resulted in the conveyance of a warning to the doctor without the preferment of charges.

SOURCE: Alfred Lindesmith's introduction to *Drug Addiction Crime or Disease: Interim and Final Reports on the Joint Committee of the American Bar Association on Narcotic Drugs*, vii–xiv. Copyright (c) 1961. Reprinted with permission from Indiana University Press.

ANALYSIS

An important effect of the Harrison Act of 1914 was the impact it had on physicians' prescribing practices. The clear intent of the law was to reduce the availability of narcotics and it was successful in this regard, at least for a time. By the time the Harrison Act was passed, the Pure Food and Drug Act, which had been in place for eight years, had already sharply curtailed narcotic distribution via patent medicines by virtue of its requirement that product labels accurately indicate the ingredients. However, in those intervening eight years, physicians could still freely prescribe narcotic drugs to patients as analgesics (i.e., to relieve pain) or to treat patients addicted to narcotics without federal oversight. Pharmacists were also able to provide clients with "medications" that included narcotics so long as the labels indicated as much. At their professional discretion, physicians could treat narcotics addiction by gradually titrating the prescription dosages in the hope of weaning their patient off drugs. Physicians could also prescribe maintenance doses for patients who had become so habituated to drug use that, in the estimation of the physician, they could not function properly without drugs and would never be able to discontinue their use.

This changed dramatically following passage of the Harrison Act, which provided for close monitoring of narcotic prescriptions using the taxing authority of the federal government (see section 1d). A series of Supreme Court rulings in the years immediately following enactment of the law determined that the rather vague clause, "in the course of his professional practice only," did not support prescribing narcotics for the purpose of maintaining an addiction or for merely providing "comfort" to the addict. As a consequence, physicians determined to be prescribing narcotics to drug addicts in such a manner as to maintain rather than to "cure" the addiction could be prosecuted under the provisions of the Harrison Act. Thus, from a legal standpoint, physicians who prescribed drugs that sustained the drug use of those who seemed hopelessly addicted were as liable to be prosecuted as were the small minority of unscrupulous profiteers who prescribed narcotics solely for financial gain without regard to patient safety or need and often without the bother of a physical examination.

While few would question the use of sanctions in the latter instance, federal oversight of and sanctions for maintaining addicts who could not be "cured," rankled many within the medical profession who believed the practice to be legitimate and under the purview of physicians. The oversight of physician prescribing practices by federal agents in the Treasury Department was not well received and seen as intrusive and as federal tax agents with no medical qualifications determining what constituted sound medical practice. Despite these professional disgruntlements, however, and facing the prospect of rather severe sanctions, many physicians simply abandoned prescribing narcotics for their patients addicted to these drugs (mostly heroin and morphine, rarely cocaine) eliminating any legal risk entirely. Ethical physicians who sought to help their drug addicted patients had to proceed with extreme caution, maintain detailed records, and justify their prescribing practices at the request of inquiring federal agents. In subsequent years, as both federal and state laws continued to ratchet up criminal sanctions, any upside to helping addicted patients manage their drug use diminished further.

In the four years following the Harrison Act, narcotics clinics were established by the states. These are the clinics referenced in the excerpted summary statement. The clinics functioned to provide treatment to addicts whose legal access to narcotic drugs had been sharply and abruptly curtailed. The narcotics clinics arose, in part, out of concern that the sudden loss of access to drugs would lead to a black market and to an extensive crime wave by addicted individuals growing increasingly desperate to obtain their drugs by any means possible. This concern was further fueled by gross overestimates of the number of drug addicts, estimates that, ironically, had been propagated in the first place to muster support for narcotics control legislation.

The clinics varied widely with respect to whether they supported maintenance or whether they functioned primarily to taper the narcotic dosage in an attempt to end a client's addiction. The policies and practices of each clinic were largely determined at the local level by clinic administrators and physician practitioners in lieu of any national treatment model and guidelines. Public support for the clinics was never more than tepid at best, however, and physicians were divided on the issue of whether maintenance was a legitimate therapeutic goal. There was even less political enthusiasm for maintenance as a treatment method, particularly at the federal level. Then too, some clinics clearly abused their license to operate and served as little more than drug distribution centers, attracting addicts to the surrounding neighborhoods thereby providing additional ammunition for those politically opposed to their operation and for those who saw addiction maintenance as little more than fostering a bad habit and increasing the number of addicts.

The result was that the narcotics clinics were shuttered after only a few years of operation leaving virtually no legal channels by which narcotics addicts could get drugs. At the time, there was also little in the way of community treatment available. Lacking legal access to drugs and with few to no treatment options, narcotics addicts did, in fact, create a black market for buying drugs from street dealers much in the same way that prohibition would create markets for bootleggers and speakeasies. Because drugs sold on the black market are many times more expensive than those obtained legally, crime also increased. This in turn fostered the impression that drug addicts were criminally inclined sociopaths who should rightly be dealt with by the criminal justice system if those addicted to drugs were unwilling to discontinue their drug use and to commit crimes to support continued access to drugs. With the closing of the narcotics clinics, maintenance as a viable, necessary treatment strategy for those with intractable addictions would not again be revisited in any systematic way in the United States until the 1960s when Dole and Nyswander began their clinical experiments to test the effectiveness of methadone as a prescribed substitute for heroin and morphine.

Physicians and others who advocated treating addiction as a public health issue and having discretion to treat patients addicted to drugs would continue to fare poorly in the decades following passage of the Harrison Act. Shunning the arguments in favor of allowing physicians medical discretion, legislators at the state and federal levels passed a series of laws that increased criminal penalties for drug use and possession up to and including the death penalty. With the exception of the two narcotics "farms" established in Lexington, Kentucky, in 1935 and Fort Worth, Texas, in 1938, little attention was paid to federal backing of expanding treatment for drug addiction through the 1960s. When AMA representatives attempted to testify at congressional hearings called to inform drug-policy legislation, their testimony was dismissed and ignored. As a result, the AMA and its supporters had little influence on drug policy from the 1930s through the 1960s. Instead, Commissioner Anslinger, who testified often at congressional hearings and who helped orchestrate the list of those invited to testify, paid scant attention to the medical literature and to formal research on addiction, such as it was, and relied on exaggerated newspaper accounts, unsubstantiated arrest reports, and states attorneys accounts of especially lurid crimes ostensively committed while under the influence of drugs; the more lurid, the better.

Facing the familiar prospect of having their views disregarded in hearings held prior to what would become the Narcotic Control Act of 1956, representatives of the AMA and sympathetic colleagues in the ABA formed a joint commission to study the problem of addiction and to issue their own report that was to include policy recommendations. Members of the joint commission hoped the report's conclusions would influence Congress to take a less punitive stance toward drug addiction and to consider at least trying on a limited basis, alternatives such as that practiced in Great Britain whereby physicians were permitted to prescribe heroin for patients they felt were unable to function normally without the drug, known somewhat informally and inaccurately as the British system (described in some detail in the Appendix B excerpt).

Many of the arguments put forth in the ABA-AMA report have a very modern feel to them, much in the same way that elements of the Kefauver Commission report did (see Section 2d). It is very possible to take the substance of the ABA-AMA Interim and Final Reports and construct a summary of current criticisms of drug policy: the damage to communities and individuals caused by emphasizing a criminal justice as opposed to public health approach to drug addiction; the impossibility of locking away forever all drug addicts; the limited value of the deterrent effect of law enforcement and criminal sanctions on discouraging drug use; the creation of a lucrative black market for selling illegal drugs that virtually ensures these drugs will continue to be available to those who want them badly enough and creates a host of related crimes; the need for additional treatment research and expanded treatment options; the importance of having aftercare following treatment within a residential facility, jail, or prison; and the importance of treating the psychiatric problems that commonly co-occur with and foster or are exacerbated by drug addiction. All of these critiques (and others) of America's punitive drug policies continue to resonate through the present day but were prominently featured 50 years ago in the ABA-AMA report.

Despite the report recommendations for a more measured approach to the country's drug problem, Congress pressed ahead, urged on by Commissioner Anslinger, with a singular focus on increasing criminal sanctions. Not surprisingly, Commissioner Anslinger was extremely displeased by the report's substance and conclusions and resented that such a commission was even convened in the first place. For him, the joint commission and their report was a direct challenge to his authority and expertise and flat-out wrong in its particulars. Anslinger ignored repeated invitations to meet with members of the ABA-AMA joint commission to discuss their findings. He used his considerable influence to persuade the foundation that would have funded publication of the report to rescind their offer. He even requested multiple copies of the report from the few that had been printed using the ruse that the reports were needed by his staff for review. Siphoning off the limited number of copies in this way effectively limited the availability of the report to others. Commissioner Anslinger published his own report (of sorts) in response based on the recommendations of a committee he constructed and that never actually met. The ersatz committee rejoinder, in contrast to the ABA-AMA report was widely distributed by the federal government and, although it was not an official government document, was bound in such a way as to appear that it was. Had Alfred Lindesmith not shown the initiative to publish the ABA-AMA report, it likely would have languished in virtually complete obscurity.

Not surprisingly given the aforementioned response, the ABA-AMA report's admonishments against relying solely on criminal sanctions for managing drug addiction were ignored. And they would continue to be ignored for most of the rest of the century. In the early 1970s, when there was a resurgence of heroin use associated with returning Vietnam War vets, and in the mid-1980s, when a violent crime wave surrounding crack cocaine distribution alarmed the country. The legislative response in both cases was to enact punitive laws that featured long mandatory sentences (i.e., required minimums not subject to judicial discretion) for drug-related crimes. Shortly thereafter, the police, the criminal courts, probation and parole officers, and jails, and prisons, would be overwhelmed by the rapid and large influx of arrestees, defendants, probationers, parolees, detainees, and inmates into the criminal justice system. That illegal drugs continued to flow into the United States throughout and a never-ending stream of drug addicts would continue to be arrested and prosecuted

ALFRED R. LINDESMITH—CHAMPION OF A PUBLIC HEALTH APPROACH

For most of his long career as a sociologist who studied drug addiction and who tenaciously advocated for substantial changes in drug policy, Alfred R. Lindesmith fought a lonely battle against the prevailing perceptions (at the Federal level at least) that drug addicts were malevolent, morally deficient psychopaths prone to committing unpredictable acts of violence. His publication of the ABA-AMA report exemplified his support of efforts to rethink and to change drug policy.

Based on research conducted while he was a graduate student at the University of Chicago, Lindesmith believed that anyone could become addicted to drugs given the right circumstances. His research involved conducting lengthy, in-depth interviews with people who had developed addictions in order to understand how the person experienced their addiction and the events that led up to it. Many of the people Lindesmith interviewed had become addicted following administration of opiates for relieving pain due to a medical condition. They were largely middle-class and were not the stereotypical, inner city, minority, and poor street addict as often portrayed in the press and in political contexts whenever public support was needed for passing the latest get-tough anti-drug legislation.

The sociological theory that Lindesmith developed as a result of his research required a specific chain of events before addiction occurred. First, the person taking the drug had to know what drug they were taking. Second, the drug must be taken over a long enough time and in high enough doses to produce withdrawal symptoms during periods of abstinence. And third, the person must associate continued use of the drug with relief from withdrawal symptoms. According to the theory, all three steps are necessary: craving for and ultimately addiction to a specific drug will not occur if the drug in question is unknown to the user, if use does not produce withdrawal symptoms, and if relief from withdrawal is not associated with the drug. The theory has the further implication that animal models of research used to study drug addiction are inadequate because animals cannot know what particular drug they are having administered to them in the same way a human can. This implication gave rise to a curiously titled paper by Lindesmith that rhetorically asked whether chimpanzees could become drug addicts.

(continued)

no matter how many were already incarcerated provides credence to Judge Ploscowe's observation that "all confirmed addicts cannot be incarcerated, permanently, there will always be addicts at liberty to serve as customers for an illicit drug traffic." Indeed.

FURTHER READING

Carroll, R. (2004). The Narcotic Control Act triggers the great nondebate: Treatment loses to punishment. In J. Erlen & J. E. Spillane (Eds.), *Federal drug control* (pp. 101–144). Binghamton, NY: Haworth Press.

Galliher, J. F., Keys, D. P., & Elsner, M. (1998). Lindesmith v. Anslinger: An early government victory in the failed war on drugs. *Journal of Criminal Law and Criminology*, 88(2), 661–682.

Lindesmith, A. R. (1938). A sociological theory of drug addiction. *American Journal of Sociology*, *43*, 593–613.

Lindesmith, A. R. (1946). Can chimpanzees become morphine addicts? *Journal of Comparative Psychology*, *39*, 109–117.

McAuliffe, W. E., & Gordon, R. A. (1974). A test of Lindesmith's theory of addiction: The frequency of euphoria among long-term addicts. *American Journal of Sociology*, 79(4), 795–840.

Musto, D. (1999). *The American disease: Origins of narcotics control, 3rd edition*. New York: Oxford University Press.

Pearson, G. (1991). Drug-control policies in Britain. *Crime and Justice*, *14*, 167–177.

Stimson, G. V., & Oppenheimer, O. (1982). *Heroin addiction: Treatment and control in Britain*. London: Tavistock.

Strang, J. Ruben, S., Farrell, M., et al. (2005). The history of prescribing heroin and other injectable drugs as addiction treatment in the UK. In J. Strang and M. Gossop (Eds.), *Heroin addiction and the British system: Treatment and policy responses (volume 2)* (pp. 1–16). New York: Routledge.

On the Internet

A copy of the full ABA-AMA report on drug addiction is available online from the Schaffer Library of Drug Policy at: http://www.druglibrary.org/schaffer/library/studies/dacd/default.htm.

The full text of the 1926 Rolleston Report, the recommendations of which strongly influenced policy as to the medical management of addicted patients that became known as the British system, is available at the International Substance Use Library at: http://www.drugtext.org/Table/Rolleston-Report.

Reevaluations of the British system in 1958 and 1964, which are summarized in what are cited as the Brain Reports 1 and 2, are also available at the International Substance Use Library at: http://www.drugtext.org/Table/

First-Brain-Report/ http://www.drugtext.org/Table/Second-Brain-Report/.

The Schaffer Library has most of the text of Commissioner Anslinger's report written in response to the ABA-AMA report at: http://www.druglibrary.org/special/king/caba/cabamenu.htm.

The Drug Policy Alliance (DPA) website is at: http://www.drugpolicy.org/homepage.cfm.

The National Institute on Drug Abuse (NIDA) publication *Drug Abuse and Addiction* explains current thinking on the causes and consequences of drug addiction, with heavy emphasis on the underlying neurological changes caused by long-term drug use and on the role played by genetic factors: http://www.nida.nih.gov/scienceofaddiction/addiction.html.

ALFRED R. LINDESMITH—CHAMPION OF A PUBLIC HEALTH APPROACH

(continued)

Lindesmith is remembered as an unwavering champion of a compassionate view of people addicted to drugs as well as a proponent of a public health response to drug addiction. For most of his professional career, however, he was the target of personal and professional smears and attempts at intimidation by the equally unwavering Harry Anslinger.

3

THE 1960s THROUGH THE MID-1990s: AMPHETAMINES AND BARBITURATES, THE COUNTERCULTURE, LSD, VIETNAM, THE HEROIN EPIDEMICS, COCAINE REEMERGES, CRACK COCAINE, HIV/AIDS, HARM REDUCTION, SENTENCING DISPARITIES

"Better Living through Chemistry"

- ***Document:*** Drug Abuse Control Amendments of 1965 (PL 89–74)
- ***Date:*** December 18, 1965
- ***Where:*** Washington, DC
- ***Significance:*** Until the 1960s, federal and state drug laws had been mainly concerned with opiates, cocaine, and marijuana. But America had a substantial and largely unaddressed problem with the legal and illegal use and misuse of prescription drugs. Faced with the growing misuse and illegal trafficking of prescription drugs such as amphetamines, tranquilizers, and barbiturates, Congress passed legislation to bring the manufacturing, distribution and sale of these drugs under tighter control and, as usual, provide for criminal sanctions for violating the law. Intentionally vague wording that the

amendments applied to any drug with a potential for abuse owing to hallucinatory effects meant drugs such as LSD were included. The amendments also contained a provision designed to provide law enforcement the means with which to combat drug counterfeiting whereby copies of legitimate drugs were being produced and sold on the black market. However, the law did nothing to address the widespread problem of the legal production and misuse of prescription drugs.

Of particular significance was the fact that the 1965 amendments to the 1938 Food, Drug, and Cosmetics Act cited the powers of the federal government under the commerce clause of the Constitution as the basis for its authority over interstate drug production, distribution, and sales. This was a significant change of course away from using the federal government's taxing powers as the basis for that authority as was the case under the Harrison Act of 1914 and the Marihuana Tax Act of 1937. The law created a new federal entity, the Bureau of Drug Abuse Control within the Food and Drug Administration, for enforcing the law's provisions. Only short excerpts of the law are included as most of the provisions detail who could manufacture and distribute depressant and stimulant drugs and under what circumstances.

DOCUMENT

An Act

To protect the public health and safety by amending the Federal Food, Drug, and Cosmetic Act to establish special controls for depressant and stimulant drugs and counterfeit drugs, and for other purposes.

Be it enacted by the Senate and House of Representatives of the United States of America in Congress assembled, That this Act may be cited as the "Drug Abuse Control Amendments of 1965."

Findings and Declaration

SEC. 2. The Congress hereby finds and declares that there is a wide-spread illicit traffic in depressant and stimulant drugs moving in or otherwise affecting interstate commerce; that the use of such drugs, when not under the supervision of a licensed practitioner, often endangers safety on the highways (without distinction of interstate and intrastate traffic thereon) and otherwise has become a threat to the public health and safety, making additional regulation of such drugs necessary regardless of the intrastate or interstate origin of such drugs; that in order to make regulation and protection of interstate commerce in such drugs effective, regulation of intrastate commerce is also necessary because, among other things, such drugs, when held for illicit sale, often do not bear labeling showing their place of origin and because in the form in which they are so held or in which they are consumed a determination of their place of origin is often extremely difficult or impossible; and that regulation of interstate commerce without the regulation of intrastate commerce in such drugs, as provided in this Act, would discriminate against and adversely affect interstate commerce in such drugs.

Control of Depressant and Stimulant Drugs

SEC. 3. (a) Section 201 of the Federal Food, Drug, and Cosmetic Act (21 U.S.C. 321) is amended by adding at the end thereof the following (v) The term "depressant or stimulant drug" means—

(1) any drug which contains any quantity of (A) barbituric acid or any of the salts of barbituric acid; or (B) any derivative of barbituric acid which has been designated by the Secretary under section 502(d) as habit forming;
(2) any drug which contains any quantity of (A) amphetamine or any of its optical isomers; (B) any salt of amphetamine or any salt of an optical isomer of amphetamine; or (C) any substance which the Secretary, after investigation, has found to be, and by regulation designated as, habit forming because of its stimulant effect on the central nervous system; or
(3) any drug which contains any quantity of a substance which the Secretary, after investigation, has found to have, and by regulation designates as having, a potential for abuse because of its depressant or stimulant effect on the central nervous system or its hallucinogenic effect; . . .

Depressant and Stimulant Drugs

Sec. 511

(a) No person shall manufacture, compound, or process any depressant or stimulant drug, except that this prohibition shall not apply to the following persons whose activities in connection with any such drug are solely as specified in this subsection:

(1) (A) Manufacturers, compounders, and processors registered under section 510 who are regularly engaged, and are otherwise qualified, in conformance with local laws, in preparing pharmaceutical chemicals or prescription drugs for distribution through branch outlets, through wholesale druggists, or by direct shipment, (i) to pharmacies or to hospitals, clinics, public health agencies, or physicians, for dispensing by registered pharmacists upon prescriptions, or for use by or under the supervision of practitioners licensed by law to administer such drugs in the course of their professional practice, or (ii) to laboratories or research or educational institutions for their use in research, teaching, or chemical analysis. "(B) Suppliers (otherwise qualified in conformance with local laws) of manufacturers, compounders, and processors referred to in subparagraph (A).
(2) Wholesale druggists registered under section 510 who maintain establishments in conformance with local laws and are regularly engaged in

supplying prescription drugs (A) to pharmacies, or to hospitals, clinics, public health agencies, or physicians, for dispensing, by registered pharmacists upon prescriptions, or for use by or under the supervision of practitioners licensed by law to administer such drugs in the course of their professional practice, or (B) to laboratories or research or educational institutions for their use in research, teaching, or clinical analysis.

(3) Pharmacies, hospitals, clinics, and public health agencies, which maintain establishments in conformance with any applicable local laws regulating the practice of pharmacy and medicine and which are regularly engaged in dispensing prescription drugs upon prescriptions of practitioners licensed to administer such drugs for patients under the care of such practitioners in the course of their professional practice.

(4) Practitioners licensed by law to prescribe or administer depressant or stimulant drugs, while acting in the course of their professional practice.

(5) Persons who use depressant or stimulant drugs in research, teaching, or chemical analysis and not for sale.

(6) Officers and employees of the United States, a State government, or a political subdivision of a State, while acting in the course of their official duties.

(7) An employee or agent of any person described in paragraph (1) through paragraph (5), and a nurse or other medical technician under the supervision of a practitioner licensed by law to administer depressant or stimulant drugs, while such employee, nurse, or medical technician is acting in the course of his employment or occupation and not on his own account. . . .

Counterfeiting of Drugs Sec. 9

(a) The Congress finds and declares that there is a substantial traffic in counterfeit drugs simulating the brand or other identifying mark or device of the manufacturer of the genuine article; that such traffic poses a serious hazard to the health of innocent consumers of such drugs because of the lack of proper qualifications, facilities, and manufacturing controls on the part of the counterfeiter, whose operations are clandestine; that, while such drugs are deemed misbranded within the meaning of section 502(i) of the Federal Food, Drug, and Cosmetic Act, the controls for the suppression of the traffic in such drugs are inadequate because of the difficulty of determining the place of interstate origin of such drugs and, if that place is discovered, the fact that the implements for counterfeiting are not subject to seizure, and that these factors require enactment of additional controls with respect to such drugs without regard to their interstate or intrastate origins.

SOURCE: Drug Abuse Control Amendments of 1965. Public Law 89–74 (H.R. 2), July 15, 1965.

ANALYSIS

The 1960s continuing into the 1970s is commonly thought of as the time when drug use achieved its broadest cultural acceptability, at least among young Americans. However, it would be a mistake to think that drug use simply exploded from out of nowhere. It's true that the use of drugs such as heroin, cocaine, and marijuana was largely relegated to marginal social groups in the 1940s and 1950s, despite some increase in heroin and marijuana use following the end of World War II. But over roughly the same time period, large numbers of Americans had already begun gulping down potent prescription drugs such as amphetamines, barbiturates, and tranquilizers. Prominently known citizens were not immune to the trend and regular users/abusers of prescription drugs included a president (John F. Kennedy), famous artists (Andy Warhol), movie stars (Marilyn Monroe), singers (Judy Garland), and athletes (Jim Bouton). By the time Timothy Leary and his acolytes began extolling the virtues of LSD and other drugs as sacraments that could change peoples' lives and foster in a better social order, they were treading down a well-worn path. Pharmaceutical ads in medical journals had been making more or less the same pitch for many years.

While it is important to consider the distinction between drugs that have legitimate medical benefits and drugs that are used solely for "recreational purposes," this boundary can be very blurry. Analgesic drugs clearly have their place in reducing physical pain from injury and illness but are also highly addictive and subject to widespread abuse. A person who is depressed and who has access to health insurance and prescribed drugs might take an anti-depressant to feel better. Another depressed person without health insurance or the finances to afford regular access to a physician might use alcohol, cocaine, and/or marijuana for the same purpose. (Clinicians in the drug treatment field refer to the latter as "self-medicating.") An ethos that promotes the message that drugs are a means by which one can feel better is pervasive and cannot be well bounded. As such, it motivates drug use across economic, racial/ethnic, and generational groups and across legal and illegal means of acquiring drugs.

The rise and fall of the use (and misuse) of the prescription drugs that achieved wide popularity in the 1950s and 1960s followed a common trajectory that would become increasingly familiar. A new drug was developed or an old drug rediscovered that was touted as providing significant relief for some ill or that simply helped people feel much better. On the basis of evidence from scientifically limited clinical trials that were funded by the drug makers and with much less federal oversight than today, the drug was touted as a wonder drug. The drug was then promoted as being highly effective; more effective than anything that had come before. Its side effects were minimized or not yet well known and the drug was proclaimed to be safe and non-addicting. As the new drug rapidly gained popularity, it received positive press coverage that served to further increase its popularity. The press stories featured anecdotal reports from sometimes-prominent users who extolled the drug's benefits. As the drug's popularity continued to increase, black and gray markets developed to support the burgeoning demand leading to the illegal production and trafficking of the drug along parallel channels.

Over time, as more people used the drug and with greater frequency, the drug's serious side effects and limitations became apparent. The drug proved to be addicting after all and, when used under some circumstances such as in combination with alcohol, lethal. The problems the drug was designed to help manage better did not go away and, ultimately, were not alleviated to any great extent: work remained tedious; life's uncertainties, disappointments, and losses still led to anxiety and sadness; important relationships still could end poorly or remain unfulfilling. As evidence weighing against unfettered access to and over prescribing the drug and illegal distribution and use mounted, federal and state laws played catch-up to try and reign in the production, sale, and use of the drug.

The classes of prescription drugs Americans began using in the 1940s and 1950s, the successors of which they continue to use through the present day, became available as part of a trend toward the increased use of drugs to treat the full spectrum of psychiatric disorders and symptoms ranging from mild cases of depression and anxiety to profoundly disruptive conditions such as schizophrenia and major depression. The shift marked the beginnings of a movement in psychiatry away from Freudian psychoanalysis and other forms of "talk therapy" as well as from other less congenial interventions such as frontal lobotomy and insulin therapy toward using medication as the primary means of treatment. The drug chlorpromazine is perhaps the most famous example of this shift. Chlorpromazine is an antihistamine that was initially intended for use with anesthetics to boost their effectiveness and to reduce post-surgical shock and nausea. During clinical trials, its striking effectiveness reducing symptoms such as hallucinations and delusions seen in schizophrenia, bipolar disorder and other severe psychiatric disorders became readily apparent. In the mid-1950s, chlorpromazine was marketed under the trade name Thorazine as a treatment for psychotic disorders and quickly came into wide use for that purpose. It helped usher in—along with the creation of Medicaid and Social Security—what became the community mental health movement whereby large numbers of psychiatric patients who had been indefinitely consigned to hospital back wards could be discharged to the community. By any measure, Thorazine was a success although serious side effects that contributed to poor treatment adherence and ultimately to patients frequently recycling between the community and the hospital would become more apparent over time.

Like Thorazine, the discovery of the psychotropic effects (i.e., affecting emotional states, mood, and perceptions) of the drugs that came into wide use from 1940 to 1970 was accidental. For example, beta-phenylisopropylamine (i.e., amphetamine) was first synthesized in 1887 by a German chemist but its neurophysiological effects were not realized. It was rediscovered by chemist Dr. Gordon Alles in 1929 during his attempt to synthesize a drug that mimicked the effects of the naturally produced hormone adrenaline, which was useful as a decongestant and for treating asthma but which was difficult and expensive to harvest in quantity. One of the compounds he tested, amphetamine sulfate, worked reasonably well as a bronchodilator and decongestant.

Operating on a separate but parallel track, the pharmaceutical firm Smith, Kline, & French (SK&F) had developed a liquid form of amphetamine, which they marketed under the trade name Benzedrine. The drug was available to the public for the relief of nasal congestion in an inhaler that was used in the same way as decongestant inhalers are today. Initially a metal and subsequently a plastic tube encased a paper insert that had been soaked in liquid amphetamine. In this form, amphetamine is volatile and vaporizes when the tube is opened allowing for inhalation. Users seeking an immediate and potent high could easily crack open the Benzedrine inhaler and either ingest the amphetamine-laced paper directly or dissolve it in coffee or alcohol. The inhaler was sold over the counter until 1959 when mounting pressure from reports of abuse and addiction forced the Food and Drug Administration to require a prescription.

The solid form of amphetamine synthesized by Alles, amphetamine sulfate, was tested in clinical trials by SK&F to determine if it had other uses beyond being a decongestant. The testing revealed the drug also had the psychological effect of providing a sense of euphoria or well-being as Alles had jotted down in his notes when he first tested the drug on himself. Subjects also reported feeling more alert and energetic after taking amphetamine and perceived themselves to be more competent. Based on the results of these trials, SK&F aggressively and successfully marketed amphetamine to the general public as a treatment for mild cases of depression and for narcolepsy, a condition characterized by frequent and unpredictable episodes of drowsiness and falling asleep. When additional clinical trials revealed that amphetamine use promoted weight loss (at least in the short term), it was heavily marketed as a diet drug for treating obesity.

Amphetamine was widely used by the military in World War II to boost the energy and performance of the troops although there was scant clinical evidence the drug was effective for improving performance. It seemed, instead, that amphetamine users felt greater confidence and perceived themselves as being better able to perform assigned tasks when, in fact, their performance was no better than when they were not using the drug or when they used a milder stimulant such as caffeine. Nevertheless, the United States military—perhaps in the belief that amphetamine's temporary boost to morale and self-confidence were sufficient rationales—continued providing amphetamine to American soldiers and pilots throughout World War II, and persisted in providing it to American troops during the Vietnam War. At the beginning of World War II during their initial bombing runs over Great Britain, the German Luftwaffe had experimented with methamphetamine for use by their pilots to improve their alertness and combat fatigue for these long missions. But they eventually abandoned using the drug after a short time when they determined it was ineffective. Parenthetically, the discovery of the drug's ineffectiveness did not deter Adolph Hitler from receiving daily injections of methamphetamine from his personal physician, Theodor Morell. Great Britain's military also tested methamphetamine but came to a similar conclusion as the Germans and abandoned using it as well before the war's end.

Barbiturates were also prescribed widely in the 1950s and 1960s. Barbiturates are in the class of drugs known as sedative-hypnotics and their primary use is as tranquilizers and to induce sleep. They were often used to counteract the side effects of amphetamines and because of this many people used both drugs regularly. SK&F and other manufacturers made this a convenience by combining amphetamine with barbiturate into a single pill. SK&F's combination pill was called Dexamyl. In some respects, it was the medically prescribed equivalent of a "speedball" whereby injection drug users combine heroin with cocaine or another stimulant to attain a better, smoother high. The addition of barbiturate to amphetamine counteracted amphetamine's side effects like jitteriness and sleeplessness. Dexamyl was promoted as both an anti-depressant and as a diet aid. Drug manufacturers targeted much of their advertising toward some of their best customers, women, a point not lost on feminists who later decried such tactics as abusive. As one advertisement in a medical journal proclaimed, "Thanks to Dexamyl, she can say 'No thank you' to the praline sundae."

As successful as the promotions and sales of amphetamine and barbiturates were, they were far eclipsed by the first true blockbuster psychiatric drug. Meprobamate was a tranquilizer that was given a brand name based on the bucolic borough Milltown,

New Jersey near where it had first been developed at Wallace laboratories. (Wyeth, a competitor, also marketed meprobamate under the trade name Equanil.) Structurally, Miltown was similar to another drug discovered while looking for compounds that could preserve penicillin from rapidly deteriorating and losing potency. Miltown was introduced in 1954 and became wildly popular shortly thereafter. It was the toast of the town in Hollywood and elsewhere. Milton Berle, a popular comedian and television personality at the time and known as Uncle Miltie is quoted in a 1956 *Time* magazine article as avidly promoting Miltown stating it had been so good to him, he was considering changing his name to Miltown Berle.

At its peak, Miltown was so popular that pharmacies rationed the drug and placed signs outside to indicate when they did not have any left in stock to avoid facing disappointed throngs of customers. Miltown's rapid rise was followed by an equally rapid fall owing to its soon-discovered high potential for misuse and addiction. No worries! Waiting in the wings to quickly take its place were the benzodiazepines, a different drug class but also prescribed for their tranquilizing effects and as muscle relaxants. Marketed under the still familiar trade names such as Librium and Valium, benzodiazepines continue to be prescribed for millions and while they have legitimate medical purposes, they have also been overprescribed and have considerable potential for misuse.

Stimulants such as Benzedrine, tranquilizers such as Miltown, and barbiturates such as Nembutal were used regularly and legally by millions of Americans at the peak of their popularity in the 1960s. In his detailed history of amphetamine use in the United States, Nicholas Rasmussen provides figures that indicate the extent to which these drugs were being used. Rasmussen writes that in 1963, 15 percent of the adult U.S. population (30 million) was taking prescription drugs for psychiatric problems. These figures do not take into account the additional millions of Americans who used the same or equivalent drugs after acquiring them illegally without a prescription. For many Americans then, as the decade of the 1950s came to a close and transitioned into the 1960s, these truly were *Happy Days*, albeit drug-induced and courtesy of pharmaceutical manufacturers, their physicians, and their local drug stores.

The 1960s has long been characterized as a time of transition marked by the escalation of a growingly unpopular war and turbulent social changes punctuated by jarring events: the assassinations of President Kennedy, his brother Robert Kennedy, and civil rights leaders Malcolm X and Martin Luther King; the Tate-LaBianca murders; and the Watts riots. Further reflecting the transitional character of the era, drug policy-related legislation enacted during the sixties marked a clear change from the increasingly punitive legislation enacted in the fifties. The Kennedy and Johnson administrations and Congress moved closer to the view that drug addiction was a public health concern and not solely a moral issue or criminal justice problem. However, even under these two rather liberal administrations, America's drug policy continued to emphasize a criminal justice approach.

Further underscoring that this was a time of change for drug policy was the retirement in 1962 of Harry Anslinger who, from his post as Commissioner of the Federal Bureau of Narcotics (FBN), had dominated federal (and state) drug policy for over three decades. His successor was pharmacist Henry Giordano, who began in the FBN as an undercover field agent charged with capturing drug kingpins. Giordano rose through the ranks of the FBN, eventually becoming a Deputy before being named the new Commissioner by President Kennedy. Giordano held conservative, pro-law enforcement views and strongly resisted proposed changes to the FBN. However, his power was much diminished under the Johnson administration, which would eventually abolish the FBN and redistribute its functions to new agencies within the Departments of Justice and Health Education and Welfare.

Several important events led up to the passage of the Drug Control Amendments of 1965 that set the tone for subsequent legislation. In 1962, President Kennedy, fulfilling a campaign promise, convened a two-day White House Conference to bring together leading experts to evaluate and discuss drug policy, problems, and possible solutions. The Conference led to the appointment of a Presidential Advisory Commission on Narcotic and Drug Abuse in January 1963. Also known as the Prettyman Commission for its chair, Judge E. Barrett Prettyman, the Commission issued a final report only a few weeks before President Kennedy's assassination in November 1963. It would not be published until January 1964 under the Johnson administration. The final report included 25 recommendations some of which called for reorganization of and better coordination among the departments and agencies, such as the FBN, that handled drug-related issues. Reflecting a greater emphasis on a public health approach, seven of the recommendations dealt specifically with the need for expanding treatment and rehabilitation. The recommendations also included repealing mandatory minimum sentences for low-level dealers and users and for civil commitment laws by which convicted drug law violators could be sentenced to participate in treatment rather than incarceration. This recommendation would be incorporated into the Narcotic Addict Rehabilitation Act of 1966, which provided for civil commitment in lieu of prosecution for addicts charged with nonviolent criminal offenses and for civil commitment to treatment for convicted addicts in lieu of sentencing to prison. The Act was restrictive in terms of who qualified, however, and the results of the civil commitment program were, at best, mixed.

Most relevant to the Drug Abuse Control Amendments of 1965 is the following recommendation, excerpted from the Commission's Interim Report: "The Commission recommends that all drugs which are medically useful and valuable but which have a potential for abuse resulting in psychotoxic and antisocial behavior should be brought under strict control by Federal statute" (p. 10).

The interim report continues on to note that laws in existence were covered under the Food, Drug, and Cosmetics Act, but that despite this act's requirement that the drugs should be sold and dispensed by prescription only, there was "nonetheless, extensive illicit sales of these drugs." The 1965 Amendments sought to directly address this issue. Included among the Amendments' provisions was the creation of the Bureau of Drug Abuse Control (BDAC), located within the Food and Drug Administration, to provide oversight for the new laws governing the production of prescription stimulants and tranquilizers. As drug policy historian David Musto has pointed out, however, this arrangement soon led to conflicts between BDAC and the FBN. Drug traffickers do not always divide their trade into channels that neatly correspond to federal or state law. The same dealer could, for instance, sell amphetamine (under the purview of BDAC) and marijuana (under the purview of FBN) leading to the conundrum of which agency should have jurisdiction. BDAC's existence was short-lived. After its formation in 1968, it was merged with the Federal Bureau of Narcotics into the Bureau of Narcotics and Dangerous Drugs (BNDD), the predecessor of the Drug Enforcement Administration (DEA) formed in 1973.

DR. MAX JACOBSON (AKA DR. FEELGOOD)—"HE'S STILL MY GOD"

If you lived in New York City in the 1950s and 1960s and, in particular, if you were a celebrity of some note wanting a pick-me-up, Dr. Max Jacobson was your guy. Receiving his medical training in Germany and immigrating to the United States in 1936, Dr. Jacobson set up shop on the Upper East Side of Manhattan. He was known as a personable, empathic physician with a warm bedside manner and good listening skills. His thriving practice was restricted to seeing outpatients, as he never established an affiliation with any hospital. His specialty was injecting patients with concoctions that consisted of varying amounts of vitamins, placenta, steroids, and methamphetamine. His preference for methamphetamine reflected his European training. At that time methamphetamine was more popular in Europe than amphetamine. For patients whose growing dependence required frequent, sometimes daily injections, Dr. Jacobson would provide them with vials of the mixture and a prescription for syringes so they could self-inject at home. Patients were never told exactly what was in the mixtures and many believed they were receiving only vitamins and enzymes.

Dr. Jacobson was especially fond of cultivating celebrity patients with whom he liked to hobnob. In this regard, he was extremely successful. His patient list included author Truman Capote, Congressman Claude Pepper of Florida, movie director Cecile B. DeMille, playwright Tennessee Williams (who sometimes had to be refused treatment because he showed up intoxicated), and entertainer Eddie Fisher who wrote "He's still my God" on a poster that was on display at Dr. Jacobson's wedding to his third wife.

Dr. Jacobson's most famous patient, however, was President John F. Kennedy. President Kennedy was plagued by a number of serious and debilitating medical conditions such as Addison's disease, a chronic endocrine disorder that results in fatigue, muscle weakness, and joint pain among its other symptoms. The reality of a chronically ill, physically weak President ran counter to the public image of a youthful, vigorous presence in the White House. Dr. Jacobson had just the tonic and began treating President Kennedy in 1960. His treatment included providing Kennedy with an injection just prior to Kennedy's debate with Richard Nixon; an appearance that is often credited with helping Kennedy narrowly defeat Nixon for the Presidency that same year. Jacobson would continue to provide Kennedy with injections over

(continued)

The Drug Abuse Control Amendments of 1965 recognized the country's sizeable problem with the illegal manufacturing, sale, and use of prescription drugs. But ironically, it was moot on the much more substantial problem of prescription drug abuse when the drugs were produced and obtained legally through the main source of such drugs, the pharmaceutical industry. Legislation that brought greater oversight to the pharmaceutical industry would come several years later. In the meantime, the use and abuse of prescription drugs, particularly amphetamine and tranquilizers, and of LSD, marijuana, and heroin, would continue to grow unabated through the end of the decade and well into the 1970s.

A culture that encouraged drug use to improve mood, lose weight, increase stamina and productivity, and get some rest when needed, helped set the stage for younger Americans to congregate in the city of San Francisco in January 1967 for a "Be-In." There, at least initially, they would celebrate a growing countercultural movement that was motivated in part by the belief that drugs, particularly hallucinogenic drugs like LSD, were tools for expanding consciousness, leading to a new vision that would in turn lead to the creation of a better, more personally fulfilling and just social order. It didn't end in exactly that way.

FURTHER READING

Angell, M. (2006). *The truth about the drug companies: How they deceive us and what to do about it*. New York: Random House.

Dallek, R. (2004). *An unfinished life: Kennedy, 1917–1963*. New York: Back Bay Books.

DeGrandpre, R. (2006). *The cult of pharmacology: How America became the world's most troubled drug nation*. Durham, NC: Duke University Press.

Frank, G. (1999). *Judy*. New York: Da Capo Press.

Herzberg, D. (2007). *Happy pills in America: From Miltown to Prozac*. Baltimore, MD: Johns Hopkins University Press.

Musto, D. F., & Korsmeyer, P. (2002). *The quest for drug control: Politics and Federal policy in a period of increasing substance abuse, 1963–1981*. New Haven, CT: Yale University Press.

President's advisory commission on narcotic and drug abuse—final report. (1963). Washington, DC: Government Printing Office.

Rasmussen, N. (2009). *On speed: The many lives of amphetamine*. New York: New York University Press.

Rensenberger, B. (1972, December 4). Amphetamines used by a physician to lift moods of famous patients, *New York Times*, 1, 34–35.

Speaker, S. (1997). From "Happiness Pills" to "National Nightmare": Changing cultural assessment of minor tranquilizers in America, 1955–1980. *Journal of the History of Medicine and Allied Sciences*, *52*, 338–376.

Tone, A. (2009). *The age of anxiety: America's turbulent affair with tranquilizers*. New York: Basic Books.

DR. MAX JACOBSON (AKA DR. FEELGOOD)— "HE'S STILL MY GOD"

(continued)

the next few years. He also treated first lady Jacqueline Kennedy as well as other members of the Kennedy family. As quoted by Robert Dallek in his book, *The Kennedy Presidency,* when brother Robert Kennedy and others in Kennedy's personal inner circle expressed their concerns over the safety and mysterious ingredients in Jacobson's injections, Kennedy replied: "I don't care if it's horse piss. It works."

On the Internet

Bruce Jackson's article "White collar pill party" describes a Hollywood party circa the 1960s where pills are the center of attention: http://www.theatlantic.com/past/docs/issues/66aug/pparty.htm.

The April 1963 Interim Report of the President's Commission on Narcotics and Drug Abuse is available from the John F. Kennedy Presidential Library and Museum at: http://www.jfklfoundation.org/Search.aspx?nav=N:4294953483.

A *New Yorker* magazine article on how pharmaceuticals are priced and marketed: http://www.newyorker.com/archive/2004/10/25/041025crat_atlarge?currentPage=2.

A May 2011 article in *Vanity Fair Magazine* describing Judy Garland's memorable 1961 performance at Carnegie Hall as well as the toll drugs took on her is available at: http://www.vanityfair.com/hollywood/features/2011/05/judy-garland-201105.

Details on Dr. Max Jacobson's amphetamine "treatments" for President John F. Kennedy as well as a brief history of the discovery and rise in popularity of amphetamine is available at: http://www.semp.us/publications/biot_reader.php?BiotID=678.

A *Time* magazine article "Medicine Don't-Give-a-Damn Pills" describes the popularity of the new "miracle drug" Miltown in 1956: http://www.time.com/time/magazine/article/0,9171,866832,00.html.

National Institute on Drug Abuse Research Report Series. (2001, July). *Prescription drugs abuse and addiction* (NIH Publication No. 05-4881). Bethesda, MD: U.S. Department of Health and Human Services, National Institutes of Health. http://www.nida.nih.gov/ResearchReports/Prescription/Prescription.html.

"We Really Thought That Drugs Were Going to Change the World"

- ***Document:*** "Inside the Hippie Revolution," *Look Magazine*
- ***Date:*** Summer 1967
- ***Where:*** Haight-Ashbury and elsewhere, San Francisco, California
- ***Significance:*** The summer of 1967 came to be called the "summer of love." That summer, tens of thousands of mostly young Americans converged on the Haight-Ashbury district in San Francisco, California. They came for many reasons: to show their dissatisfaction with a society they believed was materialistic and spiritually empty; to protest the escalating war in Vietnam; to experiment with an alternative communal lifestyle; or to simply be at the epicenter of what was perceived as an historic moment and turning point in our nation's history. Drugs played a prominent role. In particular, LSD and other psychedelic drugs, were promoted, most famously by Timothy Leary but by many others, as the means for attaining higher levels of consciousness, expanding awareness, fostering personal growth, and increasing spirituality. Advocates believed those who experienced drug-induced psychological changes would then have the self-awareness, vision and insight to change society for the better. However, by the end of the summer the large crowds overwhelmed the city's infrastructure. What had been intended as a noble experiment to engender social change instead drifted into excess, purposelessness, drug use for its own sake, and living conditions that went beyond squalid. The "summer of love" became both the high water mark as well as the beginning of the end of the countercultural movement by which the decade of the 1960s would come to be characterized. William Hedgepeth was a young reporter for *Look Magazine* sent undercover to report on the

events in Haight-Ashbury during the "summer of love." Following is the account he wrote of his experiences.

DOCUMENT

Inside the Hippie Revolution

By William Hedgepeth

Heeeere, Jake. Lovely thing. La, la, la, lee. Come to sissy, beautiful, gorgeous red love. Oh star in heaven. La, la, dee, dee, dee, dee."

It was all wispy and faint at first, and I couldn't tell where the oddly liberated little singsong voice was coming from until I had groped through the thick vines and greenery nearly all the way down into the small secluded glen, almost to the edge of the tiny, lily-padded lake. There, over near the trees at one end of the lake—with her head almost hidden by the low-hanging branches and her legs mostly covered by patches of high grass and tall yellow flowers—a brightly beaded, long-haired, Ophelia-like girl of about 19 or 20 knelt in an orange-and-blue robe knotting in a 15-foot-long chain of flower blossoms and reeling off detached, mindless little utterances in a soft, girlish voice. The only other sound was the dim, slow wail of a harmonica from the far end of the glen where a lone boy with shoulder-length hair sat on a rock improvising a Southern Negro-style blues tune.

I was fairly near the girl now, but as I got closer, I realized she was skimming farther and farther away in her drug-stretched mind. "Oh, loo, loo, blue, blue, blue. Jakejakejakejake," she sang with her deranged eyes still fixed on the lengthening flower chain in her hands. Suddenly, out of a thick clump of bushes, bounded a huge Irish setter—Jake, apparently—what was just far enough away so that I was able to claw my way wildly back up the bank and out of the valley before he had a chance to pounce on me.

A young hippie couple enjoy a festival in San Francisco's Golden Gate Park on August 8, 1967, during what became known as the Summer of Love. The countercultural movement that embraced drug use as a means for expanding consciousness arguably reached its peak that summer after which it quickly devolved into hedonism, incoherence, and drug abuse. Nevertheless, social changes brought on by the countercultural movement, including drug use, and the conservative backlash against these changes continue to reverberate through the present day. (AP/Wide World Photos)

Earlier that morning, I had strolled into San Francisco's huge Golden Gate Park—which borders the Haight-Ashbury district—with a barefoot, blanketed veteran hippie from Minneapolis named MacGregor, who claimed a major portion of his waking hours were usually spent wandering through the foliage or rolling down the park's grassy slopes. "Man, just smell all the flowers and all the dope," he smiled as soon as we passed between the stone pillars at the Haight St. entrance. The morning fog had cleared and scores of other hippies were walking about to the soft accompaniment of their jangling, ankle bells or sunning themselves on the ground or gathered in tiny groups under the bushes smoking "grass" (marijuana) or clustered in larger numbers around the endless, hypnotic beating of bongo drums, with each one lost in the swirl of his own private planetary orbit.

MacGregor and I walked through the clearing into a woodsy area and up hills and over fences until we came upon what seemed an infinity of huge bushes bursting with pink and white rhododendrons and blue hyacinths and vivid explosions of yellows and reds and purples. Almost as if on cue, though without thinking, we separated and faded wordlessly into the flowers to become lost in the thick maze of colors, making absentminded figure eight's and lazy circles. I drifted out later on to a wooded path and was maneuvering back to the park entrance when I saw coming toward me two girls in sandals and somber, full-length gowns. They would have looked like women from India if it had not been for the large, clanging cowbells around their necks and the drug-induced lumpy litheness of their walk. As we passed, one of them glanced up at me with a benign smile and warm, dazed-looking eyes, and without breaking stride, cooed, "I love you." and floated away without waiting for a reply—which saved me some embarrassment, since my initial, stunned, stupid reaction was to mutter, "Well . . . uh . . . uh . . . thank you" in a lame, small voice. At that point, I had been living in Haight-Ashbury only two days, and in spite of my beads and long hair and short beard, I was still a blatant amateur as hippies go.

Two days earlier, it had been even worse. Less than an hour and a half after flying in from New York and dressing for the part, I bounced out of a cab at Haight and Ashbury Streets, and the best I had been able to do was ogle openmouthed at the wild, shaggy milling and dancing up and down Haight, the major avenue of the largest hippie ghetto in the world. ("Haight is love," and signs everywhere.) After a few minutes, a hairy fellow with a ring in his nose and red designs painted on his cheeks stopped and asked me for some help in raising his rent money. In return, he directed me to the free store where he said I could get some food and a place to "crash" that night.

The free store is exactly that: Anything in the place is yours if you need it—second- and thirdhand clothing of any description, old magazines and books and whatever food may be lying around. The store is run by the Diggers, a sort of hippie civic association whose members spend their time scrounging about for clothes and other goods they can give away.

Since it was chilly, I had bought a blanket in town, and now I took a straw hat and an old suit coat several sizes too large. I was hungry and was about to ask where one could get something to eat when a ragged, dumpy-looking, straggle-haired girl with wire-rim glasses and feathers in her headband loped into the store carrying a sack. She plopped it in the middle of the room and, with an air of shy authority as she started back out the door, said "Food." Then she disappeared down the street as everyone in the store leaped to the bagful of cookies and peanut butter and radishes.

After wolfing down the groceries I could get hold of, I asked a tall, intense-looking hippie beside me if he knew of a place to sleep. At once, his eyes widened as he leaned toward me conspiratorially and asked in a low voice, "Have you ever done any writing?" I said yes, I had, and before I could say anything more, we were half-way down the street on the way to his pad. He told his name was Dunbar, and thanks to this meeting, I not only now had a nice piece of messy floor to sleep on, with about eight other semipermanent hippie tenants, but also a job as a writer for Fusion magazine, an underground hip publication for which he was assembling enough material to put out a first issue. The total contents at this point consisted of 30 terrible poems, a maudlin story about a coyote and an incomprehensible essay. But Dunbar had just acquired a tiny portable typewriter, and so things seemed to him to be looking up, journalistically speaking.

The next morning, I set out to find some good material for Fusion. But before leaving the pad, I made the mistake of asking the time from a hippie who had just washed his beard and was strolling around aimlessly thumping a tambourine. He looked astonished and said, "Naw, man we never know what time it is." As I came to learn, time is one of many things that mean nothing here. The days blur namelessly into one another without regard to date or hour or light or darkness.

It was worth the effort, however, to find out when Sundays rolled around because of all-day "happenings" that were staged in the Panhandle, a narrow strip of land extending from the park. Hundreds of hippies would gravitate to the Panhandle each Sunday and huddle around a large truck that served as the stage for one or more local rock groups. Rock music—referred to as "love-rock" or "acid-rock"—is a vital ingredient in this whole way of life.

In its ideal form—fast and almost too loud for the normal ear to withstand—it blanks the mind, stuns the senses and forcibly reaches out and commandeers all the nerve fibers and viscera of the body, so that you find yourself leaping and twitching to the contagious drum-thump-twang rhythm with total and unconscious abandon.

This Sunday's program features a nondescript group of makes with hair shagging well past their shoulder blades. Without a word of warning, they ripped out their electronically amplified guitar-drum-bass beat through a solid phalanx of five-foot-tall speakers systems, powered by a portable generator chugging away behind the truck bed. As the pelvic pulsing began to soak into the audience, a narcotized girl in Levis, wearing only a loose poncho with nothing underneath, and a glassy-eyed rail of a boy dangling a single unfired flashbulb on a cord around his neck began writhing in a trancelike rhythmic rite around an old bicycle tire lying on the ground. Other dancers began at once to flap and jump and gyrate in stuporous ecstasy and dead seriousness with eyes half-closed, oblivious to everyone, including their partners.

The rock group geared up and poured themselves into a long, improvised, semi-melodic stream of notes held together only by the steady, flagrantly sensual reverberating beat of the drums. Propelled by shear atavistic instinct, everyone danced or shook or rolled uncontrollably on the ground. It was an infectious Indian ritual in which all—momentarily—were warriors. A grandmother type twitched her shoulders like a Ziegfeld Follies flapper. An elderly work-a-daddy in a wide-brimmed hat and a 1940's-style suit, who had just stopped to watch, began waving his arms at the sky like a Hallelujah shouter at a Baptist camp meeting. Everything became a part of this expanding megabeat momentum that built up and up and on and on until, at last, the day cooled and darkened and the frenzy calmed and the music quieted and those of the crowd who were still able to walk inched their way back to Haight St.

I walked back with Rick, a small, wiry artist wearing circular earrings, and Kathy, his pregnant, unofficial wife. Kathy had admired the colorful Indian-design blanket I had around me, which established, as far as we three were concerned, a lifelong bond of affection. Although it didn't seem to bother them, they had less than a dollar between them and were going to be evicted from their pad the next day, along with about 30 others, for nonpayment of rent. When I heard this, I have them half of the $20 in my wallet. Thinking I was homeless, they responded by inviting me to spend the night at their place. (I later learned they used part of my $10 to buy food and drugs and then gave the rest to people they thought were destitute.)

Unlike Dunbar's pad, full of sober utopian-minded idealists ("Let's abolish money; let's set up pilot communities of love all over the country," etc.), Rick and Kathy's place was a filthy litter-strewn, swarming dope fortress that was a good deal less savory and sanitary than a sewer, since people attempted to live in it. Along the hallway when we walked in there was at least a half-dozen hippies lying in various stages of drug stupor. And in the darkened bedrooms, blank-faced males and females sat stupefied on the floors as rock music howled full volume from radios and hundreds of flies churned through the layers of sweet-smelling marijuana smoke. A past face in a coonskin cap rolled a fresh "joint" of grass and passed it around for all to smoke, except for two in the corner who were shooting their arm veins full of "speed," or Methedrine, a super powerful pep drug.

About one that morning, "The Bat" drifted into the pad, accompanied by two Negro hip types, one of whom I was told had been a "nark" (narcotics agent) until he became turned on to the glories of "acid" (LSD) and other glories of the inner universe. The Bat wore an ankle-length black cape with a little red collar poking up into thick kinky black hair that poofed out about eight inches on each side of his head. The Bat was so stoned when he arrived that he was talking in a whiny, scary falsetto voice—yet whatever he had been taking still wasn't enough. Around five a.m., I woke up briefly to catch sight of him sitting in the hall, wrapped in his cape, talking in an even higher falsetto than before and shooting sugared water into the veins of his neck, since he had run out of real drugs as well as available places to stick the needle. Each time he injected himself, he would moan "Ooooohhh, ooooohhh, this is my thing . . . this is my thing," and would "freak out" by rolling around the floor, thrashing and flopping and hooting like an owl.

By the time everyone came to and cleared out the next morning, the pad had been rented by a burly hippie named Ed, who made good money hanging pennants for used-car lots. Rick, Kathy and I had met Ed the night before, and now we were asked to be the nucleus of a new communal "family"—under the condition that we would keep our rooms clean and not allow any friends to the pad who happened to be "speed freaks." Taking too much Methedrine over a time can cause bizarre mental effects of blow people's minds so that they end up walking around like wild freaky vegetables. Speed is not a hallucinatory drug and is avoided not only by most hippies but even by the strangely non-violent variety of Hell's Angels who wander around the "Hashbury."

With these ground rules, our new communal family took shape. One of the earlier residents, a genial dealer in grass and acid named Janice, asked if she could live in the hall closet where she could close herself in and not bother with people when she was coming off a drug high. Frank, a soft-spoken Venezuelan, also asked to stay, though he was not particular about his sleeping arrangements. It turned out that he rarely slept anyway. He spent his days panhandling on Haight St. and his evenings slumped in the front hall hopped up on one chemical or another, endlessly drawing pictures of Jesus in pencil or adding to some interminable prose work he was writing in Spanish—while a radio pumped constant rock music into his ears.

Rabbit, a Bostonian with a voice like Bullwinkle the moose, and Linda, his chick, moved in a few days later. When I first saw them, they were both so stoned and giggly on acid that they seemed lost and helpless. First, he tried selling hippie papers on Haight St., and then he became a full-time panhandler; but no matter what he did, at the end of the day, he would almost always wind up giving away the money he had collected. Then he would come home and mope hungrily until someone gave him some food.

Somehow, our pad soon became an all-night civic center for itinerant speed freaks. When Kathy, who was pregnant, became a steady speed user, I gave her a bottle of vitamins I had brought to ward off creeping malnutrition. I don't know if I looked underfed—actually, I had been eating huge quantities of rice as well as some cans of chicken-flavored cat food that wasn't bad at all. And if that weren't enough, I could go to the Panhandle around four every day to fight my way to the day-old bread and free pots of food left over from restaurants, all of which the Diggers collected and served up to hungry hippies and to any brooding, groggy, middle-aged winos who happened to be standing around. Nevertheless, Rick became concerned about my health and offered to suggest a drug to suit my mood. "Man," he said, "you know I feel everyone's my better half. Like we're all part of the same sideshow. I mean there may be some who'd call you and me freaks and maybe we are. But by whose standards? LBJ and his boys? I think what you need is some smack, some scag. Groovy stuff. If you're feeling up-tight, it makes you loose and fills in all the blank spaces." I asked him if scag was like acid and he said, "No, man, no. It's smack, you know, smack—heroin, man!"

I declined, but Rick didn't mind since he was feeling pepped up and philosophical. As he looked around his and Kathy's room, with its religious symbols and drawings all over the walls, he changed pace and said, "Hell, this isn't what we want—to live like this. This isn't our whole trip. We're out to bust up the concrete, man—to let the flowers grow. What we're really looking for is a new beginning."

He winced and shook his head. "Everything's too sterile. Man's creative spirit is being destroyed. He's become so unnatural that he's freaked out the order of the universe, and now the universe is trying to restore itself. A radical change is taking place in this generation. Middle-aged people just can't accept that their children are prophesying to them. The proof is that there's no communication between the generations." Rick was prancing fiercely around his room, and a candle on the floor cast his shadow huge against the wall. "Back to the land!" he shouted as his shadow gestured wildly. "I'll groove with the elements." He paused and said more quietly, "We're a threat to the world, you know. But it's God's plan. There are more people 25 and under now that there are of 'Them.'"

The dark reference to "Them" means the "straight people, the non-hip, tuned-out guardians of the Establishment and the status quo—in other words, just about everyone else. Straight society is seen here as an irrelevant, cruel, sneaky, dehumanizing, soul-devouring fraud. The hippies' attitude toward it is not one of rebellion but of rejection. "The Establishment's falling apart. Why fool with it?" my friend MacGregor had said. To take its place, hippies are working toward an open, loving, tension-free, nature-oriented world of their own. On an individual basis, each hippie simply seeks to "do his thing"—to lead the private, personalized way of life that grooves him and turns him on. Out of respect for this, hippie philosophy cautions that "you don't try to force your 'thing' on anyone else." On this basis, a few hippie zealots have been persuaded, at least for the moment, to abandon their idea of polluting San Francisco's water system with enough LSD to turn the whole straight city on.

But the straight people are not similarly content to leave the Hashbury in peace. Every day—and unbearably so on Sundays—Haight St. is choked with automobiles stuffed with sightseers who snap photos of the hippies from behind locked car doors and window glass rolled up as tightly as if this were a tour through the reptile house at the zoo. Little children peer wide-eyed from the back seat; white-haired grannies stare in near shock with mouths agape; Mr. and Mrs. So-and-so in the front seat point and smirk nervously in their voyeurism—and then they talk of returning next week.

Of course, there are a number of would-be hippies and mixed-up teenyboppers who dress outlandishly on the weekends and drive over to the Hashbury so they can parade around gaudily and feed the public's "image" appetite. But these types usually don't know what's going on any more than the tourists. They may have even nodded approvingly with the "respectable" citizenry when a local politician described by the press as a "smiling 48-year-old Republican," announced his candidacy for mayor and "came out four-square against hippies."

That the generation gap yawns widest here was proved further when the transit company announced in June that certain bus lines were to be rerouted to avoid "the Sodom of Haight-Ashbury." This fearful and distorted public view of the whole scene came home to me very pointedly when a writer on contract to a confession magazine picked me as a candidate for an interview, and then went on to ask questions too sexual and bizarre to repeat here. Within the limits of decency and accuracy and fantasy, I "confessed" to everything she suggested and everything I could think of—except that I was with Look—until she left, satisfied and smacking her lips.

Besides the nameless strangers who would be found each morning sleeping all over the floors, our family took in some new members. The first was Don, a sophisticated East Coast hippie who was a large-scale dealer in drugs. Morton, a practicing Buddhist from Chicago, served to help the rest of us get high each night by leading us in The Great Mantra, a slow, hypnotic Buddhist chant. Eileen was an 18-year-old who served any kind of cloth she could get her hands on. And finally, there was a second Kathy, who wore glasses. The Kathy With Glasses was a mystical sort of borderline paranoid who—when she was not immersed in her comic books—spouted dark intuitive revelations. A suspicious, paranoid style of thinking is really very common here, partly because hippies are so passive in almost all that they do. When they are on "trips," the drugs are the agents in control; in their normal states, their emotions are allowed to direct their actions. The Establishment is seen as controlling the country as a whole; and on the local level, the hippies' almost-unanimous faith in astrology and fatalism further convinces them they are powerless to cope with anything that might happen.

Kathy With Glasses, among others, claims to have a vision predicting that the President was going to declare war sometime this summer, at which time the hippies—as vocal pacifists—would be branded as traitors and herded into concentration camps. She also foresaw a colossal earthquake that would send part of the State of California sliding into the Pacific Ocean. No one really minded the earthquake idea especially, but the concentration-camp business was a source of genuine fear within the community.

In spite of these omens, the hippies all share the confident belief that they are on the right astrological track and that their gentle, anachronistic mode of life is in line with the universal plan. In the life-style they are evolving, in which the goal is not to hoard but to contribute, survival is no problem and money is of no special value. Happiness, to them, is not just the old material goal of "three hots and a place to flop," it is a matter of what you can create and give to other people.

But what do you do?" I heard visitors on the street asking hippies over and over again. Actually as far as regular jobs are concerned, a great many work for the Post Office Department. Otherwise, they may play in rock bands, sell papers to tourists, get unemployment checks, receive money from home, deal in drugs, or panhandle on the street. There is a Hip Job Co-op that acts as a low-key employment service. But the general motto in all things is "Don't do it if it doesn't groove ya."

What the hippies say they are "doing" in the more important sense is living creatively, experimenting with new styles of living and generally appreciating the wonder and changeability of human life. The have consciously "dropped out," or detached themselves from what they consider the regimented, stultifying, dog-eat-dog "games" of the straight world, and have redefined "progress" and "success" in purely human terms. No boundaries are drawn between art and life. Everyone is creative and can realize his own full creative potential in everything he does, whether it is scandal making or song-writing. Hippie paintings and music are created not for public display but for the supreme private joy of spontaneous artistic creation itself.

To a large extent, this road to hippieness may be a one-way avenue: To some who have made the trip, the straight life may seem totally artificial, biologically unsound and suitable only for dropping out of. Straight life, I the eyes of most hippies, is a long stifling process designed to thwart and hem in all that is natural and spontaneous in humans. They believe that social conditioning, mass taste-making and indoctrination steadily stunt and narrow the individual human potential, with the result that society itself has become fragmented, specialized and narrow—and thereby tense, alienated and lonely. By contrast, as Rick put it, "Hippies don't separate and pigeonhole and categorize. All is one. All is love. And love is where it's at."

If life to the hippies has any "purpose" in the ordinary context of the word, the purpose is religious discovery. For religion is not only consciousness-expanding but it offers a further sense of identification and common understanding among those who have "seen the light." To the hippies, LSD is a sort of sacrament, which, as one 35-trip veteran said, "turns the keys to the inner doors." It's impossible to say what each individual finds behind his own door—that's "his thing" or "his trip." But basically, an acid voyage breaks down the ego and, as Court, an on-and-off padmate put it, "lifts the veil of illusion to show the holiness and oneness of the universe."

Most others claim the psychedelic experience reveals a unity with God, an effusion of joy and a feeling of love, compassion and identity with everything. Darlene said: "It's like seeing the world again through a child's eyes—a transcendental glory. A wonder. Everything all at once. Oh, beautiful." (I met Darlene in the faint early grayness of the morning as she sifted through sand crystals in the park with her senses far out in space on a magic carpet of acid.)

The common denominator in the psychedelic experience, whether achieved through hallucinatory drugs or grass or religious chanting or sex—with sex as the most accessible of psychedelics among hippies. Psychedelic drugs are used by some as an immediate plunge into the sensation of personal divinity and fusion with the universe, as sought by Eastern religions—a sort of instant Buddhist satori, available at last through the chemical fruits of American technology. To others, acid is an avenue to primitive Christianity. In the park, I fell in with about 40 hippies all sitting on the ground rhythmically pounding the concrete sidewalk with rocks and tin cans to the chant: "Let's all be Jesus till it starts to hurt." Two nuns stopped and smiled and swished slightly in their black robes as they patted their feet to the tin-can beat before passing on. "I mean, some guy dies for you, it can't help but turn you on emotionally, man," one of the pounders said to me.

Allen Cohen, the editor of the hippie Oracle, has been in the Hashbury almost from the start of the movement. He calls this a "prophetic community." The Victorian-era houses in this lower-middle-class run-down neighborhood were large enough and cheap enough to be rented by family-style groups of young people who soon learned to live and think and trust each other and act communally. More and more of the young were attracted until they realized that this new common unity there were developing was a "different style of life than the whole culture had."

When LSD came on the scene in 1963, its power to "decondition the mind" to old social values of separatism and individualism, he said, led its users to a greater personal trust in the deep feelings and desires of men that had been smothered in straight society. Also LSD "taps and releases the collective unconsciousness. If you feel, on your trip, the Indian or the peasant or Christ within yourself, you can don the robes and see how it feels to be that person and to discover his inner meaning for use in your own life."

The hippies' belief in the spiritual oneness of all men makes any kind of violence or aggressiveness appear as a monstrous biological crime. In the same way, property ownership and the financial arrangements of society lead to a sense of separation and tension among people. As Cohen insisted, "Human beings must be ready to give away the property they think they own but which no one really owns except God."

The whole Hashbury scene is one of rapid, constant, fluid change. The evolution of the movement thus far has led hundreds to apply their sense of unity with themselves and with nature by setting up communal farms. Even further evolutionary developments are the Indian-style "tribes" of hippies now springing up in remote rural areas—"an instinctive response by the human organism to a society that's become unnatural." as one tribesman called it.

For Haight-Ashbury to remain the same next year would signal a failure of this whole hippie experiment in gentle anarchy. Even while I was there, the "short-hairs," the college kids on vacation and the teenyboppers with braces on their teeth and brand-new beads around their necks, were showering in by the thousands, looking for excitement or all that loose sex they'd heard about or a place to hide from the draft board. The important upshot of this is that the gurus and older hippies are steadily moving elsewhere, making new converts and turning new people on. For unlike the nihilistic "Beat Generation" of the 1950s, this is a proselytizing, revolutionary kind of soft-sell Mass Movement. What it offers, the hippies say, are new depths of sensitivity and feeling between people and new styles of perception. But along with the abstract ideas of this crusade, there are casualties. Cases of hepatitis and syphilis are nearly keeping pace with the hippie population growth; immature minds are sometimes permanently derailed almost every day by powerful chemicals their users neither understand nor often can even pronounce; and in many cases, the Hashbury becomes simply a sanctuary for the shiftless.

Still, there is an enormous "spill over" of hippie art and music and language into the otherwise straight world. Amid the swirling colored lights of San Francisco's Fillmore Auditorium, surrounded by hippies with their long hair flopping up and down and their beads and amulets jangling, admen and bank-teller types dance to the visceral, biologic rock beat of groups like the Grateful Dead or Moby Grape.

"The hippies are more honest with themselves than anyone else is, " said the cab-driver who carried me, in hippie attire, from the Hashbury for the last time. "Most people spend all their time working and then enjoy life only as a sideline. With the hippies, life comes first, and work is the sideline."

The driver had picked me up at one of the sandal shops on Haight St., where I was saying good-bye to some of my friends and padmates. "I'll tell you what we'll do," one of them wearing a cape and a long blonde beard said to me as we walked outside. "I'll send you something in the mail in a few weeks. There may not be anything in the envelope, but be sure to lick the stamp. I'll put some acid on it, and I guarantee it'll turn you on. Don't forget."

The cab started down Haight St. I looked back to see my hippie friend growing smaller in the distance, with his hands cupped to his mouth, yelling the reminder: "LICK . . . THE . . . STAMP . . . Turn . . . on . . ."

SOURCE: William Hedgepeth, "Inside the Hippie Revolution," *Look Magazine*, August 22, 1967.

ANALYSIS

The late 1960s was a time when drug use, not only the use of marijuana and LSD but also the use of amphetamine, spread broadly outward from the small venues played by jazz musicians, the hovels where the beats and their followers held poetry readings, and racial-ethnic minority enclaves in large urban centers. As discussed in the previous section, drug use was never as confined to these areas as the legislative focus and the attention of enforcement agencies suggested (especially if alcohol is included as a drug). Millions of Americans spanning socioeconomic and geographical spectrums used and misused all manner of drugs, whether by prescription or made and obtained illegally. But the drugs that were the focus of federal and state laws and enforcement efforts—marijuana, heroin, and cocaine—were used by only a small percentage of the population, one that was primarily urban and minority. That changed in the 1960s, especially with respect to marijuana. And when Vietnam veterans began coming home from the war in large numbers in the late 1960s, many would return having used heroin, marijuana, and other drugs during their time overseas.

It is important, however, to keep the extent of the increase in drug use in perspective. Contrary to what a reading of press accounts from the 1960s might suggest, the number of Americans who would ever use illegal drugs such as LSD and marijuana remained in the minority. This was true then and it remains true today even when press accounts might suggest that half of the country is trying methamphetamine or OxyContin. It may be similarly surprising to consider that only a minority disapproved of the Vietnam War. After all, these were the times when conservative politicians such as Richard Nixon and Ronald Reagan were elected to the presidency and governorship of California, respectively, both by comfortable margins over liberal opponents. Still, the increase in acceptance of drug use by middle-class youth in particular, many of whom were coming-of-age baby boomers in their mid-twenties to mid-thirties is undeniable and striking.

The epicenter of the countercultural movement that embraced drug use in the 1960s was the Haight-Ashbury district in San Francisco named for the intersection of the two streets at the center of the district. At the time, Haight-Ashbury was a haven for bohemian artist types and those attracted to a more communal lifestyle that eschewed material possessions and pursuit of financial wealth. The movement evolved out of the beatnik culture that preceded it and was influenced by a fluid amalgam of Eastern religions and philosophies, the philosophical writings of authors such as Herman Hesse, and American Indian culture.

Rejecting what they perceived as the individually stultifying conventions of Western society, those who were (one) part of the countercultural movement adopted a look and wore clothes that were outward manifestations of their desire to break with mainstream culture. They did away with clothes that, to them, symbolized convention and constraint. Instead, they dressed in long, buttonless flowing shirts and dresses that were sometimes tie-dyed to create a mix of bright, intermingled colors that also represented the hallucinatory experience of acid "trips." They grew their hair long and eschewed hair-care products such as the gels and greases that were favored in the 1950s. Many of the men grew beards. Rather than wearing jewelry made of precious metals or stones, they wore "love beads" made of inexpensive materials and pinned on peace signs as symbols of protest against the Vietnam War and the military-industrial complex against which Eisenhower warned in his farewell address. They would come to be named hippies as derived from *hep-cats*, *hips*, and *hipsters*, terms first used in the jazz culture and later adopted by the beats to describe someone who was in the know and cool.

Hippies were social as opposed to political radicals. As such, music, sex, and drugs rather than political protest were central to the hippie-led aspect of the countercultural movement. These elements were often combined, most conspicuously, in large, musical events such as Woodstock that have, in retrospect, come to characterize the era and the movement. The iconic musical events and gatherings had their origins in the much smaller "acid test" parties first held in San Francisco in the mid-1960s as a way to introduce the curious to the purported mind-expanding benefits of LSD, which was distributed freely to attendees. The acid test parties were the idea of novelist Ken Kesey, who first experienced LSD when he volunteered for a CIA experiment while a graduate student at Stanford. Quickly sold on LSD's benefits, and with the proceeds from his successful novel, *One Flew Over the Cuckoo's Nest,* Kesey put together a rag-tag band of like-minded free spirits, nicknamed the Merry Pranksters, and together they roamed the country doing LSD and other drugs in a neon-colored bus they named "Furthur." Their exploits on the extended journey from California to the east coast and back would be famously chronicled in the book *The Electric Kool-Aid Acid Test*.

Returning to the San Francisco area, Kesey began throwing what were essentially LSD parties that he called "acid tests." To heighten the LSD-induced hallucinatory experiences, the acid tests included light shows and loud musical accompaniment, sometimes provided by the yet-to-be-famous Grateful Dead. Although LSD received most of the publicity, marijuana use was also prevalent and on the increase. But unlike LSD, marijuana was illegal. LSD was not made an illegal drug in California until October 6, 1966. To mark the occasion, the *Oracle,* a tabloid that chronicled and celebrated the drug counterculture in San Francisco, sponsored a Love Pageant Rally in the Panhandle next to Golden Gate Park. A few thousand attended the event. Rock bands provided free entertainment and, at one point in the evening, those in attendance took LSD in unison.

The success of the Love Pageant Rally led to a larger undertaking, the Human Be-In that would be held several months later. The Human Be-In—named after student sit-ins at various universities to protest the Vietnam War and academic administration policies—was held January 14, 1967, in Golden Gate Park. The main goal was to bring together the factions that represented the political and social aspects of the counterculture in a show of unity and to herald the ambitious possibility of combining forces to create a new social order. To this end, those whose main concern was militantly protesting the Vietnam War such as Jerry Rubin were invited to speak alongside the likes of Allen Ginsberg and Timothy Leary, who represented advocating for personal growth through drug use and pacifism. An estimated 25,000 attended to listen, do drugs, or just to be there for the experience. Bands such as the Grateful Dead and Jefferson Airplane, then relatively unknown outside the San Francisco area, provided music gratis. The Hells Angels, somewhat incongruous but ever-present participants in the countercultural movement, provided security of a sort.

The Be-In was deemed a success by the organizers and they saw the peaceful gathering as evidence for the beginnings of the sweeping social changes they hoped would come about as a result of the new movement. The event attracted considerable publicity and, in the months following, a steady stream of immigrants would be drawn to Haight-Ashbury from across the country. The song "San Francisco" sung by Scott McKenzie and written by John Phillips of the Mamas and Pappas with its refrain, "If you're going to San Francisco, be sure to wear some flowers in your hair," was an international hit. Its romantic view of a gentle hippie culture became a siren song and an unofficial anthem that further inspired the migration to the Hashbury that summer. The result was that many more came than had been expected or for which the city was prepared to absorb. By the time William Hedgepeth showed up in San Francisco to write his piece for *Look* magazine, the Haight was already becoming overcrowded and transformed for the worst.

The large influx—estimates are that over 100,000 traveled to Haight-Ashbury that summer—created numerous problems that began to undermine the countercultural movement. Many of those who came to San Francisco in the summer of 1967, were drawn by the lure of being able to use drugs for no greater purpose than to get high or they simply came out of curiosity to personally experience what had become a well-publicized scene. Others were social outcasts or disenchanted youth just looking for an escape to a happier place, better than the one from which they came. Regardless of purpose, they milled together in the Haight's increasingly crowded streets. The growing crowds strained the city's infrastructure. Many of the people who came to the Haight that summer had no means of income and little money on hand. People slept on the streets or in the nearby parks or massed together in filthy, trash-strewn apartments. Getting enough to eat was a problem despite attempts by local groups such as the Diggers to provide free food to anyone in need. Crime increased and there were frequent run-ins with the police.

Bus tours and sightseers riding in their cars drove through the area to gawk first-hand. Merchants seeking to capitalize on the moment moved into the Haight and began selling hippie-related paraphernalia to the tourists, in direct contradiction to the anti-commercialization ethos of the countercultural movement. The deteriorating atmosphere as well as his own sensibilities led Ronald Reagan, then California's governor, to quip dismissively, "A hippie is someone who dresses like Tarzan, has hair like Jane, and smells like Cheetah."

The drug use that had started with LSD as a means of expanding consciousness took a darker turn. Amphetamine and methamphetamine became increasingly popular. The Free-Clinic that had been established in Haight-Ashbury to provide treatment for drug users went from treating those experiencing the occasional bad LSD trip to treating those coming down from the ravages of having injected amphetamine for multiple days or who were experiencing an amphetamine-induced psychosis. None other than Allen Ginsberg was moved to expound on the dangers of amphetamine use, which he said led to a "Hitlerian fascist mentality." He recommended the government establish farms with log cabins where speed freaks could overcome their addictions by getting back to nature. As with the pharmaceutical companies that had aggressively promoted specific drugs for specific ills, Ginsberg too did not seem to understand that promoting use of one drug or class of drugs as promise of a better life leads to non-specific experimentation with and use of other drugs. Potent and dangerous hallucinogens such as STP were marketed on the streets as LSD to the unsuspecting, sending many to emergency rooms experiencing a three-day nightmare that seemed as if it would never end. Sexually transmitted diseases and other health problems from the overcrowded conditions spread rapidly throughout the community.

Many of the original hippies who had lived in the Haight before 1967 fled to the surrounding countryside to form communes, many of which were short-lived. By the end of the summer of love, the Haight-Ashbury district had been transformed from a relatively quiet, urban haven for bohemian types, students, and artists into a scene marked by social chaos, tourism and crass commercialization, crime, congestion, and squalor. Most of those who crowded into the Haight to share in the experience that summer returned home later that year. Retrospective interviews with those who had migrated to the Haight hoping for a better life or at least a good experience indicated a general feeling of disenchantment. As a final metaphor, in the fall of 1967, a theater group called the Diggers that was a prominent part of the street culture of the district staged a mock funeral procession in the Haight whereby they carried a coffin filled with the effigy of a hippie through the streets.

And just that quickly, the countercultural movement that had started with such optimism only a few years before by a loosely organized collection of bohemians, young eccentrics, artists, musicians, the socially and spiritually disaffected, and political and civil rights activists dissipated into incoherence. As a movement for inspiring social change in a broad sense, the counterculture was not completely finished in the fall of 1967 but it was the beginning of the end. Hippie-inspired communities continued to spring up within cities across the country but on much smaller scales than in San Francisco.

Processed through the maw of America's particular genius for merchandizing, hippie-style clothing and artifacts were mass marketed for consumption by the general public devoid of any particular social significance other than to promote looking "groovy." Even the language of the movement that once set it apart from the mainstream was co-opted and commercialized as when a television network named the successful show starring comedians Dan Rowan and Dick Martin the *Laugh-In*. By 1977 when the cast of the *Brady Bunch* stepped onstage with their permed, hippie-inspired longish hair and sequined bell-bottoms to tap out a few show tunes for one of their horrendous televised specials, the gas had clearly gone out of the countercultural balloon.

Political protest and the civil rights movement, two aspects of the broader countercultural movement that never really meshed with the hippie aspect (the Be-In was an attempt to bring these diverse elements together) other than adopting the same outward appearances, did continue unabated for several more years. Protests against the expanding Vietnam War grew, as did civil unrest resulting in race riots in cities throughout the United States. An anti-war demonstration at the Democratic National Convention in 1968 and the police brutality used to suppress the demonstrators drew headlines and fomented further civil unrest. Similarly, a Kent State student protest of the expansion of the Vietnam War into Cambodia by Nixon resulted in the National Guard shooting and killing four of the student protestors further deepening resentments and dividing the country.

Although many continued to use and to try LSD, it would be made illegal nationally by the end of the decade and use would decline in the early 1970s.

Those who espoused using LSD and other hallucinogenic drugs as sacraments that raised consciousness and fostered personal growth would eventually join the disenchanted and look for inspiration elsewhere such as through religion, mysticism, yoga, or meditation. Ken Kesey retreated to Oregon where he parked his bus Furthur and left the Merry Pranksters behind for good. Even Timothy Leary would turn away from LSD and look toward space travel and computers as alternative ways of raising his consciousness.

Marijuana, despite its long-standing illegal status and harsh criminal sanctions for possession or distribution per the Boggs and Narcotic Control Acts, would continue to increase in popularity through the end of the next decade. That many were regularly using marijuana and not becoming the crazed assassins portrayed in the writings and testimony of Harry Anslinger and other government officials simply added to a growing distrust of government and the political establishment. But marijuana was used as a recreational drug with the main goal of getting high and having a good time rather than as a means for achieving some higher individual or social purpose.

Using hallucinogenic drugs as a means to transform society and achieve a better life was, in the end, a resounding failure. Instead, the next decades would see a surge in popularity of two drugs, heroin and cocaine, that had for the most part been relegated to society's margins since the 1920s, particularly cocaine. Over the next 30 years, the new popularity of heroin and cocaine and the emergence or reemergence of other drugs like Oxycontin and methamphetamine would wax and wane as successive generations experimented with drugs that, for them, were new and at least initially seemed harmless enough. This is the phenomenon of "lived experience" as described by policy analyst Mark Kleinman. Despite the best efforts at prevention, it seems each generation must experience firsthand the effects of using drugs before the consequences of use are fully appreciated.

FURTHER READING

Anthony, G. (1995). *The summer of love: Haight-Ashbury at its highest.* San Francisco, CA: Last Gasp.

Grim, R. (2009). *This is your country on drugs.* Hoboken, NJ: John Wiley & Sons.

Inciardi, J. (2007). *The war on drugs IV: The continuing saga of the mysteries and miseries of intoxication, addiction, crime, and public policy, 4th edition.* Boston, MA: Allyn and Bacon

Lattin, D. (2011). *The Harvard psychedelic club: How Timothy Leary, Ram Dass, Huston Smith, and Andrew Weil killed the fifties and ushered in a new age for America.* New York: HarperCollins.

Leary, T. (1999). *Turn on, tune in, drop out*. Oakland, CA: Ronin Publishing.
Lee, M. A., & Shlain, B. (1992). *Acid dreams: The complete social history of LSD; The CIA, the sixties, and beyond*. New York: Grove Press.
Lytle Mark H. (2006). *America's uncivil wars: The sixties era: From Elvis to the fall of Richard Nixon*. New York: Oxford University Press.
Perry, C. (2005). *The Haight-Ashbury: A history*. New York: Wenner Media.
Warner-Smith, M., Darke, S., Lynskey, M., & Hall, W. (2001). Heroin overdose: Causes and consequences. *Addiction*, 96, 1113–1125.
Wolfe, T. (1999). *The electric kool-aid acid test*. New York: Oxford University Press.

PSYCHEDELICS

Before its adoption by the counter-cultural movement, LSD was tested as a potential therapeutic agent for treating psychiatric disorders and alcoholism in the 1940s and 1950s as exemplified by the research of Dr. Humphry. In the 1950s and 1960s, the CIA conducted a research program called MK-ULTRA. One of its purposes was to explore the usefulness of LSD for mind control as a *truth serum* and as an agent for chemical warfare. Among its many breaches of research ethics, the secretive program used prostitutes to slip LSD into the drinks of their unsuspecting clients whom CIA agents would then surreptitiously film and observe through two-way mirrors to monitor their reactions. The highly questionable methods and research goals of MK-ULTRA came to light in a subsequent Congressional investigation that was hampered by the orders of the CIA director to destroy all documents related to the project, although some misfiled documents survived the purge.

Other drugs that are considered hallucinogenic include psilocybin (from mushrooms), mescaline, MDMA (ecstasy), ketamine (special-K), phencyclidine (PCP or angel dust), DMT, DXM, STP, and nitrous oxide (laughing gas). The drugs differ widely in their potency and also as to whether their primary psychological effects are hallucinatory (e.g., LSD, psilocybin, mescaline) or dissociative (e.g., ketamine, PCP, MDMA). Dissociative effects include feelings of being detached from one's surroundings, the perception of the world as unreal or dream-like, or feeling detached from one's own body. The 2010 Monitoring the Future Survey, which annually assesses U.S. high school students for changes in drug use, found that 1.8 percent of high school students in the 8th, 10th, and 12th grades used LSD at least once in the past year with 3.8 percent reporting past-year use of any hallucinogenic drug (excluding MDMA). Since 1991, the first year the survey began being conducted annually, hallucinogen use peaked at 7.2 percent in 1996 and has slowly declined to the current level.

On the Internet

A. Hoffman, the scientist who discovered LSD during his chemistry experiments, writes about his discovery in the 1980 book *LSD, My problem child: Reflections on sacred drugs, mysticism and science*. Full text of the book as well as other full text books on psychedelic drugs are available at: http://www.psychedelic-library.org/bookmenu.htm.

American Experience: Documentary video of the events at Golden Gate Park during the summer of 1967 is available for viewing at: http://www.pbs.org/wgbh/amex/love/program/

Full text of the 1969 Supreme Court decision that determined the Marijuana Tax Act of 1937 was unconstitutional based on a case originally filed by Timothy Leary in response to his arrest and conviction under the Tax Act (Leary v United States, 395 U.S. 6) is available at: http://www.druglibrary.net/schaffer/History/e1960/learyvus.htm.

A transcript of a 1977 congressional hearing on MK-ULTRA with supporting documents is available at: http://www.nytimes.com/packages/pdf/national/13inmate_Project-MKULTRA.pdf.

Findings from the most recent survey of drug use, including use of hallucinogenic drugs, among high school youth in the United States is available at: http://monitoringthefuture.org/pubs/monographs/mtf-overview2010.pdf.

National Institute on Drug Abuse Research Report Series. (March 2001). Hallucinogens and dissociative drugs (NIH Publication No. 01-4209). U.S. Department of Health and Human Services, National Institutes of Health: Bethesda, MD. available at: http://www.nida.nih.gov/ResearchReports/hallucinogens/hallucinogens.html.

Alan Ginsberg's warnings on the danger or amphetamines is available at: http://doitnow.org/pages/ginsberg.html.

A 2007 story in *Rolling Stone* magazine reprinted on the occasion of his death in 2011, details the life of Stanley Owsley, particularly his years as sound manager and patron for the *Grateful Dead*, is available at: http://www.rollingstone.com/culture/news/owsley-stanley-the-king-of-lsd-20110314?page=1.

"Crapping around Will Not Be Tolerated"

- ***Document:*** Comprehensive Drug Abuse Prevention and Control Act of 1970 (PL 91–513)
- ***Date:*** October 27, 1970
- ***Where:*** Washington, DC
- ***Significance:*** Along with the Harrison Act of 1914, the Comprehensive Drug Abuse Prevention and Control Act of 1970 is one of the most important pieces of drug policy legislation enacted in the 20th century. It has become the cornerstone of federal drug policy and the model for state policies. The Comprehensive Control Act effectively did away with the Harrison Act and superseded other federal drug statutes such as the Marihuana Stamp Tax Act of 1937, the Boggs Act of 1951, and the Drug Abuse Control Amendments of 1965, among others. Title II is the heart of the Comprehensive Control Act and is called the Controlled Substances Act. It is excerpted below. The Controlled Substances Act created five schedules for classifying drugs based on their potential for abuse weighed against established medical benefits. This framework for classifying and controlling drugs remains in effect through the present day. The law also did away with mandatory minimum sentences for drug possession but it included a controversial provision allowing for "no-knock" search warrants that gave law enforcement the right to enter and search a building without notice when drugs were suspected of being kept and/or manufactured on the premises. In future years, the law would be amended and made more stringent with mandatory sentencing re-instated and toughened in the mid- and late 1980s amid concerns over the spread of crack cocaine use and violent crime.

DOCUMENT

Title II—Control and Enforcement

Part A—Short Title; Findings and Declaration; Definitions Short Title

Sec. 100. This title may be cited as the "Controlled Substances Act"

Findings and Declarations

Sec. 101. The Congress makes the following findings and declarations:

(1) Many of the drugs included within this subchapter have a useful and legitimate medical purpose and are necessary to maintain the health and general welfare of the American people.
(2) The illegal importation, manufacture, distribution, and possession and improper use of controlled substances have a substantial and detrimental effect on the health and general welfare of the American people.
(3) A major portion of the traffic in controlled substances flows through interstate and foreign commerce. Incidents of the traffic which are not an integral part of the interstate or foreign flow, such as manufacture, local distribution, and possession, nonetheless have a substantial and direct effect upon interstate commerce because -
    (A) after manufacture, many controlled substances are transported in interstate commerce,
    (B) controlled substances distributed locally usually have been transported in interstate commerce immediately before their distribution, and
    (C) controlled substances possessed commonly flow through interstate commerce immediately prior to such possession.
(4) Local distribution and possession of controlled substances contribute to swelling the interstate traffic in such substances.
(5) Controlled substances manufactured and distributed intrastate cannot be differentiated from controlled substances manufactured and distributed interstate. Thus, it is not feasible to distinguish, in terms of controls, between controlled substances manufactured and distributed interstate and controlled substances manufactured and distributed intrastate.
(6) Federal control of the intrastate incidents of the traffic in controlled substances is essential to the effective control of the interstate incidents of such traffic.
(7) The United States is a party to the Single Convention on Narcotic Drugs, 1961, and other international conventions designed to establish effective control over international and domestic traffic in controlled substances.

Part B—Authority to Control; Standards and Schedules

Authority and Criteria for Classification of Substances

Sec. 201. (a) The Attorney General shall apply the provisions of this subchapter to the controlled substances listed in the schedules established by section 812 of this title and to any other drug or other substance added to such schedules under this subchapter. Except as provided in subsections (d) and (e) of this section, the Attorney General may by rule -

(1) add to such a schedule or transfer between such schedules any drug or other substance if he-

(A) finds that such drug or other substance has a potential for abuse, and
(B) makes with respect to such drug or other substance the findings prescribed by subsection (b) of section 812 of this title for the schedule in which such drug is to be placed; or

(2) remove any drug or other substance from the schedules if he finds that the drug or other substance does not meet the requirements for inclusion in any schedule.

Rules of the Attorney General under this subsection shall be made on the record after opportunity for a hearing pursuant to the rulemaking procedures prescribed by subchapter II of chapter 5 of title 5. Proceedings for the issuance, amendment, or repeal of such rules may be initiated by the Attorney General (1) on his own motion, (2) at the request of the Secretary, or (3) on the petition of any interested party.

(b) Evaluation of drugs and other substances The Attorney General shall, before initiating proceedings under subsection (a) of this section to control a drug or other substance or to remove a drug or other substance entirely from the schedules, and after gathering the necessary data, request from the Secretary a scientific and medical evaluation, and his recommendations, as to whether such drug or other substance should be so controlled or removed as a controlled substance. In making such evaluation and recommendations, the Secretary shall consider the factors listed in paragraphs (2), (3), (6), (7), and (8) of subsection (c) of this section and any scientific or medical considerations involved in paragraphs (1), (4), and (5) of such subsection. The recommendations of the Secretary shall include recommendations with respect to the appropriate schedule, if any, under which such drug or other substance should be listed. The evaluation and the recommendations of the Secretary shall be made in writing and submitted to the Attorney General within a reasonable time. The recommendations of the Secretary to the Attorney General shall be binding on the Attorney General as to such scientific and medical matters, and if the Secretary recommends that a drug or other substance not be controlled, the Attorney General shall not control the drug or other substance. If the Attorney General determines that these facts and all other relevant data constitute substantial evidence of potential for abuse such as to warrant control or substantial evidence that the drug or other substance should be removed entirely from the schedules, he shall initiate proceedings for control or removal, as the case may be, under subsection (a) of this section.

(c) Factors determinative of control or removal from schedules In making any finding under subsection (a) of this section or under subsection (b) of section 812 of this title, the Attorney General shall consider the following factors with respect to each drug or other substance proposed to be controlled or removed from the schedules:

(1) Its actual or relative potential for abuse.
(2) Scientific evidence of its pharmacological effect, if known.
(3) The state of current scientific knowledge regarding the drug or other substance.

(4) Its history and current pattern of abuse.
(5) The scope, duration, and significance of abuse.
(6) What, if any, risk there is to the public health.
(7) Its psychic or physiological dependence liability.
(8) Whether the substance is an immediate precursor of a substance already controlled under this subchapter.

(d) International treaties, conventions, and protocols requiring control; procedures respecting changes in drug schedules of Convention on Psychotropic Substances (1) If control is required by United States obligations under international treaties, conventions, or protocols in effect on October 27, 1970, the Attorney General shall issue an order controlling such drug under the schedule he deems most appropriate to carry out such obligations, without regard to the findings required by subsection (a) of this section or section 812(b) of this title and without regard to the procedures prescribed by subsections (a) and (b) of this section.

Schedules of Controlled Substances

Sec. 202. There are established five schedules of controlled substances, to be known as schedules I, II, III, IV, and V. Such schedules shall initially consist of the substances listed in this section. The schedules established by this section shall be updated and republished on a semiannual basis during the two-year period beginning one year after the date of enactment of this title and shall be updated and republished on an annual basis thereafter.

(b) Except where control is required by United States obligations under an international treaty, convention, or protocol, in effect on the effective date of this part, and except in the case of an immediate precursor, a drug or other substance may not be placed in any schedule unless the findings required for such schedule are made with respect to such drug or other substance. The findings required for each of the schedules are as follows:

(1) Schedule I.—(e.g., heroin, LSD, marijuana, peyote, and ecstasy)
  (A) The drug or other substance has a high potential for abuse.
  (B) The drug or other substance has no currently accepted medical use in treatment in the United States.
  (C) There is a lack of accepted safety for use of the drug or other substance under medical supervision.

(2) Schedule II.—(e.g., morphine, opium, methadone, OxyContin, amphetamine, methamphetamine, Ritalin, cocaine)
  (A) The drug or other substance has a high potential for abuse.
  (B) The drug or other substance has a currently accepted medical use in treatment in the United States or a currently accepted medical use with severe restrictions.
  (C) Abuse of the drug or other substances may lead to severe psychological or physical dependence.

(3) Schedule III.—(e.g., Vicodin, buprenorphine, anabolic steroids, Tylenol with codeine)
  (A) The drug or other substance has a potential for abuse less than the drugs or other substances in schedules I and II.

(B) The drug or other substance has a currently accepted medical use in treatment in the United States.

(C) Abuse of the drug or other substance may lead to moderate or low physical dependence or high psychological dependence.

(4) Schedule IV.—(e.g., Xanax, Klonipin, Valium, Halcion, Ativan)

(A) The drug or other substance has a low potential for abuse relative to the drugs or other substances in schedule III.

(B) The drug or other substance has a currently accepted medical use in treatment in the United States.

(C) Abuse of the drug or other substance may lead to limited physical dependence or psychological dependence relative to the drugs or other substances in schedule III.

(5) Schedule V.—(e.g., Robitussin)

(A) The drug or other substance has a low potential for abuse relative to the drugs or other substances in schedule IV.

(B) The drug or other substance has a currently accepted medical use in treatment in the United States.

(C) Abuse of the drug or other substance may lead to limited physical dependence or psychological dependence relative to the drugs or other substances in schedule IV.

SOURCE: Comprehensive Drug Abuse Prevention and Control Act of 1970, Pub. L. No. 91-513, 84 Stat. 1236, October 27, 1970.

ANALYSIS

In the wake of the countercultural movement, as the 1960s were drawing to a close, America had a drug problem that was worsening. It was not simply that more people were using all manner of drugs; it was equally if not more important that there was a dramatic shift in who was using *illegal* drugs that was causing political and social consternation. After all, use and abuse of *prescription* drugs by middle class Americans was nothing new. Millions had been regularly using prescription drugs (legally and illegally obtained) for several decades. In the 1960s, the annual production of barbiturates was estimated as being over one million pounds. Enough amphetamines were being produced each year to provide every adult U.S. resident with at least 50 doses. Use and abuse of illegal drugs—opiates, cocaine, and marijuana—by inner-city minorities and the socially marginalized was also nothing new. Harry Anslinger and the Federal Bureau of Narcotics had been leading the fight on this front for 30 years. To be sure, increasing crime rates that were attributed to increased heroin use in major urban areas—only one of a number of heroin epidemics that would occur in the 20th century in the United States—was also causing concern as was the return of Vietnam War veterans, many of whom had used heroin and other drugs while overseas.

But it was the changing profile of those using illegal drugs, as much as the increase in the numbers of illegal drug users that was causing consternation among the public and politicians. In the 1960s, the use of illegal drugs, particularly marijuana, went mainstream. The American middle class, particularly college students, was using drugs in unprecedented numbers. A 1972 report issued by President Nixon's

National Commission on Marijuana and Drug Abuse notes the central importance and repercussions of this demographic shift:

> More than anything else, the visibility of marihuana use by a segment of our population previously unfamiliar with the drug is what stirred public anxiety and thrust marihuana into the problem area. Marihuana usage in the United States has been with us for a very long period of time, dating back to the beginning of the century. For decades its use was mainly confined to the underprivileged socioeconomic groups in our cities and to certain insulated social groups, such as jazz musicians and artists. As long as use remained confined to these groups and had a negligible impact on the dominant social order, the vast majority of Americans remained unconcerned. From the other side, the insulated marihuana user was in no position to demand careful public or legislative scrutiny.
>
> However, all this changed markedly in the mid-1960's. For various reasons, marihuana use became a common form of recreation for many middle and upper class college youth. The trend spread across the country, into the colleges and high schools and into the affluent suburbs as well. Use by American servicemen in Vietnam was frequent. In recent years, use of the drug has spanned every social class and geographic region. . . .
>
> Public confusion, anger, and fear over this development became increasingly apparent during the mid and late 1960's. Such mass deviance was a problem and the scope of the problem was augmented by frequent publicity. The topic of the usage of marihuana by the young received considerable attention from newspapermen and television reporters. The drug's youthful users abetted the media in this regard by flaunting their disregard of the law. Few of us have not seen or heard of marihuana being used en masse at rock concerts, political demonstrations and gatherings of campus activists.

In 1968, presidential candidate Richard Nixon called drugs "the curse of youth," which were "decimating a generation of Americans." He promised that if elected, he would take decisive action against the countries that were the source of illegal drugs and crack down on drug use generally. Once elected, Nixon began to make good on his campaign promises. Nixon's concern about drug use was motivated by his belief that drug use and crime were closely associated and that successfully combating crime required reducing drug use. Paralleling the increase in drug use, crime had been on the rise in America in the 1960s. National surveys suggested it was a more important issue for the American public than drug use per se, which always polled far below the Vietnam War, the economy, and crime as the country's main problems.

Nevertheless, pushing ahead with an anti-crime agenda early in his first administration, President Nixon identified drug use as a serious national threat and communicated to the American public his belief that the increase in crime was attributable to increased drug use. Underscoring the drugs-crime association and fusing the two issues Nixon described drug use as public enemy number 1.

The metaphor was not simply a rhetorical flourish; the emphasis on drug use as a criminal and not public health issue was substantive and consequential. Despite repealing mandatory minimum sentences for drug possession and moderating the law enforcement emphasis in federal policy that reached an apogee in the 1950s, drug policy passed during the Nixon administration was strongly motivated by a desire to reduce crime. Reducing drug use was seen as a means of accomplishing that end. Nixon also knew that the public was concerned about crime more than drugs but did not necessarily see the two issues as related. He saw explicitly linking the two issues as a way of gaining public support for a broad drug policy agenda.

There have also always been suspicions that Nixon's drug-crimes agenda had racist undertones. A contemporaneous diary entry by Nixon adviser H.R. "Bob" Haldeman, White House Chief of Staff, noted, "[President Nixon] emphasized that you have to face the fact that the whole problem really is blacks. The key is to devise a system that recognizes this while not appearing to." Tapes of Nixon also revealed bizarre rantings directed at Jewish psychiatrists and homosexuals as supporting drugs and being used by the communists to infiltrate and weaken America.

Nixon indicated to his staff that friend and foe alike would be confronted if they were found to be in some way supporting drug importation into the country. In his blunt style that would become familiar to Americans when White House recordings were made public after the Watergate scandal, Nixon told his staff that "no crapping around would be tolerated." While interdiction and source country eradication were important parts of the administration's overall strategy, treatment and prevention were greatly expanded under President Nixon. With the exception of the Carter administration, which favored the decriminalization (i.e., elimination of criminal sanctions replaced by small fines for possession of small amounts but short of full legalization) of marijuana, the first Nixon administration was arguably among the most moderate and balanced in its approach to drug control policy in the modern era.

On June 17, 1971, President Nixon publicly and famously (or infamously depending on perspective) declared the first "war on drugs," choosing for this occasion a militaristic metaphor to frame his vision for revising federal drug control efforts. Declaring war on a social problem was not new and did not begin with President Nixon. President Johnson had declared a "war on crime" in 1965 for instance. In this case, it was intended to convey the extent to which drug use was perceived by the administration as a major social problem that required an all-out effort at the federal level.

As part of the new drug "war," the Nixon administration gave funding to the Turkish government to ban poppy production and to encourage farmers to substitute other crops. At the time, poppies grown in Turkey yielded as much as 80 percent of the heroin entering the United States. Efforts were also made to encourage French law enforcement to crack down on the Corsican mafia (the French Connection) whose illegal laboratories in Marseille processed the Turkish opiate paste, converting it to heroin powder before shipment to the United States via Italy and Mexico. The Nixon administration also launched the largest peacetime interdiction campaign to date, known as Operation Intercept, to reduce the amount of marijuana and other drugs entering the United States from Mexico.

The effects of these programs on the amount of drugs entering the country were tangible but ephemeral. Operation Intercept decreased the supply of marijuana and as a result the potency of the marijuana that remained available decreased while price increased. Busting the labs that supplied the French Connection caused a shortage of heroin on the east coast sending addicts in the throes of withdrawal to detoxification centers and emergency rooms. However, marijuana supply routes were soon reestablished and would later be supplanted by increases in domestic production. New supply routes for heroin were also soon reestablished.

Despite their limited benefits, source country eradication and interdiction became a standard part of American drug control policy. These were not new by any means; Harry Anslinger firmly believed in and pursued international policies to limit drug production in other countries throughout his tenure. As early as the Kefauver Commission, proponents of the approach knew that it had limited value for reducing supplies but argued for its symbolic importance and deterrent effects. But interdiction and source country eradication have continued to evolve into an expansive and expensive hi-tech and diplomatic game of "whack-a-mole"; eliminate or reduce the supply of drugs from one source and another springs up to take its place. Reduce cocaine production in Colombia, production moves to Peru and Guatemala. Shut down the supply routes for cocaine in the Caribbean and they are rerouted through Mexico. Understandably, government pronouncements supporting the effectiveness of the ongoing drug war tout the successes and downplay or ignore the re-establishment of new sources and supply routes.

Another enduring legacy of the Nixon administration was the passage of the Comprehensive Drug Abuse Prevention and Control Act. The Control Act (CA) superseded and brought under one statutory framework all previous federal drug laws including the mainstay for nearly six decades, the Harrison Act. There were multiple motivations for overhauling federal drug policy. One was the 1968 merger of the Bureau of Drug Abuse Control and the Federal Bureau of Narcotics to create the BNDD. (The BNDD underwent additional reorganization and expansion to become the DEA in 1973.) The different drug policy laws governing the two merged organizations meant that the BNDD inherited responsibility for disparate laws that were created with no overarching framework for adding in new drugs or changing the penalties for older drugs without the lengthy process of amending existing law or passing a new law. The BNDD was responsible for enforcing a rather unwieldy statutory jumble that provided for different regulatory structures, enforcement procedures, and sanctions.

A more surprising impetus for overhauling drug policy was provided by none other than Timothy Leary, who filed suit challenging his arrest for marijuana possession under the Marihuana Tax Act of 1937. Dr. Leary's suit claimed the Tax Act unconstitutionally required an individual to self-incriminate. In 1969, the Supreme Court (*Leary v. United States*) unanimously agreed. The case had potential repercussions for other existing drug laws, which were also based on federal taxing authority and which could be susceptible to similar challenges to their constitutionality.

Legislation to craft the CA began under the Johnson administration. However, disputes over who would have the authority to determine what drugs to schedule, and when to add, remove, or change a drug's assigned schedule delayed passage of the law. Liberal members of Congress wanted primary authority to rest in the Department of Health, Education, and Welfare (HEW) reflecting their desire to emphasize the public health aspects of drug use and the role of science and research. Reflecting a criminal justice emphasis, conservatives wanted authority to rest in the Department of Justice where the recently created BNDD resided.

The final legislation reflected a compromise: the Attorney General would have primary scheduling authority and could initiate changes to the schedule. However, the Secretary of HEW could initiate changes as could a third party via petition. If HEW recommended a drug for control, the Justice Department had discretionary authority for determining the schedule taking into consideration the medical and research findings and HEW's recommendations. HEW could also veto scheduling a drug if, after scientific and medical review, they made such a determination. HEW's veto authority, however, would be effectively circumvented by subsequent amendments that gave the DEA greater authority.

The CA fully shifted the basis of federal authority for controlling illegal drugs (alcohol and tobacco are still taxed) away from taxation to its authority over interstate commerce. The CA thus removed the uncertainty around the constitutionality of federal drug law. It also provided a framework by which new drugs could be added or rescheduled as information about their medical use, harm, or abuse potential became available. Sanctions for possession, use, and distribution were tied to the schedules rather than to individual drugs or drug classes meaning that, for instance, changing a drug from a lower to higher schedule (e.g., from Schedule IV to Schedule III or II) automatically increased the penalties associated with that drug. In this regard, the CA provided a flexible and comprehensive drug policy framework that could readily incorporate new drugs of potential abuse without requiring new legislation.

The determination of which drugs are included in which schedule continues to be controversial. The most glaring anomaly to critics of the scheduling system is the inclusion of marijuana on Schedule I, while morphine, amphetamines, and cocaine are all Schedule II. Alternative classification schemes such as that being considered in Great Britain (see the Nutt and Caulkin references in additional readings for an example and critique) have been proposed but the system provided for in the original legislation remains in effect. Marijuana remains on Schedule I despite recent changes in some states, most notably California and a growing number of other states, that have approved its use for medical purposes.

Critics of the criminal justice emphasis of America's drug policies continue to use the date of Nixon's war on drugs proclamation as an anniversary to launch public events decrying the war metaphor, to pronounce America's drug policies a failure, and to advocate for a greater public health emphasis (using many of the same arguments put forth in the ABA-AMA Joint Commission Report and by Alfred Lindesmith in the 1950s). Compared with subsequent legislation and administrations, however, the first Nixon administration followed a moderate course that strongly supported treatment. In the same speech in which he declared a drug war, Nixon requested \$155 million in additional funds, \$105 million of which was to be allocated to treatment. (Subsequent administrations—through the present day—would reverse this ratio and allocate one-third of the federal budget for treatment and two-thirds for interdiction and enforcement). Title I of the CA provided HEW with additional funding to expand prevention and treatment through existing community mental health centers and increased research and training at the National Institute of Mental Health.

These initiatives, together with the repeal of mandatory minimum sentencing provisions marked, for a brief time, a movement away from criminal sanctions as the primary means for controlling drugs toward a broader approach that provided sentencing flexibility and funding for expanding prevention and treatment. Although it is difficult to determine definitively owing to the complexities of the drug problem and how drug use waxes and wanes over time, the initiatives begun under President Nixon's drug war appeared to have reduced heroin use and at least moderated the rising crime rate. But overall drug use continued to increase throughout the 1970s, particularly marijuana use, which peaked in 1979. The increase in marijuana use was likely due to broader cultural acceptance as well as to decriminalization laws passed in a number of states. Possession of small amounts of marijuana was decriminalized in Oregon in 1973. By 1978, eight other states including California and New York followed suit. Cocaine use also began to increase rapidly in the late 1970s.

President Nixon largely abandoned a progressive approach during his second administration. In 1972, Nixon created by executive order the Office of Drug Abuse Law Enforcement (ODALE) in the Justice Department. Among ODALE's charges was targeting communities with high rates of drug use and through the use of strike forces and "any legal means possible" including the use of no-knock warrants, busting low and midlevel drug traffickers. He rejected outright the recommendations of a 1972 report by the National Commission on Marihuana and Drug Abuse (the Shafer Commission) that marijuana possession be decriminalized. Instead, enforcement of the laws against marijuana increased dramatically under Nixon. He also proposed legislation that would again increase criminal sanctions—the Heroin Trafficking Act—modeled after but not quite as severe as the Rockefeller Drug Laws in New York. The Trafficking Act was never enacted and political scandal soon consumed the Nixon administration.

President Carter would have his own difficulties in relation to drug policy. His special assistant to the president for health issues and top adviser on drug policy, Dr. Peter Bourne, resigned following the fallout of a series of scandals that included the revelation Bourne had snorted cocaine at a Christmas party with the likes of gonzo journalist Hunter S. Thompson. Carter eventually abandoned his campaign pledge to decriminalize marijuana as other issues such as the country's deepening economic crisis and Iran's taking American embassy workers in that country hostage became the focal points during the last years of his one-term administration.

"FIRST, I WOULD LIKE TO INTRODUCE MYSELF. I AM ELVIS PRESLEY."

A most surreal moment in American history occurred December 21, 1970, at the White House where singer Elvis Presley met with President Richard Nixon to volunteer his help in bringing an anti-drug message to "people of all ages." Presley also hoped to obtain a badge from the Bureau of Narcotics and Dangerous Drugs, the successor to the Bureau of Narcotics and the predecessor to the Drug Enforcement Agency. In Presley's mind, the badge would demonstrate that he was an officially sanctioned "agent at large," a true patriot helping the president to fight America's war on drugs. Elvis had concocted the idea while flying to D.C. with some of his entourage and after discussion with U.S. Senator George Murphy of California, who happened to be on the same flight.

This awkward publicity photo shows President Nixon and Elvis Presley at their hastily arranged meeting in December 1970. Presley requested the meeting to receive a badge signifying him as an honorary drug enforcement agent. Likely high on prescription drugs at the time, Presley's premature death just a few years later, hastened by years of drug abuse, brought a dark irony to this unlikely meeting. (National Archives)

(continued)

FURTHER READING

Belair, F. (1969, September 22). Drug drive opens at Mexico border, *New York Times*, A1, 39.

Caulkins, J. P., Reuter, P., & Coulson, C. (2011). Basing drug scheduling decisions on scientific ranking of harmfulness: False promises from false premises. *Addiction*. Epub ahead of print.

Claiborne, W. (1977, June 21). N.Y. drug crackdown called a failure. *Washington Post*, A3.

Courtwright, D.T., 2004. The Controlled Substances Act: How a "big tent" reform became a punitive drug law. *Drug and Alcohol Dependence*, *76*, 9–15.

Guralnick, P. (1999). *Careless love: The unmaking of Elvis Presley*. New York: Little, Brown, and Company.

Hollister, L. E. (1969). Criminal laws and the control of drugs of abuse: An historical view of the law (or, it's the lawyer's fault). *Journal of Clinical Pharmacology*, *9*, 345–348.

Jonnes, J. (1996). *Hep-cats, narcs, and pipe dreams: A history of America's romance with illegal drugs*. New York: Scribner.

Kohler-Hausmann, J. (2010). "The Attila the Hun law": New York's Rockefeller drug laws and the making of a punitive state. *Journal of Social History, 44*, 71–95.

Krogh, E. (2002). Heroin politics and policy under President Nixon. In D. F. Musto (Ed.), *One hundred years of heroin* (pp. 39–42). Westport, CT: Greenwood Publishing.

Musto, D. F., & Korsmeyer, P. (2002). *The quest for drug control: Politics and federal policy in a period of increasing substance abuse, 1963–1981*. New Haven, CT: Yale University Press.

Nutt, D. J., King, L. A., & Phillips, L. D. (2010). Drug harms in the UK: A multicriteria decision analysis. *Lancet, 376*, 1558–1565.

Spillane, J. F. (2004). Debating the controlled substances act. *Drug and Alcohol Dependence, 76*, 17–29.

On the Internet

The 1972 report of the National Commission on Marihuana and Drug Abuse is available from the Shaffer Library of Drug policy at: http://www.druglibrary.org/schaffer/library/studies/nc/ncmenu.htm.

A 1972 *Time* magazine article on the Corsican Mafia, which supplied much of the heroin in the United States, is available at: http://www.time.com/time/magazine/article/0,9171,910391-1,00.html.

A 2002 interview with Dr. George Nichopolous, the physician who provided Elvis Presley with prescription drugs in the last years of Presley's life, is available at: http://www.guardian.co.uk/theobserver/2002/aug/11/features.magazine27.

The online encyclopedia of drugs, alcohol, and addictive behavior has a succinct and balanced summary of Operation Intercept at: http://www.enotes.com/drugs-alcohol-encyclopedia/operation-intercept.

A current listing of controlled substances and assigned schedules is available at the Drug Enforcement Administration's website: http://www.deadiversion.usdoj.gov/schedules/index.html. The DEA website also has fact sheets on drugs of abuse at: http://www.justice.gov/dea/pubs/abuse/.

Time magazine has a brief online article summarizing the history of the Rockefeller Drug Laws at: http://www.time.com/time/nation/article/0,8599,1888864,00.html.

The Schaffer Library of Drug Policy has a paper by Peter Goldberg that details the federal government's efforts to control illicit drugs from 1969 to 1978 at: http://www.druglibrary.org/schaffer/library/studies/fada/fada1.htm.

On June 17, 2011, to mark the 40th anniversary of President Nixon's war on drugs, President Carter wrote an op-ed piece for the *New York Times* that described his administration's position on drug control policy and his recommendations for changes in current policy: http://www.nytimes.com/2011/06/17/opinion/17carter.html.

"FIRST, I WOULD LIKE TO INTRODUCE MYSELF. I AM ELVIS PRESLEY."

(continued)

While en route, Presley wrote a letter of introduction on airlines stationary that he would later hand deliver to the White House via a security guard after he arrived in Washington. The brief letter began with the title quote of this section as Elvis' introduction and went on to note that Elvis wished to meet the president to help him fight the drug war against the likes of "hippie elements, the SDS, and the Black Panthers." In a PS to the letter, Elvis indicated he would like to bring a gift to the President, which turned out to be a commemorative World War II Colt 45 pistol.

Nixon's aides saw the meeting as an opportunity to enhance his popularity with youth by appearing with Presley and to promote a positive message to discourage drug use. The President agreed and they hastily arranged the impromptu and improbable meeting. Other than publicity photos snapped by the White House photographer, an awkward moment at the end of the meeting when Presley spontaneously hugged a surprised Nixon, and Presley taking the time during small talk to point out he believed the Beatles typified anti-Americanism and the promotion of drug use, nothing much happened. Nor did much come about as a result of the meeting. Elvis got his badge, which he proudly displayed to family and friends when he arrived home at Graceland. And then it probably went into a drawer or display case together with the many other law enforcement badges Presley had collected over the years.

The dark irony of the Presley-Nixon meeting and eventual tragedy was that Presley was already severely addicted to prescription drugs at the time and had been so for many years. In fact, photos taken during the meeting clearly show Presley's glazed eyes, suggesting he was likely on some kind of drug or, more likely, multiple drugs during the meeting. As have many others, including other celebrities such as Anna Nicole Smith and Heath Ledger, Presley made the profound mistake of thinking that because the drugs he was using were by prescription they were safe. Only seven years later, Presley's drug addiction played a significant if not primary role in ending his life prematurely at the age of 42.

"'Junky Johnny' Comes Marchin' Home"

- ***Document:*** "Our Most Dangerous Epidemic," *Nation's Business*
- ***Date:*** July 1971
- ***Where:*** South Vietnam, Burma, Laos, and Thailand
- ***Significance:*** As President Nixon was getting set to announce his domestic war on drugs, a growing concern was what to do about the war veterans who were using heroin while in Vietnam and who were beginning to return home in large numbers. The heroin epidemic in South Vietnam began in 1970, abetted by corrupt and profiteering South Vietnamese government officials. Their extensive network of local minions marketed the cheap and very pure heroin that was produced in the neighboring countries of Burma, Laos, and Thailand to U.S. GIs stationed in Vietnam. Within a short time, military officials estimated as many as 15 percent of the troops had used heroin and that at least 7 percent had become regular users. The following article, written by one of two U.S. Congressmen—Robert Steele, a Connecticut Republican and Morgan Murphy, an Illinois Democrat—who traveled to Vietnam to study the drug problem among the troops, brought public attention to the issue and put additional pressure on the Nixon administration to act.

DOCUMENT

Our Most Dangerous Epidemic

By Rep. Robert H. Steele

The most serious, most tragic and most baffling problem in our nation today is drug abuse.

No child, no school, no home is immune from the epidemic dangers of narcotics.

No business, big or small, is safe from the thefts, absenteeism, turnover, decreased productivity or shattered morale caused by the burgeoning drug problem.

Like snowflakes, a white plague of heroin has blanketed the U.S. military command in Indo-China. The bleak prognosis is that, in an Asian version of an ancient Greek tragedy, thousands upon thousands of American boys will be discharged into society hooked on the heinous "white poison."

Just look at these chilling statistics:

- There are 250,000 "known" heroin addicts in the United States, according to the National Institute of Mental Health.
- The cost of stolen goods to pay for the heroin these addicts need is an estimated $10 billion a year.
- Better than 50 per cent of all urban crime in the United States is drug-related.
- At a minimum, between 30,000 and 40,000 of our troops now in Viet Nam are addicted to heroin.
- In five major U.S. cities last year, according to the Bureau of Narcotics and Dangerous Drugs, drug-related deaths totaled 1,273. The breakdown: Miami—38; District of Columbia—63; Chicago—46; Philadelphia—71; and New York—1,055. Addiction is the single largest cause of death for those between the ages of 15 and 25 in New York City.

A Growth Industry

Unquestionably, the fastest-growing industry in this nation today is the illicit traffic in drugs. Moreover, it is one of the most profitable industries on earth.

For example, 2.2 pounds of raw opium, the base for heroin, costs roughly $30 at the source. Processed and packaged, it can bring in approximately $300,000 at retail level—with profits ranging from 15 per cent to 1,000 per cent for everyone along the line.

Spawned in the ghetto, drug addiction has hedgehopped to middle-class suburbs, colleges and high schools, to the armed services and, now, to corporations across the country. To support their habit, on-the-job users often become pushers and ensnare co-workers into narcotics addiction.

It is estimated that one out of every 40 workers in the U. S. uses drugs illegally and that three out of every four plants with 50 or more employees have a drug problem.

The coffee break has become the "drop" (swallow a pill) or "fix" (injection) break. Liquor in the locker room has been replaced as the scourge of industry by the secreted barbiturate or amphetamine capsule, the sneakily-dragged marijuana in the stairwell or the hastily dumped syringe in the washroom.

Dilated eyes, shaky coordination, impaired depth perception and drowsiness the addict's symptoms—result in accidents, lost productivity and thievery.

"Strung out" workers reportedly account for much of the $2.5 billion worth of tools, office machinery and other goods stolen from corporations and stores each year. For example, in New York City, which conservatively counts 100,000 heroin addicts, 80 per cent of the shoplifting is attributed to drug users, particularly those employed in the stockrooms of major department stores.

As little as two years ago, drug abuse in industry was considered a rarity. Today it is an exploding problem because new workers, fresh out of school, are imbued with the drug culture.

There is a bad parallel between corporate officials who once denied their firms had a drug problem—and are trying now to cope with it and the armed services, which once unsuccessfully tried to kick the menace under the rug.

When Johnny Staggers Home

It took, frankly, a Congressional trip to bring home the horrendous statistics and focus attention on the fact that this nation has a tremendous problem on its hands as "Junkie Johnny" comes marchin' home from Viet Nam.

I recently returned from a 22-day, nine-nation narcotics probe—which Congressman Morgan F. Murphy of Illinois and I conducted for the House Foreign Affairs Committee—with the sickening news that 10 to 15 per cent of American troops in Viet Nam are using heroin.

Top government officials have not only verified there is an epidemic troop addiction rate, but report our statistics, fearfully, may be on the "conservative" side.

This is the Greek tragedy alluded to earlier. In return for the sacrifice of 50,000 American lives and billions of dollars, the U. S. is getting a homeward-bound military force riddled with drug addicts.

At least 60 GI's now die each month from overdoses of the super-grade heroin supplied by our "allies" and marketed with the blessing of corrupt Southeast Asian officials. Both Army Secretary Stanley R. Resor and John E. Ingersoll, director of the U. S. Bureau of Narcotics and Dangerous Drugs, have been in Saigon recently giving President Nguyen Van Thieu a belatedly blunt list of demands to curb the heroin traffic directed at American servicemen.

It could be a case of too little and too late.

At least 1,000 tons of raw opium are illicitly produced yearly in the Shan States of Burma, the border area of China's Yunnan Province, northern Thailand and northwestern Laos—the so-called "Fertile Triangle "In laboratories in the Burmese-Laotian border area, in Vientiane, Laos, and in Bangkok, Thailand, the bulk of the opium is eventually refined into 94 to 97 per cent pure heroin produced exclusively for the U. S. market and for U. S. troops in South Viet Nam.

The stuff can be bought anywhere, from combat zone to Saigon cabaret, and by American standards of income—even military income—It is dirt cheap. A 97 per cent-pure quarter-gram sells for as little as $2.20. In New York City, a fourth as much sells for an estimated $8, and it's nowhere near as pure. In this country, the strength of heroin is usually only 4 to 6 per cent.

A Handy "High"

Although marijuana has always been a problem, there was very little heroin use among U. S. troops in Viet Nam until December, 1969.

Then, GI's discovered that this almost pure heroin could be smoked or snuffed, producing the same "high" they would get from injecting American heroin directly into the bloodstream. Also, there is no odor from smoking heroin, as there is with marijuana. It is less bulky, easier to hide.

And suddenly, the Army found itself in a new crisis. Fifty-nine overdose deaths in Viet Nam were confirmed by autopsy last year and more than 30 others were suspected. At first, commanders refused to believe they had a troop addiction problem. Now, they are scurrying to find a solution.

But the sorry fact remains that a once-magnificent fighting machine has suffered heavy losses in discipline, morale and effectiveness—not because of the enemy, but because of an insidious white powder. The number one domestic crisis facing this nation in days to come will be in dealing with GI users and addicts when they return to the States. After sniffing or smoking the pure stuff in Viet Nam, many will be forced to use the needle in this country to achieve the "high" they are now accustomed to.

And this means higher crime rates to pay for the higher priced, less-pure heroin available Stateside.

Once, the services simply kicked out drug users with dishonorable or bad conduct discharges. But after the scope of the problem hit home, the Department of Defense in October offered a rehabilitation program featuring an olive leaf of amnesty held out to those turning themselves in.

Few servicemen, however, have availed themselves of the program. The big reason is that there are no "cookbook" solutions to the drug habit and the ready availability of narcotics. The Veterans Administration started a rehabilitation program only a year ago. At present there are five facilities, with eight more planned by 1972. Adequate funds, oddly enough, are not a problem. But finding trained personnel and workable techniques are.

There are, of course, a few bright spots. Administration officials quietly are making control of the international traffic in narcotics a top priority of U. S. foreign policy. The Bureau of Narcotics and Dangerous Drugs, the Customs Bureau and other law enforcement agencies have intensified crackdowns on the flood of high-grade heroin and other hard narcotics coming into the country—a lot of it in military mail parcels.

In Viet Nam, the II Field Force has opened a "Pioneer House" which realistically provides drug information, counselors and medication—and complete amnesty. At home, similar projects have been started at various bases. And the Pentagon has formed an all-service drug abuse committee.

All in all, there is now a great awareness in industry—as in the services—of the drug abuse crisis. But for corporations, as for the services, the newness of the problem makes it difficult to deal with.

Today, our nation of 200 million has an estimated six million alcoholics; tomorrow, that tally may be surpassed by the growing number of heroin addicts.

Corporations should expect that as they recruit from among students and Viet Nam veterans, they risk hiring drug users.

But until all of labor and all of business face the facts, the cost in lower output and lost careers will be exorbitant.

Now that drug abuse has spread to all age groups and social levels, the nation can no longer excuse it by hiding behind cries of "generation gap" or "communications gap."

Omnibus Legislation

Implementing recommendations in a report we made on the heroin menace, Rep. Murphy and I have introduced omnibus legislation to provide for detection, detoxification and rehabilitation of GI addicts, using both military and civilian services.

The legislation, which has attracted more than 75 cosponsors, would require that the Defense Department start an extensive urinalysis program to identify military heroin addicts; and that if rehabilitation efforts prove unsuccessful, a military addict may be civilly committed—prior to his discharge—to the Veterans Administration for up to three years of treatment.

Rep. Murphy and I also have conferred with many Executive branch officials. On June 17, after several months of preparation, the President unveiled a far-reaching drug abuse program which closely parallels many of the recommendations in our report.

We hope our input played a role in the formulation of these policies. The war on drug addiction must be our top national priority. We cannot begin to solve our social problems until we win it.

Let me put it, another way. When our country's security is threatened, the threat is met by total mobilization. If we had an epidemic of malaria or polio moving as fast as heroin addiction is, we would declare a national emergency.

We have such a national emergency on our hands. We must fight it with total mobilization of all forces—government, industry and labor.

SOURCE: Robert H. Steele, "Our Most Dangerous Epidemic," *Nation's Business*, July 1971.

ANALYSIS

If America's drug policy in the 1970s was, as Nixon proclaimed, a war, it was a war that would have to be fought on two fronts. Domestically, heroin use had become far more prevalent than at any previous time following World War II. Inner-city neighborhoods, especially those that were predominantly poor and black were particularly hard hit. In these neighborhoods, the ethos of using heroin to be hip spread outward from the jazz clubs to engulf entire communities. Claude Brown, in his autobiography *Manchild in the Promised Land,* described growing up in Harlem in the 1940s and 1950s when the heroin epidemic of the 1970s had its beginnings. He wrote about his initial perceptions of heroin users providing a glimpse of the temptations that led to the spread of its use:

> The guys I had seen using it, like Butch and Danny and the others, had just started [using heroin], of course, but it wasn't doing anything bad to them. They seemed to feel good. That's what really made me want to use it. Those guys seemed to feel like they were flying, like they were way up in the air; they felt a way that they'd never felt before. And to see so many people going around on those streets feeling so good—I just knew I was missing out on something really big.

As more and more people in his neighborhood became addicted, the adverse consequences became more apparent. Crime, social disorganization, and death soon followed. Brown later perceived heroin use as a kind of plague but noted the community culture was such that those who used heroin seemed to feel "somewhat superior, more hip than I was because they were into drugs." This attitude would foster the continued spread of heroin throughout many of America's inner cities despite the increasingly obvious consequences.

The second war front, literally in this case, was in South Vietnam where American GIs began using heroin at alarming rates in late 1970. In *The Politics of Heroin*, Alfred McCoy describes how the CIA's support of corrupt officials at the highest levels of government in South Vietnam (namely, President Nguyen Van Thieu, Vice President Nguyen Cao Ky, and Prime Minister Tran Thien Kiem) and of anticommunist Chinese Taiwanese insurgents in Laos, Burma, and Thailand (the Golden Triangle) led to the rise in heroin use among U.S. troops. The insurgents controlled much of the poppy production in the area as well as the processing and distribution of heroin, morphine, and opium. After they developed the capacity to create a highly refined and pure form of heroin, and to ship the heroin to South Vietnam using planes bought with CIA money, the South Vietnamese regime targeted American GIs as a new and lucrative market for their product:

> The sudden spread of heroin addiction among GIs in 1970 was the most important development in Southeast Asia's narcotics traffic since the region attained self-sufficiency in opium production. . . .
>
> Once large quantities of heroin became available to American GIs in Vietnam, heroin addiction spread like a plague. Previously unavailable in South Vietnam, suddenly no. 4 heroin was everywhere: fourteen-year-old girls were selling heroin at roadside stands on the main highway from Saigon to the main U.S. army base at Long Binh; Saigon street peddlers stuffed plastic vials of 95 percent pure heroin into the pockets of GIs as they strolled through downtown Saigon. . . . With this kind of aggressive sales campaign, the results were predictable. . . . U.S. army medical officers were estimating that about 10 to 15 percent, of 25,000 to 37,000, of the lower-ranking enlisted men serving in Vietnam were heroin users.

Congressman Steele's article and report to Congress on May 25, 1971, raised the possibility that heroin use in South Vietnam would merge with and create a much larger heroin epidemic in America when addicted soldiers returned from the war. The Nixon administration moved quickly on both fronts to prevent this from happening. In the 1970s, under the direction of Robert DuPont, the administration had already begun an ambitious treatment program to reduce crime in Washington, D.C., by providing methadone to heroin addicts. DuPont had tested arrestees in the District and found that 44 percent tested positive for recent heroin use. Dupont's methadone program would serve as a model for the national treatment program. The man the Nixon administration selected to develop treatment programs to reduce drug use in America as well as among GIs in Vietnam was Dr. Jerome Jaffe.

As detailed in *The Fix*, by Michael Massing, Dr. Jaffe was trained in psychopharmacology and his early research involved testing drug effects in laboratory animals. During his early years post–medical school, he worked in the detoxification unit at the Lexington Narcotics Farm followed by a stint in New York City at Albert Einstein College. At Lexington and in New York, Jaffe became interested in the use of methadone, a synthetic opiate, for the treatment of heroin addiction. In New York, he witnessed firsthand and was impressed by the research of Drs. Vincent Dole and Marie Nyswander, who were using methadone not to detoxify heroin addicts but to maintain them indefinitely on the drug.

Because methadone is longer acting (24 to 36 hours) than heroin (2 to 6 hours), a single daily dose can reduce or eliminate craving, stave off withdrawal symptoms, and block the effects of heroin. Methadone produces a milder, less euphoric high than heroin and is non-sedating. As a result, Dole and Nyswander's patients were able to resume normal activities of daily life such as working and maintaining a stable residence rather than spending most of their time acquiring and using drugs or committing crimes to obtain money for drugs. Patients also did not develop a rapid tolerance to methadone as they did during trials of administrations of heroin or morphine. This meant patients could be maintained at a stable dosage level indefinitely.

While in New York, Dr. Jaffe also learned about and was impressed by other forms of treatment such as the newly developing therapeutic communities (TC). TCs are long-term (18 months or longer) residential, peer-led programs by addicts who successfully completed treatment in a TC. Because TCs do not espouse the use of any drugs during treatment, including methadone, they are one of a group of treatment modalities referred to as drug free. TC programs are still in operation throughout the country including in prisons, but the typical duration has been shortened to three to six months.

When Illinois wanted to revamp its drug treatment system in 1965, they called on Dr. Jaffe to be the main architect. Implementing what he had learned in New York and adding his own innovations such as a computerized system that tracked the progress of patients (revolutionary at the time) Jaffe built the Illinois Drug Abuse Program (IDAP) into a multifaceted, flexible model that included methadone maintenance as well as drug-free programming such as TCs. IDAP was widely viewed as a success, catching the attention of Nixon administration officials. They invited Jaffe to Washington, D.C., to discuss building a national treatment system and for his advice on designing a program to reduce heroin use among Vietnam veterans. Dr. Jaffe was subsequently appointed Director of the newly created Special Action Office of Substance Abuse Prevention (SAODAP), through which he developed and implemented his plans for reducing substance use on both fronts.

At a meeting with Nixon administration officials and top military brass at the Pentagon, Dr. Jaffe proposed a urine-testing program for all returning Vietnam veterans. Those who tested positive for heroin would remain in Vietnam at least several weeks for detoxification but they would otherwise not be court-martialed or dishonorably discharged (the military's existing policy). Jaffe reasoned that the certain and immediate threat of having to remain in Vietnam would act as a more powerful deterrent than the less likely, more distant military sanctions. Once word of the testing program spread, he believed that GIs using heroin would stop using in order to return home as soon as possible. This meant they would have been free of heroin at least a few days before returning, thereby reducing the chance they would resume heroin use once home.

At first, military officials balked at the plan arguing that it would be logistically difficult for them to implement a broad-based testing program on such short notice. Demonstrating a forthrightness that impressed but took his high-ranking Washington hosts by surprise, Jaffe commented, "I cannot believe that the mightiest army on earth can't get its troops to piss in a bottle." "Operation Golden Flow," as the military dubbed it, began shortly thereafter.

The effects of the program were dramatic. Within a month, the rate of positive tests dropped from 9 percent to about 5 percent. By 1972, the rate of positive tests dropped further to only 2 percent. Jaffe's program of deterrence through urine testing and delayed returns home was an unqualified success. A study of Vietnam veterans to determine the extent to which they returned to using heroin once back in the states, conducted by Dr. Lee Robins and her colleagues at Washington University in St. Louis, yielded surprising findings. Eighty-five percent of the returning veterans interviewed said they had been offered heroin while in Vietnam, 35 percent said they tried it, and 19 percent said they had become addicted. All of these figures are much higher than the military estimated and are due to sampling differences. Most surprising, however, was that only 1 percent of the veterans who were addicted to heroin while in Vietnam were re-addicted during their first year back and only 2 percent were re-addicted within three years. The reasons for the low re-addiction rates are complex. The main point in the current context is that the returning veterans clearly had not contributed to a second wave of heroin addiction as feared.

On the domestic front, the program Dr. Jaffe developed was modeled after IDAP and although multifaceted in terms of the kinds of treatment offered, the centerpiece was methadone. With large increases in funding from the Nixon administration and under the leadership of Dr. Jaffe, methadone maintenance programs expanded dramatically in just several years. The number of patients in methadone treatment went from 10,000 in 1970 to 60,000 by the end of 1972. As with his testing program in Vietnam, Jaffe's national treatment program yielded immediate results. Together with the successful, albeit brief disruption of heroin supplied through the Turkish-French pipeline, there were significant reductions in crime and deaths due to heroin overdose in cities across the country.

Under Jaffe's leadership, SAODAP also implemented national epidemiological surveys to scientifically assess the extent of drug use. These included the Drug Abuse Warning Network (DAWN), which monitors drug use "mentions" in hospital emergency rooms and the National Household Survey on Drug Abuse (now the National Survey on Drug Use and Health), an annual survey of the noninstitutionalized American population. Both surveys continue to provide trend information on drug use through the present day.

The accomplishments achieved by SAODAP and Jerome Jaffe would be short-lived. The Nixon administration would back away from their support of treatment as the issue lost urgency and would become embroiled in the Watergate scandal. Dr. Jaffe resigned from his post as SAODAP Director in May 1973, having tired of Washington politics. He would return to doing research at the National Institute on Drug Abuse (NIDA), SAODAP's successor. Dr. Jaffe is presently on faculty at the University of Maryland School of Medicine.

Methadone remains controversial despite its proven effectiveness. Most often, methadone treatment is opposed on the grounds it is "substituting one addiction for another." Communities oppose methadone programs fearing they attract addict congregations with the potential for spreading crime and mayhem. Methadone obtained at clinics can be diverted and sold on the streets for other drugs and it does not prevent the use of non-opioid drugs such as cocaine, alcohol, or benzodiazepines (e.g., Valium). Community disapproval and the difficulties it creates in opening and maintaining methadone clinics, the stigma associated with being identified as a patient receiving methadone over the long-term, and restrictive federal regulations (e.g., Narcotic Treatment Act of 1974, PL 93-281) have all served to limit the further expansion of methadone treatment.

On the horizon, near the time Nixon's presidency was ending abruptly in scandal, shrewd, ruthless Colombian entrepreneurs were perfecting the means for producing and shipping large quantities of cocaine across the world. Their timing could not have been better. Just as Freud had once been, many Americans, particularly those with money, became enthralled with a new *inamorata*. Reemerging from long-term obscurity, cocaine became a much desired drug once again and chic status symbol. Powerful cartels were formed to maintain the lucrative cocaine trade. They reaped unprecedented and huge profits but spawned violent political and social turmoil that roiled (and continue to roil) Colombia and other South American countries for decades. When the abundant supply of powder cocaine was reformulated into cheap, smokable *rocks* to expand the market, a wave of lethal drug-related violence would visit America as well. American policy makers would respond in a familiar way by reverting to a *zero-tolerance* stance and implementing tough new criminal sanctions.

FURTHER READING

Brown, C. (1999). *Manchild in the promised land*. New York: Simon & Shuster.

Dole, V. P., & Nyswander, M. E. (1967). Heroin addiction—a metabolic disease. *Archives of Internal Medicine, 120*, 19–24.

Dupont, R. L. (2002). Heroin addiction in the nation's capital, 1966–1973. In D. F. Musto (Ed.), *One hundred years of heroin* (pp. 67–90). Westport, CT: Greenwood Publishing.

Jaffe, J. H. (2002). One bite of the apple: Establishing the Special Action Office for Drug Abuse Prevention. In D. F. Musto (Ed.), *One hundred years of heroin* (pp. 43–54). Westport, CT: Greenwood Publishing.

Jaffe, J. H. (2010). A follow-up of Vietnam drug users: Origins and context of Lee Robins classic study. *American Journal on Addictions, 19*, 212–214.

Kleber, H. (2008). Methadone maintenance 4 decades later: Thousands of lives saved but still controversial. *Journal of the American Medical Association, 300*, 2303–2305.

Massing, M. (1998). *The fix*. New York: Simon & Shuster.

McCoy, A. W. (1991). *The politics of heroin: CIA complicity in the global drug trade, 1st edition*. Brooklyn, NY: Lawrence Hill Books.

Musto, D. F., & Korsmeyer, P. (2002). *The quest for drug control: Politics and federal policy in a period of increasing substance abuse, 1963–1981*. New Haven, CT: Yale University Press.

Robins, L. N., Helzer, J. E., Hesselbrock, M., & Wish, E. (2010). Vietnam veterans three years after Vietnam: How our study changed our view of heroin. *American Journal on Addictions, 19*, 203–211.

Sneader, W. (1998). The discovery of heroin. *Lancet, 352*, 1697–1699.

Veilleux, J. C., Colvin, P. J., Anderson, J., York, C., & Heinz, A. J. (2010). A review of opioid dependence treatment: Pharmacological and psychological interventions to treat opioid addiction. *Clinical Psychology Review, 30*, 155–166.

On the Internet

Information on heroin is available from the National Institute on Drug Abuse at: http://www.nida.nih.gov/infofacts/heroin.html.

The transcript of an interview for the PBS television show *Frontline* conducted in 2000 with Dr. Jerome Jaffe about his experiences while Director of SAODAP is available at: http://www.pbs.org/wgbh/pages/frontline/shows/drugs/interviews/jaffe.html.

The *Frontline* website also has a 30-year chronology of significant events in America's War on Drugs beginning in the late 1960s at: http://www.pbs.org/wgbh/pages/frontline/shows/drugs/cron/

Data and findings from the Drug Abuse Warning Network (DAWN) survey are at: https://dawninfo.samhsa.gov/default.asp.

Data and findings from the National Household Survey on Drug Use and Health (NHSDUH) are at: https://nsduhweb.rti.org/.

An overview of medication assisted treatment for substance abuse, including methadone maintenance and detoxification and the more recently approved physician-based treatment, buprenorphine, is available through the Substance Abuse and Mental Health Services Administration (SAMHSA) at: http://dpt.samhsa.gov/index.aspx.

A dated but comprehensive source on the history and medical use of Buprenorphine (*Buprenorphine: An Alternative Treatment for Opioid Dependence*) is available from the National Institute on Drug Abuse as part of their research monograph series at: http://archives.drugabuse.gov/pdf/monographs/download121.html.

Text of the Narcotic Addict Treatment Act of 1974, which amended the Controlled Substances Act of 1970 to more strictly regulate methadone treatment is available at the National Alliance of Advocates for Buprenorphine Treatment at: http://www.naabt.org/laws.cfm.

OPIATES AND OPIOIDS

There are many terms used to describe drugs derived from or similar in action to those derived from the *Papever somniferum* plant (opium poppy). Raw opium is obtained from the resin created when the green seedpod of the opium poppy is sliced open. The resinous raw opium contains many chemical compounds (alkaloids) including morphine, codeine, and thebaine that can be extracted with further processing. These naturally occurring compounds are called *opiates* and have similar psychoactive properties when ingested: sedation, euphoria, and analgesia (i.e., pain reduction), as well as systemic effects including depressed respiration, nausea, and constipation. The drug called morphine is named after the Greek god of dreams Morpheus, as tribute to its sedating properties and induction of dream-like states.

Named after the Greek god *Heros* (heroic), heroin is the best-known semi-synthetic opioid. Heroin's chemical name is diacetylmorphine reflecting the fact it consists of two conjoined morphine molecules. After ingestion, the body rapidly decomposes the heroin into morphine. Before its addictive properties and potential for abuse were fully appreciated, and before the event of antibiotics, heroin was marketed as a safer and more effective alternative to morphine and codeine as a cough suppressant. Other semi-synthetic opioids include lower potency drugs such as hydrocodone (Vicodin) and higher potency drugs such as oxycodone (OxyContin, Percodan, Percocet). A very long list of fully synthetic opioids includes fentanyl (Fentora) and methadone (Dolophine).

"Like Dom Perignon and Caviar"

- ***Document:*** The Cocaine Scene, *Newsweek Magazine*
- ***Date:*** May 30, 1977
- ***Where:*** New York, Miami, Chicago, Los Angeles, Washington, DC (and elsewhere)
- ***Significance:*** Relegated to jazz clubs and poor urban enclaves for decades, cocaine reemerged in the 1970s in a big way. Initially an expensive drug, cocaine was a status symbol associated with prosperity, sex, partying, and celebrity. The drug's addicting potential, its damaging effects on health and President William Taft's 1910 declaration that cocaine was "Public Enemy Number 1," had long been forgotten or were discounted. Because cocaine did not cause the same kind of physical dependence as drugs such as heroin many, including prominent public health officials, wrongly believed it to be non-addicting. As the price of cocaine dropped and as more people used the drug more often, however, this belief was challenged and eventually disproved (again). This *Newsweek Magazine* article captures the extent to which a generation of Americans embraced cocaine as a harmless but prized accoutrement of *la dolce vita*. This and similar media portrayals only added to cocaine's rapidly growing allure. Only a few years later, the drug would again be demonized.

DOCUMENT

The Cocaine Scene

Richard Steele with Susan Agrest in New York, Sylvester Monroe in Chicago, Paul Brinkley Rogers in Los Angeles, Stephan Lesher in Washington and bureau reports

Pinstriped Wall Street lawyers take it from 14-karat gold spoons at elegant parties. Ghetto kids huddle in tenements and sniff it off matchbook covers. Graduates of a North Miami high school hold a reunion every December to take it at a "White Christmas" bash, and a California corporate president dishes it out as a holiday bonus to his favorite secretaries. Some aficionados use nothing but $10 silver straws from Tiffany & Co. while others sniff it through rolled-up $100 bills. Cocaine—"the Cadillac of drugs"—was once known as the plaything of jazz musicians, kinky movie stars and the dissolute rich. No longer. To the delight of some and the alarm of others, cocaine is regularly bought, used and lavishly praised by hundreds of thousands of Americans. "Cocaine usage today is about where marijuana was four or five years ago," says one dealer. And its popularity has yet to peak.

Cocaine is expensive and illegal—and, if abused, can be dangerous or even fatal. Yet, an estimated 4.8 million Americans have tried it, and the U.S. Drug Enforcement Administration (DEA) says that the cocaine traffic has become at least a $1 billion-a-year business. Known by a variety of nicknames—"snow," "flake," "blow," "C," "white girl" and, of course, "coke"—the drug costs between $1,200 and $2,500 an ounce at street prices, depending on purity.* More cocaine is being smuggled into the U.S. today than ever, and police estimate that they seize a trifling 10 per cent of the supply—at best. "It's coming in here like a rolling ball," says a Chicago police official, "and we can't stop it."

Penalties for the sale of cocaine or even the possession of more than a minimal amount are harsh. In New York, for instance, a person convicted of possessing 2 ounces of cocaine—57 grams—can be sentenced to life imprisonment. Cocaine ranks third on the DEA's list of law-enforcement priorities for dangerous drugs, behind heroin and amphetamines, barbiturates and hallucinogens, and just above marijuana. But cocaine is not a narcotic, is not addictive and causes no withdrawal symptoms. Taken in moderation, cocaine probably causes no significant mental or physical damage and a number of researchers have concluded that it can be safer than liquor and cigarettes when used discriminately. In a recent court case, a judge in Massachusetts ruled that since cocaine is not a dangerous narcotic drug, a state law barring its possession was unconstitutional. And there is today growing pressure to lessen the penalties for its use—and some arguments to de-criminalize cocaine altogether.

Cocaine's popularity has spread so vastly within the last few years that it has become the recreational drug of choice for countless Americans. Businessmen use it to get going in the morning and entertainers use it to keep going at night. College students and housewives use it, stockbrokers and fashion designers use it, rock singers and used-car salesmen use it. A Miami teen-ager estimates that 5 to 10 per cent of her classmates used cocaine "fairly frequently," and one Hollywood producer reportedly budgeted $250,000 to keep his cast and crew happily high on cocaine during the filming of his new movie last summer.

Like Dom Perignon and Caviar

At certain restaurants in Aspen, Colo.—which one DEA official called "the cocaine capital of the U.S."—devotees can ask for "Booth D" to be assured of a table where

*Cocaine is an expensive high. A typical evening's dose—about 150 milligrams of cut cocaine—cost $15 to $25.

they can safely take the drug. A University of California law student who pays her tuition with the money she makes from dealing cocaine concedes that she does have one problem. "Most of my profits go right up my nose," she says.

Among hostesses in the smart sets of Los Angeles and New York, a little cocaine, like *Dom Perignon* and beluga caviar, is now de rigueur at dinners. Some party-givers pass it around along with the canapés on silver trays; some fill ashtrays with cocaine and set them on the table. Others dispense it more grudgingly. "Hostesses say it ruins appetites," says one Hollywood partygoer, "and they get upset to see their guests playing with the beef Wellington." Even in circles where cocaine has long been popular, it is now taken far more openly. "Before, you would go to parties and the bathroom door was always locked," says one film star's manager. "I could never get into a bathroom when I needed to because people were in there sniffing cocaine . . . now it's become socially acceptable to see people doing it."

The drug itself has a fairly quick effect. When inhaled through the nose, it goes to the back of the nasal cavity, combines with mucus and drips down the back of the throat. The nose and upper gum go numb—and then the "high" begins. Cocaine is a stimulant—an "up"—and produces none of the blurred perception or memory lapse that often accompanies the use of marijuana. The user experiences a feeling of potency, of confidence, of energy. A Miami nurse reports: "I have such a beautiful feeling—like I could touch the moon." Even doctors who have studied the effects of cocaine agree that users generally experience an uplifting sensation. "It is one of the closest things to a pure feel-good drug," says Dr. Robert Byck of Yale University's School of Medicine.

Critics contend that the drug turns people unduly aggressive and hostile. "They become snappy," says one New Yorker who has sworn off. "And besides, coke talk is even more stupid than drunk talk." Cocaine also takes some getting used to. One New York City woman describes her first sniff: "My initial sensation was the same stinging, pungent feeling you get when you use nose drops. Within seconds, I developed a postnasal drip, and within minutes a numb nose. When the coke finally took hold of me, it was an exceedingly mild high—and it seemed to me that the whole thing was an expensive hype."

"Frosties" and "Lines"

There are many ways of taking cocaine. It can be dissolved in water, sprinkled into cocktails or dabbed onto a cigarette and smoked. It can be burned and the fumes inhaled or, like heroin, it can be taken intravenously. Some cocaine fanciers like what they call "frosties"—having a friend put cocaine on a piece of paper and blowing it into the back of their mouths. Most often it is sniffed—"snorted," in the argot of the cocaine culture—and the ritual at times seems as important as the drug itself. The cocaine powder is gently poured onto a clean flat surface, often a mirror to make it easier to spot each granule. Taking a razor blade, the user divides the powder into "lines," with a precision and concern for detail that a surgeon would envy. Then, using anything ranging from a plastic straw (the cocaine granules would stick to a paper straw) to rolled-up currency, the drug is inhaled into the nose.

The accouterments of the cocaine culture seem to be part of the kick. Some coke buffs wear neck chains with a razor blade and a tiny spoon dangling like amulets. Maxferd's a San Francisco jewelry store, provides diamond-encrusted razor blades for

$500 and custom-designed spoons that sell for as much as $5,000. The store, which sold $40,000 worth of cocaine spoons last year, also offers a double spoon. "We have to use calipers to measure the distance from one nostril to the other," says Maxferd's owner, Howard Cohn. "It can get quite funny."

Bookstores around the country have sold 50,000 copies of a slim, "how-to" volume called "Cocaine," and a Los Angeles store called Propinquity stocks vials of glass and 14-karat gold at $4,000 as well as bargain-basement coke kits (mirror, razor blade, spoon and cocaine container) at $10. At an L.A. boutique, a $150 sterling-silver fountain pen has a chamber to hold cocaine—and, just in case the buyer actually wants a pen, a cartridge that holds ink.

Cocaine powder is made from the leaves of the coca plant, which grows in the Andean valleys of South America. It was used by the Incas, who regarded the coca plant as "a living manifestation of divinity," according to historian W.G. Mortimer. Divinity was not something the early Inca leaders wanted to share with the masses, and they doled out coca leaves as special favors to the nobility, as a reward to victors in athletic contests—or to sacrificial victims just before their execution. It took centuries before cocaine found its way into Western European society, where one of its most avid enthusiasts was Sigmund Freud. "One senses an increase of self-control and feels more vigorous," Freud wrote in 1884. "Long-lasting, intensive mental or physical work can be performed without fatigue . . . doses of coca produce no compulsive desire to use the stimulant further."

In 1886, an Atlanta, Ga., pharmacist named John Styth Pemberton mixed cocaine and caffeine in a syrup he called "the intellectual beverage"; later he named it Coca-Cola. "Coke" contained coke until 1903, when the company agreed to remove the drug from its product to comply with the new Pure Food and Drug Act. (Chemists at the U.S. Customs office still analyze random samples of Coca-Cola syrup to make certain that all traces of cocaine have been removed.)

"I Get No Kick from Cocaine"

Cocaine's escapist properties were quick to spread among the rich and the famous. It is believed that Jean Cocteau, Aldous Huxley and Arthur Conan Doyle used it—as well as Doyle's fictional friend Sherlock Holmes. When Cole Porter wrote "I Get a Kick Out of You" in 1934, he said "I get no kick from cocaine": "I'm sure that if/I took even one sniff/That would bore me terrif/ic'ly too." And the snooty magazine *Vanity Fair* took uncritical note of coke's sway among the West Coast's beautiful people in 1922: "'Will you come to my Snow-Ball' read the clever invitations. In one corner of the living room was a miniature drug-store where (the host) kept the company in a roar as he dispensed little packages of cocaine, morphine and heroin."

Today, only one firm, the Maywood Division of the Stepan Chemical Co., is legally permitted to import coca leaves to the U.S. It converts some of the leaves to cocaine for medicinal use, while the majority is processed to produce the non-cocaine flavoring waxes for Coca-Cola. But Stepan's legal operation pales in comparison with the illegal traffic in cocaine conducted by amateur and professional criminals. "Traffic is booming and the problem is now outracing us," says Robert Nickoloff, the DEA's special agent in northern California.

The criminal underworld smuggles the drug from South America on ships (bound usually for California, Florida or New York) or by couriers, called "mules." The mules are often South American workers, and the operation is made to order for organized-crime syndicates. "They get someone who earns about $300 a year and pay him $1,000 to carry a case to the U.S.," says Marino Milano, the DEA's agent in charge in the Washington, D.C., area. "If he doesn't get caught, he's made three years' pay and is eager to go again. . . . In most cases, (mules) are caught—and then they're deported. When others see that the worst thing that can happen is to be sent back home again, they too will take the chance to make what to them is a great deal of money."

Most cocaine smugglers, however, are amateurs and independents. College students pool their funds and send a courier to South America to buy relatively large amounts. Tourists bring the drug back, planting it on their young children in hopes of escaping detection. One Hollywood movie mogul and a group of friends recently purchased 200 pounds—and turned more than $2 million profit in a space of five weeks. The ruses that the smugglers employ are many and varied, though not always successful. Customs agents and DEA officials have found cocaine sewn into an antique rug being imported by a 74-year-old woman, in a cage full of boa constrictors and pythons, in aerosol cans, in scuba divers' oxygen tanks, in diplomatic pouches and in bottles of Scotch (when the liquor is poured into a pan and evaporates, the cocaine remains).

No Ebb in the Flow

Last year, DEA officials seized 571 pounds—up from 295 pounds in 1972. At San Francisco International Airport, the number of cocaine-smuggling arrests has increased 150 per cent in the last three years. About 60 per cent of the cocaine seized by American officials is confiscated in Puerto Rico or Florida, and last year in Tampa, customs officials intercepted 181 pounds—worth $40 million at street prices—hidden on board a freighter arriving from Colombia. Still, there is no reason to believe that the flow is being stemmed.

Once the pure cocaine is in the hands of a dealer, it is invariably "stepped on," diluted by mixing it with substances such as lactose, dextrose or quinine. On the average, a supply purchased from a drug dealer will contain about 10 to 20 per cent pure cocaine. The adulterated dosages can then be resold at astounding profits. One 24-year-old Boston dealer, who has been selling narcotics since he was 13, has been able to pay for and renovate a triplex apartment and purchase a downtown bar with his profits. His income over the past five years: $700,000.

In some areas, cocaine dealers compose a genteel underworld. "When we bust someone, we always ask them what they know about heroin trafficking," says an agent in Detroit." Most of them are quite outraged. They say things like, 'How would I know about that? That stuff ruins people's lives.'" Other narcotics agents, however, contend that the subterranean world of cocaine dealers has grown increasingly violent. "A few years ago, none of the coke dealers armed themselves," notes a DEA official. "Now they're all packing pieces." Last year, an American agent was murdered in the course of a cocaine investigation in Bogota, Colombia.

As cocaine use rises, more people have come to regard the penalties for moderate, social indulgence as far too severe. Cocaine busts often net celebrities—and sometimes they are given only moderate sentences. Last May, for instance, television star Louise Lasser of "Mary Hartman, Mary Hartman" pleaded guilty to possession of cocaine, but the judge let her off on condition that she see a psychiatrist. A number of recent developments have encouraged cocaine cultists who look toward the day when the drug can be taken openly. The Massachusetts court's ruling last December was considered one important step in this direction. Spurred by the decision, the Judiciary Committee of the Massachusetts House of Representatives began hearings last month to put cocaine in a new—and lower—drug classification, and was considering lowering the penalty for possession from one year in jail to a mandatory six-month probation for first offenders.

President Carter's special assistant for health issues, Dr. Peter Bourne, says, "There's not a great deal of evidence of major health consequences from the use of cocaine." But Bourne, whom Carter has named to run the Office of Drug Abuse Policy, believes that if cocaine were less expensive and more easily obtained, users would indulge more heavily, perhaps creating greater health problems. There is little likelihood that Federal statutes will be revised in the immediate future. Despite the medical evidence that cocaine is a relatively harmless substance, the popular view is still that sniffing it can be dangerous to one's health—and few politicians seem inclined to risk the consequences of trying to lessen the penalties for doing so. But it is equally true that U.S. officials believe that "recreational" users of the drug are no more deterred by laws than marijuana smokers are. In short, the cocaine culture is sure to grow in coming months—and seems all but certain to hit a new high.

SOURCE: Richard Steele, "The Cocaine Scene," *Newsweek Magazine*, May 4, 1977.

ANALYSIS

An important question concerning the history of drug use in America (and in other countries for that matter) is why one drug or another seems to become popular with great suddenness. The unsatisfying answer to that question is that each drug "epidemic" has occurred owing to a unique confluence of circumstances. In very general terms, cultural events converge to provide the context for broader acceptance of a drug (or for drugs generally) creating increased demand. Drug availability is an equally important factor. Drugs that are easier to obtain are more likely to be tried, used regularly, and then abused. These two factors—cultural context plus availability—spiral into a feedback loop of increasing demand and supply that then lead to what is often called an epidemic but would be more accurately characterized as simply a spike or increase in use. Sometimes it has been the increased availability of a drug that creates the initial demand and sometimes it has been the reverse.

However, in every instance the circumstances driving cultural acceptance and increased demand on the one hand and drug supply on the other have been unique. This makes it difficult to be more specific about the causes of drug epidemics and it is hard to predict when the next epidemic will occur and for which drug. It's like trying to predict the next big pop music star or fashion trend. In the 1950s, for instance, heavy marketing by pharmaceutical firms, celebrity endorsements, and physician practice patterns created an appetite for stimulants and tranquilizers. In the 1960s, the countercultural movement fostered in LSD and marijuana use and set the stage for the broader, albeit more limited social acceptance of other drugs such as heroin and cocaine. The reemergence of cocaine in the 1970s and its rebranding as being the "champagne of drugs" after decades of marginalization provides another good illustration of how historically unique contextual factors interact with unique supply factors to create an "epidemic."

After the Harrison Act of 1914, cocaine was no longer available in over-the-counter patent medicines or other products. The supply of coca leaves that had been processed into cocaine also came under strict regulation. This drove down availability and increased price. Moreover, cocaine is a stimulant. As such it soon had plenty of competition from the growing production and marketing of amphetamine in the 1930s, which was inexpensive and widely available. It's not that cocaine could not be had. There were always small numbers of cocaine users throughout the years, post–Harrison Act. There is even indication that crack cocaine was first created and used as early as the 1960s. It's just that the demand was not great for a relatively expensive and hard to get drug like cocaine when cheaper and potent alternatives like amphetamine were readily available and popular.

This changed in the 1960s and 1970s when Congress passed laws that more tightly regulated amphetamine production and prescribing (see Drug Abuse Control Amendments of 1965 and the Controlled Substances Act of 1970). Those seeking stimulants thus had to look elsewhere when amphetamine became harder to get. Cocaine fit the bill. Still rather costly and somewhat scarce in the early 1970s, it was first embraced by wealthier Americans and the glitterati as a status symbol and harmless diversion.

Perhaps the best representation of cocaine's newfound status was the large, "Man in the Moon with a Cocaine Spoon" animated display at the trendy 1970s Manhattan nightclub, Studio 54. As the unselected masses waited outside behind a velvet rope in hopes of gaining admission, the chosen few danced, drank, sexed, and drugged the night away inside; cocaine was the popular drug of choice. At the appointed time—usually while Donna Summer's paean to orgasms "Love to Love You, Baby" was playing—the cocaine spoon arced gracefully across the back curtains ending up at the man in the moon's nose. This touched off a sequenced line of lights that led from nose to brain, cheering dance crowd, mission accomplished.

Articles such as "The Cocaine Scene" in *Newsweek Magazine* and others appearing in prominent periodicals such as *Time* and *Rolling Stone* fostered the perception that cocaine provided for a rollicking good time that was devoid of any ill aftereffects. That perception helped create an increased demand for cocaine that in turn encouraged profiteering distributers to increase supply. The *Newsweek* article notes that most cocaine suppliers were amateurs who used human "mules" to bring the drug into the country keeping the supply limited and the price high. But that changed rapidly too.

The capacity to import cocaine in large quantities was facilitated by a number of people and events that occurred in South America, Mexico, the Caribbean, and the United States. Suppliers perceived the growing demand for the drug in the United States and found ways to meet it. Among the more important are the following:

- The World Bank paid for the construction of the Pan American Highway through the Upper Huallaga River Valley in Peru. This portion of the highway, which extends throughout South and Central America, provided an expedient means by which the coca leaves grown and harvested in Peru could be transported to the processing facilities in Colombia. Mules (regular ones in this case) carrying packs of cocaine over rough terrain were replaced with speedy cars and vans traveling over a highway thereby increasing the amount of coca leaves available for processing.
- Through the early 1970s, Chilean traffickers largely controlled the South American cocaine trade. They hired Colombians as intermediaries to produce and transport the drug. They did so to take advantage of an existing trafficking network of Colombian *contrabandistas* that illegally imported high tariff items from the United States such as cigarettes, coffee, and appliances and then sold the items at a profit in Colombia. Instead of heading back to the United States with no cargo, the return trips for more contraband were used to export cocaine. Chilean control of the cocaine trade came to an abrupt end in 1973 when General Augusto Pinochet came to power. Pinochet sought to end drug trafficking because he feared the profits could be used to fund an insurgent-led counter-coup. The Colombians were more than willing to take full control of the distribution channels that had formerly been overseen by the Chileans.
- Cuban exiles that came to Miami after Fidel Castro took power in 1959 brought a small but significant cocaine trade with them that helped establish Miami as an import destination. Wealthy expatriate Cubans from Havana brought their expensive, pre-Castro habits with them, including sniffing cocaine (the poor smoked marijuana). At first, Colombians began selling cocaine from Queens, New York, where there was an existing and sizable community of Colombian émigrés. But it was only a matter of time before they infiltrated and then violently took control of the cocaine markets in Miami. Leading the way was Griselda Blanco ("La Madrina," see sidebar). Once they secured Miami, Colombians controlled cocaine production, importation, and distribution throughout South America and the United States running a highly efficient operation.
- The successful eradication of marijuana in Mexico and reduction of the importation of that drug into the United States in the 1970s left marijuana traffickers with little product to sell. As supplies of cocaine became more plentiful, the existing networks that had formerly provided marijuana were used to sell the new drug for which there was a steadily growing demand. This is a good example of how, when the supply of one drug is reduced in one place, a new drug emerges to take its place or drug production is moved to another place.
- In the United States, a German Colombian immigrant named Carlos Lehder Rivas developed a plan for importing cocaine by the ton instead of by the kilogram. Using his own transportation fleet, Lehder's fly-by-night (literally) operations brought unprecedentedly massive quantities of cocaine to the United States. A steady stream of small planes and speedboats brought ton after ton of cocaine into the Miami area, the Carolinas,

and Georgia where it was distributed to the rest of the country. Pilots reported flying hundreds of sorties without experiencing any hindrance from law enforcement.

- Panamanian dictator Colonel Manuel Noriega was deeply involved in drug trafficking for many years. Drug officials in the United States knew it but for political reasons, looked the other way. Noriega was allowed to thrive as a major drug dealer by virtue of his involvement with the CIA and because of his assistance to the Reagan administration in support of the Nicaraguan Contras. As a result, during Noriega's dictatorship in the 1980s, Panama served as a major transshipment point for cocaine. Its secretive and corrupt banking system, particularly the Bank of Credit and Commerce International, was a repository for laundering the enormous sums of money that were made. Noriega became a rich man from his role in drug trafficking.
- Nixon, Ford, and Carter administration officials focused their anti-drug efforts on marijuana and heroin. They regarded cocaine as a minor nuisance, perhaps believing as many American's did that cocaine was a relatively safe, non-addicting drug, especially in comparison to heroin. They ignored or downplayed the reports of DEA field and law officers who warned of the growing crime and violence in Miami and in other parts of the country as a result of the cocaine trade. For a time, this willful neglect allowed cocaine traffickers to run their business with impudence, virtually unfettered by law enforcement.
- On the clinical side, influential figures such as Dr. Robert DuPont, who was the head of National Institute on Drug Abuse in the 1970s, underestimated cocaine's addicting potential. The 1980 edition of *The Comprehensive Textbook of Psychiatry* indicated that "if it is used no more than two or three times a week, cocaine creates no serious problems." Because cocaine does not produce physical withdrawal symptoms like opioids such as heroin, it was believed cocaine was less addicting. The clinical understanding of addiction had not yet evolved to consider fully a drug's potential for compulsive use or for more subtle symptoms indicative of withdrawal such as anxiety and depression. This underscored the broader public perception—reinforced by articles such as the one in *Newsweek*—that cocaine was a relatively benign drug and reflected a surprising lack of appreciation for the historical precedent of the late 1800s to early 1900s when the harmful effects of cocaine use had been clearly in evidence.

By the mid- to late 1980s, the supply of cocaine in the United States was as bountiful as the demand. For instance, the DEA reported seizing 200 kilograms (440 pounds) of cocaine in 1977. Ten years later, the amount seized was 36,000 kilograms (79,200 pounds). Despite the increase in seizures, the price of cocaine had fallen dramatically over roughly the same period while the purity had increased; both indicators of an abundant supply. The price per kilogram of cocaine in 1982 ranged from $47,000 to $70,000 with an average purity of about 50 percent. By 1991, the kilogram price had dropped to between $10,000 and $38,000 with an average purity of 80 percent.

With the increased supply and reduced cost, cocaine use spread from the well-to-do to the hoi polloi, who were attracted by cocaine's euphoric effects as well as by its association with wealth and status; the drug-using equivalent of keeping up with the Jones's. Miami remained at the center of it all. The violent cocaine trade there would be portrayed in a highly stylized way in the popular television show *Miami Vice* and the movie *Scarface*. Whatever national concern there might have been over the large increase in cocaine use, that concern did not translate into political action until the highly publicized death of the popular basketball player Len Bias and professional football star Don Rogers in 1986 forced the issue. The increase in violence associated with gangs vying for control of the crack cocaine trade provided additional incentive. The result would be a return of mandatory minimum sentences, a policy of zero-tolerance, and the beginnings of what has been termed an "experiment in mass incarceration."

FURTHER READING

Antonowicz, A. (2001, January 30). Woman with the golden gun; America's evil drugs godmother . . . true-life face of the film *Traffic*. *Mirror*, Section 1, 24–25.

Bowden, M. (2001). *Doctor dealer: The rise and fall of an All-American boy and his multimillion-dollar cocaine empire*. New York: Grove Press.

Crittenden, A., & Ruby, M. (1974, September 1). Cocaine: The champagne of drugs. *New York Times Magazine*, 14–17.

Eddy, P., Sabogal, H., & Walden, S. (1989). *The cocaine wars*. New York: Bantam Books.

Gugliotta, G., & Leen, J. (1989). *Kings of cocaine: Inside the Medellin cartel—an astonishing true story of murder, money, and international corruption*. New York: Simon and Schuster.

Jonnes, J. (1996). *Hep-cats, narcs, and pipe dreams: A history of America's romance with illegal drugs*. New York: Scribner.

Karch, S. B. (2006). *A brief history of cocaine, 2nd edition*. New York: CRC.

Kerr, P. (1988, August 24). Cocaine glut pulls New York market into drug rings' tug-of-war. *New York Times*, B1.

Kerr, P. (1987, February 13). From center of cocaine trade to a Florida jail. *New York Times*, A1.

Massing, M. (1998). *The fix*. New York: Simon & Schuster.

Rinfret, M. (1991). Cocaine price, purity, and trafficking trends. In S. Schober & C. Schade (Eds.), *The epidemiology of cocaine use and abuse* (pp. 297–303). *NIDA Research Monograph Series 110* (ADM 91-1787).

GRISELDA BLANCO—"LA MADRINA"

On the afternoon of July 11, 1979, when Griselda Blanco wanted to settle a score with a rival Colombian cocaine dealer, she dispatched several men in a white Ford Econoline van to the Dadeland Mall, located ten miles south of Miami. Far from being the inconspicuous warehouse chosen by Al Capone for his 1929 massacre, the Dadeland Mall was the largest in the Miami area and busy with mid-day shoppers. The outside of the van was crudely disguised by hand-stenciled lettering that said "Happy Time Complete Party Supply" on one side and "Happy Time Complete Supply Party" on the other. Inside the "war wagon" the walls of which were reinforced with steel plates, were police-issue bulletproof vests and a cache of weaponry suitable for a small military detachment. Leaving the vehicle idling, the Colombian hitmen (part of a group of Blanco's paid assassins called *Pisteleros*) followed their target and his bodyguard into a liquor store where they opened fire with a Beretta automatic handgun and an Ingram Mac-10 machine pistol. The Dade County coroner stopped counting the bullet holes in the two victims saying they looked like "Swiss cheese."

The Dadeland Mall Massacre marked the beginning of Miami's "cocaine wars" and the brief, violent reign of Griselda Blanco who became known as Miami's "Queen of Cocaine." Other nicknames she received along the way were less flattering: the "Black Widow" (all 3 of her husbands were murdered), the "Female Scarface," La Gaga ("the Stutterer), and La Madrina ("the Godmother"). She named her German shepherd Hitler and her youngest son Michael Corleone after the character in *The Godfather*. Before, she was deported back to Colombia in 2004, she would be responsible for as many as 200–250 murders. She ordered killings for almost any reason: because people owed her money; because she owed them money; and for perceived slights no matter how small. She ordered that a restaurant parking lot be sprayed with bullets because of bad service. Some of her intended victims included her targets' small children. In fact, she would be angry if her hitmen spared a child's life for any reason. She killed her second husband by shooting him in the face in a parking lot.

Blanco ordered the killings of at least eight female strippers that she hired to perform at the lavish orgiastic parties she threw for customers, associates, and Miami's well connected. She suspected the strippers were sleeping with her husband although the openly bisexual Blanco also frequently slept with the paid entertainment. Tons of cocaine, imported from Colombia and distributed throughout the country, financed the madness on

(continued)

GRISELDA BLANCO—"LA MADRINA"

(continued)

a scale worthy of Caligula. At her peak, she was generating at least 80 million dollars of income *per month.* Blanca was eventually arrested and served a long sentence in a federal prison in California, where she continued to run her drug enterprise. Released from prison in 2004, she was immediately deported to Colombia. The last known picture of her was taken in 2007 at the Bogota airport. She is believed to be alive but her exact whereabouts are unknown.

Rockville, MD: U.S. Department of Health and Human Services.

Siegel, R.K. (1992). Repeating cycles of cocaine use and abuse. In D.R. Gerstein & H.J. Harwood (Eds.), *Treating drug problems—Volume 2* (pp. 289–316). Washington, DC: National Academy Press.

On the Internet

Information on cocaine abuse and addiction is available from the National Institute on Drug Abuse at: http://www.nida.nih.gov/researchreports/cocaine/cocaine.html.

The July 2008 issue of *Maxim* magazine has an article titled "The Female Scarface: The Rise and Fall of the Deadliest Woman Alive" that details the life and criminal career of Griselda Blanco at: http://www.charlescosby.com/charles-cosby-and-griselda-blanco-in-maxim-magazine.

The Office of National Drug Control Policy has information on cocaine including the report *Cocaine Smuggling in 2009* at: http://www.whitehousedrugpolicy.gov/drugfact/cocaine/index.html.

The PBS show *Frontline* has the transcript of an interview with Fernando Arenas who was a pilot for Carlos Lehder at: http://www.pbs.org/wgbh/pages/frontline/shows/drugs/interviews/arenas.html.

"We Are Fighting a Disease, Not People"

- ***Document:*** The Surgeon General's Report on Acquired Immunodeficiency Syndrome
- ***Date:*** October 22, 1986
- ***Where:*** Washington, DC, and the nation
- ***Significance:*** The Reagan administration was criticized for being slow to recognize the extent of the public health problem presented by HIV/AIDS and even slower to marshal resources to combat the growing epidemic. President Reagan gave only two speeches on the topic, both occurring late in his second term in office. Dr. C. Everett Koop was the nation's Surgeon General at the time. After months of meeting with scientists, advocates, and others affected by the expanding epidemic, Dr. Koop concluded—contrary to what many among the administration's conservative base believed—that policies based in moralizing, advocating for sexual abstinence, quarantining immigrants infected with HIV, and universal testing would not reach or help many Americans and could be counterproductive and stigmatizing. Instead, Dr. Koop wrote a balanced, nonjudgmental report that in blunt, candid terms described the epidemic and the means by which HIV/AIDS was spread. Koop's report described ways to minimize the risk of contracting HIV that went beyond advocating sexual abstinence such as recommending condom use during intercourse and maintaining sterile needles for injection drug use. Koop's report also advocated sex education in schools to teach young children about HIV/AIDS. Until the report's release, he kept strict control of early drafts for fear of censure and meddling by administration advisors. A revised, shorter version of the report was mailed to every American household in 1988. Koop's reports deeply angered conservatives and he was derisively dubbed the "condom

king." In other circles, however, he earned considerable respect and praise for his candor and integrity. The report was the first large-scale effort to allay public fears on how HIV/AIDS is spread and it changed the public dialogue. Excerpts highlight aspects of the report that were the most controversial at the time.

DOCUMENT

This is a report from the Surgeon General of the U.S. Public Health Service to the people of the United States on AIDS. Acquired Immune Deficiency Syndrome is an epidemic that has already killed thousands of people, mostly young, productive Americans. In addition to illness, disability, and death, AIDS has brought fear to the hearts of most Americans—fear of disease and fear of the unknown. Initial reporting of AIDS occurred in the United States, but AIDS and the spread of the AIDS virus is an international problem. This report focuses on prevention that could be applied in all countries.

My report will inform you about AIDS, how it is transmitted, the relative risks of infection and how to prevent it. It will help you understand your fears. Fear can be useful when it helps people avoid behavior that puts them at risk for AIDS. On the other hand, unreasonable fear can be as crippling as the disease itself. If you are participating in activities that could expose you to the AIDS virus, this report could save your life.

In preparing this report, I consulted with the best medical and scientific experts this country can offer. I met with leaders of organizations concerned with health, education, and other aspects of our society to gain their views of the problems associated with AIDS. The information in this report is current and timely.

This report was written personally by me to provide the necessary understanding of AIDS.

The vast majority of Americans are against illicit drugs. As a health officer I am opposed to the use of illicit drugs. As a practicing physician for more than forty years, I have seen the devastation that follows the use of illicit drugs—addiction, poor health, family disruption, emotional disturbances and death. I applaud the President's initiative to rid this nation of the curse of illicit drug use and addiction. The success of his initiative is critical to the health of the American people and will also help reduce the number of persons exposed to the AIDS virus.

Some Americans have difficulties in dealing with the subjects of sex, sexual practices, and alternate lifestyles. Many Americans are opposed to homosexuality, promiscuity of any kind, and prostitution. This report must deal with all of these issues, but does so with the intent that information and education can change individual behavior, since this is the primary way to stop the epidemic of AIDS. This report deals with the positive and negative consequences of activities and behaviors from a health and medical point of view.

Adolescents and pre-adolescents are those whose behavior we wish to especially influence because of their vulnerability when they are exploring their' own sexuality (heterosexual and homosexual) and perhaps experimenting with drugs. Teenagers often consider themselves immortal, and these young people may be putting themselves at great risk.

Education about AIDS should start in early elementary school and at home so that children can grow up knowing the behavior to avoid to protect themselves from exposure to the AIDS virus. The threat of AIDS can provide an opportunity for parents to instill in their children their own moral and ethical standards.

Those of us who are parents, educators and community leaders, indeed all adults, cannot disregard this responsibility to educate our young. The need is critical and the price of neglect is high. The lives of our young people depend on our fulfilling our responsibility.

AIDS is an infectious disease. It is contagious, but it cannot be spread in the same manner as a common cold or measles or chicken pox. It is contagious in the same way that sexually transmitted diseases, such as syphilis and gonorrhea, are contagious. AIDS can also be spread through the sharing of intravenous drug needles and syringes used for injecting illicit drugs.

AIDS is *not* spread by common everyday contact but by sexual contact (penis-vagina, penis-rectum, mouth-rectum, mouth-vagina, mouth-penis). Yet there is great misunderstanding resulting in unfounded fear that AIDS can be spread by casual non-sexual contact. The first cases of AIDS were reported in this country in 1981. We would know by now if AIDS were passed by casual, non-sexual contact.

Today those practicing high-risk behavior who become infected with the AIDS virus are found mainly among homosexual and bisexual men and male and female intravenous drug users. Heterosexual transmission is expected to account for an increasing proportion of those who become infected with the AIDS virus in the future.

At the beginning of the AIDS epidemic many Americans had little sympathy for people with AIDS. The feeling was that somehow people from certain groups "deserved" their illness. Let us put those feelings behind us. We are fighting a disease, not people. Those who are already affected are sick people and need our care as do all sick patients. The country must face this epidemic as a unified society. We must prevent the spread of AIDS while at the same time preserving our humanity and intimacy.

AIDS is a life-threatening disease and a major public health issue. Its impact on our society is and will continue to be devastating. By the end of 1991, an estimated 270,000 cases of AIDS will have occurred with 179,000 deaths within the decade since the disease was first recognized. In the year 1991, an estimated 145,000 patients with AIDS will need health and supportive services at a total cost of between $8 and $16 billion. However, AIDS is preventable. It can be controlled by changes in personal behavior. It is the responsibility of every citizen to be informed about AIDS and to exercise the appropriate preventative measures. This report will tell you how.

The spread of AIDS can and must be stopped.

C. Everett Koop, M.D., Sc.D.

Aids

Caused by Virus

The letters A-I-D-S stand for Acquired Immune Deficiency Syndrome. When a person is sick with AIDS, he/she is in the first stages of a series of health problems caused by a virus (germ) that can be passed from one person to another chiefly during sexual contact or through the sharing of intravenous drug needles and syringes used for "shooting" drugs. Scientists have named the AIDS virus HIV or HTIV-III or LAW. These abbreviations stand for information denoting a virus that attacks white blood cells (T-Lymphocytes) in the human blood. Throughout this publication, we will call the virus the AIDS virus. The AIDS virus attacks a person's immune system and damages his/ her ability to fight other disease. Without a functioning immune system to ward off other germs, he/she now becomes vulnerable to becoming infected by bacteria, protozoa, fungi, and other viruses and malignancies, which may cause life-threatening illness, such as pneumonia, meningitis, and cancer. . . .

No Risk from Casual Contact

There is no known risk of non-sexual infection in most of the situations we encounter in our daily lives. We know that family members living with individuals who have the AIDS virus do not become infected except through sexual contact. There is no evidence of transmission (spread) of AIDS virus by everyday contact even though these family members shared food, towels, cups, razors, even tooth- brushes and kissed each other. . . .

Control of Certain Behaviors Can Stop Further Spread of AIDS

Knowing the facts about AIDS can prevent the spread of the disease. Education of those who risk infecting themselves or infecting other people is the only way we can stop the spread of AIDS. People must be responsible about their sexual behavior and must avoid the use of illicit intravenous drugs and needle sharing. We will describe the types of behavior that lead to infection by the AIDS virus and the personal measures that must be taken for effective protection. If we are to stop the AIDS epidemic, we all must understand the disease—its cause, its nature, and its prevention. *Precautions must be taken.* The AIDS virus infects persons who expose themselves to known risk behavior, such as certain types of homosexual and heterosexual activities or sharing intravenous drug equipment.

Risks

Although the initial discovery was in the homosexual community, AIDS is not a disease only of homosexuals. AIDS is found in heterosexual people as well. AIDS is not a black or white disease. AIDS is not just a male disease. AIDS is found in women; it is found in children. In the future AIDS will probably increase and spread among people who are not homosexual or intravenous drug abusers in the same manner as other sexually transmitted diseases like syphilis and gonorrhea.

Sex between Men

Men who have sexual relations with other men are especially at risk. About 70 percent of AIDS victims throughout the country are male homosexuals and bisexuals. This percentage probably will decline as heterosexual transmission increases. *Infection results from a sexual relationship with an infected person.*

Multiple Partners

The risk of infection increases according to the number of sexual partners one has, *male or female*. The more partners you have, the greater the risk of becoming infected with the AIDS virus.

How Exposed

Although the AIDS virus is found in several body fluids, a person acquires the virus during sexual contact with an infected person's blood or semen and possibly vaginal secretions. The virus then enters a person's blood stream through their rectum, vagina or penis.

Small (unseen by the naked eye) tears in the surface lining of the vagina or rectum may occur during insertion of the penis, fingers, or other objects, thus opening an avenue for entrance of the virus directly into the blood stream; therefore, the AIDS virus can be passed from penis to rectum and vagina and vice versa without a visible tear in the tissue or the presence of blood.

Prevention of Sexual Transmission—Know Your Partner

Couples who maintain mutually faithful monogamous relationships (only one continuing sexual partner) are protected from AIDS through sexual transmission. If you have been faithful for at least five years and your partner has been faithful too, neither of you is at risk. If you have not been faithful, then you and your partner are at risk. If your partner has not been faithful, then your partner is at risk, which also puts you at risk. This is true for both heterosexual and homosexual couples. Unless it is possible to know with *absolute certainty* that neither you nor your sexual partner is not carrying the virus of AIDS, you must use protective behavior. *Absolute certainty* means not only that you and your partner have maintained a mutually faithful monogamous sexual relationship, but it means that neither you nor your partner has used illegal intravenous drugs.

AIDS: You Can Protect Yourself from Infection

Some personal measures are adequate to safely protect yourself and others from infection by the AIDS virus and its complications. Among these are:

- If you have been involved in any of the high risk sexual activities described above or have injected illicit intra venous drugs into your body, you should have a blood test to see if you have been infected with the AIDS virus.
- If your test is positive or if you engage in high risk activities and choose not to have a test, you should tell your sexual partner. If you jointly decide to have sex, you must protect your partner by always using a rubber (condom) during (start to finish) sexual intercourse (vagina or rectum).
- If your partner has a positive blood test showing that he/she has been infected with the AIDS virus or you suspect that he/she has been exposed by previous heterosexual or homosexual behavior or use of intravenous

drugs with shared needles and syringes, a rubber (condom) should always be used during (start to finish) sexual intercourse (vagina or rectum).

- If you or your partner is at high risk, avoid mouth contact with the penis, vagina, or rectum.
- Avoid all sexual activities, which could cause cuts or tears in the linings of the rectum, vagina, or penis.
- Single teenage girls have been warned that pregnancy and contracting sexually transmitted diseases can be the result of only one act of sexual intercourse. They have been taught to say NO to sex! They have been taught to say NO to drugs! By saying NO to sex and drugs, they can avoid AIDS, which can *kill* them! The same is true for teenage boys who should also not have rectal intercourse with other males. It may result in AIDS.
- Do not have sex with prostitutes. Infected male and female prostitutes are frequently also intravenous drug abusers; therefore, they may infect clients by sexual inter course and other intravenous drug abusers by sharing their intravenous drug equipment. Female prostitutes also can infect their unborn babies.

Intravenous Drug Users

Drug abusers who inject drugs into their veins are another population group at high risk and with high rates of infection by the AIDS virus. Users of intravenous drugs make up 25 percent of the cases of AIDS throughout the country. The AIDS virus is carried in contaminated blood left in the needle, syringe, or other drug related implements and the virus is injected into the new victim by reusing dirty syringes and needles. Even the smallest amount of infected blood left in a used needle or syringe can contain live AIDS virus to be passed on to the next user of those dirty implements.

No one should shoot up drugs because addiction, poor health, family disruption, emotional disturbances and death could follow. However, many drug users are addicted to drugs and for one reason or another have not changed their behavior. For these people, the only way not to get AIDS is to use a clean, previously unused needle, syringe or any other implement necessary for the injection of the drug solution.

AIDS: What Is Safe

Most Behavior Is Safe

Everyday living does not present any risk of infection. You cannot get AIDS from casual social contact. Casual *social* contact should not be confused with casual *sexual* contact, which is a major cause of the spread of the AIDS virus. Casual social contact such as shaking hands, hugging, social kissing, crying, coughing or sneezing, will not transmit the AIDS virus. Nor has AIDS been contracted from swimming in pools or hot tubs or from eating in restaurants (even if a restaurant worker has AIDS or carries the AIDS virus.) AIDS is not contracted from sharing bed linens, towels, CUPS, straws, dishes, or any other eating utensil. You cannot get AIDS from toilets, doorknobs, telephones, office machinery, or household furniture. You cannot get AIDS from body massages, masturbation or any non-sexual contact. . . .

Children in School

None of the identified cases of AIDS in the United States are known or are suspected to have been transmitted from one child to another in school, day care, or foster care settings. Transmission would necessitate exposure of open cuts to the blood or other body fluids of the infected child, a highly unlikely occurrence. Even then routine safety procedures for handling blood or other body fluids (which should be standard for all children in the school or day care setting) would be effective in preventing transmission from children with AIDS to other children in school. . . .

Casual social contact between children and persons infected with the AIDS virus is not dangerous. . . .

AIDS Will Impact All

The changes in our society will be economic and political and will affect our social institutions, our educational practices, and our health care. Although AIDS may never touch you personally, the societal impact certainly will.

Concern about Spread of AIDS

While the concentration of AIDS cases is in the larger urban areas today, it has been found in every state and with the mobility of our society, it is likely that cases of AIDS will appear far and wide.

Special Educational Concerns

There are a number of people, primarily adolescents, that do not yet know they will be homosexual or become drug abusers and will not heed this message: there are others who are illiterate and cannot heed this message. They must be reached and taught the risk behaviors that expose them to infection with the AIDS virus.

High Risk Get Blood Test

The greatest public health problem lies in the large number of individuals with a history of high risk behavior who have been infected with and may be spreading the AIDS virus. Those with high risk behavior must be encouraged to protect others by adopting safe sexual practices and by the use of clean equipment for intravenous drug use. If a blood test for antibodies to the AIDS virus is necessary to get these individuals to use safe sexual practices, they should get a blood test. Call your local health department for information on where to get the test.

Anger and Guilt

Some people affected with AIDS will feel a sense of anger and others a sense of guilt. In spite of these understandable reactions, everyone must join the effort to control the epidemic, to provide for the care of those with AIDS, and to do all we can to inform and educate others about AIDS and how to prevent it.

Confidentiality

Because of the stigma that has been associated with AIDS, many al3icted with the disease or who are infected with the AIDS virus are reluctant to be identified with AIDS. Because there is no vaccine to prevent AIDS and no cure, many feel there is nothing to be gained by revealing sexual contacts that might also be infected with the AIDS virus. When a community or a state requires reporting of those infected with the AIDS virus to public health authorities in order to trace sexual and intravenous drug contacts—as is the practice with other sexually transmitted diseases—those infected with the AIDS virus go underground out of the mainstream of health care and education. For this reason current public health practice is to protect the privacy of the individual infected with the AIDS virus and to maintain the strictest confidentiality concerning his/ her health records. . . .

Sex Education

Education concerning AIDS must start at the lowest grade possible as part of any health and hygiene program. The appearance of AIDS could bring together diverse groups of parents and educators with opposing views on inclusion of sex education in the curricula. There is now no doubt that we need sex education in schools and that it include information on heterosexual and homosexual relationships. The threat of AIDS should be sufficient to permit a sex education curriculum with a heavy emphasis on prevention of AIDS and other sexually transmitted diseases.

Handicapped and Special Education

Children with AIDS or ARC will be attending school along with others who carry the AIDS virus. Some children who develop brain disease, which will produce changes in mental behavior. Because of the right to special education of the handicapped and the mentally retarded, school boards and higher authorities will have to provide guidelines for the management of such children on a case-by-case basis. . . .

Controversial Issues

A number of controversial AIDS issues have arisen and will continue to be debated largely because of lack of knowledge about AIDS, how it is spread, and how it can be prevented. Among these are the issues of compulsory blood testing, quarantine, and identification of AIDS carriers by some visible sign.

Compulsory Blood Testing

Compulsory blood testing of individuals is not necessary: The procedure could be unmanageable and cost prohibitive. It can be expected that many who test negatively might actually be positive due to recent exposure to the AIDS virus and give a false sense of security to the individual and his/her sexual partners concerning necessary protective behavior. The prevention behavior described in this report, if adopted, will protect the American public and contain the AIDS epidemic. Voluntary testing will be avails able to those who have been involved in high-risk behavior.

Quarantine has no role in the management of AIDS because AIDS is not spread by casual contact. The only time that some form of quarantine might be indicated is in a situation where an individual carrying the AID virus knowingly and willingly continues to expose others through sexual contact or sharing drug equipment. Such circumstances should be managed on a case-by-case basis by local authorities.

Identification of AIDS Carriers by Some Visible Sign

Those who suggest the marking of carriers of the AIDS virus by some visible sign have not thought the matter through thoroughly. It would require testing of the entire population, which is unnecessary, unmanageable and costly. It would miss those recently infected individuals who would test negatively, but be infected. The entire procedure would give a false sense of security. AIDS must and will be treated as a disease that can infect anyone. AIDS should not be used as an excuse to discriminate against any group or individual.

SOURCE: Surgeon General's Report on Acquired Immune Deficiency Syndrome (Washington, DC: United States, Public Health Service, Office of the Surgeon General, 1986).

ANALYSIS

The first published report of what would come to be known as AIDS (Acquired Immunodeficiency Syndrome) was in the Centers for Disease Control's (CDC) Morbidity and Mortality Weekly Report (MMWR) for June 5, 1981. The report described five cases, all younger gay men, who were suffering from a very rarely seen form of pneumonia, *Pneumocystis carinii* (PCP). Soon thereafter, gay men in greater numbers and living predominantly in large cities such as New York, San Francisco, and Los Angeles sought medical attention for PCP and other equally rare conditions such as Kaposi's sarcoma and cytomegalovirus.

Most of the first AIDS patients were already in a severely weakened state by the time they sought medical attention and died within a short time. Other than being gay and having compromised immune systems, there was little else connecting them to explain their illnesses. Some had used drugs, particularly amyl nitrites or poppers and for a time it was thought that this might have compromised their immune systems. The main risk factor appeared to be having many sexual partners but the exact cause and origins of the illness remained in question. Before it became apparent that no one was immune to infection, the syndrome manifest as a cluster of opportunistic infections and a weakened immune system was designated Gay-Related Immune Deficiency or GRID. But the disease would be renamed AIDS in July 1982 as cases began emerging among injection drug users, hemophiliacs, the female partners of injection drug users, Haitians, and infants born to infected women.

In retrospect, from a political and economic perspective, the timing of the AIDS epidemic could not have been much worse. The United States was reeling economically from high inflation and stagnant job growth (i.e., stagflation) during the Carter administration. Moreover, the United States appeared weakened internationally; its influence as a world power in decline after the Vietnam War, the humiliation of the Iranian hostage crisis, and the success of the OPEC cartel in keeping the price of oil high despite stout American opposition. A dispirited American public facing high unemployment, a declining dollar, and the loss of international prestige looked to new leadership for a clear change in direction from what a plurality perceived as the failed liberal policies of the previous two decades. They threw their support behind former film actor and two-term California Governor Ronald Reagan. Combining an avuncular likeability with polished speechifying, and an unapologetically conservative political agenda, Reagan was elected the 40th president in 1980, an event that marked the beginning of a sharply conservative political shift in America.

Although the Reagan administration is admired for restoring American confidence and President Reagan is credited with helping to win the Cold War, his public health record when it came to HIV/AIDS is not laudatory. At a time that fiscal resources were needed for research and treatment, the Reagan administration had as its centerpiece reducing the size of the federal government through decreased spending and lowered taxation (Reaganomics). This governing philosophy was crystallized in the now-famous words of President Reagan at his inaugural address on January 20, 1981: "Government is not the solution to our problem; government is the problem."

Adding to the tepid response of the Reagan administration to the growing epidemic was the fact that AIDS first appeared in gay and bisexual men. This led to the erroneous belief that AIDS was a "gay plague," a belief that persisted (and persists) even in the face of growing counterevidence that the disease was not exclusive to homosexuals. The coalition that supported President Reagan's election included a large, devoted block of fundamentalist Christians as epitomized by Jerry Falwell's "Moral Majority." They believed that homosexuality was a sin and a choice. Some, including Reverend Falwell, saw HIV as divine retribution for immoral behavior. That injection drug users were the second, hardest hit group, one that was also characterized as making immoral choices, did nothing to increase empathy for those infected with HIV and dying with AIDS.

The combination of a conservative, limited-government political philosophy with the view among many administration supporters that AIDS was God's punishment for homosexuality and injection drug use contributed to a decided lack of enthusiasm among administration officials for ushering public resources to combat HIV/AIDS. The following excerpt of a 1982 press conference captures the shockingly cavalier attitude of the Reagan administration (and the national press, note the room laughter during the Q&A) during the first years of the epidemic. The exchange is between reporter Les Kinsolving and White House Press Secretary Larry Speakes:

Kinsolving: Larry, does the President have any reaction to the announcement—the Centers for Disease Control in Atlanta, that AIDS is now an epidemic and have over 600 cases?

Speakes: What's AIDS?

Kinsolving: Over a third of [the victims] have died. It's known as "gay plague." (*Laughter.*) No, it is. I mean it's a pretty serious thing that one in every three people that get this has died. And I wondered if the President is aware of it?

Speakes: I don't have it. Do you? (*Laughter.*)

Kinsolving: No, I don't.

Speakes: You didn't answer my question.

Kinsolving: Well, I just wondered, does the President—
Speakes: How do you know? (*Laughter.*)
Kinsolving: In other words, the White House looks on this as a great joke?
Speakes: No, I don't know anything about it, Lester.
Kinsolving: Does the President, does anybody in the White House know about this epidemic, Larry?
Speakes: I don't think so. I don't think there's been any—
Kinsolving: Nobody knows?
Speakes: There has been no personal experience here, Lester.
Q: No, I mean, I thought you were keeping—
Speakes: I checked thoroughly with [Reagan's personal physician] Dr. Ruge this morning and he's had no—(*laughter*)—no patients suffering from AIDS or whatever it is.

The first administration official to speak publicly about HIV/AIDS was Reagan's Secretary of Health and Human Services, Margaret Heckler. At a U.S. Conference on Mayors, she praised the work of gay advocacy groups and said the administration considered AIDS its "number-one health priority." Despite this assertion, Heckler opposed additional funding for HIV/AIDS. She reasserted this position in a 2006 interview stating that more funding would not have helped. Recent interviews with CDC scientists who studied HIV/AIDS, however, suggest their research efforts were hampered by both the lack of funding as well as the time wasted in pursuit of funding.

Her assertion that HIV/AIDS was the administration's number-one health priority is admirable but questionable. The Reagan administration did allocate additional money for research. Annual federal spending increased from $8 million in 1982 to over $2 billion by 1989. President Reagan also appointed a special commission to study the HIV epidemic and to make policy recommendations. But he then ignored most of the commission's findings when they were published in a 1988 report (much like Nixon ignored his commission's findings on drug policy) near the end of his presidency. He did, however, sign an antidiscrimination law that protected AIDS patients from discrimination by any organization receiving federal assistance.

President Reagan rarely spoke publicly about HIV/AIDS during his two terms in office. He never even mentioned the epidemic until 1985 when he responded to a question from a reporter on HIV/AIDS funding. He would not address the issue again until 1987 when he gave a speech on AIDS at the College of Physicians in Philadelphia. During the speech, he defended his administration's funding amounts and said that "when it comes to preventing AIDS, don't medicine and morality teach the same lessons?" His last speech on AIDS was the May 1987 keynote address at the American Foundation for AIDS Research (amfAR) at the behest of his friend and amfAR's National Chairman Elizabeth Taylor. The speech drew mixed reviews because he advocated for expanded testing and denial of entry to immigrants infected with HIV.

Koop's report reflected another attempt, belated as it was, by President Reagan to address the HIV/AIDS epidemic. Koop was a pediatric surgeon when he was appointed to the position of Surgeon General. Because of his strong and well-known stance opposing abortion, his appointment dismayed many liberals who believed he would use the office primarily as a forum to promote an anti-abortion agenda. But this estimation was erroneous. Koop used his office to speak out on, among other issues, the health consequences of tobacco use and to advocate for better medical care for handicapped children. Despite political pressure and his own opposition to abortion, Dr. Koop refused to issue a report stating there were long-term health consequences for women who had abortions because he did not believe this conclusion was supported by the scientific evidence.

Relegated to the sidelines by administration officials during Reagan's first term in office, Koop was not involved in forming policy related to the HIV/AIDS epidemic until 1986 when President Reagan asked him to write a report on AIDS. At the time, there was a lack of widely disseminated and definitive information on how the virus was spread. With no vaccine or effective treatment yet in sight, misinformation that infection could occur from casual contact, mosquito bites, and toilet seats caused undue fear and anxiety among the general public. In some locales, parents refused to allow their children to attend schools with children who were HIV infected. Some police departments routinely issued rubber gloves for patrol officers and AIDS patients in hospitals were quarantined. The main intent of Koop's report was to provide the public with accurate information about the epidemic to calm these fears and to suggest ways to prevent becoming infected.

Consulting with a wide range of groups and experts that included public health officials, advocacy groups, Christian fundamentalists, scientists, and AIDS patients, Koop collected the information that he would distill into the final report. He wrote the report himself working at a stand-up desk in the basement of one of the buildings at the National Institutes of Health campus. He closely guarded early drafts of the report from Reagan's domestic policy advisors for fear that it would be altered for political reasons. The strategy worked and the final report, issued without alteration, was released in October 1986. Twenty million copies would eventually be mailed to the public.

The report surprised Koop's liberal detractors and disappointed conservative supporters. Koop explained, "My position on AIDS was dictated by scientific integrity and Christian compassion. . . . My whole career has been dedicated to prolonging lives, especially the lives of people who were weak and powerless, the disenfranchised who needed an advocate: newborns who needed surgery, handicapped children, unborn children, people with AIDS."

HIV/AIDS IN THE UNITED STATES, 2011

Although there has been considerable progress in HIV prevention and treatment, figures on the annual HIV incidence (i.e., number of new infections per year) remain grim. Each year, 56,300 Americans are infected, translating into a new infection every 9-1/2 minutes. Since the beginning of the epidemic in 1981 through the end of 2008, 617,025 people have died of AIDS or AIDS-related complications in the United States. At the end of 2009, based on the most recent estimates available from the CDC, there were 1.1 million people infected with HIV. One fifth does not know they are infected and because of this, pose a higher risk for infecting others than those who know their status.

The risk for HIV infection is not shared evenly. There are disparities by sexual preference, race/ethnicity, and gender. In the United States, men who have sex with men (MSM)—a category that includes gays, bisexuals and men who consider themselves heterosexual but who have sex with men—have been at highest risk since the beginnings of the epidemic. Though the proportion of new infections has dropped among MSM, they still account for 53 percent of all new infections and for 75 percent of all new infections among adult and adolescent males. MSM represent the only risk category where the incidence rate has increased over the past decade. Heterosexual contact presently accounts for 31 percent and injection drug use for 12 percent of new infections. The latter figure represents a substantial drop in the proportion of infections attributable to injection drug use and represents one of the few bright spots in the ongoing epidemic although some of the decline may be attributable to older, infected IV drug users dying and there being fewer new injection users to take their place.

Among racial/ethnic groups, Blacks/African Americans, which represent about 12 percent of the US population, account for a disproportionate number of both new infections (45%) and of people living with HIV/AIDS (46%). Especially, concerning is the infection rate for Black/African American women, who have been increasingly hard hit by the HIV/AIDS epidemic. They now have an HIV incidence rate that is 15 times higher than white women and 4 times higher than Hispanic/Latino women.

In 1988, he mailed a shorter version of the report to every American household. As a result of his efforts, calls for mandatory testing and the continued quarantining of AIDS patients receded, as did parental concerns about their children attending public schools and concerns about infection through casual contact. In that same year, the first advertisement for condoms appeared on national television.

America still had (and has) a long way to go with respect to the epidemic. Effective treatments for HIV/AIDS would not be developed until the mid-1990s and thousands of Americans (hundreds of thousands worldwide) continue to be infected each year (see sidebar on current HIV/AIDS statistics). The development of an effective vaccine remains elusive. The disenfranchised and stigmatized groups that Koop cared about such as gays, injection drug users, and minorities continue to have the highest HIV infection rates. But Koop's efforts helped permanently and profoundly change the public conversation on HIV/AIDS and lessened but not eliminated the associated stigma.

That HIV could be efficiently transmitted through dirty needles shared by injection drug users and through unprotected sexual encounters between already infected drug users and their sexual partners—heterosexual as well as homosexual—brought new urgency to the drug policy debate. Drug use, particularly injection use, which had always had potentially dire health consequences, had become quite literally a matter of life and death. The urgency sharpened the focus on the effectiveness/advisedness of harm reduction efforts such as needle exchange and condom distribution programs. Harm reduction, as a drug policy strategy, and the continuing debate are considered further in the document pertaining to Switzerland's social experiment known as Needle Park ("Hooked on Dogma; U.S. Drug Warriors Ignore Switzerland's Success with Heroin Addicts"). The sharply divided response to some of Dr. Koop's recommendations for reducing the spread of HIV infections and AIDS (e.g., sex education in schools, distributing condoms, and clean needles) foreshadow many of the aspects of that still contentious debate.

FURTHER READING

Altmam, L.K. (1982, May 11). New homosexual disorder worries health officials. *New York Times*, C1.

Auerbach, D.M., Darrow, W.W., Jaffe, H.W., & Curran, J.W. (1984). Cluster of cases of the acquired immunodeficiency syndrome. Patients linked by sexual contact. *American Journal of Medicine*, *76*, 487–492.

Boodman, S.G. (1988, May 5). HHS AIDS brochure: Frank, explicit, and ready to be mailed. *Washington Post*, A21.

Engel, J. (2006). *The epidemic: A global history of AIDS*. Harper Collins e-book.

Lansky, A., Brooks, J.T., DiNenno, E., Heffelfinger, J., Hall, H.I., & Mermin, J. (2010). Epidemiology of HIV in the United States. *Journal of Acquired Immunodeficiency Syndromes*, *15(Suppl 2)*, S64–S68.

Montagnier, L. (2010). 25 years after HIV discovery: Prospects for cure and vaccine. *Virology*, *20*, 248–254.

THE ORIGINS OF HIV

Two of the more puzzling aspects of HIV are when and how a virus that causes such a devastating illness could arise with such suddenness and seemingly out of nowhere. It took years of painstaking and elaborate research and the tools of molecular phylogenetics to determine the origins of HIV but there is solid evidence that answers these important questions. We now know the virus did not arise suddenly or even recently and the location and means by which it first infected humans have been identified with reasonable certainty.

The origins of HIV are now estimated to be between 1884 and 1924. The most common form of HIV (HIV-1, subtype M for main) is a mutation of a virus that infects chimpanzees (*Pan troglodytes*) that live in the forests of Cameroon, Equatorial Guinea, and the Republic of Congo in West Central Africa. That virus is named simian immunodeficiency virus (SIV) and given the suffix cpz (SIVcpz) to distinguish it from similar, related viruses that affect other non-human primates such as gorillas (SIVgor). The other major form of HIV, HIV-2, is much less common and is thought to have evolved from the simian virus that infects a monkey called the sooty mangabey.

(continued)

THE ORIGINS OF HIV

(continued)

The HIV mutation of SIVcpz first infected humans living in proximity to the forests inhabited by its chimpanzee carriers. Interspecies transmission most likely came about during the butchering of an infected animal when there was blood-to-blood contact from a bite or other wound. The relative isolation of West Central Africa at the time constrained new infections geographically for a number of years. This changed in post-colonial Africa when there was a large-scale migration from villages to larger urban centers resulting in increased contact with foreigners and where sexual practices such as prostitution that could spread the virus were more common. The advent of modern air travel further connected Africa with the rest of the world and facilitated the spread of the virus beyond its original geographical confines.

The first confirmed case of HIV infection in the United States was in 1969 and identified as a 16-year-old African-American boy from Missouri known only as Robert R. He died from Kaposi's sarcoma, another common AIDS-related opportunistic infection., The source of his infection was never discovered. Of significance is that Robert R. never traveled outside the United States, meaning that the virus was already present in this country as early as the 1960s. The most likely pathway for the wider HIV/AIDS epidemic in the United States that began in the 1970s is through Haiti. It is now believed that Haitian workers were infected with HIV while in the Congo, returned to Haiti and spread the infection to others through sexual contact. Infected Haitian immigrants or gay men vacationing in the Caribbean or both then brought the disease to the United States.

Ostrow, D. (1994). Substance abuse and HIV infection. *Psychiatric Clinics of North America. 17*, 69–89.

Ross, M.W., & Williams, M.L. (2001). Sexual behavior and illicit drug use. *Annual Review of Sex Research, 12*, 290–310.

Shattock, R.J., Warren, M., McCormack, S., & Hankins, C.A. (2011, July 1). Turning the tide against HIV. *Science, 333*, 42–43.

Shilts, R. (2007). *And the band played on: Politics, people, and the AIDS Epidemic, 20th Anniversary Edition*. New York: St. Martin's Griffin

Trafford, A., & Thompson, L. (1988, August 23). The muddled state of AIDS policy. *Washington Post*, T16.

Woodman, Z., & Williamson, C. (2009). HIV molecular epidemiology: Transmission and adaptation to human populations. *Current Opinion in HIV and AIDS*, *4*, 247–252.

On the Internet

A copy of the 1981 CDC MMWR Report that documented what would later be recognized as the first AIDS cases in the United States is available at: http://www.cdc.gov/mmwr/preview/mmwrhtml/june_5.htm.

The PBS series *Frontline* ran a two-part documentary in May 2006 called *The Age of AIDS* to mark the 25th anniversary of the AIDS epidemic in the United States. The complete documentary can be viewed online. The site also has many associated documents such as a transcript of the only speech President Reagan gave on AIDS at: http://www.pbs.org/wgbh/pages/frontline/aids/

The Centers for Disease Control maintains a site that has a large amount of historical and current information on HIV/AIDS at: http://www.cdc.gov/hiv/

The website for the international charity AVERTing HIV and AIDS has extensive information on many topics related to HIV/AIDS including the virus's origins and current status of the global epidemic at: http://www.avert.org/aids-hiv-epidemic.htm.

The website The Body provides extensive information on HIV/AIDS including the latest updates on treatment and prevention at: http://www.thebody.com/

The National Library of Medicine maintains a site with biographical information and the collected papers of Dr. C. Everett Koop including the full report on HIV/AIDS at: http://profiles.nlm.nih.gov/ps/retrieve/Collection/CID/QQ.

The full report of President Reagan's Commission on the HIV Epidemic is available at: http://www.archive.org/details/reportofpresiden00pres.

A reassessment of the Reagan administration's response to AIDS epidemic is at: http://igf culturewatch.com/2004/06/24/reagan-and-aids-a-reassessment/

A synopsis and critique of the response to the AIDS epidemic by the Reagan, Bush, and Clinton administrations is available at: http://www.thebody.com/content/art14034.html.

The Obama administration's 2010 National HIV/AIDS Strategy is available at: http://www.whitehouse.gov/sites/default/files/uploads/NHAS.pdf.

A *Time* magazine story on the first identified case of HIV infection in the United States, Robert R., is available at: http://www.time.com/time/magazine/article/0,9171,965934-1,00.html.

"From the Champagne of Drugs to the Beer of Drugs"

- ***Document:*** Anti-Drug Abuse Act (PL 99–570)
- ***Date:*** October 27, 1986
- ***Where:*** Washington, DC
- ***Significance:*** During the first part of the 1980s, prodded by politically active groups of conservative parents, the Reagan administration focused its drug control efforts on marijuana, justifying that focus with a renewal of the gateway hypothesis. Two events: the highly publicized death of basketball star Len Bias and the spread of crack cocaine to the inner cities, accompanied by violent, gang-related crime for control of the crack trade refocused the administration's (and all politicians') attention on cocaine. No longer viewed as the "champagne of drugs," cocaine became the demonic drug du jour, particularly crack cocaine, which was often wrongly characterized as "instantly addicting." Enacting the Anti-Drug Abuse Act of 1986, just one week before a national election, politicians in both major political parties scrambled to appear "tough on drugs." With little thought to the long-term implications and costs, legislators brought back lengthy mandatory minimum prison sentences and a "zero-tolerance" policy; no illegal drug use would be viewed as minor. The act contained especially severe sanctions for crack cocaine possession and distribution relative to powder cocaine but the magnitude of the sentencing disparities (100 to 1) had little justification. The Anti-Drug Abuse Act marked a sharp turn away from the nation's brief adoption of a public health oriented policy approach and a return to using the legal system and criminal justice sanctions as the primary underpinnings of drug control policy.

DOCUMENT

Anti-Drug Abuse Act of 1986

An Act to strengthen Federal efforts to encourage foreign cooperation in eradicating illicit drug crops and in halting international drug traffic, to improve enforcement of Federal drug laws and enhance interdiction of illicit drug shipments, to provide strong Federal leadership in establishing effective drug abuse prevention and education programs, to expand Federal support for drug abuse treatment and rehabilitation efforts, and for other purposes.

Be it enacted by the Senate and House of Representatives of the United States of America in Congress assembled,

Section 1. Short Title

This Act may be cited as the "Anti-Drug Abuse Act of 1986."

Title 1—Anti-Drug Enforcement

Subtitle A—Narcotics Penalties and Enforcement Act of 1986

Sec. 1001. Short Title

This subtitle may be cited as the "Narcotics Penalties and Enforcement Act of 1986."

Sec. 1002. Controlled Substances Act Penalties

Section 401(b)(1) of the Controlled Substances Act (21 U.S.C. 841(b)(1) is amended—

(1) by redesignating subparagraph (C) as subparagraph (D); and
(2) by striking out subparagraphs (A) and (B) and inserting the following in lieu thereof:

"(1) (A) In the case of a violation of subsection (a) of this section involving—
"(i) 1 kilogram or more of a mixture or substance containing a detectable amount of heroin;
"(ii) 5 kilograms or more of a mixture or substance containing a detectable amount of—

"(I) coca leaves, except coca leaves and extracts of coca leaves from which cocaine, ecgonine, and derivatives of ecgonine or their salts have been removed;
"(II) cocaine, its salts, optical and geometric isomers, and salts of isomers;
"(III) ecgonine, its derivatives, their salts, isomers, and salts of isomers; or

"(IV) any compound, mixture, or preparation which contains any quantity of any of the substance referred to in subclauses (I) through (III)";

"(iii) 50 grams or more of a mixture or substance described in clause (ii) which contains cocaine base;
"(iv) 100 grams or more of phencyclidine (PCP) or 1 kilogram or more of a mixture or substance containing a detectable amount of phencyclidine (PCP);
"(v) 10 grams or more of a mixture or substance containing a detectable amount of lysergic acid diethylamide (LSD);
"(vi) 400 grams or more of a mixture or substance containing a detectable amount of N-phenyl-N-{142-phenylethyl)-4-piperidinyl) propanamide or 100 grams or more of a mixture or substance containing a detectable amount of any analogue of N-phenyl-N-(142-phenylethyl)-4-piperidinyl] propanamide; or
"(vii) 1000 kilograms or more of a mixture or substance containing a detectable amount of marihuana;

such person shall be sentenced to a term of imprisonment which may not be less than 10 years or more than life and if death or serious bodily injury results from the use of such substance shall be not less than 20 years or more than life, a fine not to exceed the greater of that authorized in accordance with the provisions of title 18, United States Code, or $4,000,000 if the defendant is an individual or $10,000,000 if the defendant is other than an individual, or title 18, United States Code, or $2,000,000 if the defendant is an individual or $5,000,000 if the defendant is other than an individual, or both. . . .

"(B) In the case of a violation of subsection (a) of this section involving—

"(i) 100 grams or more of a mixture or substance containing a detectable amount of heroin;
"(ii) 500 grams or more of a mixture or substance containing a detectable amount of—

"(1) coca leaves, except coca leaves and extracts of coca leaves from which cocaine, ecgonine, and derivatives of ecgonine or their salts have been removed;
"(II) cocaine, its salts, optical and geometric isomers, and salts of isomers;
"(III) ecgonine, its derivatives, their salts, isomers, and salts of isomers; or
"(IV) any compound, mixture, or preparation which contains any quantity of any of the substance referred to in subclauses (I) through (III)";

"(iii) 5 grams or more of a mixture or substance described in clause (ii) which contains cocaine base;
"(iv) 10 grams or more of phencyclidine (PCP) or 100 grams or more of a mixture or substance containing a detectable amount of phencyclidine (PCP);

"(v) 1 gram or more of a mixture or substance containing a detectable amount of lysergic acid diethylamide (LSD);

"(vi) 40 grams or more of a mixture or substance containing a detectable amount of N-phenyl-N-[1-(2-phenylethyl)-4-piperidinyl] propanamide or 10 grams or more of a mixture or substance containing a detectable amount of any analogue of N-phenyl-N-[1-(2-phenylethyl)-4-piperidinyl] propanamide; or

"(vii) 100 kilograms or more of a mixture or substance containing a detectable amount of marihuana;

such person be sentenced to a term of imprisonment which may not be less than 5 years and not more than 40 years and if death or serious bodily injury results from the use of such substance shall be not less than 20 years or more than life, a fine not to exceed the greater of that authorized in accordance with the provisions of title 18, United States Code, or $2,000,000 if the defendant is an individual or $5,000,000 if the defendant is other than an individual, or both. If any person commits such a violation after one or more prior convictions for an offense punishable under this paragraph, or for a felony under any other provision of this title or title III or other law of a State, the United States, or a foreign country relating to narcotic drugs, marihuana, or depressant or stimulant substances, have become final, such person shall be sentenced to a term of imprisonment of not less than 10 years and not more than life imprisonment and if death or serious bodily injury results from the use of such substance shall be sentenced to life imprisonment, a fine not to exceed the greater of twice that authorized in accordance with the provisions of title 18, United States Code, or $4,000,000 if the defendant is an individual or $10,000,000 if the defendant is other than an individual, or both. Any sentence imposed under this subparagraph shall, in the absence of such a prior conviction, include a term of supervised release of at least 4 years in addition to such term of imprisonment and shall, if there was such a prior conviction, impose a term of supervised release of at least 8 years in addition to such term of imprisonment. Notwithstanding any other provision of law, the court shall not place on probation or suspend the sentence of any person sentenced under this paragraph. No person sentenced under this subparagraph shall be eligible for parole during the term of imprisonment therein. . . .

Note: N-phenyl-N-[1-(2-phenylethyl)-4-piperidinyl] propanamide is fentanyl, a synthetic opioid similar to morphine but much more potent. It is used as an analgesic to relieve pain and is a Schedule II prescription drug. Fentanyl is often mixed with heroin to enhance the effects. Occasionally, because fentanyl is more potent than heroin, a batch of heroin-fentanyl sold on the streets as if it were pure heroin can result in a spate of overdose deaths among unsuspecting users.

SOURCE: Anti-Drug Abuse Act. Public Law 99–570 (100 Stat. 3207 to 3207–192)

ANALYSIS

The Boston Celtics were an NBA powerhouse at the end of the 1986 season led by a trio of still great but aging stars: Larry Bird, Kevin McHale, and Robert Parish. After winning the NBA championship in 1985, the Celtics again went to the finals in 1986 but lost to Magic Johnson and the Los Angeles Lakers. Normally, successful NBA teams have lower draft picks to select college prospects turning professional. This is to provide the poorer teams an opportunity to improve by giving them the chance to select the most talented college players available. But in 1986, by virtue of a trade several years earlier, the near-champion Celtics had the second draft pick. They used that pick to select 22-year-old Len Bias, who had just completed an outstanding basketball career at the University of Maryland.

Len Bias was a promising basketball player at the University of Maryland who died at the age of 22 after overdosing on cocaine. The publicity surrounding Bias's death shortly after he signed with the NBA as a high draft pick led to hastily crafted federal legislation that provided especially severe penalties for crack cocaine possession and distribution. (Focus on Sport/Getty Images)

NBA talent scouts saw Bias as having superstar potential. The Celtics hoped he would be the beginning of a new, young nucleus of stars who would help the franchise continue their winning tradition. In Landover, Maryland, he was known simply as "the man" because of his basketball prowess and his good citizen status as a clean-living role model. On June 17, 1986, with much fanfare, Bias attended a ceremony in Boston to sign a contract with the Celtics. Photos show a beaming Bias wearing a Celtics cap surrounded by equally happy team officials. Two days later, after an evening of celebrating his new fame and future fortune, Len Bias was dead.

The initial reports of the cause of Bias's death—an overdose of crack cocaine—created quite a public stir and reinforced the growing perception that crack was an especially dangerous form of cocaine. But these reports proved to be inaccurate. An eyewitness account indicates Bias was snorting powdered cocaine just before he died. The immediate cause of death determined at autopsy was cocaine intoxication that disrupted the electrical control of his heartbeat resulting in seizures and cardiac arrest. Nevertheless, the news was stunning not only because of Bias's prominence as an athlete but also because of his reputation as a model citizen. Eight days later, Don Rogers, a young professional football player with the Cleveland Browns, suffered a similar fate. The high-profile deaths of two prominent and popular athletes meant that cocaine could no longer be dismissed as a harmless party drug.

At the time of Rogers's and Bias's deaths, there were already press reports on the spread of crack cocaine in the nation's inner cities and the increased violence attributed to turf wars between gangs vying to sell the lucrative new product. Sometimes the gunfights were literally for control of one street corner and resembled the violence of the cocaine wars waged by Colombians in Miami for control of national distribution. The violence caught the attention of both law enforcement and the press. The following excerpt from a *Newsweek Magazine* article that appeared just days before Bias died quotes public officials who were already making the case for tougher sentencing. After describing the growing trafficking and violence surrounding crack cocaine, the article continues:

> Crack and rock are spreading because cocaine is so widely available in the United States and because the justice system has been unable to thwart the cocaine trade at any level. Police in every city where crack is now a major problem argue that the courts are too lenient with drug offenders, and they

may be right. In New York, special narcotics prosecutor Sterling Johnson recently argued for mandatory jail sentences even in plea-bargained drug cases—and warned that some neighborhoods now have "more crack stops than bus stops.

Prosecutor Johnson would get his wish and then some. Following Bias's and Roger's deaths, the coverage of the crack cocaine epidemic grew exponentially. A Lexis-Nexus search using the terms "crack" and "cocaine" for the two years prior yields 21 articles. The same search applied to the following two years yields 715 articles. The press accounts now included descriptions of how crack cocaine was spreading from the inner cities to the suburbs, causing further public alarm. By the fall of 1986, the steady stream of press accounts of the dangers and violence surrounding the crack cocaine trade was barraging an increasingly fearful public. In September of that year CBS aired *48 Hours on Crack Street*, a *cinema verite* documentary that featured SWAT team raids on the residences of suspected drug dealers. It drew an audience estimated at 15 million viewers.

The heightened media profile, the reality of increased violence related to the drug trade, growing public concern about drugs generally, and rapidly approaching elections in November, sent politicians in both major political parties scrambling to craft new legislation to deal emphatically with a drug problem that was perceived as being suddenly out of control and worsening. Even though national surveys such as the *Monitoring the Future Study*, which annually surveys drug use among high school students, showed that drug use had peaked in the late 1970s and that use of all drugs, including cocaine, was declining, the public perception of increasing drug use, the new crack cocaine "menace," and the violent drug trade demanded political action. Punctuating the importance of the issue, President Reagan and Vice President George H. W. Bush peed into cups and had their urine samples tested for drugs (both test results were negative).

The legislation that passed a month later might have been reassuring to a fearful public and politically advantageous, but it was hardly sound policy based on scientific evidence and well-informed decision making. Chief among those who heeded the call to action was the politically powerful Speaker of the House, Tip O'Neill. House Speaker O'Neill was from Boston, where the buzz surrounding Bias's drug-related death was particularly acute. O'Neill was especially concerned that the Democratic Party would be perceived as being "soft on drugs." His concern, in part, was reflective of the fact that legislation passed by a relatively liberal Congress in the 1960s and 1970s had done away with mandatory minimum sentences and placed a greater emphasis on treatment and prevention. Although this legislation might have had little relevance as the cause of increased drug use over that time—broader cultural acceptance of drug use was the more likely immediate cause—the perception was there and could easily be exploited in political campaigns, which have never been bastions of nuanced policy discussion.

And so, with little time to waste before the next election, legislation was hastily crafted that had as its centerpiece the return of mandatory minimum sentences for drug possession and trafficking. Mandatory minimum sentences for illegal drugs were in vogue during the decade of the 1950s when successive pieces of legislation increased prison terms. The fact that those new laws proved largely ineffective during the 1960s when drug use attained broader cultural acceptance was obviously not considered during the creation of the 1986 legislation. Nor were the effects of the 1973 "Rockefeller Drug Laws" passed in New York State. Those laws also provided for long mandatory minimum sentences, did little to deter drug use, and clogged the criminal courts because more cases went to trial to contest the charges and avoid the long sentences.

The length of the new mandatory minimum sentences were tied exclusively to the amount of the drug confiscated at the time of arrest and were particularly steep for crack cocaine relative to powder cocaine; a 100 to 1 ratio. For example, the 1986 law imposed a minimum of five years imprisonment for possessing 500 grams of powder cocaine or for possessing five grams of crack cocaine (incorrectly designated as cocaine base in the legislation).

The mandatory minimum sentences included in the 1986 Anti-Drug Abuse Act also pertained to marijuana, reflecting a return to a policy of "zero tolerance" for any illegal drug. This reversed a trend toward decriminalizing marijuana that had begun in the 1960s. Marijuana use was already in sharp decline by 1986 so the inclusion of the drug in the mandatory minimum sentencing provisions seems especially gratuitous and puzzling. Its inclusion marked the return of the thesis that marijuana is a gateway drug that leads to the use of harder drugs. Politically active, conservative, grass roots parent groups were especially influential during the Reagan administration (see sidebar on Nancy Reagan) and pushed the administration to focus policy on preventing marijuana use among children. In a 1982 speech, reflecting this change in attitude from the Carter administration, which favored decriminalizing marijuana, President Reagan said: "We are making no excuses for drugs, hard, soft, or otherwise. Drugs are bad and we are going after them." The influence of the parent groups was particularly keen in the first term of Reagan's Presidency and, in part, explains the inclusion of marijuana in the lengthy mandatory sentencing provisions. The policy of zero tolerance would be made even more explicit in the 1988 National Drug Control Strategy released by Bill Bennett, the first Director of the newly created Office of National Drug Control Policy (ONDCP) (see next section).

It is reasonable to ask how the exact sentence lengths and drug amounts that would trigger them were determined. It would be equally reasonable to think that the substantial changes enacted were the result of intense and well-informed hearings and deliberations.

If you thought that, you would be profoundly mistaken. There was neither reasonableness nor scientific evidence informing the process. The bill was drafted in a committee in August when many academics and officials were vacationing. No public hearings were held and there was no input from judges, prison authorities, or clinicians with experience working with substance abusers. Eric Sterling, who was the assistant counsel to the House Subcommittee on Crime, which drafted much of the legislation, is quoted as saying about the drug amounts and mandatory minimums: "The numbers were being pulled out of thin air." It was as if politicians were in a high stakes poker game, raising each other in terms of years of imprisonment for smaller and smaller amounts of drugs in order to be perceived as the toughest on drugs.

The disparity in mandatory minimums was not quite pulled out of thin air. They were based, in part, on the Congressional testimony of Johnny St. Valentine Brown Jr., a police investigator and, as described by Alyssa Beaver in her article "Getting a Fix on Cocaine," Brown was also the "resident narcotics expert" of the Superior

Court of Colombia. As such, he was called to testify as a government witness in thousands of criminal cases. Claiming a doctorate in pharmacology from Howard University and board certification as a pharmacist, Brown testified before Congress that his "independent research" showed 20 grams of crack was as dangerous as 1,000 grams of powder cocaine. Brown's testimony was an important influence on the decision to go with a 100 to 1 ratio for determining sentence lengths for powder versus crack cocaine. Some years later, it would be revealed that Dr. Brown was neither a pharmacist nor a doctor and had never attended Howard University. In 2000, he was charged with and convicted of perjury for which he was sentenced to a year in prison. By then, irreparable damage to the lives of many thousands serving or already having served long prison sentences as a result of the sentencing mandates influenced by his testimony had been done. Since its enactment in 1986, Congress's repeatedly refused (until very recently) to reconsider the sentencing disparities introduced in the 1986 law and there has been no consideration given to the fraudulent basis of the original rationale.

Facing the public perception of an out-of-control drug epidemic and looming elections, only 16 Congressmen voted against the legislation in the House. It passed on a simple voice vote in the Senate. One of the lone voices to speak out against the act was Representative Barney Frank of Massachusetts who made these prescient comments:

> I am afraid that this bill is becoming the legislative equivalent of crack. It is going to give people a short-term high, but it is going to be dangerous in the long run to the system and expensive to boot.

With many of its provisions still in effect—the disparity in sentences for crack and powder cocaine were only recently repealed in 2010—the 1986 Drug Abuse Act ushered in the modern era of drug policy. That era has been characterized by a return to an emphasis on law enforcement and supply side reduction (e.g., reducing the amount of drugs available at the source and entering the country and using the deterrence of the criminal justice system) to control drug use.

On October 14, 1982, Ronald Reagan (re)declared a "war on drugs" but the form his administration's drug war would take was very different than that of President Nixon's war on drugs. The Reagan administration, with its focus on marijuana use, had already begun dismantling the national treatment system put into place by Jerome Jaffe during the Nixon administration. While President Reagan paid lip service to treatment as important at the beginning of his first administration, over time it became clear the emphasis would be on law enforcement. Under Reagan, law enforcement and interdiction were expanded, in part, with resources that were reallocated from treatment. The expanded interdiction efforts included the National Narcotics Border Interdiction System that deployed radar balloons and AWAC planes across the southern border but chiefly in south Florida to intercept drug-smuggling boats or drug traffickers flying into the country from the Caribbean.

Reagan administration drug budgets flipped the Nixon formula of two-thirds for treatment, one-third for law enforcement. The federal drug budget has maintained roughly those same proportions ever since. In the end, while the beefed-up law enforcement efforts resulted in record seizures of drugs, impressive arrest statistics, and numerous photo opportunities, it did little to stem the overall flow of illegal drugs into the country. The price of cocaine remained low and the purity high. One year after enactment of the Anti-Drug Abuse Act, the National Narcotics Intelligence Consumers Committee Report indicated that cocaine "wholesale prices during the year were the lowest ever reported and the purity remained at high levels, reflecting widespread availability."

The law did increase arrests and incarcerations, however. Federal prisons began to fill with a growing number of offenders convicted of possessing relatively small amounts of drugs. In 1985, there were 27,700 federal prisoners of which 34 percent were incarcerated for a drug-related offense. In 2009, there were 208,759 federal prisoners of which 51 percent were incarcerated for a drug-related offense. Many of those incarcerated are serving lengthy sentences for drug possession. Because of the sentencing disparities between crack and powder cocaine, which were not repealed until 2010, and because African Americans disproportionately used crack cocaine, many of those imprisoned under the new drug laws were African American who comprise 39 percent of the federal prison population but only 12 percent of the general population.

When the states followed suit and enacted similar laws, state jail and prison censuses also increased dramatically setting off a minor boom in new prison construction, which became a welcome source of jobs and tax revenues in the rural areas in which they were built. The prison building boom marked the beginnings of what some feared would be a self-perpetuating "prison-industrial complex" motivated mainly by maintaining local economies in the same way that President Eisenhower warned of a "military-industrial complex" that would motivate the country to war for economic purposes. Until an economic recession began squeezing state budgets, few save some academics and civil rights advocates seemed to mind the growing number of prisons and the rapidly increasing numbers of prisoners.

Despite the change in sentencing and a focus on law enforcement, crime rates continued to rise over the next few years. Rather than reconsidering the emphasis on law enforcement, Congress decided to up the ante further. Get tough measures continued in 1988 when as part of a military defense-spending bill, Congress amended the obscure, Civil War–era Posse Comitatus Act. Posse Comitatus forbade the military from enforcing civilian laws. The law was amended to allow the military to participate in drug interdiction efforts on the border. For good measure, Congress included drug possession as an offense warranting a mandatory minimum sentence and again zeroed in on crack for particularly harsh punishment. In a book highly critical of the war on drugs, *Smoke and Mirrors*, author Dan Baum, describes the rationale for and expectations behind the 1988 amendment:

> With no time for hearings, legislators informed themselves from television, magazines, constituents' letters, and each other's increasingly florid statements to the TV cameras. Clay Shaw of Florida declared drugs "the biggest threat that we have ever had to our national security." . . .
>
> Drugs are a "threat worse than any nuclear warfare or any chemical warfare waged on any battlefield," South Carolina Republican Thomas Hartnett said,

> sponsoring a measure to force the president to stop all drug smuggling within forty-five days. Senator Sam Nunn of Georgia called it "the equivalent of passing a law saying the president shall, by Thanksgiving, devise a cure for the common cold."

The measure passed by a vote of 385 to 23 in the House. Forty-five days came and went. Drugs continued flowing into the United States despite the authorization to use the military to stop them. Nevertheless, somewhere, Harry Anslinger was surely smiling.

FURTHER READING

Baum, D. (1996). *Smoke and mirrors: The war on drugs and the politics of failure, 1st edition*. New York: Little, Brown, and Company.

Beck, J. (1998). 100 years of "Just Say No" versus "Just Say Know": Reevaluating drug education goals for the coming century. *Evaluation Review, 22,* 15–45.

Inciardi, J. A. (1987). Beyond cocaine: Basuco, crack, and other coca products. *Contemporary Drug Problems, 14,* 461–492.

Kerr, P. (1986, November 17). Anatomy of the drug issue: How, after years, it erupted. *New York Times,* A1.

Massing, M. (1998). *The fix*. New York: Simon & Schuster.

Miller, B. (2000, February 4). Narcotics "expert" said to be fraud: Witness to D.C. criminals cases is charged with perjury. *Washington Post*, B8.

Morganthau, T., Greenberg, N. H., Murr, A., Miller, M., & Raine, G. (1986, June 16). Crack and crime. *Newsweek Magazine*, National Affairs, 16.

Provine, D. M. (2007). *Unequal under the law: Race in the war on drugs*. Chicago: University of Chicago Press.

Reinarman, C., & Levine, H. G. (1997). The crack attack: Politics and media in the crack scare. In C. Reinarman & H. G. Levine (Eds.), *Crack in America: Demon drugs and social justice* (pp. 18–52). Berkeley: University of California Press.

Reinarman, C., Waldordf, D., Murphy, S. B., & Levine, H. G. (1997). The contingent call of the pipe: Bingeing and addiction among heavy cocaine smokers. In C. Reinarman & H. G. Levine (Eds.), *Crack in America: Demon drugs and social justice* (pp. 77–97). Berkeley: University of California Press.

Reuter, P. (1992). Hawks ascendant: The punitive trend of American drug policy. *Daedalus, 121,* 15–52.

Rouse, B. (1991). Trends in cocaine use in the general population. In S. Schober & C. Schade (Eds.), *The epidemiology of cocaine use and abuse* (pp. 5–18). *NIDA Research Monograph Series 110* (ADM 91–1787). Rockville, MD: U.S. Department of Health and Human Services.

Siegel, R. K. (1987). Cocaine smoking: Nature and extent of coca paste and cocaine free-base abuse. In A. M. Washton & M. S. Gold (Eds.), *Cocaine: A clinician's handbook* (pp. 175–191). New York: Guilford Press.

Vaughn, M. G., Perron, B. E., & Howard, M. O. (2010). Is crack cocaine use associated with greater violence than powdered cocaine use? Results from a national sample. *American Journal of Drug and Alcohol Abuse, 36,* 181–186.

On the Internet

An analysis of the genesis and effects of the mandatory minimum sentencing laws by Eric Sterling, who was counsel to the U.S. Committee on the Judiciary where the laws were drafted is available at: http://www.pbs.org/wgbh/pages/frontline/shows/snitch/primer/

An analysis of Reagan administration drug policy with recommendations for policy changes in prepared testimony before the House select committee on Narcotics Abuse and Control by Dr. Steven Wisotsky, Nove University Law Professor is available at: http://www.druglibrary.org/schaffer/other/wisotsky.htm.

An article written by Eric Schlosser published in the *Atlantic Monthly* titled "Reefer Madness" describes in detail the origins of the 1986 legislation as well as subsequent legislation that imposed additional sanctions on drug offenders. The full text is available at: http://www.theatlantic.com/past/docs/issues/97apr/reef.htm.

An *ESPN* article on the death of Len Bias, its immediate affects on the public, and his mother's enduring crusade to warn others about drug use as a cautionary tale is available at: http://www.theatlantic.com/past/docs/issues/97apr/reef.htm.

Maykuth, A. (1989, September 16). Drug abuse invades the Andes. *Philadelphia Inquirer*. This article describes the rise of basuco smoking in Medellin Colombia: http://www.maykuth.com/Archives/basuco89.htm.

The National Families in Action website is at: http://www.nationalfamilies.org/

The National Family Partnership website is at: http://www.nfp.org/.

Parents, Peers, and Pot written by Marsha Manatt (aka Keith Schuchard), one of the founders of the parents movement, is available at: http://www.eric.ed.gov/ERICWebPortal/search/detailmini.jsp?_nfpb=true&_&ERICExtSearch_SearchValue_0=ED185485&ERICExtSearch_SearchType_0=no&accno=ED185485.

NANCY REAGAN AND "JUST SAY NO"

First Lady Nancy Reagan's advisors were at first reluctant for her to take on drug use as her social cause. Mrs. Reagan had expressed an interest in speaking out against drugs recalling that in her Hollywood days, she had seen the lives of many of her friends and colleagues ruined by drug use. However, her advisors believed drugs might be too negative an issue. The parent movement's campaign against marijuana use among children, however, provided a means for Mrs. Reagan to address the issue she wanted to focus on in a manner that was politically acceptable to her advisors. A grassroots organizing effort, the parent movement brought parents together to help children resist or stop using drugs, oppose the decriminalization of marijuana, and change what was perceived as society's permissive attitude toward drugs.

The "Just Say No" campaign, wherein Mrs. Reagan would speak at rallies held mainly at middle-class, suburban schools to encourage children to "say no" if offered drugs, produced one of the best known slogans in drug prevention but was also one that has been widely derided. Opponents believed the campaign was simplistic, did not reach the children who were at most risk for abusing drugs, and did nothing to address the emerging crack-cocaine problem in the inner cities. Proponents point to national surveys indicating declining numbers of school children using marijuana as evidence the campaign was effective. This observation is tempered by the fact that the same surveys showed marijuana use was already declining prior to the start of the "Just Say No" campaign while over the course of the campaign crack cocaine use increased substantially in the inner cities.

"He Liked the Prop. It Drove the Point Home"

- ***Document:*** Address to the nation on the national drug control strategy
- ***Date:*** September 5, 1989
- ***Where:*** Washington, DC
- ***Significance:*** Making his first address to the nation, President George H. W. Bush spoke about the continuing drug problem and the efforts his administration would take to reduce drug use and drug-related crime. Public polls indicated drugs were a principal concern at the time. To illustrate the pervasiveness of the problem, President Bush held up a bag of crack cocaine that had been purchased recently by an undercover DEA agent in Lafayette Park, near the White House. President Bush also announced the newly created Office of National Drug Control Policy's first national strategy report. In his speech, reflecting the policies advocated in the national strategy and during the Reagan administration, President Bush emphasized "zero tolerance" for any drug and along with it a major expansion of domestic and international enforcement efforts. The budget recommendations reflected this emphasis allocating two-thirds for enforcement and interdiction—more police, prisons, jails, and source country eradication programs—and one-third for treatment and prevention. While the use of marijuana continued its decline from 1979 levels and while cocaine use among the middle class also declined, the use of crack cocaine in the inner cities and the use of cocaine among frequent users, to whom Bush refers in the speech, were increasing. Moreover, state jail and prison censuses continued increasing dramatically, straining state budgets but doing little to reduce the drug supply or the number of users addicted to cocaine and/or heroin.

DOCUMENT

Good evening. This is the first time since taking the oath of office that I felt an issue was so important, so threatening, that it warranted talking directly with you, the American people. All of us agree that the gravest domestic threat facing our nation today is drugs. Drugs have strained our faith in our system of justice. Our courts, our prisons, our legal system, are stretched to the breaking point. The social costs of drugs are mounting. In short, drugs are sapping our strength as a nation. Turn on the evening news or pick up the morning paper and you'll see what some Americans know just by stepping out their front door: Our most serious problem today is cocaine, and in particular, crack.

Who's responsible? Let me tell you straight out—everyone who uses drugs, everyone who sells drugs, and everyone who looks the other way.

Tonight, I'll tell you how many Americans are using illegal drugs. I will present to you our national strategy to deal with every aspect of this threat. And I will ask you to get involved in what promises to be a very difficult fight.

This is crack cocaine seized a few days ago by Drug Enforcement agents in a park just across the street from the White House. It could easily have been heroin or PCP. It's as innocent looking as candy, but it's turning our cities into battle zones, and it's murdering our children. Let there be no mistake: This stuff is poison. Some used to call drugs harmless recreation; they're not. Drugs are a real and terribly dangerous threat to our neighborhoods, our friends, and our families.

No one among us is out of harm's way. When 4-year-olds play in playgrounds strewn with discarded hypodermic needles and crack vials, it breaks my heart. When cocaine, one of the most deadly and addictive illegal drugs, is available to school kids—school kids—it's an outrage. And when hundreds of thousands of babies are born each year to mothers who use drugs—premature babies born desperately sick—then even the most defenseless among us are at risk.

These are the tragedies behind the statistics, but the numbers also have quite a story to tell. Let me share with you the results of the recently completed household survey of the National Institute on Drug Abuse. It compares recent drug use to 3 years ago. It tells us some good news and some very bad news. First, the good. As you can see in the chart, in 1985 the Government estimated that 23 million Americans were using drugs on a "current" basis; that is, at least once in the preceding month. Last year that number fell by more than a third. That means almost 9 million fewer Americans are casual drug users. Good news.

Because we changed our national attitude toward drugs, casual drug use has declined. We have many to thank: our brave law enforcement officers, religious leaders, teachers, community activists, and leaders of business and labor. We should also thank the media for their exhaustive news and editorial coverage and for their airtime and space for antidrug messages. And finally, I want to thank President and Mrs. Reagan for their leadership. All of these good people told the truth: that drug use is wrong and dangerous.

But as much comfort as we can draw from these dramatic reductions, there is also bad news, very bad news. Roughly 8 million people have used cocaine in the past year. Almost 1 million of them used it frequently—once a week or more. What this means is that, in spite of the fact that overall cocaine use is down, frequent use has almost doubled in the last few years. And that's why habitual cocaine users, especially crack users, are the most pressing, immediate drug problem.

What, then, is our plan? To begin with, I trust the lesson of experience: No single policy will cut it, no matter how glamorous or magical it may sound. To win the war against addictive drugs like crack will take more than just a Federal strategy: It will take a national strategy, one that reaches into every school, every workplace, involving every family.

Earlier today, I sent this document, our first such national strategy, to the Congress. It was developed with the hard work of our nation's first Drug Policy Director, Bill Bennett. In preparing this plan, we talked with State, local, and community leaders, law enforcement officials, and experts in education, drug prevention, and rehabilitation. We talked with parents and kids. We took a long, hard look at all that the Federal Government has done about drugs in the past—what's worked and, let's be honest, what hasn't. Too often, people in government acted as if they're part of the problem—whether fighting drug production or drug smuggling or drug demand—was the only problem. But turf battles won't win this war; teamwork will.

Tonight, I'm announcing a strategy that reflects the coordinated, cooperative commitment of all our Federal agencies. In short, this plan is as comprehensive as the problem. With this strategy, we now finally have a plan that coordinates our resources, our programs, and the people who run them. Our weapons in this strategy are the law and criminal justice system, our foreign policy, our treatment systems, and our schools and drug prevention programs. So, the basic weapons we need are the ones we already have. What's been lacking is a strategy to effectively use them.

Let me address four of the major elements of our strategy. First, we are determined to enforce the law, to make our streets and neighborhoods safe. So, to start, I'm proposing that we more than double Federal assistance to State and local law enforcement. Americans have a right to safety in and around their homes. And we won't have safe neighborhoods unless we're tough on drug criminals—much tougher than we are now. Sometimes that means tougher penalties, but more often it just means punishment that is swift and certain. We've all heard stories about drug dealers who are caught and arrested again and again but never punished. Well, here the rules have changed: If you sell drugs, you will be caught. And when you're caught, you will be prosecuted. And once you're convicted, you will do time. Caught—prosecuted—punished.

I'm also proposing that we enlarge our criminal justice system across the board—at the local, State, and Federal levels alike. We need more prisons, more jails, more courts, more prosecutors. So, tonight I'm requesting—all together—an almost billion-and-a-half dollar increase in drug-related federal spending on law enforcement.

And while illegal drug use is found in every community, nowhere is it worse than in our public housing projects. You know, the poor have never had it easy in this world. But in the past, they weren't mugged on the way home from work by crack gangs. And their children didn't have to dodge bullets on the way to school. And that's why I'm targeting millions to fight crime in public housing projects—to help restore order and to kick out the dealers for good.

The second element of our strategy looks beyond our borders, where the cocaine and crack bought on America's streets is grown and processed. In Colombia alone, cocaine killers have gunned down a leading statesman, murdered almost 200 judges and 7 members of their supreme court. The besieged governments of the drug-producing countries are fighting back, fighting to break the international drug rings. But you and I agree with the courageous President of Colombia, Virgilio Barco, who said that if Americans use cocaine, then Americans are paying for murder. American cocaine users need to understand that our nation has zero tolerance for casual drug use. We have a responsibility not to leave our brave friends in Colombia to fight alone.

The millions in emergency assistance announced 2 weeks ago was just our first step in assisting the Andean nations in their fight against the cocaine cartels. Colombia has already arrested suppliers, seized tons of cocaine, and confiscated palatial homes of drug lords. But Colombia faces a long, uphill battle, so we must be ready to do more. Our strategy allocates more than a quarter of a billion dollars for next year in military and law enforcement assistance for the three Andean nations of Colombia, Bolivia, and Peru. This will be the first part of a 5-year, billion dollar program to counter the producers, the traffickers, and the smugglers.

I spoke with President Barco just last week, and we hope to meet with the leaders of affected countries in an unprecedented drug summit, all to coordinate an inter-American strategy against the cartels. We will work with our allies and friends, especially our economic summit partners, to do more in the fight against drugs. I'm also asking the Senate to ratify the United Nations antidrug convention concluded last December.

To stop those drugs on the way to America, I propose that we spend more than a billion and a half dollars on interdiction. Greater interagency cooperation, combined with sophisticated intelligence-gathering and Defense Department technology, can help stop drugs at our borders.

And our message to the drug cartels is this: The rules have changed. We will help any government that wants our help. When requested, we will for the first time make available the appropriate resources of America's Armed Forces. We will intensify our efforts against drug smugglers on the high seas, in international airspace, and at our borders. We will stop the flow of chemicals from the United States used to process drugs. We will pursue and enforce international agreements to track drug money to the front men and financiers. And then we will handcuff these money launderers and jail them, just like any street dealer. And for the drug kingpins: the death penalty.

The third part of our strategy concerns drug treatment. Experts believe that there are 2 million American drug users who may be able to get off drugs with proper treatment, but right now only 40 percent of them are actually getting help. This is simply not good enough. Many people who need treatment won't seek it on their own, and some who do seek it are put on a waiting list. Most programs were set up to deal with heroin addicts, but today the major problem is cocaine users. It's time we expand our treatment systems and do a better job of providing services to those who need them.

And so, tonight I'm proposing an increase of 1 million in Federal spending on drug treatment. With this strategy, we will do more. We will work with the States. We will encourage employers to establish employee assistance programs to cope with drug use; and because addiction is such a cruel inheritance, we will intensify our search for ways to help expectant mothers who use drugs.

Fourth, we must stop illegal drug use before it starts. Unfortunately, it begins early—for many kids, before their teens. But it doesn't start the way you might think, from a dealer or an addict hanging around a school playground. More often, our kids first get their drugs free, from friends or even from older brothers or sisters. Peer pressure spreads drug use; peer pressure can help stop it. I am proposing a quarter-of-a-billion-dollar increase in Federal funds for school and community prevention programs that help young people and adults reject enticements to try drugs. And I'm proposing something else. Every school, college, and university, and every workplace must adopt tough but fair policies about drug use by students and employees. And those that will not adopt such policies will not get Federal funds—period!

The private sector also has an important role to play. I spoke with a businessman named Jim Burke who said he was haunted by the thought—a nightmare, really—that somewhere in America, at any given moment, there is a teenage girl who should be in school instead of giving birth to a child addicted to cocaine. So, Jim did something. He led an antidrug partnership, financed by private funds, to work with advertisers and media firms. Their partnership is now determined to work with our strategy by generating educational messages worth a million dollars a day every day for the next 3 years—a billion dollars worth of advertising, all to promote the antidrug message.

As President, one of my first missions is to keep the national focus on our offensive against drugs. And so, next week I will take the antidrug message to the classrooms of America in a special television address, one that I hope will reach every school, every young American. But drug education doesn't begin in class or on TV. It must begin at home and in the neighborhood. Parents and families must set the first example of a drug-free life. And when families are broken, caring friends and neighbors must step in.

These are the most important elements in our strategy to fight drugs. They are all designed to reinforce one another, to mesh into a powerful whole, to mount an aggressive attack on the problem from every angle. This is the first time in the history of our country that we truly have a comprehensive strategy. As you can tell, such an approach will not come cheaply. Last February I asked for a 10 million increase in the drug budget for the coming year.

And now, over the past 6 months of careful study, we have found an immediate need for another billion and a half dollars. With this added 2 billion, our 1990 drug budget totals almost x billion, the largest increase in history. We need this program fully implemented—right away. The next fiscal year begins just 26 days from now. So, tonight I'm asking the Congress, which has helped us formulate this strategy, to help us move it forward immediately. We can pay for this fight against drugs without raising taxes or adding to the budget deficit. We have submitted our plan to Congress that shows just how to fund it within the limits of our bipartisan budget agreement.

Now, I know some will still say that we're not spending enough money, but those who judge our strategy only by its price tag simply don't understand the problem. Let's face it, we've all seen in the past that money alone won't solve our toughest problems. To be strong and efficient, our strategy needs these funds. But there is no match for a united America, a determined America, an angry America. Our outrage against drugs unites us, brings us together behind this one plan of action—an assault on every front.

This is the toughest domestic challenge we've faced in decades. And it's a challenge we must face not as Democrats or Republicans, liberals or conservatives, but as Americans. The key is a coordinated, united effort. We've responded faithfully to the request of the Congress to produce our nation's first national drug strategy. I'll be looking to the Democratic majority and our Republicans in Congress for leadership and bipartisan support. And our citizens deserve cooperation, not competition; a national effort, not a partisan bidding war. To start, Congress needs not only to act on this national drug strategy but also to act on our crime package announced last

May, a package to toughen sentences, beef up law enforcement, and build new prison space for 24,000 inmates.

You and I both know the Federal Government can't do it alone. The States need to match tougher Federal laws with tougher laws of their own: stiffer bail, probation, parole, and sentencing. And we need your help. If people you know are users, help them—help them get off drugs. If you're a parent, talk to your kids about drugs—tonight. Call your local drug prevention program; be a Big Brother or Sister to a child in need; pitch in with your local Neighborhood Watch program. Whether you give your time or talent, everyone counts: every employer who bans drugs from the workplace; every school that's tough on drug use; every neighborhood in which drugs are not welcome; and most important, every one of you who refuses to look the other way. Every one of you counts. Of course, victory will take hard work and time, but together we will win. Too many young lives are at stake.

Not long ago, I read a newspaper story about a little boy named Dooney who, until recently, lived in a crack house in a suburb of Washington, DC. In Dooney's neighborhood, children don't flinch at the sound of gunfire. And when they play, they pretend to sell to each other small white rocks that they call crack. Life at home was so cruel that Dooney begged his teachers to let him sleep on the floor at school. And when asked about his future, 6-year-old Dooney answers, "I don't want to sell drugs, but I'll probably have to."

Well, Dooney does not have to sell drugs. No child in America should have to live like this. Together as a people we can save these kids. We've already transformed a national attitude of tolerance into one of condemnation. But the war on drugs will be hard-won, neighborhood by neighborhood, block by block, child by child.

If we fight this war as a divided nation, then the war is lost. But if we face this evil as a nation united, this will be nothing but a handful of useless chemicals. Victory—victory over drugs—is our cause, a just cause. And with your help, we are going to win.

Thank you, God bless you, and good night.

SOURCE: George Bush, "Address to the Nation on the National Drug Control Strategy," September 5, 1989. Online by Gerhard Peters and John T. Woolley, The American Presidency Project, http://www.presidency.ucsb.edu/ws/?pid=17472.

ANALYSIS

As he took office to become the 41st president of the United States in January 1989, George H.W. Bush already had direct experience battling the nation's ongoing drug problem. In 1982, he headed the vice president's Task Force on South Florida. The intent of the task force was to stem the flow of drugs into the Miami area and it involved the joint efforts of the DEA, FBI, IRS, and the military. Publicity shots from the time show Vice President Bush flying in helicopters or zooming out to sea in a speedy task force boat, presumably looking for bundles of marijuana or cocaine dropped into the water for pick-up.

As he assumed the presidency, Bush was aware that illegal drugs remained a primary public concern. National polls consistently showed the American public was very worried about drugs and drug-related crime, especially violence surrounding the drug-trade, which had not yet abated and which continued to receive extensive media coverage. As was the case during the time of the Nixon administration, the war on drugs was as much if not more about reducing crime (and fear of crime) than it was about reducing drug use.

Towards that end, and only several years after enacting the tough new mandatory minimum sentencing provisions in the Anti-Drug Abuse Act of 1986, Congress passed the Anti-Drug Abuse Act of 1988. The 1988 legislation continued the trend of emphasizing law enforcement and interdiction over treatment and prevention. President Bush's budget request to Congress and the subsequent congressional budget supported that emphasis. The formula was similar to the budget allocations during the Reagan administration. Two-thirds of the monies allocated towards drug-control would be for law enforcement and interdiction and one-third to treatment, education, and prevention. Although the budget for drug control under President Bush would be nearly doubled over his four years in office (for $6 billion to $12 billion), including proportionate increases for prevention, the allocation of two-thirds for enforcement versus one-third for treatment remained a constant.

Among its main provisions, the 1988 act created the ONDCP in the Executive Office of the President. ONDCP would be led by a Director (a position known informally as the "drug czar") under which would be Deputy Directors for Demand (i.e., treatment) and Supply (i.e., enforcement) Reduction. ONDCP would have general responsibility for coordinating federal efforts to control drugs and for recommending to Congress and the President how money should be allocated across federal agencies and to the states to assist in those efforts. By law, ONDCP would also be required to submit a National Drug Control Strategy report annually to Congress. The report would assess the current status of America's drug issues, provide policy direction, and determine the impact of ongoing efforts. The first report was produced just prior to President Bush's address in which he highlighted some of the report's recommended strategies and statement of the problem.

The first ONDCP report clearly reflected the views of one of its principal authors, William J. Bennett, President Bush's selection to be the ONDCP Director. Bennett was the former Secretary of Education under President Reagan. He had little direct experience with either drug treatment or law enforcement but was of the opinion that because drug use among children was a major issue in schools he had a strong appreciation for the problems caused by drugs. He had equally strong ideas about what to do about the perceived problems. Openly opinionated, unabashedly combative during his many public appearances, and a hard-line neoconservative, Bennett brought to ONDCP his unwavering view that drug use, even compulsive use and addiction, was a choice and therefore a moral/values issue rather than a public health concern. In Bennett's view, those who used drugs did so because they wanted to and if they made that choice, they would have to pay a steep price for the problems they caused others. In a speech given at a Washington, D.C., synagogue he stated, "Two words sum up my entire approach: consequences and confrontation. Those who use, sell, and traffic in drugs must be confronted and they must suffer consequences."

Not surprisingly then, Bennett favored an emphasis on law enforcement and, in fact, advocated for an even greater push in that direction: more prisons, more jails, more police, more prosecutors, more DEA agents, more radar balloons, AWACS, and border patrols. Although he supported education, treatment and prevention (the first ONDCP budget did request additional money for treatment), his support was tepid at best and he openly questioned both treatment efficacy and drug addicts' willingness to enter treatment unless coerced by the legal system. As pointed out by Michael Massing in an article on the "The Two Bill Bennetts" for *The New York Review of Books* and in his book, *The Fix,* Bennett seemed to hold the criminal justice and treatment system to different standards:

> Bennett never questions the efficacy of the criminal justice system. That system, like treatment programs, suffers from serious inefficiencies. Across the country, police chiefs, judges, and prosecutors are throwing up their hands, frustrated by their inability to contain, much less defeat, the drug trade. Such problems, however, never seem to find their way into Bennett's speeches. There, police and prisons are described in only the most glowing terms. The contrast with his pronouncements on treatment could not be starker.

Herb Kleber, who was Bennett's Deputy Director for Demand Reduction and hence in charge of treatment and prevention policy, eventually resigned from ONDCP in frustration after several years when it became clear that funding allocations were never going to move in the direction of treatment and prevention no matter how bad the data on the lack of effectiveness of supply reduction efforts. In fact, the funding formulation of two-thirds for supply side and one-third for demand reduction has been maintained at ONDCP ever since and remains so under the current Director R. Gil Kerlikowske. In this excerpt from an interview done in 2000 for the PBS series *Frontline*, Dr. Kleber explains his views on the difficulty of getting Congress to approve additional treatment funding:

> Historically, funding for treatment has been a bipartisan failure. Neither Democratic congresses nor Republican congresses have voted for enough money for treatment. And that seems to be independent of who's in the White House. No matter who's running Congress, or the administration, treatment never seems to get adequate funding or adequate respect. I don't think the reasons for that are simple. There are a number of possible explanations, and I think they're probably taken together.
>
> For one, there's a real feeling that addicts brought it on themselves—that rectifying what they're doing is not worthy of taxpayer dollars. Two, the messengers are not trusted. When scientists and researchers say we know how to treat addicts, Congress tends to view them suspiciously. They feel that the bunch of liberals who want to treat the addict do not worry about the law-abiding citizen who got mugged. Three, failures are obvious, but successes are anonymous.
>
> And every congressman, probably everyone in the administration, has some family member, some neighbor, or someone they know who's been in treatment and failed. And so they think treatment doesn't work. You can give them all the statistics that you want—they know that Uncle Joe did not do well in treatment.

Of course, using the criminal justice system as the primary means of controlling substance abuse was not new to the Reagan or Bush administrations. Except for a brief period of 20 years from 1960 to 1980, this has been the favored approach to drug policy in the United States since the Harrison Act of 1914. Likewise for the view that drug addiction is a moral failing requiring swift and certain consequences to discourage drug use. Director Bennett's unique twist was to emphasize that the war on drugs should be focused on the casual user whom he saw as being at the root of the problem and the one most likely to spread drug use to others. After pointing out recent significant declines in the casual use of marijuana and cocaine excepting crack cocaine, which the national strategy report labels the "most dangerous and quickly addictive drug known to man," the report goes on to argue that the main culprit in spreading drug use is indeed the casual user:

> The non-addicted casual or regular user, however, is a different story. He is likely to have a still-intact family, social, and work life. He is likely to "enjoy" his drug for the pleasure it offers. And he is thus much more willing and able to proselytize drug use—by action or example—among his remaining non-user peers, friends, and acquaintances. A non-addict's drug use, in other words, is **highly** contagious. And casual or regular use—whether ongoing or brand new—may always lead to addiction: again we have no accurate way to predict its eventual trajectory.

This argument together with the gateway hypothesis, which posits marijuana use *causes* the transition to harder drugs such as cocaine or heroin, are key to understanding the rationale behind a zero tolerance policy that treats the use of any illegal drug as equally harmful. There are several problems with such an approach, however, leaving aside the inherent inconsistency in the report's logic whereby casual use was reported as declining while at the same time the use of crack cocaine and the prevalence of addiction to any kind of cocaine were increasing (the casual user/gateway hypothesis would predict that the frequent use of harder drugs should also be declining barring some kind of lag effect).

First, there is no support for the contention that the casual user is *highly contagious* and the national strategy report cites no data or research to that effect. The premise was based on criminologists James Q. Wilson's and George L. Kelling's "broken windows theory" whereby even small signs of social disorder such as a building with broken windows and graffiti signify the potential for larger problems such as crime. The implication is that the police and the community should immediately address even such small signs of social disorder to prevent larger problems down the road. Whatever the evidence in support of this theory as an explanation of the genesis of crime, there is not much evidence to suggest it applies equally well if at all to the how drug use is propagated.

Second, the large majority of illegal drug users are, in fact, infrequent, experimental or casual users who stop at marijuana use. Over 90 percent of those who use marijuana do not go on to use other drugs (excepting alcohol) and most of those who do use marijuana stop using within a few years. Since there are so many more marijuana users than users of all other illicit drugs combined, targeting them with criminal justice sanctions means expending a large amount of resources to arrest and incarcerate thousands and thousands of people, the majority of which would not have progressed to using other drugs, committed crimes, or encouraged by example others to use drugs. In effect, the policy ends up diverting resources away from the very users—cocaine and heroin addicts—whose drug use is the most strongly associated with all manner of social and health issues such as crime, HIV infection, homelessness, and mental illness. If the inefficiency of treatment was a concern in defending the budgetary status quo, the policy of zero tolerance was a prescription for inefficiency on a much grander scale.

The test case for implementing Bennett's take-back-the-streets strategy was Washington, D.C., which like other major urban centers had a significant crack problem and a high rate of violent crime. DEA agents were added, numerous drug busts were conducted, and the population in D.C.'s jails grew rapidly. Plans to build additional prison space nearby to house the steady stream of arrested dealers and users ran afoul of bureaucratic wrangling, however. And there was poor coordination between federal and city law enforcement. Federal and city officials subsequently pointed fingers at each other as to who was mostly to blame. The end result was that there was very little change in either drug trafficking or crime in D.C. during Bennett's tenure as drug czar. The test case was a colossal bust regardless of claims to the contrary.

Despite President Bush's desire to use a bag of crack cocaine as a prop to illustrate the pervasiveness of America's drug problem, the national drug control strategy document he brandished before the American public did not specifically focus on that troublesome drug or on major drug traffickers but instead laid out a strategy to go after the "casual user." Perhaps it is appropriate then, that the purchase of the crack cocaine used as the prop was itself something of a ruse. Crack was not typically sold in Lafayette Park, which is located near the White House, for the simple reason there were few drug buyers there. The park is heavily patrolled. The deal had been arranged by the DEA with a teenage dealer named Keith Timothy Jackson whom the DEA had been following for some time. Jackson was instructed to come to Lafayette Park for the transaction and offered the inducement of a large ($2,400.00) sale. Never having sold drugs in or frequented Lafayette Park, however, he had no idea where it was. He was even a little foggy on the current resident in the White House: "Oh, you mean where Reagan lives?" A DEA agent needed to give him a lift. According to a *Washington Post* article describing the incident, Jackson did not tune in to see President Bush's address.

FURTHER READING

Baum, D. (1996). *Smoke and mirrors: The war on drugs and the politics of failure, 1st edition*. New York: Little, Brown, and Company.

Grim, R. (2009). *This is your country on drugs: The secret history of getting high in America*. Hoboken, NJ: John Wiley & Sons.

Isikoff, M. (1989, September 22). Drug buy set up for Bush speech; DEA lured seller to Lafayette Park. *Washington Post*, A1.

Isikoff, M. (1989, October 17). Bennett's anti-drug initiative making little headway in D. C. *Washington Post*, A1.

Massing, M. (1988, December 22). The war on cocaine. *New York Review of Books*.

Massing, M. (1990, March 1). The two William Bennetts. *New York Review of Books*.

Reuter, P. (2001). Why has research had so little impact on drug policy? *Addiction*, 96, 373–376.

GARY WEBB—DARK ALLIANCE

Gary Webb was a Pulitzer prize-winning reporter for the *San Jose Mercury News*. On August 18, 1996, the *Mercury News* published the first of a three-part series of articles written by Webb. The articles made the sensational allegation that the CIA had fostered drug trafficking, specifically crack-cocaine trafficking in the inner cities, to support Contra insurgents in Nicaragua.

The Contras were a pet cause of the Reagan Administration. The administration supported the Contra effort as a bulwark against the socialist Sandinista government in Nicaragua. The administration believed that after they rose to power in 1979, the Sandinistas could spread communism throughout Latin America. Webb's articles had some resonance as they came after the Iran-Contra hearings during which it was revealed the Reagan Administration had bypassed Congressional disapproval and funded the Contras by selling arms to Iran and then sending the profits back to the Contras.

(continued)

GARY WEBB —DARK ALLIANCE (continued)

At first largely ignored by the mainstream press, Webb's articles eventually created an uproar among black Americans who saw them as evidence the American government had deliberately poisoned black neighborhoods with crack-cocaine for the sake of international politics. Congresswoman Maxine Waters, who still represents California's 35th congressional district that includes the effected LA neighborhoods, led the call for public meetings and congressional hearings on the matter. The CIA conducted an internal evaluation led by Frederick Hitz, the CIA Inspector General. Senator John Kerry chaired an Investigating Committee. Surprisingly, the mainstream press went after Webb and not the government. In multiple reports, they contended there was little evidence to support Webb's most sensational contention—that the CIA had colluded in the drug trade—and, at best, the accusations had been over-reach.

Webb's personal and professional life followed a sad and rapid downward trajectory after the publication of his articles. The *Mercury News* editor disavowed the articles as inaccurate and sensational and issued a recantation in a letter to readers. Webb quit his job with the *Mercury News* after he was reassigned to a satellite office in Cupertino, requiring him to commute 150 miles each way every day. Webb published his findings in the book *Dark Alliance* but he gained little support from the effort despite providing additional evidence for his allegations. His marriage ended in divorce. Distraught over his deteriorated financial affairs, his professional and personal isolation, and his inability to gain work with a major newspaper, Webb committed suicide in 2004. Investigative reporting after his death supports many of the major contentions in Webb's original report if not all the details and has been critical of the earlier press response. Instead of serving the public by investigating government wrongdoing, the national press served as an instrument of the government and turned on one of its own that dared to directly challenge the status quo.

Reuter, P., & Kleiman, M. (1986). Risks and prices: An economic analysis of drug enforcement. *Crime and Justice*, *7*, 289–340.

Schou, N. (2006). *Kill the messenger: How the CIA's crack-cocaine controversy destroyed journalist Gary Webb*. New York: Nation Books.

Treaster, J. B. (1992, June 14). Echoes of Prohibition: 20 years of war on drugs, and no victory yet. *New York Times*, Section 4, p. 7.

Treaster, J. B. (1992, July 28). The 1992 campaign: Candidates' records; Four years of Bush's drug war: New funds but an old strategy. *New York Times*, A1.

Webb, G. (1999). *Dark alliance: The CIA, the contras, and the crack cocaine explosion*. New York: Seven Stories Press.

Wilson, J. Q., & Kelling, G. (1982). Broken windows: The police and neighborhood safety. *Atlantic Monthly*, *249*, 29–38.

On the Internet

A chronology and description of legislation related to the creation and purview of the Office of National Drug Control Policy as well as access to current and previous national drug strategy reports are available at the ONDCP website: http://www.whitehousedrugpolicy.gov/index.html.

The full PBS interview in 2000 with Herb Kleber, the first Deputy for Demand Reduction at ONDCP is at: http://www.pbs.org/wgbh/pages/frontline/shows/drugs/interviews/kleber.html.

PBS also has detail on Gary Webb's articles charging the CIA with complicity in the cocaine trade and the subsequent investigations of that allegation at: http://www.pbs.org/wgbh/pages/frontline/shows/drugs/special/cia.html.

Manski, C. F., Pepper, J. V., & Thomas, Y. F. (1999). *Assessment of two cost-effectiveness studies on cocaine control policy*. Washington, DC: National Academy Press. http://www.nap.edu/catalog.php?record_id=9441.

A copy of the declassified CIA report that investigated Gary Webb's allegations the agency was involved in crack cocaine distribution to support the Contras in Nicaragua is available on the CIA website at: http://www.justice.gov/oig/special/9712/index.htm.

The full text of the original articles written by Gary Webb for the *San Jose Mercury News* charging the CIA with involvement in selling cocaine have been archived at: http://www.narconews.com/darkalliance/drugs/index.htm.

"Heroin and Cocaine Infected Thousands of Drug-Stunned Addicts"

- ***Document:*** "Hooked on Dogma; U.S. Drug Warriors Ignore Switzerland's Success with Heroin Addicts," *Washington Post*
- ***Date:*** December 21, 1997
- ***Where:*** The Platzspitz in Zurich, Switzerland, and Washington, DC
- ***Significance:*** The Platzspitz, or "Needle Park" as it came to be known, was the site of a social experiment carried out on a grand scale in Zurich, Switzerland, from 1986 to 1992. Within the confines of the Platzspitz, drug addicts were allowed free reign to buy, sell, use, and inject drugs without fear of police interference. In the last two years of this permissive policy, the Swiss government made extensive harm reduction programs such as needle exchanges and medical care freely available within the Platzspitz. The belief was that the problems associated with drug use such as crime and HIV infection could be confined to a single area of the city and minimized through harm reduction programs. The experiment was, however, a spectacular failure. The park became a magnet for drug addicts across Switzerland swelling their ranks in Zurich and overwhelming prevention efforts as well as the police. When theft, robbery, prostitution, and drug use spilled into the surrounding neighborhoods, the six-year experiment was abruptly ended and the park closed. While there is no dispute the policy failed, there is disagreement about the implications of that failure. Needle Park remains a point of contention between harm reduction advocates, who believe that unique aspects of the situation make it a poor representation of harm reduction strategies and that the comparison is unfair. Opponents continue to portray harm reduction as a slippery slope towards drug legalization and use the example of Needle Park

as a cautionary tale of what could happen if harm reduction efforts were adopted on a broad scale in this country. This article describes how American policy makers have misapplied the lessons of Needle Park in the interest of arguing against harm reduction policies. The specific circumstances surrounding the Swiss social experiment known as Needle Park that limit its applicability to American drug policy generally and to harm reduction efforts specifically are considered further in the analysis that follows.

DOCUMENT

Hooked on Dogma; U.S. Drug Warriors Ignore Switzerland's Success with Heroin Addicts

By Joshua Wolf Shenk

In 1986, the Swiss city of Zurich designated its Platzspitz park as a refuge for drug users, a place where they would be tolerated by police and even offered sterile needles and medical care. The goal wasn't to condone drug use, but to control its side effects—mainly the diseases contracted by users and spread to the population at large. But, by the early 1990s, "Needle Park" bulged with Europe's outcasts. As crime rose in the area and a once-charming garden became an eyesore, Zurich ended the experiment.

The shapers of American drug policy—from former czar Bill Bennett to Drug Enforcement Agency chief Thomas Constantine—often cite Needle Park as an argument against changing America's hard-line drug policies. But the Swiss, aware that dispersing the Needle Park junkies did not eliminate the serious harm they were doing to themselves and to society, have continued to pursue novel approaches toward solving their country's drug problem. For the heroin addicts who would not respond to conventional treatment, the government decided to take the radical step of offering heroin itself.

From 1994 to 1997, in 18 treatment centers around Switzerland, 1,146 male and female addicts received injections of pure heroin three times a day. Led by Ambros Uchtenhagen, an internationally renowned social scientist, the Addiction Research Institute in Zurich kept careful tabs over the experiment. The goal was not to offer the drug, in perpetuity, to all comers. Rather, the researchers hoped to mitigate the injurious behavior of a small group of addicts for whom repeated treatment regimens had failed.

The success was striking. Heroin maintenance, Uchtenhagen and his researchers found, not only improved the lives of addicts but benefited society in tangible ways. Before going on heroin maintenance, 59 percent of the Swiss addicts in the program were involved in criminal activity. Because they no longer needed cash to pay exorbitant prices on the black market, by the end of the experiment that number dropped to 10 percent. For the same reason—and also because participants in the program were required to undergo counseling—many addicts climbed out of the underworld, found housing and began to work in mainstream jobs. The rate of homelessness in the group dropped from 12 percent to near zero.

The health benefits were also unambiguous: HIV and hepatitis infections dropped sharply, and the annual death rate fell by half. Day to day, many fewer addicts contracted skin infections and other diseases. A small but significant portion of the group even left the program for abstinence treatment.

If the Swiss experiment had failed, you can be sure that American officials would trumpet the news, just as they so regularly refer to Needle Park. But the actual results are less convenient for advocates of the status quo. And so the response has been to ignore it.

For example, in the past four months, the National Institute on Drug Abuse (NIDA), which controls a $520 million budget and 85 percent of all research on the health effects of drug abuse and addiction, has organized two major conferences on heroin without considering the Swiss research.

The lesson is not that heroin maintenance ought to be embraced here. The episode illustrates, however, how discussion of America's drug policy has been constricted by the dogma of the drug war. While vigorous research and debate is taken for granted in public policy debates about, say, welfare policy or affirmative action, such discussion is largely absent from the study of drugs. To ignore innovative ideas and approaches—especially complicated, unsettling ones—is at best unsound. At worst, it will lead to outright failure.

While it is a legitimate social policy goal to eliminate heroin use entirely, the American approach of zero-tolerance has proven remarkably ineffective. About 600,000 Americans are addicted to the drug. That number has increased over the past several decades, despite billions of dollars and hundreds of thousands of arrests.

Meanwhile, these addicts are causing a great deal of harm—to themselves and to the rest of us. Intravenous drug users are now the single biggest factor in the spread of HIV. Eighty-five percent of addicts commit some kind of crime, ranging from petty burglary to homicide. The financial costs of untreated heroin addiction is an estimated $20 billion a year, according to a National Institutes of Health (NIH) panel.

And yet, for the same reasons that they wouldn't contemplate heroin maintenance, American officials have kept tight restrictions on the medical treatment with the best track record: methadone maintenance. Only 20 percent of heroin addicts have access to methadone, a synthetic opiate that often removes the craving for heroin. In November, a panel of scientists convened by NIH and NIDA urged expanded use of methadone maintenance. This treatment regimen, the panel concluded, "is effective in reducing illicit opiate drug use, in crime reduction, in enhancing social productivity, and in reducing the spread of viral diseases such as AIDS and hepatitis."

The problem, the panel reported, is a public that refuses to consider heroin addiction in a medical context. Drug therapy for addiction is viewed with suspicion because it's seen as just another addiction. "It's not the zero tolerance option and so it's unpopular," says David C. Lewis, a professor of medicine and community health at Brown University. The irony is that Americans embrace pharmaceutical treatments for every conceivable human ailment, from impotence to depression to hyperactivity to stage fright. But drug addicts are regarded as castoffs.

Even discussing heroin maintenance is strictly taboo—as was evident at the same NIH conference that concluded by lamenting the stigma attached to methadone treatment. Before the conference, NIDA assembled a bibliography that was supposed to contain every known study of the medical treatment of heroin addiction. The Swiss study was not among them. When Lewis made brief mention of the study, he was criticized by his colleagues for doing so.

"Scientists and clinicians—people I regard as leaders and look to with respect—are concerned that just bringing it up will cause difficulty," Lewis said. "You can't talk about these things in this country without causing controversy, which is a great sadness."

NIDA is a perfect example of the paralysis that permeates the discussion about American drug policy. In 1992, the institute was put under the aegis of NIH specifically to insulate it from the prejudices of public opinion—to evaluate and commission drug-related research based on science, not politics. Nevertheless, NIDA gives priority to studies that are likely to support government positions and regularly interpret science with obvious political intent.

That makes debate around scientific questions concerning drug issues difficult. "If you were at NIDA," says Peter Reuter, the director of the University of Maryland's Drug Policy Research Center, "you would say, 'How can I seriously argue that [discussing heroin maintenance] would make a difference to programs here?' " Worse than not making a difference, it could do a great deal of harm, if outraged congressmen moved to slash the institute's research budget.

So public opinion keeps researchers from considering new ideas. But the public can't reconsider its biases without being presented with new ideas.

The cycle is difficult to break, but not impossible. Consider the case of medical marijuana. For years, NIDA has stonewalled researchers trying to conduct large-scale trials of the plant's utility in treating diseases such as glaucoma and related nausea. Then, California passed an initiative legalizing marijuana for medical use and the Clinton administration finally instructed NIDA to conduct studies. "It's a case where popular politics has really driven science," says Reuter.

By contrast, Swiss scientists who, like their American counterparts, depend on government support, seem more free to conduct research in the addiction field, which citizens can then judge on the merits. Indeed, after the results of the heroin maintenance experiment were published this summer, Swiss voters were asked in a referendum whether the program should continue. More than 70 percent said "yes."

What Swiss voters seem to have realized is that there is a middle ground between condoning heroin use and insisting all addicts kick their habits immediately. As with nicotine, a drug with a similar addiction profile, heroin use is not a simple matter of exercising free will. Dependence is fierce and all consuming; withdrawal wreaks havoc on both the body and mind. The pleasure of heroin, writes David Lenson in his book, "On Drugs," takes over the body, "so that in withdrawal, ordinary consciousness is received as pain."

Anja Dobler-Micola, a member of the Swiss research team, says, "We always get this question: 'Shouldn't therapy be drug-free?' But is drug freedom the first step, or is it the last step?" Addicts in the program, she says, "realize how dependent they really are." Freed from the consuming street life and required to undergo counseling, they are able to reflect and make more rational choices about their future.

Now, if only Americans could start making rational choices about their drug policy.

SOURCE: Joshua Shenk, "Hooked on Dogma: U.S. Drug Warriors Ignore Switzerland's Success With Heroin Addicts," *Washington Post*, December 21, 1997.

ANALYSIS

As defined by Alan Marlatt in his recent review of harm reduction programs, harm reduction is a "pragmatic and compassionate approach to reduce the harms associated with substance use and other risk behaviors." Harm reduction came about in large part because of the association between HIV/AIDS and drug use. Injection drug use is the method of ingestion most clearly associated with an increased risk of HIV infection when users share injection equipment. Consequently, some of the first harm reduction programs were needle exchanges whereby injection users could obtain clean needles in exchange for their used ones, thereby lessening the need for them to share injection equipment and reducing their risk of infection with HIV and other diseases. But other programs such as opioid substitution (e.g., methadone maintenance, buprenorphine) and school prevention programs can also be considered as being harm reduction oriented.

One of the main ideas underlying harm reduction is that although abstinence might be an ideal, it is difficult if not impossible for some who are addicted to drugs to achieve permanent abstinence (although many do). In addition, strictly enforced abstinence as a requirement of drug free treatment prevents many addicts from entering or remaining in treatment. From a harm reduction perspective then the goal is to meet the person where they are at as a way of engaging them and, at the very least, helping them minimize the health risks of their drug use. If the person addicted to drugs can achieve abstinence, then abstinence is the goal. If they cannot, then perhaps helping them reduce their drug use is a good first step. If they cannot reduce their drug use, then perhaps teaching them to clean their needles and to not share their injection equipment with others is an attainable goal. Harm reduction programs can take the form of providing a drug user with stable housing where treatment and other services are readily available as the best initial step. All of these interventions, while short of the ideal of ceasing drug use, can be of benefit and improve the health of the drug addict and keep them engaged with or help them initiate treatment. For this reason, Marlatt suggests that harm reduction can also be characterized as health promotion.

Opponents of harm reduction see it much differently. They would not characterize the approach as promoting health but instead see it as doing the opposite. They see harm reduction programs like needle exchanges as encouraging continued use among existing addicts and, worse, promoting drug use to non-users. For example, harm reduction opponents characterize methadone maintenance as no better than "substituting one addiction for another." In many respects, the debate is the same as the one on whether sex education in classrooms should teach abstinence only or should promote abstinence but also advise students to use condoms correctly and consistently if abstinence is not an option. For opponents of harm reduction approaches, the issue is a moral matter: the only right choice is the morally correct choice, promoting abstinence. Anything less is indefensible. In the face of such moral certitude, scientific evidence, even if it shows positive benefits for harm reduction programs, is irrelevant. This has been precisely the case with needle exchange and methadone maintenance programs, which continue to face strong opposition despite a preponderance of research findings indicating they both have positive benefits and do not encourage drug use among non-users.

Harm reduction opponents frequently conflate harm reduction with the intent to decriminalize/legalize drugs. Consider the following excerpt from an essay published on the National Families in Action (NFIA) website by Sue Rusch, one of the founders of that organization, which coalesced with similar organizations to form the parents' movement that strongly influenced drug policy during the Reagan years and which continues to have considerable influence. In the first part of the essay, she reviews the events that led to the closing of Needle Park and argues they constitute strong evidence against harm reduction strategies:

> Health authorities distributed 15,000 clean needles a day. Observers were overwhelmed by the sight of bright, red blood coursing down arms and legs as addicts injected drugs into festering sores. Wet cotton swabs turned pink with mopped-up blood, and discarded blue needle wrappers covered the ground. In the heart of Zurich, purple and red sores infected arms and legs, pink and blue litter infected sidewalks as heroin and cocaine infected thousands of drug-stunned addicts.

In the next paragraphs, she describes the continued—and in her mind counterproductive—harm reduction efforts in Zurich post Needle Park. Although the efforts she describes include jailing drug traffickers she nevertheless contends that Zurich's policies were tantamount to drug legalization:

> By saying no to legalization, we say yes to comprehensive policies that bring together prevention, education, treatment, research, law enforcement and international drug control. Such policies have cut drug abuse in half since 1979. Then, 24 million Americans used drugs regularly. Today, 12 million do.

The portrayal of harm reduction as simply a covert way of legalizing drugs is even more explicit in testimony given to Congress in 1999 by Kevin Sabet, a 20-year-old college student at the University of California in Berkeley. Presuming to speak for his generation, Sabet offered this assessment on harm reduction to the Subcommittee on Criminal Justice, Drug Policy and Human Justice as they held a hearing on drug legalization and harm reduction:

> Come to my school in Berkeley, and you will see the crowning glory of something called "harm reduction." Where organizations like the Drug Policy Foundation, fund groups like Berkeley Cannabis Consumers Union, and the Cannabis Action Network. These organizations not only don't reject drug use, they claim its use is beneficial. Or the Drug Policy Foundation's funding of the needle-exchange and handout programs in the Bay Area. All part of something in a neat little package, that they call "harm reduction," that they define as, "reducing the harm that drugs do to an individual." But that any subjective, fair-minded individual would call drug legalization.

One problem with this argument is that prevention, education, research, and treatment can all be considered harm reduction strategies. It is true that some harm reduction proponents advocate forcefully for the decriminalization or outright legalization of marijuana and other drugs in the belief that criminal sanctions increase the harms associated with drug use by driving up prices, creating profitable black markets, spawning violence, forcing users to buy drugs of unknown purity and composition, and increasing the spread of disease. But advocating for legalization or decriminalization is not a defining characteristic of the harm reduction philosophy, particularly as it is applied to treatment and prevention interventions. Hence, characterizing harm reduction as equivalent to advocacy for legalization/decriminalization is inaccurate. They are separate issues and an informed policy debate should treat them as such. Too often, slippery slope arguments (e.g., harm reduction advocates always have the secret agenda of drug legalization) get in the way of implementing moderate measures that would be helpful in reducing both drug use as well as the harms associated with it.

The events in Needle Park continue to resurface in the harm reduction debate. Needle Park represents a nightmare scenario for both opponents and proponents but for very different reasons. For those opposed to the harm reduction approach, Needle Park is what they fear drug use would become if greater leniency and, in fact, facilitation of use were allowed to take hold. There could be no clearer argument against harm reduction than Needle Park. Anti-harm reductionists believe the U.S. would see an immediate increase in the number of people using and addicted to drugs. Contrary to predictions of harm reduction proponents, crime, suffering, and disease would also increase as they did in and around Needle Park. Worse, children would get the message that drug use was socially sanctioned leading many more to experiment with drugs and eventually join the ranks of those addicted.

For proponents of harm reduction, Needle Park is the nightmare of an experiment in harm reduction run amuck; an imperfect and unfair example that opponents continue to unfairly flaunt. Interventions such as needle exchanges, low-threshold methadone maintenance programs, medical care, and the provision of food and shelter should have minimized the harms of drug use. Instead, the interventions seemed to have facilitated and worsened use. Moreover, problems such as crime and the spread of HIV that harm reduction advocates have argued are a result of the oppressive, criminal-justice oriented policies of the war on drugs did not dissipate in the more lenient environs of Needle Park but instead intensified and spilled into the surrounding neighborhoods.

Why did it all go so wrong? Is Needle Park a fair example of harm reduction interventions? There is no dispute the policies were a disaster and that the Swiss authorities did well to close the Platzspitz. It took several years and an expensive scrubbing to clean up the park before it was reopened to the public. But were there elements unique to Needle Park that limit its representativeness as a counter-argument against harm reduction? In letters that appeared in both the *New York Times* and the *Washington Post* shortly after Needle Park was closed, Arthur Trebach, a harm reduction advocate made the following points as to why Needle Park was a poor example of a social experiment generally and of a harm reduction specifically:

- The intent was more to "ghettoize" the problem of drug use and contain it within a local area rather than to minimize harms. The greater concern was for the welfare of the non-drug-using citizenry than for the drug users at least for the first four years the park was open. By containing the drug use to one location, the rest of the city could be largely free of drug addicts.

- No attempt was made to control the age of users, who could enter the park, and who could sell drugs in the park. It became a magnet of addicts and traffickers all across Switzerland. It would be as if when Prohibition was ended, only one bar was opened in New York City. The result would be chaos, as drinkers would deluge the bar and the neighborhood. This is exactly what happened in Needle Park. The huge influx of addicts to the one area of the city where drugs could be readily obtained overwhelmed the provision of services, the police, and eventually the surrounding neighborhoods.
- No attempt was made to control the drug traffickers. While the price of drugs did drop some, it was still an illegal market and the price remained relatively high and continued to spawn crime to pay for the drugs. If the experiment were one in drug legalization, drugs would be prescribed and sold legally keeping the price low and purity high.
- The most important failure was toleration of an open drug scene in combination with harm reduction programs that exacerbated the problems (e.g., providing addicts with methadone that they could then use to supplement their heroin or sell on the black market for heroin without legal repercussion).

Are these arguments persuasive to opponents of harm reduction efforts? Probably not. Needle Park will remain for them an example of why harm reduction is a bad strategy. Was the failure of the Needle Park experiment enough to dissuade harm reduction advocates? Probably not. Proponents of harm reduction will continue to point out that no harm reduction programs proposed or implemented in this country advocate for tolerating the open use of drugs. Perhaps what both opponents and proponents can agree on is that an openly tolerated drug scene combined with harm reduction interventions leads to extremely poor results. The debate will surely continue.

As postscript: Switzerland did not abandon a progressive drug policy in the aftermath of Needle Park and has continued to experiment with harm reduction programs albeit understandably none that replicate Needle Park. In particular, the Swiss have implemented a heroin maintenance program whereby addicts can get heroin by prescription at centers around the country where they receive the drug in a controlled environment. Research findings have been positive and there is widespread public support. Other countries recently implementing heroin maintenance programs include Germany, Denmark, Spain, Canada, and England.

The United States, however, continues to resist such efforts as misguided. The current Director of U.S. National Drug Policy, Gil Kerlikowske, points instead to the Swedish model, which follows a zero-tolerance policy and requires drug addicts to enter treatment. Sweden has the lowest rate of substance use of any European nation. However, critics of the Swedish policy point out that Sweden invests much more in their prevention and treatment systems than the United States and all Swedish citizens have access to affordable health care through a publicly funded system. Hence, they argue, coercion of drug addicts into treatment has not yielded the same results in this country given the lack of treatment availability, access, quality, and affordability.

FURTHER READING

Babor, T., Caulkins, J., Edwards, G. et al. (2010). *Drug policy and the public good.* New York: Oxford University Press.

Breyer, C. Malinowska-Sempruch, K., Kamarulzaman, A., & Strathdee, S. A. (2010). 12 myths about HIV/AIDS and people who use drugs. *Lancet, 376*, 208–210.

Centers for Disease Control (2010, November 19). Syringe exchange programs—United States, 2008. *Morbidity and Mortality Weekly Report, 59*, 1488–1451.

Degenhardt, L., Mathers, B., Vickerman, P., Rhodes, T., Latkin, C., & Hickman, M. (2010). Prevention of HIV infection for people who inject drugs: Why individual, structural, and combination approaches are needed. *Lancet, 376*, 285–301.

Domoslawski, A. (2011, June). *Drug policy in Portugal: The benefits of decriminalizing drug use*. Warsaw, Poland: Open Society Foundation. Available at: http://www.soros.org/initiatives/drugpolicy.

Greenwald, G. (2009), *Drug decriminalization in Portugal; Lessons for creating fair and successful drug policies*. Washington, DC: The Cato Institute. Available at: http://www.cato.org/pub_display.php?pub_id=10080.

Huber, C. (1994). Needle park: What can we learn from the Zürich experience? *Addiction, 89*, 513–516.

MacCoun, R. J. (1998). Toward a psychology of harm reduction. *American Psychologist, 53*, 1199–1208.

MacCoun, R. J. (2011). What can we learn from the Dutch cannabis coffeeshop system? *Addiction, 105*, 1899–1910.

MacCoun, R. J., & Reuter, P. (2001). *Drug war heresies: Learning from other vices, times, & places*. New York: Cambridge University Press.

Marlatt, G. A., & Witkiewitz, K. (2010). Update on harm-reduction policy and intervention research. *Annual Review of Clinical Psychology, 6*, 591–606.

Palmateer, N., Kimber, J., Hickman, M., Hutchinson, S., Rhodes, T., & Goldberg, D. (2010). Evidence for the effectiveness of sterile injecting equipment provision in preventing hepatitis C and human immunodeficiency virus transmission among injecting drug users: A review of reviews. *Addiction, 105*, 844–859.

Shah, S. (2010). Living with HIV in the shadow of the White House. *Lancet, 376*, 223–224.

Subcommittee on Criminal Justice, Drug Policy, and Human Resources, Committee on Government Reform House of Representatives (1999, June 16). *Pros and cons of drug legalization, decriminalization, and harm reduction* (Serial No. 106-99). Washington, DC: U.S. Government Printing Office.

Trebach, A. S. (1992, March 17). Lessons from Needle Park. *Washington Post*, A17.

Uchtenhagen, A. A. (2011). Heroin maintenance treatment: From idea to research to practice. *Drug and Alcohol Review. 30*, 130–137.

On the Internet

The Avert.org website covers harm reduction in the context of needle exchange and other types of harm reduction programs. The site describes the controversy over harm reduction and how policies have been enacted or rejected by different countries at: http://www.avert.org/needle-exchange.htm.

The Drug Policy Alliance website has information on issues in harm reduction at: http://www.drugpolicy.org/issues/reducing-drug-harm.

SYRINGE EXCHANGE PROGRAMS IN THE UNITED STATES

Syringe exchange programs (SEPs) have been and remain controversial in the United States although acceptance appears to be gradually broadening. A group called the Junkie Union established the first SEP in Amsterdam in 1984. In the United States, the first SEP was no more than a single individual, Jon Parker, who distributed clean needles to addicts in New Haven and Boston. The first comprehensive program providing clean syringes and other services was established in Tacoma, Washington in 1988. Having seen enough, Senator Jesse Helms of North Carolina shepherded a bill through Congress that banned all federal funding for SEPs beginning in 1988. The ban would last until 2009. Opponents such as Helms were concerned that SEPs encouraged drug use, a concern common to harm reduction programs generally. Although President Clinton agreed with the research showing that SEPs do not encourage drug use, his administration did not lift the ban. President George W. Bush did not support SEPs and pressured the United Nations Office on Drugs and Crime to suppress data showing the success of such programs.

The ban was lifted in 2010 when the House of Representatives voted in support of the Labor-Health and Human Services-Education appropriations bill, which included language to lift the ban on federal funding for needle exchange programs. The effects of the recently available funding will not be known for several years but it seems reasonable to assume that more such programs will become available throughout the country and existing programs will be better staffed and offer more services.

Partially as a result of the efforts of these programs, the incidence of HIV among injection drug users (IDUs) has declined by 80 percent from 1988–1990 to 2003–2006 in the United States. This is the only adult transmission category to show a decline of this magnitude although IDUs continue to account for approximately 12–15 percent of new HIV infections annually depending on whether cases with multiple risk factors are included in the total.

The *Global State of Harm Reduction 2010* is a report by Harm Reduction International. The report describes the status of harm reduction strategies in countries across the world. The full text of the report can be downloaded or viewed by section at: http://www.ihra.net/global-harm-reduction.

The Harm Reduction Coalition is an agency dedicated to promoting harm reduction policies and interventions. Their website is at: http://www.harmreduction.org/

Information on the supervised injection site operated in Vancouver and other harm reduction efforts in Canada are available at the Vancouver Area of Drugs Users (VANDU) website at: http://www.vandu.org/

The North American Syringe Exchange Network website is at: http://www.nasen.org/

A 2005 *Salon* magazine article by Maia Szalavitz describes the George W. Bush administration's attempts at suppressing information on needle exchange programs: http://www.salon.com/news/feature/2005/03/24/needle_exchange.

The full text of Sue Rusch's essay on the lessons of Needle Park is available at the National Families in Action website at: http://www.nationalfamilies.org/publications/by_nfia/needle%20_park.html.

"The Experiment in Mass Incarceration"

- ***Document:*** "Young Black Americans and the Criminal Justice System: Five Years Later"
- ***Date:*** October 1995
- ***Where:*** National
- ***Significance:*** The Anti-Drug Abuse Acts of 1986 and 1988 provided long mandatory minimum sentences for selling or possessing even small amounts of crack cocaine and, to a lesser extent, other drugs. Many states followed suit and enacted similar laws. Soon after, the prison population began to grow at an extremely rapid pace. The new laws took an especially heavy toll on young African American men who were disproportionately arrested and incarcerated for drug-related offenses. Eventually, as this report indicates, nearly one in three were under the supervision of the criminal justice system (jail, prison, probation, parole). While crime rates have moderated to some extent, the degree to which that can be attributed to the increase in incarcerations is debatable. Moreover, the impact of these laws on drug use and availability has been marginal. Drug use was already in decline when the laws were enacted. The effects on the communities left behind have been severe, creating many single-parent homes, generations of children growing up in the absence of a father, and generations of men with dim employment prospects. Whether the emphasis on crack cocaine in the enacted laws was racially motivated continues to be the subject of a contentious debate. Whatever the original intent, however, the result has been a significant disparity in the arrest and incarceration rates of African American men compared with other racial-ethnic groups. For years, until 2010, Congress resisted the recommendations

of the U.S. Sentencing Commission to reduce the sentencing disparities for crack and powder cocaine.

DOCUMENT

Young Black Americans and the Criminal Justice System: Five Years Later

By Marc Mauer and Tracy Huling

The Sentencing Project

Overview

In 1990, The Sentencing Project released a report that documented that almost one in four (23%) African American males in the age group 20–29 was under some form of criminal justice supervision—in prison or jail, on probation or parole. That report received extensive national attention and helped to generate much dialogue and activity on the part of policymakers, community organizations, and criminal justice professionals.

Despite these efforts, many of the factors contributing to the high rates of criminal justice control for African American males remain unchanged or have worsened during the succeeding five years. Public policies ostensibly designed to control crime and drug abuse have in many respects contributed to the growing racial disparity in the criminal justice system while having little impact on the problems they were aimed to address.

The key findings of this report . . . are the following:

- Almost one in three (32.2%) young black men in the age group 20–29 is under criminal justice supervision on any given day—in prison or jail, on probation or parole.
- The cost of criminal justice control for these 827,440 young African American males is about $6 billion a year.
- In recent years, African American women have experienced the greatest increase in criminal justice supervision of all demographic groups, with their rate of criminal justice supervision rising by 78% from 1989–94.
- Drug policies constitute the single most significant factor contributing to the rise in criminal justice populations in recent years, with the number of incarcerated drug offenders having risen by 510% from 1983 to 1993. The number of Black (non-Hispanic) women incarcerated in state prisons for drug offenses increased more than eight-fold—828%—from 1986 to 1991.
- While African American arrest rates for violent crime—45% of arrests nationally—are disproportionate to their share of the population, this proportion has not changed significantly for twenty years. For drug offenses, though, the African American proportion of arrests increased from

24% in 1980 to 39% in 1993, well above the African American proportion of drug users nationally.
- African Americans and Hispanics constitute almost 90% of offenders sentenced to state prison for drug possession.

The criminal justice control rates documented in this report should prove even more disturbing than those revealed five years ago. Combined with the potential impact of current social and criminal justice policies, they attest to the gravity of the crisis facing the African American community.

The current high rates of criminal justice control are also likely to worsen considerably over the next several years. In addition to the steady twenty-year increase in criminal justice populations, the impact of current "get tough" policies in particular suggests continuing increases in criminal justice control rates and increasing racially disparate impacts. . . .

Impact of the "War on Drugs"

While debate will continue on the degree to which the criminal justice system overall contributes to racial disparities, there is increasing evidence that the set of policies and practices contained within the phrase "war on drugs" has been an unmitigated disaster for young blacks and other minorities.

Whether or not these policies were consciously or unconsciously designed to incarcerate more minorities is a question that may be debated. In essence, though, what we have seen are policy choices that have not only failed to reduce the scale of the problem but have seriously eroded the life prospects of the primary targets of those policies. The main elements of these policies have been the following:

Increased Arrests

Arrest policies beginning in the 1980s have disproportionately affected African Americans and other minorities: first, through greatly increased numbers of drug arrests, and second, through an increased rate of minority drug arrests. Drug arrests increased dramatically in the 1980s, rising from 471,000 in 1980 to 1,247,000 by 1989. As the number of arrests grew, so did the proportion of African Americans, from 24% of all drug arrests in 1980 to 39% by 1993.

Some persons would contend that African Americans are arrested in larger numbers because of their higher rates of drug use and sales. There are no reliable data on the overall composition of drug sellers in the total population, but we have reasonably good data available on drug possession through the annual household surveys of the National Institute on Drug Abuse (NIDA). Their most recent survey reveals that African Americans comprise 13% of monthly drug users, compared to the 1993 arrest proportion of 39%. Even if we only consider arrests for drug possession, which should be reflective of drug use, African Americans still constitute 34.7% of such arrests. Although the NIDA surveys have some limitations, the degree of disparity between drug use and drug possession arrests is of such magnitude that it clearly points to disproportionate arrest practices.

A recent analysis by James Lynch and William Sabol points to additional significant racial effects of law enforcement practices. Lynch and Sabol analyzed data on incarceration rates, race, and class during the period 1979–91. They identified inmates as either being "underclass" or "nonunderclass" (working class or middle class) based on educational levels, employment history, and income. They concluded that the most significant increase in incarceration rates was for working class black drug offenders, whose rates increased six-fold from 1.5 per 1,000 in 1979 to match that of underclass blacks at 9 per 1,000 in 1991. The trends for whites, on the other hand, were just the opposite, with the underclass drug incarceration rate being double that of the non-underclass by 1991.

Lynch and Sabol suggest several factors that may explain these trends. The "spill-over" effect of residential racial segregation, along with law enforcement targeting of black neighborhoods, may sweep more non-underclass blacks into the criminal justice system than is the case in the more stratified white housing patterns. They conclude that:

All of the processes described above lead to the same result, an increased targeting of black working and middle class areas for discretionary drug enforcement and ultimately increased incarceration for drug offenses. The immunity that working and middle class status used to bring in the black community (and still does among whites) may have been lost. While the processes that produced these outcomes may not have been racially motivated in intent, they have resulted in racially disparate outcomes.

Prosecution Policies

Aggravating the racial disparities in arrest patterns are decisions made by prosecutors which can increase the severity of the impact of drug policies on minorities. A recent survey of prosecutions for crack cocaine offenses conducted by the Los Angeles Times revealed that not a single white offender had been convicted of a crack cocaine offense in the federal courts serving the Los Angeles metropolitan area since 1986, despite the fact that whites comprise a majority of crack users. During the same period, though, hundreds of white crack traffickers were prosecuted in state courts. While federal prosecutors contend that they target high-level traffickers, the Times analysis found that many African Americans charged in federal court were low-level dealers or accomplices in the drug trade.

The consequences of this prosecutorial discretion are quite serious since federal mandatory sentencing laws require five- and ten-year minimums even for first offenders. The study found that whites charged with crack offenses and prosecuted in California state courts received sentences as much as eight years less than in the federal courts.

Sentencing Policies

Compounding the higher arrest rates for drug offenses have been changes in sentencing policies that have also disproportionately affected African Americans. The advent of a renewed generation of mandatory minimum sentencing statutes, now in place in all states and the federal system, has led to dramatic increases in the number of incarcerated drug offenders. The impact of these policies can be seen in several ways. First, the risk of incarceration per drug arrest increased more than 400% from 19 per 100,000 in 1980 to 104 per 100,000 by 1992, far greater than for any other offense during that period. . . . this has led to a 510% increase in the number of incarcerated drug offenders between 1983 and 1993, with one out of four inmates now serving time or awaiting trial for a drug offense.

The full impact of these policies has yet to be seen, since many of the mandatory sentences only began to be applied in large numbers in the late 1980s. In state prison systems, therefore, while average time served in prison has not changed appreciably in recent years, we can expect it to rise in the years ahead due to the impact of mandatory sentencing and other harsh policies.

In the federal system, the impact of these changes is already being felt, with the average time served by drug offenders increasing 50% from 22 months in 1986 to 33 months by 1992. Compounding this has been the much-discussed disparity in sentencing between crack cocaine and powder cocaine, whereby those persons convicted of crack possession receive a mandatory prison term of five years by possessing only one-hundredth of the quantity of cocaine as those charged with powder cocaine possession. Fourteen states also have statutes that distinguish between crack and powder cocaine in sentencing. The U.S. Sentencing Commission found that blacks accounted for 84.5% of federal crack possession convictions in 1993, while comprising 38% of those who report using crack in the past year. The Sentencing Commission has also calculated that a person convicted of trafficking in five grams of crack with a maximum retail value of $750 will receive the same sentence as an offender charged with selling 500 grams of powder cocaine retailing for $50,000.20

Impact of High Rates of Control on the African-American Community

The high rate of incarceration of African American males raises concerns about its impact not only on the individuals who are incarcerated, but on their communities, as well. As increasing numbers of young black men are arrested and incarcerated, their life prospects are seriously diminished. Their possibilities for gainful employment are reduced, thereby making them less attractive as marriage partners and unable to provide for children they father. This in turn contributes to the deepening of poverty in low-income communities.

The large-scale rates of incarceration may contribute to the destruction of the community fabric in other ways as well. As prison becomes a common experience for young males, its stigmatizing effect is diminished. Further, gang or crime group affiliations on the outside may be reinforced within the prison only to emerge stronger as the individuals are released back to the community. With so few males in underclass communities having stable ties to the labor market, the ubiquitous ex-offenders and gang members may become the community's role models.

The cumulative impact of these high rates of incarceration has been to postpone the time at which large numbers of African American males start careers and families. While we should not ignore the fact that these men have committed crimes that led to their imprisonment, current crime control policies may actually be increasing the severity of the problem, particularly when other options for responding to crime exist.

SOURCE: Marc Mauer and Tracy Huling, "Young Black Americans and the Criminal Justice System: Five Years Later," The Sentencing Project, Washington, DC, October 1995. Used by permission of the Sentencing Project.

ANALYSIS

> The whole law-and-order movement is—in operation—anti-black and anti-underclass. Not in plan, not in design, not in intent, but in operation.
> —Norval Morris—Professor, University of Chicago Law School

Were the sentencing policies enacted in the 1986 and 1988 Anti-Drug Abuse Acts racially motivated? Does the original motivation matter if the practical effect of the laws has been to disproportionately incarcerate young, undereducated black men? These are the kind of deeply troubling, divisive questions that have been asked repeatedly in the wake of federal and state legislation that returned mandatory minimum sentences providing for lengthy sentences for distributing or possessing even small amounts of crack cocaine.

As might be expected, the dispute over the motivations and practical effect of the laws has fallen along ideological lines. Conservatives continue to support the criminal justice emphasis of drug policy and the resulting mass incarceration. They deny the laws were racially motivated and argue that the disparate incarceration rates reflect the reality of higher crime rates among minorities and that most offenders sentenced under the provisions of the drug laws have histories of multiple offenses. Conservatives point to decreases in crime rates as evidence the policies are effective and protecting the rights of the law-abiding public. Keeping the public safe justifies the expense of incarceration.

Progressives/liberals decry these policies, perhaps conveniently forgetting that the federal measures had strong bipartisan support when passed. They suggest there was a covert if not overt racial motivation behind the laws and point to the racial and class disparities among those arrested and incarcerated under the laws' provisions as evidence. They cite national surveys showing comparable levels of drug use by whites and blacks and argue that racial profiling by the police, a law enforcement focus on black neighborhoods, and prosecutorial bias as driving the differential arrest and conviction rates. They also cite studies showing that only a small proportion of the decrease in crime rates can be attributed to the increase in incarceration rates and argue that there are more effective and less costly alternatives such as providing more funding for treatment, education and employment and focusing law enforcement efforts on higher level drug dealers rather than street dealers.

There is little dispute that historically drug policy has had racist overtones and intentions. In the early to mid-20th century, the racism was explicit as evidenced by the essay on the (exaggerated) effects of cocaine on southern blacks (see the section on "A hitherto inoffensive negro") and characterizations of opium-smoking Chinese as intent on seducing white women. Overt racism was also evident when publisher William Randolph Hearst escalated his personal vendetta against Mexicans into a public flogging played out in Hearst's publications as portrayals of Mexicans as crazed, murderous, marihuana smoking ne'er-do-wells intent on spreading their drug use to American children.

Federal Bureau of Narcotics (FBN) Commissioner Harry J. Anslinger was only too happy to incorporate Hearst's distortions into his own writings and testimony along with other wild mischaracterizations in his efforts to portray marihuana as the "Assassin of Youth" and legislate that drug into oblivion. Anslinger was not above using racist statements and fears to win political support. In internal FBN documents he referred to "ginger-colored niggers." In writings intended for public consumption, his racism was only marginally less apparent. Coming to the aid of white women throughout the country he warned:

> There are 100,000 total marijuana smokers in the U.S. and most are Negroes, Hispanics, Filipinos and entertainers. Their Satanic music, jazz and swing, result from marijuana use. This marijuana causes white women to seek sexual relations with Negroes, entertainers and any others.

By the 1970s, however, after the Civil Rights Movement, racially overt and charged language such as this had begun disappearing from legislative discourse (if not from the backrooms of the Nixon White House). The thin amount of information in the Congressional record in the five-week rush to draft the Anti-Drug Abuse Act of 1986 is mostly filled with the recitation of press accounts of the dangers and violence surrounding crack cocaine, the new "most dangerous drug in the world" and self-congratulatory statements about the degree of bipartisanship in attacking the nation's drug problem. However, it could not have been lost on Congress that crack was concentrated in black, impoverished, inner-city neighborhoods with little evidence that it was spreading further. When the federal mandatory minimums singling out crack cocaine were enacted and the states largely followed suit, an era of mass incarceration had begun that, as the Sentencing Project's excerpted report shows, began disproportionately consigning generations of young black men to lengthy prison sentences.

In a cogent if speculative analysis of the possible motivations of law makers as they considered the Anti-Drug Abuse Act, Doris Provine in her thoughtful book *Unequal Under the Law* suggests that the goal of the Reagan administration was to expand the Republican Party's post-Watergate base by appealing to moral conservatives. To that end, they wanted to "replace social welfare with social control as the principle of state policy." She notes further that "their political strategy took advantage of racial tensions without ever openly revealing a racial agenda" and that crack was a perfect issue because "media attention ensured that no one would miss its connection with the terrifying inner city and its restless Black youth." Referring to political conservatives, she adds:

> They used it (crack cocaine) and the drug issue as an ideological fig leaf to place over the unsightly urban ills that had increased markedly under the Reagan Administration's social and economic policies . . . For the Reagan Administration and others on the right, America's drug problems functioned as opportunities for the imposition of an old moral agenda and the appearance of a new social concern . . . Such remedies avoided all questions about the economic and political sources and solutions to America's social problems.

Perhaps, but one problem with this analysis is that it neglects the fact that support for the 1986 and 1988 legislation was overwhelmingly bipartisan, including even many prominent members of the Black Congressional Caucus. It is difficult to ascribe covert racist intentions to such a broad representation of Congress, many of whom clearly did not support the political agenda of the Reagan administration and its conservative supporters. But to ask the question again: Even if covert racist intentions are difficult to ascribe to the legislation, does that really matter if, as Professor Morris suggests in the quote above that the law and order movement is "anti-black and anti-underclass in operation." The data cited in the Sentencing Project's report certainly support this contention.

Statistics compiled in a recent analysis of racial disparities in incarceration rates by Western and Pettit in a paper published in *Daedalus* provide further support. They note that between 1980 and 2008, the U.S. incarceration rate increased from 221 to 762 per 100,000 following a 50-year period during which the rate had been stable at 100 per 100,000. Most of the disparity in incarceration rates has occurred among young black men who did not graduate from high school. The 1980 incarceration rate among undereducated black men was 10%. By 2008, this rate increased to 37%! Although the incarceration rates for whites and Latinos without a high school education also increased, the increases were much smaller; from about 1% to 10% for whites and from about 2% to 6% for Latinos. The rates of increase for all racial/ethnic groups were much smaller for those with a high school education or greater. Western and Pettit attribute most of the increase and the disparities to drug laws generally and to the provisions that target low level crack cocaine dealers and users specifically.

Why have the sentencing laws had such a disproportionate effect on young black men? The first and most obvious point is one that has already been made, that being the higher rates of crack cocaine use by blacks as compared with whites but even this difference does not account for the full disparity in incarceration rates. A second point has to do with where drugs are sold. Whereas crack cocaine trafficking tends to occur in open-air markets with purchases made from street vendors, powder cocaine sales occur in more secluded and harder to detect locations. In much the same way it is easier for police to identify and arrest prostitutes who are street walkers as opposed to call girls, it is easier for police to detect and arrest crack cocaine dealers working on the streets than dealers who cater to a more secluded and exclusive clientele who are more likely to purchase powder rather than crack cocaine.

Glasser and Siegel, in their essay on the erosion of civil rights and liberties under the drug war describe other factors related to police tactics and procedural justice that further contribute to racial disparities in the criminal justice system. As an example of the former they note the sweeps of public housing residents whereby police could search residences for drugs without a warrant. If any drugs are found on the premise residents can be immediately expelled. Black Americans disproportionately occupy public housing. In terms of procedural justice, Glasser and Siegel note that charged with the same or an even worse crime, white defendants are more often able to afford a private lawyer who helps them plea bargain to a lesser charge whereas blacks of less financial means must rely on public defenders, who are often less skillful attorneys. They provide the example of a white defendant in Indianapolis charged with possessing nearly *10 grams* of cocaine. His private lawyer plea-bargained and obtained a sentence to community service for six weeks. A black defendant in the same jurisdiction was arrested for selling less than *3 grams* of cocaine. With a large degree of sarcasm, Glasser and Siegel write: "His public defender worked out a deal: He pled guilty and was sentenced to six years in prison."

So many drug users came under the purview of the criminal justice system that expanding drug treatment came to mean expanding drug treatment *within* the criminal justice system where attendance could be mandated. Special courts called, understandably enough, "drug courts" arose. Drug courts were designed specifically to deal with the overflow of drug using offenders and to conduct "therapeutic jurisprudence." That is, judges in drug courts not only meted out justice, they also closely monitored convicted drug users throughout the treatment process. Therapeutic communities, residential treatment programs whereby the milieu or environment is seen as the primary therapeutic agent were incorporated into prisons, extensively studied and modified to accommodate the unique circumstances of prison environments. Boot camps for first time offenders convicted on lesser charges were developed on the theory that instilling discipline military style was what was needed to change drug use (they don't work too well). Re-entry programs designed to help prisoners returning to the community post-incarceration are the newest wrinkle.

In the years following the Sentencing Project report, the prison population continued to expand with much of the expansion driven by enforcement of the mandatory minimum drug laws. Racial disparities in arrests and sentencing continued. Only within the last three years has the growth rate in state and federal prison populations abated, showing declines at the state level between 2006 and 2009. The U.S. Sentencing Commission, an independent agency of the federal judicial branch, was established by the Sentencing Reform Act provision of the Comprehensive Crime Control Act of 1984. Among the Commission's charges are establishing advisory sentencing guidelines for the federal courts and advising Congress on effective crime policy. In the same year as the Sentencing Project report, the Sentencing Commission recommended to Congress that the sentencing disparities be reduced. For the first time, Congress overrode the Commission's recommendation. It would take 15 more years before the Fair Sentencing Act of 2010 reduced (but did not eliminate) the sentencing disparity between crack and powder cocaine from 100:1 to 18:1. In 2011, the Sentencing Commission determined the revised provisions should be applied retroactively to those already sentenced effectively reducing the sentences of over 12,000 federal prison inmates. The debate about the fairness of the mandatory minimum laws, whether they are racially motivated, their effectiveness in controlling drug use and crime, and the relative benefits given the fiscal and social costs is ongoing.

FURTHER READING

Adler, W. M. (1996). *One family's quest for the American dream in the age of crack.* New York: Penguin Group.

Beaver, A. L. (2010). Getting a fix on cocaine sentencing policy: Reforming the sentencing scheme of the Anti-Drug Abuse Act of 1986. *Fordham Law Review, 78,* 2531–2575.

Bourgois, P. (2003). *In search of respect: Selling crack in El Barrio.* New York: Cambridge University Press.

Duster, T. (1997). Pattern, purpose, and race in the drug war. In: C. Reinarman & H. G. Levine (Eds.) *Crack in America: Demon drugs and social justice* (pp. 260–287). Berkeley, CA: University of California Press.

Glasser, I., & Siegel, L. (1997). "When Constitutional rights seem too extravagant to endure": The crack scare's impact on civil rights and liberties. In: C. Reinarman & H. G. Levine (Eds.) *Crack in America: Demon drugs and social justice* (pp. 229–248). Berkeley, CA: University of California Press.

Goldstein, P. (1985). The drugs/violence nexus: A tripartite conceptual framework. *Journal of Drug Issues, 39,* 143–174. Available at: http://www.drugpolicy.org/docUploads/nexus.pdf.

LAURIE HIETT—"OH MY GOD. I'M SO WIRED!"

Laurie Hiett was the wife of Army Colonel James C. Hiett, who for one year had served as the head of the U.S. embassy's military group in Bogota, Colombia. Colonel Hiett's job was to advise the Colombian military on antinarcotics strategies. The daughter of a Panamanian mother and American father, Laurie met James Hiett while she was working as a secretary in the Canal Zone. The two seemed an unlikely couple. James Hiett had a reputation as a straight-laced, by-the-books, lifetime military man whereas Laurie was a free spirit who was already experimenting with drugs and alcohol. Proving the adage that opposites sometimes attract, the two married in 1989.

While the couple was in Fayetteville, NC, Laurie began leading a double life: a high school Spanish teacher by day, a cocaine-snorting party-girl by night who ran with a social network of strippers and ex-prostitutes. Even then, her teaching colleagues noticed she was using drugs during recesses and at the lunch break. Hiett's drug use worsened and in 1995, she voluntarily entered a treatment program to try to regain control of her life. She managed to avoid using drugs for only a short time before resuming her cocaine and alcohol use.

Shortly after moving to Colombia, a bored Laurie asked an embassy employee, Jorge Ayala, to chauffeur her to a bar in Bogota's red light district called *La Zona Rosa*. The area was generally off-limits to embassy staff as it was a known drug haven. En route, she asked if he knew where to get some cocaine. In a country that was supplying an estimated 80 percent of the cocaine used in the United States, this proved to be an easy matter. But instead of returning with the expected one or two grams, Ayala brought Laurie a one pound brick and for cheap. Snorting the near-pure cocaine in the bar's bathroom a surprised and giddy Laurie observed: "Oh my God. I'm so wired . . . It was a beautiful thing."

Laurie and Ayala hatched a plot to sell cocaine and heroin after seeing how easy it was for her to bring cocaine in her carry-on bag when she traveled back to the United States to visit friends. They began mailing cocaine and heroin in brown paper packages from the embassy in Bogota to one of Ayala's contacts in Queens, New York, who would sell the drug and share the profits.

The ruse was sniffed out, literally, when a Customs drug dog took interest in one of Hiett's parcels. When the package was opened, Customs agents found it did

(continued)

Jonsson, P. (2011, June 30). US prisoners sentenced under strict crack cocaine laws get relief. *The Christian Science Monitor*. Available at: http://www.csmonitor.com/USA/Justice/2011/0630/US-prisoners-sentenced-under-strict-crack-cocaine-laws-get-relief.

Kornblum, W. (1991). Drug legalization and the minority poor. *Millbank Quarterly*, 69, 415–435.

Massing, M. (1996, February 1). Crime and drugs: The new myths. *New York Review of Books*.

Nurco, D.N., Ball, J.C., Shaffer, J.W., & Hanlon, T.E. (1985). The criminality of narcotic addicts. *Journal of Nervous and Mental Disease*, *173*, 94–102.

Provine, D.M. (2007). *Unequal under the law: Race in the war on drugs*. Chicago: University of Chicago Press.

Shapiro, B. (2000, July 5). The corruption of Col. James Hiett. *Salon*. http://www.salon.com/news/feature/2000/07/05/hiett/index.html.

Taxman, F.S., & Bouffard, J. (2002). Treatment inside the drug treatment court: The who, what, where, and how of treatment services. *Substance Use and Misuse*, *37*, 1665–1688.

Werb, D., Rowell, G., Guyatt, G., Kerr, T., et al. (2011). Effect of drug law enforcement on drug market violence: A systematic review. *International Journal of Drug Policy*, *22*, 87–94.

Western, B., & Pettit, B. (2010). Incarceration and social inequality. *Daedalus*, *139*, 8–19.

White, H.R., & Gorman, D.M. (2000). *Dynamics of the drug-crime relationship*. In G. LaFree (Ed.), *Criminal justice 2000, volume I the nature of crime: Continuity and change* (pp. 151–218). Washington DC: U.S. Department of Justice.

Zimring. F. (2011, August). How New York City beat crime. *Scientific American*, *305*, 74–79.

On the Internet

A 2006 report prepared by the ACLU titled *Cracks in the System: Twenty Years of the Unjust Federal Crack Cocaine Law* is available at: http://www.aclu.org/drug-law-reform/cracks-system-20-years-unjust-federal-crack-cocaine-law.

An Associate Press article by Tom Hays titled "Army Wife Preferred Drug Enjoyment to Enforcement" describing the Laurie Hiett debacle is available at: http://articles.latimes.com/2000/aug/27/news/mn-11099.

The latest data on state and federal prison populations and trends in incarceration rates are available from the Bureau of Justice Statistics website at: http://bjs.ojp.usdoj.gov/index.cfm?ty=tp&tid=13

Families Against Mandatory Minimums, an advocacy organization, has a website at: http://www.famm.org/

The Federal Bureau of Prisons (FBOP) report on drug treatment in U.S. federal prisons is available at: http://www.bop.gov/news/index.jsp and the most recent annual FBOP report providing statistics on federal prison facilities and inmates is available at: http://www.bop.gov/news/publications.jsp.

Full text of the Fair Sentencing Act of 2010, which reduced the sentencing disparities between crack and powder cocaine is available at: http://www.fd.org/odstb_CrackCocaine.htm#fair.

The National Association of Drug Court Professionals (NADCP) has extensive information on drug courts at: http://www.nadcp.org/nadcp-home/

The National Center on Addiction and Substance Abuse at Colombia University publishes regular reports on various aspects of substance use policy and issues at their website. A 2010 report entitled *Behind Bars II: Substance abuse and America's prisons* is available at: http://www.casacolumbia.org/templates/publications_reports.aspx.

The National Sentencing Project website has many links and documents related to sentencing policies, drug laws, and racial disparities including the full text of the excerpted report at: http://www.sentencingproject.org.

The U.S. Sentencing Commission website is at: http://www.ussc.gov/index.cfm.

LAURIE HIETT—"OH MY GOD. I'M SO WIRED!"

(continued)

not contain coffee, toys, and sweets as listed on the declarations page but instead concealed three pounds of high-quality cocaine. Hiett, Ayala, and his contact in New York were soon arrested. At first, James Hiett was not implicated. But after an investigation showed he attempted to launder money from the drug sales by using it to pay for expenses on a trip to Florida, he too was indicted. Laurie Hiett was sentenced to five years in prison and Colonel James Hiett was sentenced to five months in jail.

4

THE MID-1990s TO 2011: MEDICAL MARIJUANA, BLACK TAR HEROIN, OXYCONTIN, METHAMPHETAMINE, THE MEXICAN DRUG WAR, THE WAR ON DRUGS CONTINUES

"Any Other Illness for Which Marijuana Provides Relief"

- ***Document:*** Proposition 215 (Compassionate Use Act of 1996)
- ***Date:*** November 5, 1996
- ***Where:*** California
- ***Significance:*** Marijuana has been an illegal drug per federal law since 1937, classified (incorrectly) as a narcotic with heroin and cocaine. In practice, enforcement of federal laws pertaining to marijuana has been uneven but nevertheless, considerable resources have been expended to suppress marijuana use, growing, and distribution. Despite these efforts, marijuana has been and remains the most widely used illegal drug and by a large margin. Until the 1990s, calls to reduce criminal penalties for marijuana use and distribution (depenalization) or to remove criminal penalties outright in lieu of civil penalties such as fines (decriminalization) did not gain much traction outside of dedicated groups of reformists. However, persistent anecdotal reports and some research evidence that smoked marijuana provides relief from the symptoms of a variety

Jasmine, behind the counter, helping clients select marijuana from jars at the La Brea Collective medical marijuana dispensary in Los Angeles. Such dispensaries often feature many "brands" of marijuana that are displayed in canisters such as those depicted in this photo. The different brands are often given whimsical names such as "Charlie Sheen" and "OG Baby Ivy." (AP/Wide World Photos)

of medical conditions led to growing public support to pass laws legalizing marijuana use for medical purposes. In 1996, California was the first state to pass such a law, known as Proposition 215. Since then 16 other states and Washington, D.C., have enacted medical marijuana laws. However, the status of medical marijuana remains in legal limbo, as the federal government continues to resist petitions to reclassify the drug from Schedule I to Schedule II, which would allow more research to be done to formally test the claimed medical benefits in large-scale clinical trials. Moreover, ambiguities in the state laws and varying provisions have allowed for abuses. The result has been a backlash in some states to strengthen provisions in the laws to reduce the excesses and the "gaming" that has occurred by limiting distribution.

DOCUMENT

Compassionate Use Act of 1996

Health and Safety Code Section 11362.5

Sec. (1) a–b The people of the State of California hereby find and declare that the purposes of the Compassionate Use Act of 1996 are as follows:

(A) To ensure that seriously ill Californians have the right to obtain and use marijuana for medical purposes where the medical use is deemed appropriate and has been recommended by a physician who has determined that the person's health would benefit from the use of marijuana in the treatment of cancer, anorexia, AIDS, chronic pain, spasticity, glaucoma, arthritis, migraine, or any other illness for which marijuana provides relief.

(B) To ensure that patients and their primary caregivers who obtain and use marijuana for medical purposes upon the recommendation of a physician are not subject to criminal prosecution or sanction.

(C) To encourage the federal and state governments to implement a plan to provide for the safe and affordable distribution of marijuana to all patients in medical need of marijuana.

(2) Nothing in this Act shall be construed to supersede legislation prohibiting persons from engaging in conduct that endangers others, nor to condone the diversion of marijuana for nonmedical purposes.

(c) Notwithstanding any other provision of law, no physician in this state shall be punished, or denied any rights or privilege, for having recommended marijuana to a patient for medical purposes.

(d) Section 11357, relating to the possession of marijuana, and Section 11358, relating to the cultivation of marijuana, shall not apply to a patient, or to the patient's primary caregiver, who possesses or cultivates marijuana for the personal medical purposes of the patient upon the written or oral recommendation or approval of a physician.

(e) For the purposes of this section, "primary caregiver" means the individual designated by the person exempted under this act who has consistently assumed responsibility for the housing, health, or safety of that person.

Sec. 2. If any provision of this measure or the application thereof to any person or circumstance is held invalid, that invalidity shall not affect other provisions or applications of the measure which can be given effect without the invalid provision or application, and to this end the provisions of this measure are severable.

SOURCE: Compassionate Use Act of 1996. California Health and Safety Code Section 11362.5

ANALYSIS

> Orr would be crazy to fly more missions and sane if he didn't, but if he was sane, he had to fly them. If he flew them, he was crazy and didn't have to; but if he didn't want to, he was sane and had to. Yossarian was moved very deeply by the absolute simplicity of this clause of Catch-22 and let out a respectful whistle.
>
> —Joseph Heller, *Catch 22*

Since the Marihuana Tax Act of 1937, marijuana has been illegal to grow, possess, and distribute in the United States. The tax act (see "It has something to do with something that is called marihuana" for more detail and analysis) was not based on scientific evidence but instead was guided by the dubious congressional testimony of nonmedical experts and the outsized influence of one indefatigable man, Federal Bureau of Narcotics Commissioner Harry Anslinger. With an able assist from media mogul William Randolph Hearst, Anslinger succeeded in portraying marijuana (or marihuana as it was more commonly spelled at the time) as being the "assassin of youth" and the province of crazed Mexicans intent on corrupting susceptible American teenagers. Thereafter, incorrectly classified as being a narcotic with the potential for abuse on par with cocaine and heroin, marijuana was included in a series of increasingly punitive laws passed in the 1950s.

Despite the scare tactics and legal efforts to suppress marijuana use, it has been and has remained the most widely used illegal drug. It is the largest cash crop in the state of California. Along with LSD, marijuana was a symbol of rebellion in the 1960s for the countercultural movement. The pungent smell of burning marijuana—one nickname of which is skunkweed—became a fixture in college dormitories and large outdoor rock concerts. In the face of the drug's continuous and growing popularity, the punitive laws passed less than a decade earlier were only laxly enforced and had done little to deter its growing acceptance regardless.

Riding the wave, President Nixon's National Commission on Marihuana and Drug Abuse (the Shaffer Commission) issued a report in 1972 that "there is little proven danger of physical or psychological harm from the experimental or intermittent use of the natural preparations of cannabis." The report went on to recommend decriminalizing marijuana. Nixon angrily rejected the report's conclusions, and transcripts from White House recordings made at the time reveal Nixon's thoughts about the dangers presented by drugs including marijuana and his bizarre representation of the threat the drugs posed. He linked the push for legalization to Jewish psychiatrists, communists, and homosexuals in the service of subverting the U.S. government:

> It's a funny thing, every one of the bastards that are for legalizing marijuana is Jewish. What the Christ is the matter with the Jews, Bob? What is the matter with them? I suppose it is because most of them are psychiatrists.
>
> Dope? Do you think Russians allow dope? Hell no. Not if they can catch it, they send them up. You see, homosexuality, dope, immorality in general: These are the enemies of strong societies. That's why the Communists and the left-wingers are pushing it. They're trying to destroy us.

Earlier, the Controlled Substances Act of 1970 placed marijuana on Schedule I right along with heroin and LSD as drugs having a high potential for abuse, no known medical benefits, and lacking accepted safety under medical supervision. The designation means the federal government believes marijuana is more dangerous than cocaine or morphine, which are Schedule II drugs, making for a tricky argument that marijuana is a "gateway drug" leading to the use of "harder drugs" (see sidebar on the gateway hypothesis, this section).

True to his anticrime pledge, Nixon pushed for greater law enforcement efforts to crack down on all drug use, including marijuana use, and under his administration, arrests increased. No matter, marijuana use continued to grow in popularity reaching its apotheosis at the end of 1979. In that year, 60 percent of high school seniors reported trying marijuana and 10 percent reported daily use. In 2010, the corresponding rates for high school seniors were 44 percent reporting ever using marijuana and 6 percent reporting daily use. President Carter campaigned on a platform that proposed decriminalizing marijuana use but economic concerns, the Iran-hostage crisis, and a scandal that led to the resignation of his top drug policy adviser ensured that proposal was never brought before Congress.

The use of marijuana declined in the 1980s as the influence of the countercultural movement waned and the public turned away from drugs (excepting cocaine). Increasing numbers no longer viewed drugs as benign or beneficial. Nancy Reagan's Just Say No campaign and the beginnings of what became the *parent's movement* (see sidebar) refocused government efforts on reducing marijuana use. These efforts ignored perhaps that by the mid-1980s marijuana use was already in sharp decline. Focus on the *casual user* (i.e., including and especially those who used marijuana or other drugs occasionally but not compulsively) only intensified in the late 1980s with the creation of the Office of National Drug Control Policy (ONDCP) under President George H. W. Bush and the first ONDCP Director, Bill Bennett. Thousands would be arrested and millions spent on the prosecution and confinement of marijuana users, growers, and distributors. Throughout, marijuana remained the most commonly used illegal drug, albeit at levels below the peak in 1979–1980 as indicated by prevalence data. All of these things remain true through to the present day.

Calls to legalize marijuana or to allow the use of marijuana for medical purposes were fairly muted in the 1980s but grew in volume in the 1990s as more people began openly questioning the wisdom of arresting and incarcerating millions of citizens while, at the same time, grossly underfunding treatment and prevention. Marijuana use began regaining in popularity among the general public and high school youth but prevalence remained below the rates of the late 1970s. Additionally, people with medical conditions such as HIV/AIDS, cancer, multiple sclerosis, and glaucoma who used marijuana were reporting it was highly effective in relieving symptoms related to these conditions; more effective than existing legal treatments including Marinol, which is the trade name for synthesized tetrahydrocannabinol (THC), the main active ingredient in smoked marijuana.

As efforts to legalize marijuana or make it available for medical use increased, they were met with equally sharp resistance from those who believed marijuana is a dangerous drug on many levels and has no medicinal value. An important part of the debate for and against reducing or eliminating criminal sanctions is the idea that marijuana use is not only harmful in and of itself but also that it leads users to try "harder drugs" such as heroin and cocaine. This idea, known as the gateway hypothesis, is not new and has been used as justification for the passage of laws restricting marijuana use since the 1930s.

In November 1996, with growing public support, California passed the Compassionate Use Act, put to a direct vote on the ballot. Arizona would shortly follow suit. The California law passed easily garnering 55 percent of the vote. Lack of specificity in the law, however, has led to abuses. For example, the law allowed physicians to recommend marijuana for a variety of medical conditions including those covered by the very ambiguous phrase "any other illness for which marijuana provides relief." The law was also ambiguous on how patients or their primary caregivers should acquire marijuana. As a result, numerous co-ops or cannabis clubs began springing up and patients began growing marijuana in their homes or gardens. In some instances, the number of such co-ops was excessive and clearly beyond any legitimate medical need. Some co-ops were ill advisedly (or perhaps intentionally) located near high schools. Also not specified were the number of marijuana dispensaries permitted nor the necessity for and definition of a legitimate doctor-patient relationship (leaving open the possibility of obtaining a prescription from a script-doc). To clarify some of these ambiguities and protect marijuana patients from arrest, California passed a new law in 2003, SB 420, that provided for medical marijuana ID cards and information on application and registration for the cards and stipulated that the cannabis co-ops should be not-for-profit organizations. The main purpose of the ID cards is to provide medical marijuana users a way of legitimizing their possession or growing of marijuana if challenged by the local police.

As described in a very recent article by Cohen, similar vagueness in Colorado's medical marijuana law, passed in 2000, led to "innovations such as a 5,000-square-foot dispensary, dispensaries with hair stylists on site, and even one dispensary that claims to have the country's only medical-marijuana restaurant." Cohen argues that the vagueness and inconsistency from one state law to another have resulted in subterfuge and the de facto legalization of medical marijuana whereby even those without a medical need are now able to easily purchase the drug at the legal outlets.

While the complete legalization of marijuana may be the ultimate goal for some, it undermines the argument that medical marijuana can be restricted to users with legitimate medical needs and risks the repeal of current medical marijuana statutes on the grounds that distribution cannot be adequately controlled. Hence, abuse of the medical marijuana laws have led to a backlash in some California counties and elsewhere to legislate restrictions that would reduce the perceived abuses of the law's original intent and place restrictions on the number and sales practices of cannabis co-ops. The backlash was evident to an extent in November 2010 when by a 54 percent to 46 percent margin, Californians voted down full legalization of the drug (Proposition 19 or the Regulate, Control, & Tax Cannabis Act). However, earlier that same year, Governor Schwarzenegger signed into law SB 1449, which decriminalized possession of less than 1 ounce of cannabis from a misdemeanor to a "civil infraction" punishable by a $100 fine.

New Jersey is among the most recent of 16 other states and the District of Colombia to join California in passing a medical marijuana law. The New Jersey law could be a model for redrafting existing legislation in states with existing laws and a template for states considering new legislation. The 2010 New Jersey law, known as the Compassionate Use Medical Marijuana Act, provides strict definitions and controls on the prescribing of medical marijuana similar to the controls on prescribing OxyContin and other restricted drugs. The law further stipulates there be a "*bona-fide* physician-patient relationship" and requires the physician take a full medical history and conduct a complete physical examination. Moreover, medical marijuana in New Jersey can only be obtained at state-monitored dispensaries. Growing marijuana for personal use is prohibited. The recency of the New Jersey law means there has not yet been time to determine if its provisions have curbed the abuses seen in other states.

The status of medical marijuana at present has been described as being in legal limbo. This is because the state laws permitting medical marijuana are at odds with the Controlled Substances Act, which prohibits the dispensation and use of marijuana under any circumstances. In 2005, the Supreme Court ruled in *Gonzalez v. Raich* that federal law supersedes state law—via federal authority over interstate commerce—leaving open the possibility of federal arrests and prosecutions in states that have medical marijuana laws. In 2009, Eric Holder, the current Attorney General indicated that federal resources would not be used to enforce the law but he seems to have reversed himself on this position. The DEA has continued to conduct raids on medical marijuana dispensaries since that time.

Opponents of medical marijuana present the circular argument that smoked marijuana has no known medical uses and has the high potential for abuse, citing verbatim the language pertaining to Schedule I drugs. However, the fact that marijuana is a Schedule I drug means that it is difficult (not impossible, but difficult) to conduct the kind of large-scale clinical trials necessary to determine if marijuana is medically useful (although limited, smaller scale trials have shown that it is effective for a variety of conditions). Researchers must first get a license from the DEA qualifying them to conduct such research and they then must acquire marijuana through the National Institute on Drug Abuse, the only legal source for conducting marijuana research. The FDA must also approve the study protocol. Resistance to permitting research into the possible medical benefits of marijuana has been met at all three levels of the approval process.

On June 21, 2011, the DEA denied a petition filed by the Coalition for Rescheduling Cannabis to initiate proceedings to reclassify marijuana as a Schedule II drug. Medical marijuana advocates were happy to receive this decision from the DEA. Their petition to reschedule marijuana had languished since 2002. The decision can now be appealed in the federal courts. The letter explaining the denial lists the

Schedule I criteria and explains why marijuana meets the criteria. Here is the response to the criterion that medical marijuana has no currently accepted medical use in treatment in the United States:

> According to established case law, marijuana has no "currently accepted medical use" because: The drug's chemistry is not known and reproducible; there are no adequate safety studies; there are no adequate and well-controlled studies proving efficacy; the drug is not accepted by qualified experts; and the scientific evidence is not widely available.

In other words, there is no evidence that marijuana is medically effective and, therefore, it is a Schedule I drug. And because it is a Schedule I drug, such research cannot be done without considerable difficulty. With a limited possibility of large-scale research clinical trials, laws regarding marijuana use will continue to be unduly guided by intransigence and entrenched political ideology rather than grounded in scientific evidence. It might very well be that marijuana is not as medically effective as its adherents proclaim. But this cannot be determined until large, randomized clinical trials are permitted and funded. That does not seem likely in the near term.

FURTHER READING

Cohen, P.J. (2011). Medical marijuana 2010: It's time to fix the regulatory vacuum. *Journal of Law, Medicine, & Ethics, 38*, 654–666.

Conant, E. (2010, November 1). Pot and the GOP; Is the party of "Just Say No" morphing into the part of "Just Say Grow"? *Newsweek Magazine*, p. 30.

Earlywine, M. (2005). *Understanding marijuana: A new look at the scientific evidence*. New York: Oxford University Press.

Fergusson, D.M., Boden, J.M., & Horwood, J. (2006). Cannabis use and other illicit drug use: Testing the cannabis gateway hypothesis. *Addiction, 101*, 556–559.

Goodnough, A., & Zezima, K. (2011, July 16). An alarming new stimulant, legal in many states. *The New York Times*, http://www.nytimes.com/2011/07/17/us/17salts.html.

Hall, W., & Lynskey, M. (2009). The challenges in developing a rational cannabis policy. *Current Opinion in Psychiatry, 22*, 258–262.

Hoffmann, D.E., & Weber, E. (2010). Medical marijuana and the law. *New England Journal of Medicine, 362*, 1453–1457.

Johnston, L.D., O'Malley, P.M., Bachman, J.G., & Schulenberg, J.E. (2011). *Monitoring the Future: National survey results on drug use, 1975–2010, Volume 1*. Ann Arbor, MI: Institute for Social Research, University of Michigan, http://www.monitoringthefuture.org/pubs.html#reports.

Kandel, D.B. (2002). *Stages and pathways of drug involvement: Examining the Gate-way hypothesis*. Cambridge, MA: Cambridge University Press.

THE GATEWAY HYPOTHESIS

The proposition that marijuana use inevitably leads to or at least strongly predisposes youth to using *harder* drugs such as cocaine and heroin is called the gateway hypothesis. It has been used as justification for passing strict laws related to marijuana possession and trafficking since the 1930s and was a favorite rationale for Federal Narcotics Bureau Director Harry Anslinger in his 30-year crusade against marijuana and other drugs. Testimony before the Kefauver Commission in 1951 stated the hypothesis as fact using the argot of the time: "They go from sneaky pete to pot to horse to banging." (Translation: They go from concealed liquor in a bag, to marijuana, to snorting heroin, to injecting drugs.) The reality of such testimony was largely unchallenged and led to the increasingly tough anti-drug laws in the 1950s that were among the first to impose mandatory minimum sentences for marijuana possession and trafficking. After a surge in marijuana use in the 1960s and 1970s, the parents' movement in the 1980s resurrected the gateway hypothesis and made it a centerpiece of the Reagan Administration's redeclaration of a War on Drugs and a rationale for Nancy Reagan's "Just Say No" prevention campaign.

It the gateway hypothesis was simply a political prop lacking any supporting evidence it could be easily dismissed as such. But that is not the case. Recent work suggests there is at least some validity to the gateway hypothesis but that if marijuana does cause use of other

(Continued)

THE GATEWAY HYPOTHESIS (continued)

drugs, the effects are small and time-limited. The question then becomes why does this happen. What is the causal mechanism? One theory is that there is cross-sensitization between the cannabinoid and opioid receptors in the brain such that marijuana use "primes the pump" for use of opiates by sensitizing the person to the effects of opioids such as heroin, morphine, and oxycodone. Animal models have, in fact, demonstrated that cross-sensitization between the two classes of drugs and receptors does occur. A competing and completely different theory that is sociological suggests that because drugs are illegal and must be obtained on the black market, a person who uses marijuana is more likely to come into contact with sellers and users of other illegal drugs, leading to experimentation and the eventual regular use of the other drugs (for some).

These competing explanations of the causal connection between marijuana use and the use of other illicit drugs are not simply academic. They have very different implications for prevention and policy. If neurological sensitization is the main issue, then retaining strict sanctions on marijuana use makes sense. However, if the illegal drug market explanation is more correct, then depenalizing or decriminalizing marijuana makes more sense, as it would separate the two markets. Countries like the Netherlands have followed the course of separating drug markets through decriminalization of marijuana whereas countries like the United States have maintained strict sanctions against marijuana use, at least at the federal level.

Macleod, J., & Hickman, M. (2010). How ideology shapes the evidence and the policy: What do we know about cannabis use and what should we do? *Addiction, 105*, 1326–1330.

McKinley, J. (2008, June 10). California pulling back on medical marijuana. *The International Herald Tribune*, p. 2.

Room, R., Fischer, B., Hall, W., Lenton, S., & Reuter, P. (2010). *Cannabis policy: Moving beyond the stalemate*. New York: Oxford University Press.

Samuels, D. (2008, July 28). How medical marijuana is transforming the pot industry. *New Yorker, 84*, 49.

Swift, W., Coffey, C., Degenhardt, L., et al. (2011). Cannabis and progression to other substance use in young adults: Findings from a 13-year prospective population-based study. *Journal of Epidemiology and Community Health*, eprint.

Van Gundy, K., & Rebellon, C. J. (2010). A life-course perspective on the "Gateway Hypothesis." *Addiction, 51*, 244–259.

Yardley, W. (2011, May 8). New federal crackdown confounds states that allow medical marijuana. *The New York Times*, A13.

On the Internet

The *Los Angeles Times* report on the DEA's 2011 decision to deny an appeal for reclassifying marijuana from a schedule I to a schedule III, IV, or V drug under the Controlled Substances Act is available at: http://www.latimes.com/news/local/la-me-marijuana-20110709,0,1346255.story.

The California Department of Public Health has information on the current status of the state's Medical Marijuana Program including data and statistics at: http://www.cdph.ca.gov/programs/mmp/Pages/Medical Marijuana Program.aspx.

The full text of the DEA's response to the petition to reclassify marijuana along with supporting documents was published in the *Federal Register* and is available at: http://www.ofr.gov/(S(ztclq22gsjl5u42mfotcq3cv))/OFRUpload/OFRData/2011–16994_PI.pdf.

Arguments for and against medical marijuana are presented by an organization called ProCon. The site includes information on the medical conditions for which marijuana is used, legal issues, medical risks, and medical value. Their website is at: http://medicalmarijuana.procon.org/

The ProCon website also has pages that provide detailed information on the medical marijuana laws by state (http://medicalmarijuana.procon.org/view.resource.php?resourceID=000881) as well as a timeline of the history of the medical uses of marijuana dating back to 2900 BC through the present day http://medicalmarijuana.procon.org/view.resource.php?resourceID=000143

"Heroinville"

- ***Document:*** "Texas Heroin Massacre," *Rolling Stone*
- ***Date:*** May 27, 1999
- ***Where:*** Plano, Texas
- ***Significance:*** Just as cocaine reemerged and increased in popularity in the 1970s and 1980s, heroin was discovered by a new generation—Generation X—in the 1990s. As with the resurgence in cocaine use (see "Like Dom Perignon and Caviar"), unique social-contextual factors and greater availability combined to drive the newfound popularity of heroin. Increasingly, the source countries for the heroin sold in the United States were Colombia and Mexico. Youth unfamiliar with the addicting potential of heroin started by snorting the drug before progressing to injection use. Countercultural analogs of the 1960s, grunge rock and heroin chic, romanticized heroin use in the 1990s before it took its predictable toll on the proselytizers. This 1999 article from *Rolling Stone* describes an improbable outbreak of heroin use in the wealthy Dallas suburb of Plano. Heroin use had become so extensive in Plano that local teens began referring to it as Heroinville. Before law enforcement identified and shut down the heroin traffickers, 18 teenagers died from an overdose and numerous others showed up in emergency rooms. Mini heroin epidemics in small town and suburban America continue through the present, exacerbated by more recent increases in the diversion and abuse of prescription opiates such as OxyContin and Vicodin.

DOCUMENT

Texas Heroin Massacre

By Mikal Gilmore

The Jocks and Preps of Plano, Texas, Couldn't Get Enough of a New Drug. By the Time They Found Out What the Fine Brown Powder Really Was, Kids Had Already Started Dying.

IN 1996, DR. LARRY ALEXANDER, an earnest young medic with sandy hair and a stylish goatee, came back to Plano, Texas, after a residency at an inner-city hospital in Kansas City that had left him reeling. He had seen enough murder there, enough coke, crack and crank to last a lifetime. Plano, by contrast, was a wealthy corporate nesting ground north of Dallas—good schools, big houses, smoked-glass business parks and a hundred lighted ball fields—and statistically, the safest city in Texas. It had fewer murders in a year than Kansas City had on any given Saturday night. This smooth exterior, however, concealed a certain hollowness. Plano is a pop-up city, having risen from empty rangeland in less than a generation. During the last couple of decades, some 200,000 people have moved there to work for corporate giants like 7UP, JC-Penney and Frito-Lay. In the wide-open land to the west of the new freeway, developers built a sea of gated communities and subdivisions that have been described as "tract mansions."

The city went through a bad patch in the early Eighties, when seven teenagers committed suicide and a dozen others attempted it in a one-year period. The national press blamed Plano's status as a sterile corporate dormitory where children had too much money and too little attention. And while Plano's 200,000 citizens are the same decent, well-meaning folks you'd find anywhere in Middle America, they hardly know one another. Once again, Plano was about to pay a terrible price for its splendid isolation, and one of the first to spot the impending danger was Larry Alexander. ER physicians like Alexander belong to a fairly exclusive club, and they tend to compare notes from one hospital to the next. In the fall of 1996, friends at Parkland Health and Hospital in Dallas, and at Methodist and Baylor, were telling him that heroin was back in style. His first reaction was that this was a Dallas problem; Plano had nothing to worry about. Then on New Year's Day 1997, he found himself looking at the body of Adam Wade Goforth, a nineteen-year-old Marine who had come home for the holidays only to die of a heroin overdose.

During the next few weeks, Alexander saw a parade of overdose victims rushed into his emergency room, usually dropped off by terrified friends. "They're banging on the door, screaming, 'He's not breathing!'" Alexander says. "We drag the kid out of the back of a Suburban. He's blue. We put him on a gurney and run him back into the ER. The next thing I hear is tires peeling out. His friends take off, and we don't even know who he is." Less than a month after Goforth died, Alexander's ER team lost another teen; and six weeks after that, Victor Garcia, a middle-school soccer player who was barely fifteen, was found face down in a church parking lot. His friends had left him there after driving around with his dead body for a day and a half

By now it was clear that something was deeply wrong in Plano. Alexander checked with his contacts in the Dallas police department and they said that cheap black-tar heroin was flooding into the area from Mexico. What distinguished this stuff from anything they had seen before was its astonishing quality. The product on the street was five times more potent than the heroin that authorities were accustomed to seeing. Because it was so powerful, you didn't have to shoot it. You could just snort the powder. Soon, Alexander was handling three or four overdoses a night. He knew he had to get the word out about what was quickly becoming an epidemic, but his superiors suggested he keep quiet. In the next few months, he cornered one official after another and kept getting the same nervous response. "People don't want the community to be known as having a drug problem," says Alexander. "The city council, the police department, big business, whatever. They don't want to talk about it." In three years, eighteen teenagers from Plano and its suburbs would die of heroin overdoses. In 1997 alone, another 75 to 100 would be brought back from the brink of death by Alexander and his colleagues.

THE RIO DE LAS BALSAS, a wild mountain stream for most of its 500-mile tumble to the Pacific, divides the Mexican states of Michoacin and Guerrero, and somewhere up this river, in the jungle between the coast and the provincial capital of Ciudad Attamirano, is a tiny collection of adobe huts known as Pinzandaro. Watched over by the 12,000-foot peaks of the Sierra Madre del Sur, the village is distinguished by its moderate climate and its crushing poverty. One day in 1994, Irma Lopez Vega, a diminutive nineteen-year-old mestiza, decided she'd had enough. Ever since she quit school in the third grade to help feed her siblings, she had been working like a dog—cleaning other people's houses, putting in a full shift at the flour mill, selling enchiladas on the side—and all she had to show for it was the food on her table. Her husband, Ecliserio Martinez Garcia, a respected figure in the community, had grander dreams for his family, and when he decided to make the 500-mile trek north to the U.S. border, Irma was with him.

They crossed the Rio Grande at Laredo, Texas, that summer and made their way to McKinney, about thirty miles north of Dallas and fifteen miles from Plano. Once there, they moved in with friends from home, Salvador Pineda Contreras and his wife, Marcruz. Salvador had a wood-frame bungalow on Walnut Street, within hailing distance of the Southern Pacific railroad. Once again, Irma Lopez was working like a slave, but now she was getting paid for it. The two women held down jobs at a local dry cleaner while helping their husbands build a business steam-cleaning the driveways and patios of the gringos. But they were sending, every spare nickel back home, and it was a struggle.

When Ectiserio Martinez Garcia first laid eyes on Plano, he must have thought he was looking at El Dorado. The median household income, $54,000, beat the U.S. national figure by eighty percent, and the kids all drove sport utility vehicles. It was an upscale market for everything from jaguars to Learjets, but somehow nobody had thought to supply the place with high-quality heroin. Drugs, of course, were already on the scene, but you had to go all the way to Dallas, into unsavory neighborhoods. As one ghetto dealer puts it, "These white kids, they're scared to come to my neighborhood, so they come and buy double and triple what my people buy." Martinez was in a position to solve that problem.

The village of Pinzandaro may have its drawbacks, but its climate is perfect for growing opium poppies. Of the sixty tons of heroin that Mexico produces each year, at least half comes from these mountains above Acapulco.

The setup was simple. In these high mountain valleys, the poppies grow like weeds. Using friends and family, Martinez processed the local crop into high-grade black-tar heroin, shipped it north to the border at Laredo and hired couriers to mule the product into the U.S. a few ounces at a time. Once it got to McKinney, the heroin was ground into powder with an electric coffee mill, then cut with Dormin, an over-the-counter sleep aid, and packaged in gel caps. It was nerve-racking and desperate work, but for men like Ecliserio, accustomed to backbreaking jobs and the routine dangers of life in Mexico, this was nothing.

Late in 1996, Ecliserio delivered his first batch to his Plano contacts, four young Mexican-Americans who had lived in the area all their lives and had established a modest business selling cocaine to Plano teenagers. The three Meza brothers, all in their early twenties, and their sidekick, Santiago Mejia, 17, had known one another since childhood. They started offering free samples of the new stuff to their regular customers from the Plano high schools, and all of a sudden, demand went through the roof.

The purity, even after the heroin was cut, was an astonishing thirty-five percent—so powerful, there was no need to search for a vein, or a spike, or a men's room, or a belt to tie off with. What's more, Dormin contains antihistamines, so it eliminated the telltale signs of heroin use: red eyes and a runny nose. As for terms, they were pretty good: ten bucks a cap and the first one's free.

The Meza brothers operated out of "the Blue House," a saltbox at 1120 Avenue I, where a couple of the brothers usually lived full time. It was in the old part of Plano, east of the freeway. By late 1996, the scene at the Blue House was off the scale. "They were parked three deep all hours of the day and night," says a neighbor, who remembers kids in Beemers and Jeeps dashing in and out with their engines running.

The stuff was called chiva, and the kids thought it was just the next drug in line—marijuana, LSD, ecstasy . . . chiva. But this shit was fantastic. "Heroin is about as mellow as you can get," says one Plano college student who's been dealing since the eighth grade. "Nice vibrations, you have your eyes roll back for a couple hours, and at these wholesale prices, you can afford to do as much as you want."

The party scene in Plano took an exciting and sinister turn. You would get a beep on your pager, summoning you to somebody's house where the parents weren't around, or maybe to a motel room, and there you'd find football players, cheerleaders, geeks and honor-roll students all doing chiva. The crowd was not the expected stoners and rebels. These were the students you were supposed to emulate. And they clearly had no idea what they were into. Collin County drug counselor Sabina Stern was stunned.

"I would say, 'Have you ever used chiva?'" she says.

"'Well, yeah.'

"'Have you ever used heroin?'

"'Oh, I'd never touch heroin."

"They didn't know the difference. And I don't think it was a deliberate attempt to fool kids on the part of the Mexicans. Chiva is just the Mexican word for heroin."

There was also a certain glamour attached to being on the inside. You'd see hand signals at a party and a bunch of kids would disappear into the back bedroom, or a car would pull up in the driveway and your boyfriend would duck out with part of the football squad and come back with a whole different attitude.

Chris Cooper, a gentle, easygoing twenty-year-old African-American with a quick smile, recalls those days. "It was not peer pressure," he says, "but it was just, my friends had moved on to it, and I was kinda wondering, what did it feel like? I had five or ten close friends. We'd go clubbin' in downtown Dallas, Fort Worth, anywhere there's a party. "But very shortly, weekends degenerated into finding a place that you didn't have to move from.

"I can remember doing it with a friend," says Cooper, "and he was telling me, 'Man, I heard if you do it seven days in a row, you start feeling bad.'" And I was like, "Hey, I've been doing it about eight or nine days in a row." So I didn't do it for a day and I was like, "Yeah, what is this? This is kinda weird." And then I did some, and right when I did it, I was feeling like crap and then whoo!"

That was Chris Cooper's first clue that maybe he was in over his head. His mother, a TV newswoman, had moved to Plano, she says, "because it was safe." Chris had been using for several weeks before he began to get nervous about it, and by the time it dawned on him and everybody else that they were dealing with a major addiction, it was too late. Dozens of kids were deeply involved, and some who had started as users were about to become dealers.

John Aaron Pruett, 18, was one of the first serious users to get busted. Initially his parents were supportive, and they got him into rehab. But when he relapsed, they were told that tough love was the answer. So they cut off his income, which cured his cash surplus but not his addiction. Pruett, slight and dark-haired, started dealing. He'd buy the chiva uncut from the Mezas and mix it with the Dormin himself. His apartment, on Preston Road, a couple of minutes from the Plano senior high schools, became a major branch of the Blue House.

Emily Stevenson, a cute, long-haired former cheerleader and an honor student, got into chiva like you get into ice cream. "I did it and I liked it and kept on doing it," she says. She became such a fixture at the Blue House that they invited her into the business. She and Santiago Mejia became best friends, and Emily wound up handling the books for him, She also provided the wheels for the resupply runs to McKinney until her parents took her car away. Later, when Santiago needed a place to lay low, she stashed him in her bedroom closet.

In spite of the growing awareness about the downside of this new craze, there were still plenty of people willing to try chiva. For one thing, not everyone who used it got addicted. According to the U.S. Department of Health, most people who try heroin do not become addicted. And when the kids in Plano saw that some of their friends were able to take it or leave it, they decided that chiva couldn't be all that dangerous.

The kids who did get hooked, however, were in for a jolt. Milan Malina, 19, was a sensitive-artist-and-poet type. His mother, Joanne, had raised him on opera. "I used to play Pavarotti while he was still in the crib," she says. The family was extremely close. His father, George, suffered a heart attack some months earlier and Milan had said, "If you die, I don't want to go on living."

Likable and outgoing, Milan made friends easily. He had some problems with school, though, and dropped out in his senior year. But he finished his GED, and in January '97 he was checking out the University of California at Santa Barbara campus when he was busted for driving while intoxicated. He spent three days in jail before his girlfriend was able to bail him out. In the fallout from this brush with the law, he confessed to his parents what they had already suspected: that he was in trouble with drugs and desperate to quit. They made a few quick phone calls and found Dr. John Talmadge, a psychiatrist and addiction expert at the University of North Texas.

Right from the start, Talmadge was encouraged. "Milan was poised, intelligent, very natural," says Talmadge. "He looked like the cover of GQ—kind of a young Al Pacino. I was expecting somebody tough or street-wise. He struck me as almost innocent." Talmadge's evaluation was glowing. "We have an acronym, YAVIS: young, attractive, verbal, insightful and successful. If somebody has all five, they have a good prognosis. Milan had an excellent chance." Talmadge felt that Milan was so motivated that outpatient therapy alone would do the trick. Events proved Talmadge right. When Milan celebrated his twentieth birthday, at the beginning of June, he had been clean for four months. He was enrolled in the local junior college, scheduled to start classes the following Monday. His parents were beaming. But there was an ominous note in the otherwise upbeat celebration. When he spoke to a friend in California that night, he told her, "My friends here don't like me anymore. They like the high Milan. They don't like the clean Milan."

That Saturday night, he decided to give his friends a treat: the high Milan. A bunch of the guys were getting together to watch a hockey game at a house on a golf course where one of the boys lived with his father. With Dad gone for the weekend and the maid in another part of the house, they passed around joints and champagne. Chris Cooper was there. He and Milan had been friends since freshman gym class. When the discussion got around to chiva, everybody was in. Chris and Milan made the drug run together.

Along with his friends, Milan snorted a couple of caps of chiva. By the end of the evening, he couldn't stay on his feet. His pals put him to bed and told him to sleep it off. When Chris decided to call it a night, Milan seemed safely asleep. Chris didn't think twice about him—people passed out all the time.

Any junkie will tell you not to sit around drinking while you're waiting to score. Alcohol and heroin don't mix. They are both downers, and they reinforce each other, shutting off the part of the brain that reminds you to breathe. But the alcohol wasn't Milan's only problem. He was also seriously asthmatic, and though he had been told since he was a small boy not to take certain cold medications containing antihistamines—which dry out the lungs and can trigger asthma attacks—he probably did not realize that the chiva he was snorting was full of antihistamines. On top of this, he had been clean for several months, so he had the low tolerance of a first-time user. "They said he was snoring throughout the night," recalls his dad. "The reality is, he was aspirating his vomit."

A few hours after Chris had gone home, he got an urgent phone call: Milan was in the hospital. Chris threw on some clothes and got there as fast as he could. In the waiting room, seven of his buddies were standing around in shock. A police officer was interviewing them. Then Milan's parents came out of the emergency room.

George Malina found a chaplain in the waiting room. He asked the priest to escort Milan's friends in to see the body. He wanted them to have a chance to say goodbye. And he wanted them to grasp the enormity of what had happened. The chaplain led them in and pulled back the sheet. There was Milan's face—blue, caked with blood, eyes closed for all time. Some reacted in stunned silence; the rest were sobbing. "They wanted us to see what had happened, to really took at him," says Cooper. He looks away. "It was awful."

GEORGE MALINA wanted to find out who was responsible. And he wanted to make sure none of these other kids ended up like Milan. He went to the police and demanded an investigation. The police said there was nothing to investigate. They said that Milan had brought this on himself, yes, he was a victim, but he was also a perpetrator. Case closed. "They were very condescending to us," says Joanne Malina. "They made us feel like we as the parents were at fault, that we were the cause of his death."

The determination to keep a lid on this story—spurred, no doubt, by an honest concern for property values—extended to neighboring suburbs like Richardson and Addison, as well. But Plano authorities were particularly jumpy. For years, whenever city officials showed up at conventions, it was, "Oh, Plano, the suicide capital." It had taken a decade to bury that smear. As the police chief said later, "There's no way you can package nine, ten, twelve deaths in something that is going to be positive."

But George Malina was willing to let it be known that his son had died of a heroin overdose if that could save some other kid. And when he found out that Larry Alexander had said the same thing months earlier—and was stonewalled—Malina was outraged. "Whatever guilt the parents have to carry," he says, "they carry. But shouldn't the authorities have the responsibility to give us an alert?" By then, however, it was academic. A reporter for the Plano Star-Courier had pieced the story together from the obituaries. She tracked down Alexander at work, and he gave up the whole story—the extent of heroin use, the deaths, the town's denial in the wake of the disaster. The article ran right after Milan's death, and within hours the Dallas Morning News was on the case. Before long, Diane Sawyer was on the line.

Finally unleashed, Alexander began lecturing to students all over town, trying to educate them about heroin—but for a lot of them, it was already too late. The overdoses and the deaths continued. In November 1997, sixteen-year-old Erin Baker, a Plano Senior High junior, became victim number thirteen. The authorities were mystified. The bodies piling up seemed to have no impact on the users. Kids would sometimes attend a friend's funeral and, after sobbing at a graveside, immediately go out and score. "I don't think people who don't use understand how addictive heroin is," says Sarah, 18. "I went to one funeral and got high right afterward. I felt bad, but I was just numb." Another addict agrees: "I've taken friends to the hospital and then gone right back to where we were and kept on using." Chris Cooper knows what they're talking about. "I had three or four pretty good friends die," he says. "It didn't stop me." But after that scene with Milan in the ER, he quit using and was clean for nearly two months—just sheer will power. One day, however, he decided to try one little cap, and in no time he was right back where he'd started. Finally he told his mom he needed help.

Chris was lucky. Decent long-term treatment usually costs a fortune, and the health insurance that most of us have will get you a ten-day detox at the most. But Chris' mom was able to find him a safe haven an hour southeast of Dallas, at the House of Isaiah, a private treatment center run by former L.A. Rams linebacker Isaiah Robertson. Modeled after Alcoholics Anonymous, the twelve-step program relies on spiritual guidance for its forty or so clients.

After he completed the six-month course, Chris decided to spend another year at the center's halfway house, in Fort Worth. Living there, he got a job working construction and cut himself off from his old life in Plano. "I thought, 'Man, I'm doing good now,' he says. But while Chris was getting his life back together in the city, events in Plano were moving along another set of rails.

The night Milan died, Chris had been interviewed by the cops, but nothing ever came of it, and he managed to convince himself he was in the clear. But just after five on the morning of July 22nd, 1998, Chris was getting ready for work when he got a frantic call from his mother: FBI agents were outside her front door.

Within a few hours he was in front of a Federal judge. The charge was something he'd never even heard of: conspiracy to distribute heroin that caused a death. Thirty minutes later he was in a cell—"the lowest, the scariest point in my life," Chris says. When his lawyer showed up, he learned that he faced a mandatory minimum sentence of twenty years.

"When I heard those words," he says, "I remember thinking, 'You fucked up, you really did it this time.' It's hard to describe that feeling. I was nineteen."

IN THE NORMAL COURSE of events, Plano police chief Bruce Glasscock rarely had to deal with anything more thrilling than an overturned semi on Central Expressway. There had always been drugs in Plano—marijuana, a little cocaine—but they were out of sight, under control. Now here was an explosion of serious narcotics right under his nose. And while the city fathers may have been reticent with the public, they weren't shy about putting heat on Glasscock. Almost immediately, one of his top detectives identified the source of the problem. In fact, he could practically see it out the back window of the police station: The Blue House was three blocks away.

As predicted, the press pegged Plano as the heroin capital of America—quite unfairly, since cities like Tampa, Florida; Baltimore; and Parsippany, New Jersey, were going through exactly the same thing at that moment. But the Plano angle had legs. For one thing, the kids there kept dying. When Prime Time Live was about to hit town, one official said, "If this goes wrong, everybody's house is gonna be worth $50,000 less."

To stem the hysteria, Glasscock needed a bold gesture. Unfortunately, Texas law doesn't allow the taking of scalps. Under state drug measures, Plano's heroin dealers would face sentences of no more than ten years. But if Glasscock called in the feds, the authorities could invoke a seldom-used law passed during the drug-war hysteria of the Eighties. That law says you can get a sentence equal to a murder rap if a drug sale leads to someone's death.

In late September 1997, when the furor following Malina's death was building, Glasscock called on assistant U.S. attorney Bill Baldwin in Tyler, Texas, and together they mobilized a Federally funded task force. By October, this enforcement team had hit Plano like a command battalion. Undercover agents were all over the place, and since most of their targets were amateurs, arrests were made in no time.

Glasscock focused his investigation on the Mezas' Blue House and reached into the schools as well, bringing in local police-academy recruits to infiltrate Plano high schools. One twenty-eight-year-old earned the trust of her new peers as she revisited her own adolescence, leaving her purse open to conspicuously show off a pack of cigarettes; she would act uninterested in class, mouthing off to her teachers, slyly revealing her newly pierced tongue. The undercover operative quickly learned where to buy marijuana and, later, chiva, and before she knew it, she was being introduced to Plano's biggest dealers.

On July 23rd, 1998, Baldwin, Glasscock and the head of the Drug Enforcement Administration held a joint press conference. A thirty-six-count Federal indictment was handed out. It named twenty-nine people, everyone from Ecliserio Martinez Garcia all the way down to Chris Cooper. Count Six made it clear to Cooper why he was essential to the case. He was the ultimate link in the chain that led from the Mexican dealers to the dead body of Milan Malina.

Of the twenty-nine people, seven were illegal aliens like Ecliserio and therefore perfectly cast as villains. Glasscock, Baldwin and the DEA also hauled in fourteen local Plano kids—the town's own: good students, sons of prominent citizens. If convicted, they would be in their forties when they got out.

Among the parents of the kids who died, George Malina seemed to have the clearest fix on what had happened in Plano, and he was outraged by the indictments. His empathy extended even to the young man who was accused of murdering his son. "Chris Cooper shouldn't be sent to jail," he said. "it could just as easily have been the other way around."

Malina, in fact, doesn't believe his son was a victim of heroin. He blames the drug war itself. "It was easier to get heroin than it was to get beer," he says. "Chiva became a party favor." He feels that the kids were let down by the very people who were supposed to protect them.

To begin with—in spite of Red Ribbon Days, Nancy Reagan and "Just Say No"—the school system left these kids totally unprepared for the arrival of heroin. At Plano-district schools, they had drug-sniffing dogs cruising the lockers, but they had not bothered to tell the students anything useful. Like the fact that chiva is the Mexican word for heroin.

But the blame goes far beyond Plano. It goes to some of the fundamental assumptions of the drug war, like the idea that we can cut narcotics off at the border. The amount of heroin needed to supply Plano for a year would fit in "a gallon jug," admits police chief Glasscock. The mules were simply walking it across on monthly trips home. It was hidden in compartments in the heels of their shoes. And it's important to remember that the only reason the Mexicans set up shop in Plano was the money. If they could have earned a decent living growing some legitimate crop down in Guerrero, they would no doubt have jumped at the chance.

SINCE ANY JURY in Plano would likely turn into a lynch mob, the trial was shifted to Beaumont, down by the Gulf Coast, some 340 miles away. When it finally got under way, on February 2nd, one thing was clear about the government's strategy: The Mexicans were going to pay. The kids from Plano had all pleaded to lesser charges. All they had had to do to reduce their prison time was give up a few Mexicans.

Armed with the testimony of the Plano kids, prosecutors set out to convince the jury that the Martinez gang was a major international drug conspiracy, overlooking the fact that none of these so-called criminal masterminds could even afford to pay for a lawyer. The defense attorneys for the Mexicans were court appointed, all gringos who had to communicate with their clients through interpreters.

One of the defendants would not even talk to his lawyer. Jose Cleotilde Solis—"Little Cocho"—was one of the part-time players associated with the Blue House. During the big sweep of '97, he was busted with ten grams of coke and six grams of heroin. Like some of the other defendants in the Federal case, he had already been tried in Texas state court, in 1998. And while it may seem unreasonable to convict somebody twice for the same events, it's not unusual in drug-war prosecutions. At the state trial, believing he would probably get probation, Solis pleaded guilty, and the judge handed him twenty-one years. These days, not surprisingly, Solis doesn't speak to lawyers. All he does is read his Bible.

The defense lawyers did their best to paint the Federal charges as arbitrary and excessive, but in the end, the prosecutors held all the cards. Ecliserio Martinez Garcia, for example, had confessed and pleaded guilty in an earlier trial; according to Martinez's lawyer, the government had agreed not to use that confession but ended up disclosing it anyway. The best that the defenders could do was to chip away at the conspiracy charges, which carried the heaviest penalties. That seemed like a possible opening, since the idea that the government had nailed some international cartel was clearly laughable.

"They were trying to make these individuals out as kingpins," says attorney Garland Cardwell. "My client was the other Solis brother [Hilario] and he had been working a steady job for five or six years at a telecommunications company. He was making monthly payments on a '95 Ford pickup. If he was making all this dough off the sale of heroin, I don't know where it was going." In fact, none of the defendants seemed to be living very high on the hog. When Martinez was busted in McKinney, he was driving a four-year-old Dodge Caravan.

But despite the whiff of class warfare and racism hovering over the proceedings, the jurors quickly returned with the inevitable conclusion. They found all the Mexicans guilty of all the charges, except for Irma Lopez Vega. But before the feds could toss her back over the border, the state of Texas announced that it would retry Irma Lopez Vega in state court on the same charges.

SENTENCING for the Plano twenty-nine will probably come down in a month or so. The betting is that most of the kids will do OK but the Mexicans will go down for the full count. Of the kids, John Aaron Pruett is looking at the longest stretch. He faces a twenty-year sentence, though he may get several years sliced off in return for his testimony. Chris Cooper ultimately pleaded guilty to using a telephone in the sale of heroin, and he's almost certainly going to do four years in the Federal pen.

In the wake of this overwhelming state and Federal effort to prosecute the dealers, the heroin deaths continue. With the March 30th death of twenty-one-year-old David Allen of Bedford, the body count for the northern suburbs of Dallas and Fort Worth rose to at least thirty-four. In Plano proper, the scene is less frantic, because kids don't bring overdose victims to the hospital there anymore. They know better. As Larry Alexander points out, the overdose rate is rising in the surrounding suburbs. And while Chief Bruce Glasscock may feel that the heroin situation in Plano is "under control," a brief tour of the old neighborhood suggests otherwise. "I could have drugs on this table in forty-five minutes," says a friend of Chris Cooper's who is still trying to kick. "It's more available now than ever. Back then I only had one guy I could call. They busted him. Now I got three guys I can call."

SOURCE: Mikal Gilmore, "Texas Heroin Massacre," *Rolling Stone*, March 27, 1999.

ANALYSIS

In the first half of the 1990s, illegal drug use began increasing after a decade of decreases but remained well below the peak of use in 1979. Per the National Household Survey on Drug Abuse (NHSDA), 13 million Americans had used an illicit drug in the past month, whereas 25 million reported using any illicit drug in the past month in 1979. The large drop is mostly attributable to a steep decade-long decline in marijuana use. Whereas the panic over crack-cocaine was subsiding as street markets became established and the violence ebbed, a surprising turn (drug epidemics always seem to be surprising) led to heroin re-emerging as a new, fashionable drug among American youth. In 1993, the NHSDA survey estimated there were 68,000 past-month heroin users. The comparable estimate was 216,000 by 1996 with the majority of new users under the age of 26. These numbers hardly register as a blip in national prevalence estimates (less than 1 percent) but they illustrate how even such a relatively small number of users can trigger concerns about and prominent media coverage of the next epidemic.

As with the surge in cocaine use in the 1970s and 1980s, the uptick in heroin use was driven by the combination of increased availability and a welcoming cultural context within a small but still significant population of youth. Prior to the 1980s, most of the heroin in the United States came from poppies grown in the Golden Triangle in the Southeast Asian countries of Laos, Burma, and Thailand or from those grown in the Golden Crescent countries of Afghanistan, Iran, and Pakistan. This changed when Colombia began to get into the business of cultivating heroin-producing poppies in 1986. Pressure on the major cocaine-producing cartels in Medellín and Cali led to their diversification into the heroin market. Using established cocaine routes, Colombian traffickers began marketing pure, cheap heroin to U.S. markets in the 1990s. The low cost and high quality of the Colombian product drove out the heroin produced in Southeast and Southwest Asia.

As Colombian traffickers increasingly used Mexico as a transshipment point for cocaine to avoid stepped-up interdiction efforts in Florida and the Caribbean, black tar heroin produced in Mexico began to be exported to the United States in greater quantity using the same newly established trafficking routes. In the years that followed, heroin produced in Colombia would dominate the eastern seaboard and southeastern states while Mexican-produced black tar heroin would predominate in the west, southwest, and Midwest states. The predominance of Colombian and Mexican-produced heroin in the American market is the reason why the ebbs and flows in poppy production in Afghanistan owing to the Taliban crackdown in 2000 and then the rapid resumption of poppy growing following the 2001 American invasion had minimal effect on heroin availability in America.

The purity of the heroin produced in Colombia and Mexico relative to the purity of the heroin produced by the Southeast and Southwest Asian countries had an important implication for the spread of heroin use in the 1990s. Whereas a typical bag of heroin confiscated and tested by the DEA in the 1970s would be between 5 percent to 10 percent pure, heroin confiscated and tested in the 1990s would be at least 30 percent to 40 percent pure (the current national average remains in this range at 35 percent purity) with some seized heroin as high as 98 percent pure. The higher purity was part of the Colombians' aggressive marketing campaign to take over the heroin markets. It allowed beginners to snort or smoke heroin (i.e., chasing the dragon) rather than inject it, a significant barrier for many who are averse to needles. Eventually, however, with the development of tolerance and addiction, many of those who began snorting heroin did end up as injection users.

In the 1990s, as the disaffected generation of Gen-X youth were coming of age, they echoed the youthful, countercultural ambitions of their baby boomer parents. But there was a key difference: the countercultural inclinations of the Gen-X'ers were devoid of the naïve proposition of the 1960s countercultural movement that drugs were a means of changing self and society for the better. In fact, the Gen-X counterculture was nihilistically devoid of any inclination toward positive change, period.

Drugs were simply a means of coping with a pessimistic assessment of life and the lack of any meaningful prospects for change.

There is no agreement on the dates that bracket the start and end of Generation X. (How could there be? It is a categorical abstraction imposed on a continuous phenomenon, births.) A range of 1965 through 1984 provides as good an estimate as any. In a book devoted to describing the genesis and demise of Gen-X culture, Malcom Furek provides this characterization of Gen-X'-ers:

> As they were scapegoated, marginalized, and forgotten, the experience and expectation of Generation X were considerably different from that of Baby Boomers. X'ers had little of the optimism, expectation, and promise that embraced previous generations . . . Their mission, in a hostile postmodern universe, was merely to survive.

The music most associated with Generation X is grunge rock, an amalgamation of punk and metal that originated in Seattle and which represented a counterpoint and reaction to the glitzy, heavily commercialized rock of the 1980s. Reflecting the preoccupations of Gen-X'-ers, the subject matter of the music was often the acceptance and even celebration of alienation. Popular grunge bands included: the Melvins, Alice in Chains, Malfunkshun, and Pearl Jam. But the band that most defined grunge was Nirvana and its lead singer Kurt Cobain.

Cobain used many drugs beginning with marijuana at age 13. He began taking heroin to relieve chronic gastrointestinal problems that were never diagnosed and became addicted. His ongoing problems with drugs and depression and the difficulties of dealing with the fame achieved while playing with Nirvana led to his suicide in 1994. His death is seen as heralding the beginning of the end of grunge. As with jazz and rock musicians addicted to heroin, a number of grunge musicians would lose their lives through overdose including Layne Staley and Mike Starr of Alice in Chains and Kristen Pfaff of the group Hole. Cobain's wife Courtney Love would have her own battle with heroin addiction but survived it.

One of the group's most famous and popular songs, "Smells Like Teen Spirit" became an anthem of Gen-X'-ers in its celebration of apathy and self-loathing. Within the song's inscrutable, stream-of-consciousness lyrics are moments of clarity as to the song's meanings embodied in phrases such as "I feel stupid and contagious" and "I'm worst at what I do best." For Cobain and other Gen-X'-ers, heroin was the perfect analog for the dark moods expressed in songs like "Smells Like Teen Spirit." Whereas the stimulant cocaine was used in the 1980s to socialize and to celebrate the good times, the depressant heroin was used in the 1990s to retreat into a solipsistic cocoon, sheltered from a harsh and unwelcoming world seen as offering few real prospects for change or hope.

Of course, not everyone was impressed with Gen-X's taste in or Cobain's style of music, personal philosophy, or choice of drugs. A scathing essay by Rich Lowry that appeared in the *National Review* brings to mind Norman Podhoretz's similarly critical essay on the ethos of the Beat Poets in the 1950s (see "I saw the best minds of my generation destroyed by madness"). Lowery's short essay, entitled "Heroin, Our Hero" notes:

> Grunge shares some qualities with the old 1960s counter-culture. It is hostile to the bourgeois and consumer culture. It is at the same time, like 1960s activism,

an outgrowth of wealth and leisure (it's not easy to be a tortured victim of ennui working on a factory floor). But there are important differences. Grunge is for the most part shorn of ideals and the impulse for political action. . . .

Being driven into the arms of a dangerous drug by the conviction that life is a pointless bore never looked quite so good. If Kurt Cobain had it to do over again, no doubt he'd be careful to become addicted to something else.

Oddly enough, the high fashion industry also got caught up in the same cultural crosscurrents as grunge rock, spawning what became known as heroin chic. As counterpoints to the glamorous look of 1980s models such as Christie Brinkley and Heidi Klum, heroin chic models such as Kate Moss were thin to the point of anorectic gauntness. Purposely made to look unhealthy, with dark circles under their eyes, pallid complexions, dark or black lipstick a la the Goth style, heroin chic models posed staring vacantly into the distance; fashion's embodiment of a drugged-out disconnect. Adding to the mis-en-scene, models were photographed in decidedly unglamorous locations such as on a mattress on a floor in a squalid hotel room or in an alley with garbage strewn about nearby. Some images showed models snorting drugs near a chic piece of lingerie.

The most infamous heroin chic ad campaign was for the Calvin Klein perfume "cK Be" that appeared in a 12-page spread in *Harper's Bazaar* in 1996. Jim Inciardi writes in his book *The War on Drugs IV* that the advertisers sought out heroin addicts from the streets to lend authenticity to the campaign. The photographer best known for and one of the originators of heroin chic was Davide Sorrenti. Like Cobain, Sorrenti struggled with heroin addiction. He died at the age of 21 from a chronic kidney ailment that was likely exacerbated by his heroin use but not before incurring President Clinton's public denouncement of heroin chic as promoting drug use. As Cobain's death marked the beginning of the end for grunge, Sorrenti's death was seen as the beginning of the end of the heroin chic fashion trend.

Were the teenagers that were part of the "heroin massacre" using the drug because they identified as alienated Gen-X-ers following the self-pitying tenets espoused by grunge rock lyrics? There is no evidence these were direct influences. It is possible the cultural ethos of the time might have indirectly encouraged their experimentation with heroin. Then too, it could have been the case that heroin simply came along as they were experimenting with drugs and it was added to the mix as something new to try, no complex cultural explanation necessary. As the story indicates, they were naïve as to heroin's potential for abuse, having had neither firsthand exposure to the drug nor exposure to an older generation of heroin users.

The incident in Plano was not unique although the number of deaths and the use of heroin in the unlikely setting of a wealthy suburb attracted considerable media attention. The differential legal treatment of the Mexican immigrants compared with the American teens, as described in the article, again highlights how the war on drugs continued to be prosecuted disproportionately at the expense of minorities. The long sentences received by the Mexican traffickers can be contrasted with the relatively light sentence received by Laurie Hiett (and her husband), who used her status as the wife of a high-ranking military advisor to ship pounds of heroin and cocaine to the United States from Colombia (see the sidebar about Laurie Hiett).

Things do not appear to have changed much in Texas since the 1997 incidents in Plano. On April 14, 2011, 12 individuals from or living near Flower Mound, which like Plano is a wealthy suburb located near Dallas and Fort Worth, were indicted by a federal grand jury for conspiring to sell 100 grams of heroin. Most were between the ages of 18 and 21. The investigation that led to the indictments was spurred by the overdose deaths of three teenagers. A recent posting on a Flower Mound community forum in a thread entitled "Flower Mound's new fad, heroine [*sic*]" by a teenaged local resident, seemingly unaware of the history of nearby Plano, describes the scope of the new problem:

> I'm sure y'all are aware that a lot of kids smoke weed and drink alcohol in Flower Mound. The network of these kids is huge and everybody seems to know or know of just about everybody in the social scene in Flower Mound. My point is, they are saying heroine [*sic*] is moving in on these kids like a wildfire, its the new marijuana, everybody's hooked and everybody's trying it.

According to the DEA's National Drug Threat Assessment report for 2011: "The availability of heroin in the United States—and the number of markets in which it is available—is increasing as a result of increased production in Mexico, even as Colombian production declines." Mexico is now the second largest producer of heroin in the world, second only to (but far behind) Afghanistan. In an ironic twist, heroin is now marketed as a cheaper and more potent alternative to illegally obtained oxycodone, the semi-synthetic opiate sold in a time-release formulation as OxyContin. Oxycodone users with a high tolerance may ingest as much as 400 milligrams of the drug each day costing about $400.00. In contrast, a comparable amount of heroin can cost less than half of that. Prescription drugs like oxycodone and hydrocodone (Vicodin) have become, in effect, gateway drugs for heroin.

BLACK TAR HEROIN—THE XALISCO CONNECTION

Customer service and satisfaction are their priorities. "We deliver" might as well be their advertising slogan. Were they selling any legal product, the loosely based organization of franchised dealers with connections to the obscure (to most Americans) rural area of Xalisco, Mexico might receive accolades for their entrepreneurship in respected business-oriented publications such as *Forbes Magazine* or the *Wall Street Journal.* As it is, they sell black tar heroin, a lower grade of heroin that results from using cheaper reagents during one of the main processing steps in heroin production (i.e., acetylation). Despite this, black tar heroin is as potent as more processed heroin but use entails greater health risks such as bacterial infections owing to its relative impurity, sludgy consistency, and the way it is most often injected (i.e., subcutaneously rather than intravenously).

Xalisco-based traffickers specialize in the small to mid-sized markets in the United States—Myrtle Beach,

(Continued)

FURTHER READING

Ciccarone, D. (2009). Heroin in brown, black and white: Structural factors and medical consequences in the US heroin market. *International Drug Policy, 20*, 277–282.

Friend, L. (1992, July). Heroes and heroin. *RIP Magazine*.

Furek, M. (2008). *The death proclamation of Generation X: A self-fulfilling prophecy of goth, grunge, and heroin*. Bloomington, IN: iUniverse.

Lowry, R. (1996, October 28). Our hero, heroin. *National Review, XLVII*, 75–76.

Massing, M. (1992, June 11). What ever happened to the war on drugs? *New York Review of Books*.

Prato, G. (2009). *Grunge is dead: The oral history of Seattle rock music*. Toronto, ON: ECW Press.

Spindler, A.M. (1997, May 20). A death tarnishes fashion's "heroin look." *The New York Times*, A1.

Tarabar, A.F., & Nelson, L.S. (2003). The resurgence and abuse of heroin by children in the United States. *Current Opinion in Pediatrics, 15*, 210–215.

Woestendiek, J. (1998, February 15). An old killer strikes teens/Heroin? In the affluent suburbs? *The Philadelphia Inquirer*, A01.

Wren, C.S. (1997, May 22). Clinton calls fashion ads' "heroin chic" deplorable. *New York Times*.

On the Internet

A series of articles appearing in the *Los Angeles Times* in February 2010 by reporter Sam Quinones describes the growing trade in black tar heroin produced in Mexico and the unique business model of Xalisco-based traffickers: http://articles.latimes.com/2010/feb/14/local/la-me-blacktar14–2010feb14.

A 2008 report titled *The Price and Purity of Illicit Drugs: 1981–2007* by Arthur Fries, Robert W. Anthony, Andrew Cseko, Jr., Carl C. Gaither, and Eric Schulman published by the Institute for Defense Analysis as well as other information on heroin is available at the Office of National Drug Control Policy at: http://www.whitehousedrugpolicy.gov/drugfact/heroin/heroin_ff.html.

The *Dallas News* has an article on the recent federal indictments for heroin trafficking in Flower Mound, Texas at: http://www.dallasnews.com/news/community-news/flower-mound/headlines/20110517-flower-mound-heroin-overdoses-lead-to-17-federal-indictments.ece.

The DEA National Drug Threat Assessment Report for 2011 is available at: http://www.justice.gov/ndic/topics/ndtas.htm#y2011.

Embodying withdrawal: Abjection and the popularity of heroin chic by Mary Rizzo is a critique of the heroic chic trend in the fashion industry from a feminist perspective. The full text is available at: http://hdl.handle.net/2027/spo.ark5583.0015.004.

The National Institute on Drug Abuse (NIDA) Community Epidemiological Work Group (CEWG) monitors drug use throughout the country and sentinel sites to provide surveillance at the community level. They groups composing CEWG meet semiannually to compile their findings. The NIDA website has copies of the most recent and past CEWG reports at: http://www.drugabuse.gov/about/organization/cewg/CEWGHome.html.

The United Nations Office on Drugs and Crime website has information on many aspects of the global drug trade including trafficking patterns at: http://www.unodc.org/unodc/en/drug-trafficking/index.html. The site also has information on treatment programs and prevention at: http://www.unodc.org/unodc/en/drug-prevention-and-treatment/index.html.

BLACK TAR HEROIN—THE XALISCO CONNECTION

(continued)

South Carolina, Salt Lake City, Utah, and Indianapolis—that have been overlooked by dealers trafficking in heroin produced in Colombia. By focusing on customer satisfaction and underserved markets, the Xalisco traffickers have been highly successful at what they do. Shunning the violent disputes that marred drug trafficking in, for instance crack-cocaine in the 1980s, they have been able to operate in near anonymity under the radar of law enforcement for some time. This has also contributed to their success and allowed them to add *franchises* in new markets as they branch out across the country.

The traffickers use cell phones for texting and calling clients and often deliver the drug directly to clients' homes. This obviates the need for their white, middle-class, suburban clientele to risk driving into a dangerous inner-city neighborhood to buy drugs, further expanding their markets. Xalisco-based traffickers shun African-American and even Hispanic customers and focus on the white market. As each driver only carries a small amount of the drug, there is less risk of a large bust and decentralization makes it more difficult for law enforcement to identify a central trafficking location. Arrested drivers are easily replaced and can offer little information to authorities about the organization's structure. To build customer loyalty, the traffickers will call after a delivery to check on the client's satisfaction. As a local market expands, dealers who are part of an existing network branch off to form a new dealership in the expanded territory. The competition among networks keeps prices low, leading one dealer to compare their business model favorably to that of Walmart's.

"It's Growing from Within"

- ***Document:*** "Life: Hillbilly Hell," *Observer Guardian* (UK)
- ***Date:*** April 7, 2002
- ***Where:*** Rural and small-town America
- ***Significance:*** OxyContin is a prescription painkiller and a time-release formulation of oxycodone, a semi-synthetic derivative of Thebaine, an alkaloid obtained from the opium poppy (see sidebar on opiates and opioids). Because illegal opiates such as heroin are not widely available in rural areas, OxyContin and similar prescription painkillers have become popular alternatives. Obtained mainly from friends, family, and acquaintances with prescriptions, the illicit use of OxyContin and similar drugs spread rapidly through small town and rural America in the late 1990s. Because of its association with rural communities, the drug is sometimes derisively called hillbilly heroin. But OxyContin is much more expensive than heroin and users of the drug sometimes turn to heroin as a cheaper, more potent alternative. To date, the abuse of prescription drugs such as OxyContin continues to increase. This article describes the rapid spread of OxyContin use in rural and small-town America through interviews with dealers and users. It also describes the role the drug manufacturer Purdue Pharma had in the drug's spread through an aggressive marketing campaign to physicians and the public.

DOCUMENT

Last month, 18-year-old Samantha Jenkinson from Hull became the first person in the UK to die from an overdose of OxyContin. But the prescription painkiller has already killed 300 in America. Paul Tough traces the spread of

'hillbilly heroin' from the Appalachian backwoods to the teen party scene in Britain.
—Paul Tough

The rise in abuse of prescription painkillers such as Oxycontin has been fueled, in part, by the diversion of these drugs from poorly regulated pain clinics, many of which are located in Florida. At this clinic in Tampa, a physician and his assistant try to stem access to the drugs by carefully reviewing all prescription requests. They approve only 1 of every 20 requests received. Other clinics have not been as conscientious. (Melissa Lyttle/ZUMA Press/Corbis)

Paula is taking me on a driving tour of Man, the West Virginia town where she has spent her entire life. Because I don't know my way around the hollows and gullies and creeks that carve through these hills, Paula is at the wheel. And because Paula isn't a morning person, we've set out on our tour at midnight.

The tour Paula is leading isn't sanctioned by the local chamber of commerce; it's a pill-head tour: an addict's-eye view of the radical changes that a single prescription drug, OxyContin, has brought to the town. "That's my best friend's trailer right there," Paula says, pointing out a comfortable-looking single-wide across the creek. "She's somebody that you couldn't look at and know she was an oxy addict. She was a cheerleader in junior high. She's married. You can't just look at somebody and tell."

A few years ago, Paula says, Man was like any small town in America: you could buy a variety of illegal drugs, as long as you knew the right person to talk to. Pot was big; there was occasionally some cocaine around and a few pills for recreational use. But these days, she says, the only drug for sale in Man is OxyContin, a narcotic painkiller that users crush—to disable its patented time-release mechanism—and then snort or inject for a powerful and immediate opiate high. Legally, it's sold only by prescription for the treatment of chronic pain. In practice it's available just about everywhere around here, for cash. The going rate is a dollar a milligram or $40.00 for a 40mg pill.

Paula is a thoughtful 24-year-old with wispy blonde hair, serious eyes and faded jeans. She's fidgety; as she drives with one hand, she's rummaging through her handbag with the other, looking for her pack of Marlboro Lights. She finds them, removes one and stabs the dashboard lighter. "I'll show you some places over here," she says, as she turns her car off the main road, over a bridge and down into a rough indentation that holds a couple dozen trailers and prefab homes. "This is Green Valley. We just call it the valley. It's a pretty good neighborhood," she says, then interrupts herself. "Well, except that's a dealer there."

She points to a trailer with a pickup out front and a light burning inside. I crane my neck to get a look at a real-life drug den, but the tour has already moved on. Paula is pointing out a trailer on the other side of the road: "That's a small-time dealer there, nothing big," she says. Then she points to another one, and then another: "That's a dealer. . . . That's a small-time dealer. . . . That's a dealer. . . . Her son's a dealer, but I don't know if he lives there. . . . He uses, that boy in there. . . . They use really, really big."

We're driving slowly around the circular dirt road that is the only path through Green Valley. The neighborhood doesn't feel dangerous—no graffiti, no pit bulls, no broken bottles lying around. Still, Paula is pointing out criminal activity in every second home, peering through the front windshield and gesturing left and right.

The first time Paula did an oxy (as she calls the pills), in the summer of 1999, it didn't do much for her. "That first 10mg pill, I didn't really feel nothing off it," she says. "But the second time I did it, I did two 20s, and I was high." She liked the effect. "When you get that oxy buzz," she says, "you're happy. Your body don't hurt. Nothing can bring you down. It's a high to where you don't have to think about nothing. All your troubles go away. You just feel like every-thing is lifted off your shoulders."

What Paula calls "that oxy buzz" comes from OxyContin's only active ingredient: oxycodone, an opioid, or synthetic opiate, developed in a German laboratory in 1916. Chemically, it is a close relative of every other opium derivative and synthetic: heroin, morphine, codeine, methadone. And just as every opiate does, oxycodone creates a physical dependence in most of its users and a powerful addiction in some of them. "At first you do them to get high," Paula says, "and then after you're addicted, you don't do them to get high—you do them to survive."

The earliest reported cases of OxyContin abuse were in rural Maine, rust-belt counties in western Pennsylvania and eastern Ohio and the Appalachian areas of Virginia, West Virginia and Kentucky. The problem travelled through these regions, as word spread from town to town, county to county, up and down the Appalachians. There are a few defining characteristics that the first affected regions share: they're home to large populations of disabled and chronically ill people who are in need of pain relief; they're marked by high unemployment and a lack of economic opportunity; they're remote; and they are areas where prescription drugs have been abused in the past. "There's always been a certain degree of prescription-drug abuse in this area," says Art Van Zee, a physician in Lee County, Virginia, "but there's never been anything like this. This is something that is very different and very new, and we don't understand all the reasons why. This is not just people who have long-term, substance-abuse problems. In our region, this is young teenagers, 13 and 14-year-olds, experimenting with recreational drug use and becoming addicted."

In Man, Paula said, it was like OxyContin came out of nowhere. One day no one had heard of oxys, and a month later, the pills had become a way of life for hundreds of locals. When Paula wants to buy an OxyContin pill, she simply drives to a dealer's house and knocks on the front door in broad daylight. If she knows the dealer well enough, she'll go on in and snort the pill there. If not, she'll hand over the cash, put the pill in her pocket and drive away. Sometimes she'll be the only person there; other times, there will be a dozen cars lined up out front.

The dealers have the benefit of a captive market: OxyContin, like any opioid, is very difficult to quit abusing. And given the pill's ubiquity here in Man, and the fact that the nearest rehab clinic is two hours away, this is an unusually hard place to quit using it. Nonetheless, Paula is trying. Six months ago, she and her best friend decided they were going to quit cold turkey. They took a couple of days off work, locked themselves in her friend's trailer and started to detox. "That was the worst three days of my life," Paula said. "Honestly, I prayed to God to let me die. That's how bad it is. If you can get past the third or the fourth day, you're pretty much fine, but most people don't make it.' Paula and her friend didn't make it: at the end of the third day, they went out and got a pill.

Although heroin and OxyContin have a similar unhappy effect on the lives of the people addicted to them, there is a critical and simple difference between the two: heroin is illegal; OxyContin, when used as directed, is legal. More than that: the pill is made by Purdue Pharma, a successful and well-regarded pharmaceutical company, headquartered in Stamford, Connecticut. It is prescribed to one million patients in the US for the treatment of chronic pain, and it is closely regulated at every stage of its manufacture and distribution by the Food and Drug Administration and the Drug Enforcement Administration.

This fact has meant a major conceptual shift for law-enforcement officials, who are used to combating narcotics produced by international drug lords, not international corporations. As Scott Walker, the director of Layne House, a drug treatment facility in Prestonsburg, Kentucky, says: "You don't have the Coast Guard chasing OxyContin ships. This isn't something you can stop at the border. It's growing from within."

Part of what makes the spread of OxyContin abuse so difficult to track, let alone to stop, is that the drug moves not physically but conceptually. When crack cocaine spread from the big cities on either coast toward the centre of the US, it travelled gradually, city by city. OxyContin abuse pops up suddenly, in unexpected locations: Kenai, Alaska; Tucson; West Palm Beach, Florida. At the Gateway Rehabilitation Center in Aliquippa, a suburb of Pittsburgh, Jay, a recovering OxyContin addict and a former small-time dealer, offered an explanation for OxyContin's sudden geographical shifts. "It's the idea that passes on," he told me. "That's how it spreads." There aren't mules running the drug across the country. It's dealt by word of mouth. I call a friend in Colorado and explain it to him: "Hey, I've got this crazy pill, an OC 80, an OC 40. You've got to go to the doctor and get it. Tell him your back hurts."

Jay is 26, a college graduate and former nurse. He started doing oxys in 1999, and his consumption quickly rose to 240mg a day. He was clean when we met and trying to stay that way. But when he talked about the drug's potential as a small business, he couldn't help getting excited.

Unlike heroin, Jay explained, OxyContin doesn't require investment or muscle or manpower to move across the country. OxyContin abuse is a contagious idea—a meme, if you will. Because OxyContin, the medicine, is readily available in pharmacies everywhere, all it takes to bring OxyContin, the drug, to a new place is a persuasive talker like Jay.

In order to understand the dilemma of OxyContin, you need to understand the long-fought war among doctors over pain and addiction. For centuries, opium and its derivatives have been considered a double-edged sword—the most effective painkiller on earth and also the most addictive substance. For most of the 20th century, opiates were considered too dangerous to use in all but the most critical pain treatments. The assumption was that their medical use would inevitably lead to addiction. In the late 80s, for the first time, public and medical opinion began to swing decisively in the other direction. Patient advocates and pharmaceutical companies encouraged the medical community to rethink its approach to opioids, especially in the management of cancer pain. Their campaign was persuasive. Between 1990 and 1994, morphine consumption in the US rose by 75 per cent, and in 1994, the Department of Health and Human Services issued new clinical guidelines encouraging the use of opioids in the treatment of cancer pain.

Purdue Pharma was a leading player in the pro-opioid campaign. The company contributed generously to patient-advocacy organizations, including the American Pain Foundation, the National Foundation for the Treatment of Pain and the American Chronic Pain Association, and underwrote dozens of scientific studies on the effectiveness of opioids in the treatment of pain. In 1985, the company began marketing MS Contin, a time-release morphine pill that was used to treat cancer pain. As attitudes on opioids shifted, Purdue began promoting it for non-cancer pain as well.

Dr. Russell Portenoy is chairman of pain medicine and palliative care at Beth Israel Medical Center in New York City, and the co-author of a groundbreaking 1986 study that supported the long-term use of opioids to treat non-cancer pain. "Between 1986 and 1997, within the community of pain specialists there was increasing attention on the role of opioids," Portenoy says, "but there was relatively little diffusion of that idea to family doctors and other non-specialists." That began to change, he says, with the FDA's approval of OxyContin in 1995: "There was a sea change that occurred with the release of this drug." For the first time, GPs began to prescribe strong, long-acting opioids to treat chronic non-cancer pain. Portenoy says the change was due to four factors that came together at about the same time. "The reasons were partly cultural—the attitudes of the medical and regulatory communities had been gradually shifting for a decade. They were partly medical—studies had been coming out showing that patients with low-back pain, headaches and neuropathic pain might benefit from long-term opioid therapy. They were partly pharmacological—OxyContin made it easier and more convenient for patients to receive long-term opioid therapy. And they were, finally, related to marketing, because Purdue Pharma was the first company to advertise an opioid pill to GPs in mainstream medical journals."

In addition, the company began an innovative indirect-marketing campaign just before OxyContin's release. Because of regulations on the marketing of narcotics, the company was unable to use direct-to-consumer advertising. Just as Nike advertises the concept of sports instead of shoes, so Purdue would market the concept of pain relief to consumers, but not OxyContin. In 1994, the company launched Partners Against Pain, a public-education program that at first concentrated on cancer pain and later expanded to include other forms of long-term pain. Through videos, patient-pain journals and an elaborate website, Purdue promoted three ideas to doctors and patients: that pain was much more widespread than had previously been thought, that it was treatable, and that in many cases it could, and should, be treated with opioids. Partners Against Pain didn't promote OxyContin specifically—the company's marketers knew that simply expanding the total market would also increase their bottom line.

OxyContin was seen by many doctors as the solution to the long rift between pain specialists and addiction specialists. Purdue Pharma believed that OxyContin's time-release function would mean a lower risk of addiction than other opioid medications.

Over the next few years, sales of OxyContin exploded. OxyContin prescriptions in the US have more or less doubled in number each year since its release. The company's revenues from the pill jumped to 1.14 billion dollars 2000 from 55 million in 1996. Last year, American doctors wrote more than 6.5 million OxyContin prescriptions. Purdue's attempt to expand the opioid marketplace beyond cancer patients was also remarkably successful. Five years ago, cancer patients were still the main market for long-acting opioids, but the largest group of prescribers is now family physicians.

According to Portenoy, this change in the number and kinds of doctors prescribing OxyContin is fundamentally linked to the spread of OxyContin abuse. "It's not the drug, per se," Portenoy says. "It's rapidly expanding access, plus the reality of doctors prescribing it who may not have the skill set required to prescribe it responsibly."

Purdue's field reps were the first wave of OxyContin apostles, spreading word of the pill's effectiveness door-to-door, doctor-by-doctor, pharmacist-by-pharmacist. But Purdue's officially sanctioned word-of-mouth marketing campaign was followed by another, unsanctioned one. This time the news was that the miracle pill had an Achilles heel, that its time-release matrix could be eliminated in a matter of seconds by the simple act of crushing the pill with a spoon, a lighter, even a thumbnail, and that the resulting powder, when snorted or mixed with water and injected, produced a very potent high. The apostles this time were not Purdue's reps but casual drug abusers. And just like Purdue's, their marketing campaign was enormously successful.

In a steel-mill suburb northwest of Pittsburgh, the leader of the second wave of OxyContin apostles was Curt, a young man who in 1998, at the age of 23, found himself kicked out of the Air Force and living back in his hometown. He worked the midnight shift running cranes at the mill, and he dealt a little marijuana during the day.

In April 1999, someone in his circle was prescribed OxyContin. Curt assumed that it was just like any other pain pill. But at a party, he figured out the trick of crushing the pill and snorting the powder, and he quickly spread the word. "I showed a lot of people," Curt says. 'At first they were like, "You're crazy." But then they'd do it, and that would be it. People tell me now, "Yeah, you're the one who showed me how to snort this thing."

Oxys quickly became very popular in Curt's circle of friends, and Curt found a comfortable niche for himself between supply and demand. "I knew people all over the county that were getting prescriptions," he says. "They'd call me and say, 'I'm getting OCs now and I want to get rid of them.' They knew there was money there, but they didn't know who to sell to. They usually gave me a heck of a deal. For every one I sold, I made one. And then I'd give them their money and the next month I'd get their scrip again."

Before long, he had 10 people giving him their pills to sell, mostly women in their thirties and forties on welfare or disability. "It's so weird the people that got into this," Curt says. "Some of them were innocent mothers. I had one that was in her sixties. She never did drugs. She'd sell every last one of her pills, and it would pay for all her other medication." Curt would keep careful track of which day of the month each of his suppliers filled her prescription. "A lot of times I would drive them to the pharmacy."

On the demand end, Curt had between 25 and 50 steady customers. "I had a cell phone at that time, so I was doing a lot of driving," he says. "People would gather at their houses, and they'd bring all their friends over, 10 of them that'd use it. They'd all gather when they knew I was coming, because they wanted the pill immediately."

Curt has been in recovery for a few months now; since he got out of rehab, he's been cut off from almost all his old friends, and he fills his spare time fixing up his sister's house, fishing and reading up on psychology, which he plans to begin studying. He's a man of boundless energy and focus, and he has taken to the 12-step process with an unusual intensity; in his first 60 days clean, he told me, he attended 138 Narcotics Anonymous meetings. That same energy served him well back in his oxy days, when he was cutting steel at the mill all night and driving around making pick-ups and deliveries all day.

It was only a couple of months after OxyContin arrived in town that Curt and most of his customers realized they were addicted. At first, they were happy just to take a pill whenever one was around, for fun, but soon they found themselves experiencing severe withdrawal symptoms if they didn't have a pill every day. Everyone's tolerance built up quickly—one week they were able to get by on a 20 a day, the next week they'd need a 40, and a couple of weeks later, it had to be an 80. "No one knew what was going on," Curt says. "These are a bunch of pot smokers, drinkers, just mellow people. This drug just took us by storm. A whole community, at least 100 people I know around here. They're all into the addiction. These are guys I used to smoke pot with and drink beer with in the woods. I grew up with them all, having parties and that. And now there's not one of them—not one of them—that don't use pills."

Purdue Pharma wasn't aware of significant problems with OxyContin abuse until April 2000, when a front-page article in The Bangor Daily News claiming that OxyContin "is quickly becoming the recreational drug of choice in Maine" landed on the desk of Purdue's senior medical director, Dr J David Haddox. In the summer of 2000, the company formed a response team, made up of medical personnel, PR specialists and two of the company's top executives, which has guided the company's OxyContin campaign ever since.

It's fair to say that in public-relations terms, Purdue's reaction to the OxyContin problem has been less than successful. It is now facing potential class-action suits from former patients, as well as one from the attorney general of West Virginia. John Ashcroft called OxyContin a "very, very dangerous drug." Donnie Marshall, then head of the DEA, said that unless he received "more co-operation" from Purdue, he was "seriously considering rolling back the quotas that DEA sets to the 1996 level," which would have meant a 95 per cent cut.

Purdue's PR problems seem rooted in the company's deep-seated belief in the inherent safety of and public need for its product. It is an article of faith for the company that illegal traffic in its drug is the work of "bad guys" and "professionals," in Haddox's words. In fact, Purdue says that its internal data indicates that the levels of OxyContin abuse in the country are no greater than expected. "We have had increased numbers in the past year or so," I was told by Robert Reder, Purdue's vice president of medical affairs and drug safety, "but our estimation is they're commensurate with the distribution of the drug." The abuse situation, according to Reder's numbers, is normal. The real victims, the company says, are their "legitimate patients," who would be denied OxyContin if its distribution were restricted.

The lack of co-ordination between Purdue and the government agencies that regulate it has had serious repercussions in affected communities, as local police, small-town mayors and individual doctors and pharmacies have been forced to make up their own policies on the fly. Six US states have introduced regulations making it harder for Medicaid recipients to receive OxyContin. After a spate of pharmacy robberies near Boston, dozens of drug stores pulled OxyContin from their shelves—only to be ordered by the state pharmacy board to begin carrying the drug again.

Purdue's executives see the company as an unwitting victim of criminal activity. The company's critics prefer to compare Purdue to tobacco companies and handgun manufacturers, who are likely to be found liable for deaths caused by their products.

When I returned to the Gateway Rehabilitation Center, I got a clearer sense of the way in which OxyContin is taking hold in urban and suburban America. I also learnt about an unexpected secondary effect of OxyContin abuse: in cities like Pittsburgh, the crackdown on OxyContin is resulting in a sharp rise in heroin abuse.

I sat for an afternoon in a glassed-in conference room, looking out on Gateway's parking lot and groomed grounds, and talked with Andy and B, two addicts and former low-level dealers. Before trying OxyContin, they had used their share of recreational drugs, but they didn't consider themselves part of a hardcore drug community. Aside from the track marks on his arms, B, 21, looked like every disaffected college kid in America. He was a professional sloucher, dressed in an orange T-shirt, army shorts and trainers, with a mop of brown hair. Andy wore a sparse goatee, a hooded sweatshirt and a baseball cap with a Japanese character on it. I asked him what it meant, and he said he didn't know.

B began using OxyContin in 1998, when a friend told him about the pills. He soon started dealing to support his habit, buying pills from a dozen or so people and then selling them from his apartment to friends and friends of friends. His sources were all legitimate patients, sick with cancer, carpal-tunnel syndrome, lupus or chronic back problems. But, as B explained, they would often supplement their prescriptions with something weaker and cheaper, then sell the OxyContin. "Some of them were old sick ladies who've never done drugs," B said. "They didn't understand what oxy can do to people. They just wanted that money."

Andy laughed. "Old people are supposed to keep young people off drugs," he said.

B described the casual feel of his drug deals. For the first several months that he was selling, he said, everything was friendly when he'd go to pick up pills from his suppliers. "Most would say, "Hi, honey, come on in." You go into their house and sit down and have something to drink and talk for a while and see how their family's doing, and they see how mine's doing."

But as the police and news media began to sound the alarm about OxyContin abuse, local doctors grew anxious. Many switched their patients to harder-to-abuse drugs, and B lost most of his connections. The supply dried up, prices rose and people started ripping each other off.

A friend told him that shooting heroin was just like shooting OxyContin, only cheaper. He'd never imagined he might take heroin, but the expense of OxyContin was killing him. "I was spending 100 bucks a day on oxy," B said. "That's why I switched to heroin. You get really high off two bags, which is 30 bucks a day. That's a big saving."

Andy agreed. It took him only a month and a half to go from using OxyContin for the first time to shooting heroin, he said. "I've always said that I'd never, ever touch heroin. But then oxys came along and that's the same thing, just cleaner. And that got me into shooting dope. If I'd never touched OxyContin, I wouldn't have done heroin."

In Pittsburgh, Andy and B's stories aren't unique. Gateway's doctors report a sharp increase in admissions of young heroin addicts who started out on OxyContin. "Ninety per cent of my friends that were addicted to oxys are now addicted to heroin," B says. "I know probably 30 or 40 heroin IV drug users now because of OxyContin."

OxyContin entered the lives of casual drug users as a Trojan horse, disguised as something it is not. It has never become a popular drug among existing heroin or crack addicts, who already have a cheaper mechanism for getting high. OxyContin does the most damage when it enters a community of casual drug users—Curt's pot smokers and beer drinkers—who think of pain pills as just another interesting diversion for a Saturday night. In networks like Curt's or Paula's, before OxyContin, no one ever did heroin or crack; those were seen as an entirely different category of drug: something that will take over your life.

When you hold it in your hand, an OxyContin pill doesn't seem any different than any of the mild narcotic preparations that have for years seeped out of the pharmaceutical pipeline and into the lives of casual drug users. What B and Andy and Paula and Curt failed to realize is that, despite appearances, OxyContin actually belongs on the other side of the drug divide—it might look like a casual Saturday-night drug, but it's a take-over-your-life drug.

To Art Van Zee, the doctor who has seen his small community in western Virginia "devastated" by OxyContin abuse, the answer to the crisis is to take OxyContin off the market. Van Zee is circulating a petition asking the FDA and Purdue to withdraw the pill until a safer formulation can be found. "The bottom line is, there's much more harm being created by this drug being available than good," he says. "There are already very good medicines available that are equally effective."

But for many people, "drug communities" like Curt's are not worthy of a whole lot of official sympathy or regulatory concern—especially not when their interests are considered next to those of patients in pain, who are using OxyContin the way it is meant to be used and whose lives have been improved as a result. For doctors who have seen their patients transformed by OxyContin, there is something mystifying, even infuriating, about the suggestion that it should be withdrawn or even restricted, just because a bunch of kids in Kentucky didn't know what they were snorting.

"There is no question that increasing opioid consumption for legitimate medical purposes is going to lead to some increase in the rates of addiction," Portenoy of Beth Israel says. "But the fact is, the trade-off is worth it. At the moment, the attitude is that if one housewife in Alabama becomes addicted, then the drug must be pulled and the company shut down. But we're talking about millions of people whose lives can be brought back from total disability by the proper use of opioids. Any actions taken by law enforcement or the regulatory community that increase the stigma associated with these drugs, or increase the fear of physicians in prescribing these drugs, is going to exacerbate an already terrible condition and hurt patients."

The 10th point in Purdue Pharma's 10-point plan to reduce OxyContin abuse is reformulation. The company says that it is spending millions of dollars to create a new version of OxyContin, or perhaps an entirely new medication, that would have all the benefits of OxyContin and none of its dangers.

In some recent interviews, Purdue's representatives sound enthusiastic about this idea. But when pressed, Haddox admits that what Purdue's scientists are looking for is a "holy grail," a drug that will activate the receptors in the brain that control pain relief and leave alone those that control euphoria. And this isn't a new initiative, it turns out, but one that the company has been working on for many years.

There are often suggestions from Purdue that this reformulation may take "a few years"—it's also entirely possible that it will never happen. Opioids, including OxyContin, may remain the double-edged sword they have always been. And regulators may simply decide to accept a certain amount of unintentional damage in the treatment of pain, and leave local police chiefs and drug counselors—as well as individual addicts—to find solutions to the OxyContin problem on their own.

SOURCE: Paul Tough, "Hillbilly Hell," *Observer*, April 7, 2002.

ANALYSIS

In many respects, the trajectory followed by OxyContin and similar opioid-based painkillers such as Vicodin is a familiar one. It is virtually the same trajectory followed by many previous drugs such as heroin, tranquilizers like Miltown and Valium, and amphetamine. Although not a prescription drug, cocaine was viewed in the same light in the 1970s. All were considered to be safe, but none of them were. All became widely abused. That the public continues to believe in miracle prescription drugs—at least ones with psychoactive properties—that provide only benefits and have no drawbacks after that assumption has proven false so many times in the past is testimony to the persistence of wishful thinking, the effectiveness of the marketing campaigns of pharmaceutical manufacturers, and the trust people place in the opinions of their physicians. No drug has ever been completely safe.

The full trajectory for OxyContin as well as for previous miracle drugs more or less follows this sequence: A new compound is identified as a miracle drug and is described as having low or no possibility for abuse. The drug is then aggressively marketed to physicians and, to the extent allowed by law, to potential consumers. The drug is initially well received and the number of prescriptions written rapidly expands. The benefits of the drug are extolled by those using it, fueling further increases in the number of prescriptions written. As more and more people use the drug, however, the limits of its effectiveness and its potential for abuse become apparent. The press, which initially wrote positive stories about the new miracle drug when it was released with maybe a caveat or two about *possible* downsides, now features alarmist stories about the threat of a new and growing epidemic. As knowledge of the potential for abuse grows, physicians grow more cautious about prescribing the drug and legislators look for ways to further restrict availability. But these attempts to put limits on the drug are reactionary and late. The initial campaign has already created an appetite for the drug that will be supplied by a black market that compensates for the decreased availability through legal channels.

The above report does a good job of detailing the spread of OxyContin and highlights again how the availability of a drug combined with a shift in cultural acceptance, can lead to a rapid increase in the use of the drug. In this instance, physicians and their patients embracing the idea that opioid-based analgesics had been underprescribed by non-specialists and that such drugs were safe and effective for managing chronic pain other than that attributable to cancer represented the cultural shift. Once family physicians began prescribing OxyContin for a broader class of conditions, some of which because they lack objective physical referents such as chronic lower back pain, are hard to verify and can be easily faked for the purpose of obtaining drugs. Rural areas were the first hit because there are illegal opiates such as heroin that are hard to get. And the people who live in rural areas tend to work demanding, physical jobs that require hard labor. Over a lifetime, this can lead to injury and chronic pain. As a result, when prescribing opioids to relieve pain, some of the first areas to experience that cultural shift were rural. The initial reports of OxyContin abuse were in rural Maine in the late 1990s followed by rural Appalachia, western Virginia, eastern Kentucky, and West Virginia; areas that continue to be hard hit by OxyContin abuse.

Fueling the spread of OxyContin is the fact that there is considerable financial incentive for patients with legitimate prescriptions to sell at least some of their OxyContin tablets. This is the way that most OxyContin users report obtaining the drug as opposed to from non-using dealers. As described by Jim Inciardi in *The War on Drugs IV:*

> Diversion has also occurred by means of fraud, particularly through the abuse of medical insurance programs . . . For example, a Medicaid patient may pay only $3 for a bottle of 100 80-milligram OxyContin tablets. In communities where employment and money are scarce resources, the temptation to sell some pills for the going "street price" of $1 per milligram provides an opportunity to earn money. In this example, the $3 bottle from the pharmacy can net the patient up to $8,000 on the illegal market.

Also fueling the spread has been the growth of unregulated "pain management centers" in Broward County Florida. A 2010 article in *Time Magazine* reported there were more pain clinics (115) in Broward County than there were McDonalds (70) and that the top 25 oxycodone dispensing doctors in the nation worked in Broward County. The success of the clinics in South Florida led to the expansion to other counties; and in 2009, Florida doctors wrote prescriptions for a half-billion doses of oxycodone. That is more than twice as many as any neighboring state for the same time period.

Florida's lax laws allow unscrupulous doctors (script docs) at the clinics to conduct the most cursory histories and physicals necessary to write prescriptions for OxyContin. The lack of regulation means a *patient* at one clinic can easily travel to others in the same day to obtain multiple prescriptions (i.e., doctor shopping) without leaving a trail. The drugs are then trafficked within and outside of Florida. A crack down on similar clinics in Tennessee and Kentucky has helped boost tourism in Florida where the pain management centers have become a major source of illicit OxyContin for the entire country.

Florida legislators have proposed enacting laws that would establish a centralized database to track purchases but finding funding for that purpose has proven difficult in a cost-cutting environment. Moreover, the current governor, Rick Scott, opposed the legislation stating that it intrudes on patient privacy and is too costly. In 2011, the Office of National Drug Control Policy proposed a prescription drug monitoring program to track opioid prescriptions and would require all states—including

Florida—to participate. But funding for this program is in question as well and to date it has not been implemented.

The continuing frenetic prescribing practices in Florida insure that OxyContin and like drugs remain relatively easy to obtain and initiation of use by youth remains high. The National Survey of Drug Use and Health (NSDUH) for 2010 indicates the nonmedical use of prescription pain relievers has remained stable since about 2002 but concludes that there is still a growing problem. The report notes,

> Initiation rates for nonmedical pain reliever use continue to be second only to marijuana rates, with 2 million or more new nonmedical pain reliever users each year since 2002, including over 500,000 who initiate use without ever having used another illicit drug. The sustained numbers of new and continuing users have contributed to substantial increases in indicators of problems associated with use, especially among adults. The rate of pain reliever dependence for persons aged 12 or older increased from 2002 to 2010 (from 0.4 to 0.6 percent of the population), and the number of persons with dependence increased from 936,000 to 1.4 million.

FURTHER READING

Clines, F.X., & Meier, B. (2001, February 9). Cancer painkillers pose new abuse threat. *New York Times*, A1.

Collins, T.R. (2010, April 13). Invasion of the pill mills in South Florida. *Time*, http://www.time.com/time/nation/article/0,8599,1981582,00.html.

Compton, W.M., & Volkow, N.D. (2006). Major increases in opioid analgesic abuse in the United States: Concerns and strategies. *Drug and Alcohol Dependence, 81*, 103–107.

Edwards, J. (2010, January 7). Who signed off on Purdue's misleading OxyContin Chart? Judge may want answers. *CBS Interactive Network*, http://www.bnet.com/blog/drug-business/who-signed-off-on-purdues-misleading-oxycontin-chart-judge-may-want-answers/3832.

Inciardi, J. (2007). *The war on drugs IV: The continuing saga of the mysteries and miseries of intoxication, addiction, crime, and public policy, 4th edition*. Boston, MA: Allyn and Bacon.

Leshner, A. (1999). Science based views of drug addiction and its treatment. *Journal of the American Medical Association, 282*, 1314–1316.

Manchikanti, L. (2007). National drug control policy and prescription drug abuse: Facts and fallacies. *Pain Physician, 10*, 399–404.

Mendelson, J., Flower, K., Pletcher, M.J., & Galloway, G.P. (2008). Addiction to prescription opioids: Characteristics of the emerging epidemic and treatment with buprenorphine. *Experimental and Clinical Psychopharmacology, 16*, 435–441.

Raffa, R.B., & Pergolizzi, J.V. (2010). Opioid formulations designed to resist deter abuse. *Drugs, 70*, 1657–1675.

RUSH LIMBAUGH—"IT'S TRUE. I AM ADDICTED TO PAIN MEDICATION."

Given the right circumstances, virtually no one is immune to drug addiction. Individuals who are not necessarily genetically or environmentally predisposed, who do not have an underlying mental illness, and who are not smoking or injecting drugs can also develop an addiction. No person illustrates that better than Rush Hudson Limbaugh III, known simply as "Rush" to the many regular listeners ("ditto heads") of his popular radio broadcast.

In his statements, Limbaugh made no distinction between the illegal use of prescription drugs and the use of illegal drugs. His view that drug use was *always* a personal choice made his own admission all the more shocking. Limbaugh had developed an addiction to painkillers following unsuccessful spinal surgery that left him in constant pain. Specifically, he was addicted to opiates such as oxycodone (OxyContin) and hydrocodone (Vicodin).

Wilma Cline, Limbaugh's ex-housekeeper, exposed him when she came forward to authorities for reasons that remain unclear. She claimed he was taking as many as 30 OxyContin per day; an amount far beyond what would safely be prescribed. Retribution via the national press was as swift, as certain, and as brutal as Limbaugh's judgments of liberals and their ilk.

Following the revelations of the extent of his drug use, Limbaugh was investigated but never charged for

(continued)

RUSH LIMBAUGH—"IT'S TRUE. I AM ADDICTED TO PAIN MEDICATION."
(continued)

illegally obtaining drugs through "doctor shopping." He was eventually charged with one count of fraudulently concealing information to obtain prescription drugs but the charge was dropped when Limbaugh successfully completed drug treatment. Limbaugh's high-priced lawyer, Roy Black, disputed the housekeeper's account and said that according to Limbaugh's medical records, Limbaugh was taking only 8 OxyContin per day and not the 30 as alleged by his ex-housekeeper.

Limbaugh's drug addiction makes it clear that prescription drugs are as dangerous and addicting as illegal drugs and should never be deemed safe to use simply because a doctor is willing to prescribe them and a pharmacist dispenses them in neatly labeled bottles.

Rosenberg, D. (2001, April 9). How one town got hooked. *Newsweek*, Society p. 48.

Thomas, E. (2003, October 20). "I am addicted to prescription pain medication." *Newsweek*, Society, p. 42.

On the Internet

The National Center on Addiction and Substance Abuse at Colombia University publishes regular reports on various aspects of substance use policy and issues at their website. A recent report entitled *Adolescent Substance Use: America's #1 Public Health Problem* is available at: http://www.casacolumbia.org/templates/publications_reports.aspx.

The National Institute on Drug Abuse (NIDA) has a series of publications on prescription drug abuse at: http://drugpubs.drugabuse.gov/shopdisplayproducts.aspx?id=29&cat=Prescription.

The Office of Applied Statistics, part of the Substance Abuse and Mental Health Services Administration has the full report on the findings of the 2010 National Household Survey on Drug Abuse and Health. The report contains a section detailing use of non-prescription drugs, including non-prescription opioids. It is available at: http://oas.samhsa.gov/nsduhlatest.htm.

The Office of National Drug Control Policy published a Response to the Epidemic of Prescription Drug Abuse in April 2011. The publication is available at the ONDCP website at: http://www.whitehousedrugpolicy.gov/publications/html/rx_epidemic.html.

The ONDCP Prescription Drug Abuse Action Plan is avail-able at: http://www.whitehouse.gov/ondcp/supplemental-strategies.

The Oxycontin Express is a documentary on the ease with which OxyContin/oxycodone can be obtained from poorly monitored "pain management centers" in Broward Country, Florida and sold throughout the country. The program originally aired on Current TV and can be watched in its entirety at: http://current.com/shows/vanguard/91183979_the-oxycontin-express.htm.

"I Felt My Face Just Melting"

- ***Document:*** Combat Methamphetamine Epidemic Act of 2005 (Title VII of the Patriot Act PL 109–177)
- ***Date:*** March 9, 2006
- ***Where:*** Washington, DC
- ***Significance:*** Methamphetamine surged in popularity in the United States in the late 1960s as part of the counterculture's broad acceptance of drug use and because it could be easily obtained by prescription or manufactured in home-based laboratories. Its popularity receded with the passage of the Controlled Substances Act of 1970, which made methamphetamine a Schedule II drug with limited access. It became popular again in the 1990s when Mexican drug cartels began manufacturing the drug in quantity in superlabs and distributing it in southern California and the southwest. Small, home-based labs in rural states also began springing up at this time and used readily available over-the-counter decongestants as the raw material for making methamphetamine for personal use and limited distribution. In 2005, the federal government included provisions in the Patriot Act that restricted access to the over-the-counter medications in an attempt to shut down the home-based labs. Together with the passage of a law in Mexico that restricted the importation of precursor drugs into that country, the law has had some albeit limited success in reducing methamphetamine use. This document is from the DEA Office of Diversion Control website. It describes the effective dates and main provisions of the Combat Methamphetamine Epidemic Act.

DOCUMENT

Effective March 9, 2006

The Act makes definitional changes to add "scheduled listed chemical product," "regulated seller," "mobile retail vendor," "at retail," and to modify the existing definition of "retail distributor." Definitions are as follows:

"The term *scheduled listed chemical product* means, . . . a product that—

(i) contains ephedrine, pseudoephedrine, or phenylpropanolamine; and
(ii) may be marketed or distributed lawfully in the United States under the Federal, Food, Drug, and Cosmetic Act as a nonprescription drug.

Each reference in clause (i) to ephedrine, pseudoephedrine, or phenylpropanolamine includes each of the salts, optical isomers, and salts of optical isomers of such chemical."

"The term *regulated seller* means a retail distributor (including a pharmacy or a mobile retail vendor), except that such term does not include an employee or agent of such distributor."

"The term *mobile retail vendor* means a person or entity that makes sales at retail from a stand that is intended to be temporary, or is capable of being moved from one location to another, whether the stand is located within or on the premises of a fixed facility (such as a kiosk at a shopping center or an airport) or whether the stand is located on unimproved real estate (such as a lot or field leased for retail purposes)."

"The term *at retail*, with respect to the sale or purchase of a scheduled listed chemical product, means a sale or purchase for personal use, respectively."

"The term *retail distributor* means a grocery store, general merchandise store, drug store, or other entity or person whose activities as a distributor relating to pseudoephedrine or phenylpropanolamine products are limited almost exclusively to sales for personal use, both in number of sales and volume of sales, either directly to walk-in customers or in face-to-face transactions by direct sales."

Effective April 8, 2006

a. The change to 21 U.S.C. § 830 that adds a new subsection (d) SCHEDULED LISTED CHEMICALS; RESTRICTIONS ON SALES QUANTITY; REQUIREMENTS REGARDING NONLIQUID FORMS:

   i. This sets the daily sales limit of ephedrine base, pseudoephedrine base, or phenylpropanolamine base at 3.6 grams per purchaser, regardless of the number of transactions.
   ii. Affects regulated sellers and persons required to submit mail order reports under 21 U.S.C. 830(b)(3).
   iii. Requires all nonliquid forms (including gel caps) to be in 2-unit blister packs (with exception when blister pack is not technically feasible, the product may be in unit dosage packets or pouches).

b. The change to 21 U.S.C. § 830 that adds (2) MAIL-ORDER REPORTING; VERIFICATION OF IDENTITY OF PURCHASER; 30-DAY RESTRICTION ON QUANTITIES FOR INDIVIDUAL PURCHASES:

i. This requires the mail-order seller to confirm the identity of the purchaser prior to shipping the product.
ii. Limits such sales to 7.5 grams per customer during a 30-day period.

c. The change to 21 U.S.C. § 844(a) entitled RESTRICTIONS ON QUANTITY PURCHASED DURING 30-DAY PERIOD:

i. This makes it unlawful for any person to knowingly or intentionally purchase at retail more than 9 grams during a 30 day period (of which no more than 7.5 grams can be imported by private or commercial carrier or the Postal Service).

Effective September 30, 2006

Sales Limits

a. A mobile retail vendor may not sell more than 7.5 grams of product per customer during a 30-day period.

Product Placement

b. Regulated seller must place product such that customers do not have direct access before the sale is made ("behind the counter" placement) or in a locked cabinet that is located in an area of the facility to which customers do have direct access. Regulated seller must deliver product directly into the custody of the purchaser.
c. A mobile retail vendor must place product in a locked cabinet.

Logbook Provisions

d. Seller maintains written or electronic list (logbook) of sales that identifies:

(1) Products by name;
(2) Quantity sold;
(3) Names and addresses of purchasers; and,
(4) Date and time of the sales.

The logbook requirement does not apply to any purchase by an individual of a single sales package that contains not more than 60 mg. of pseudoephedrine.

e. Seller may not sell the product unless prospective purchaser presents a photographic identification card issued by a State or the Federal Government, or a document considered acceptable for purposes of 8 CFR § 274a.2(b)(1)(v)(A) or (B).
f. Purchaser must sign the logbook and enter his or her name, address, and date and time of sale.
g. Seller must determine that the name entered into the logbook corresponds to the name provided on such identification and that the date and time entered are correct.
h. Seller must enter into the logbook the name of the product and the quantity sold.

i. The logbook must contain a notice to purchasers that entering false statements or misrepresentations in the logbook may subject the purchaser to criminal penalties under 18 U.S.C. § 1001 and such notice must specify the maximum fine ($250,000.00) and term of imprisonment (5 years).
j. Seller must maintain each entry in the logbook for not fewer than two years after the date on which the entry is made.
k. The Attorney General will issue regulations establishing restrictions on disclosure of information in logbooks. Disclosure to the Attorney General and to State and local law enforcement agencies will be authorized. Accessing, using, or sharing the logbook information for any purpose other than to comply with the Controlled Substances Act or to facilitate a product recall to protect public health and safety will be prohibited.
l. Regulated seller who in good faith releases logbook information to Federal, State or local law enforcement authorities is immune from civil liability for such release unless the release constitutes gross negligence or intentional, wanton, or willful misconduct.

Self-Certification and Training

m. Self-certification and training.

(1) Seller must self-certify to the Attorney General that each individual who is responsible for delivering such products into the custody of purchasers, or who deals directly with purchasers by obtaining payment for the products, has undergone training provided by the seller to ensure that the individual understands the requirements that apply to the sale of these products.
(2) Regulated seller may not sell any scheduled listed chemical product at retail unless the self-certification has been submitted to the Attorney General.
(3) Seller must maintain a copy of such self-certification and records demonstrating that individuals have undergone such training.
(4) The certification is not effective unless, in addition to provisions regarding the training of individuals, the certification includes a statement that the seller understands each of the requirements regarding transactional limits, blister-packs, "behind the counter" placement, photo identification, and logbook also apply and agrees to comply with the requirements.
(5) The Attorney General will issue regulations to establish the criteria for self-certifications and employee training. Separate certification is required for each place of business at which a regulated seller sells such products at retail.
(6) The Attorney General will establish a program that will:

(a) be carried out through an Internet site of the Department of Justice;
(b) inform regulated sellers that 18 U.S.C. § 1001 applies to such certifications;
(c) make available to sellers the criteria for certification and training;

(d) be designed to permit submission of certifications through the Internet site; and

(e) be designed to automatically provide the explanation of the criteria for certification and training and an acknowledgment that the Department of Justice has received a certification, without requiring direct interaction of regulated sellers with staff of the Department of Justice.

(7) Copies of certifications shall be made available to appropriate State and local officials.

SOURCE: Combat Methamphetamine Epidemic Act of 2005 (Title VII of The Patriot Act PL 109–177).

ANALYSIS

Dr. Richard Rawson is the Associate Director of the UCLA Integrated Substance Abuse Programs. He has studied the neurological and psychological effects of methamphetamine and treatment for methamphetamine abuse for many years. In presentations, he likes to compare the amount of dopamine released in the brain after ingesting methamphetamine with the release after non-drug pleasurable activities, and ingestion of other drugs. Dopamine is the neurotransmitter most affected by methamphetamine. The increase in dopamine released after use is thought to underlie the drug's pleasurable effects. Rawson's slides show that after eating, there is a release of 100 units of dopamine, whereas during sex there is a release of 200 units of dopamine. (Leading to the quip that: "One orgasm equals two cheeseburgers."). Drugs such as alcohol, nicotine, and morphine are all within the range of 100 to 300 units of released dopamine. With cocaine use, there is a release of 350 units. In contrast, ingestion of methamphetamine results in the rapid release of 1,250 units of dopamine. Because of this profound neurophysiological effect, methamphetamine use can alter normal brain function over a relatively short time, contributing to the rapid onset of addiction. Addicted meth addicts, called tweakers then need to take the drug more or less continually—usually in multi-day binges called runs—to ward off depression, anxiety, and dysphoria owing to the neurological changes in response to chronic meth use.

Methamphetamine was first synthesized in 1919 by a Japanese chemist. It was more widely prescribed in Europe than in the United States in the 1930s and was favored by German and British troops during World War II, whereas American troops were supplied with amphetamine. Methamphetamine had its first surge in use in the United States in the 1960s as part of the broader cultural acceptance of drug use. There are reports from the San Francisco-based treatment center called the Free Clinic that during the hippie heyday in Haight Ashbury, some local physicians were prescribing injectable methamphetamine as a treatment for injection heroin users. Inevitably, the heroin addicts also became addicted to methamphetamine. The drug caught on, in both injectable and non-injectable form, among the hippies, hippie wannabes, counter-culturists, and biker gangs that flooded into the Haight in 1967. College students also liked methamphetamine because it allowed them to remain alert through the night while *cramming* for exams (or just partying). But some, such as drug-proselytizer Alan Ginsberg of all people, saw methamphetamine as being contrary to what the countercultural movement stood for: the use of drugs to broaden personal awareness and change society.

The passage of the Controlled Substances Act of 1970 classified methamphetamine as a Schedule II drug, greatly restricting the circumstances under which it could be prescribed and for a time reducing availability. (It can still be obtained via prescription under the trade name Desoxyn for the treatment of ADHD, obesity, and narcolepsy. Methamphetamine is prescribed for children!) Meth faded in popularity as an abused drug, becoming the province of outlaw biker gangs (e.g., Hells Angels, the Outlaws, the Pagans) on the west coast. They used a rather complex method of production called P2P, named for the precursor drug phenyl-2-propanone that was used. This method required a skillful chemist to convert the raw material into methamphetamine. In 1980, the federal government restricted access to phenyl-2-propanone.

The biker chemists adjusted by developing a new method for manufacturing methamphetamine using ephedrine and pseudoephedrine, ingredients readily found in over-the-counter decongestants and diet products. The meth they produced became more potent over time, increasing in average purity from 30 percent in 1970 to 60 percent by the early 1980s. The nickname "crank" derives from the fact that the bikers used to stow methamphetamine in the crankcases of their motorcycles. The biker gangs used the drug themselves and also sold it—to long distance truckers and others—for profit.

In the 1980s, drug traffickers based in Mexico began producing methamphetamine in bulk, in what evolved into *superlabs*. Located in remote areas, superlabs produce as few as 10 to more than 100 pounds of methamphetamine in a single production cycle (several days), yielding millions of dollars worth of product in street value. Mexico had no restrictions on the precursor drugs used to make amphetamine, allowing the traffickers to easily divert legally purchased ephedrine and pseudoephedrine for methamphetamine production. (Ephedrine and pseudoephedrine are difficult to manufacture and require extensive facilities and a sophisticated knowledge of chemistry. Consequently, these drugs are made at only nine facilities around the world, five of which are in India.)

Mexican traffickers began peddling methamphetamine in the Southwest and in Southern California where cities like San Diego experienced a significant rise in methamphetamine abuse. From these new beginnings in the west, methamphetamine use gradually spread eastward. Methamphetamine abuse increased throughout the 1990s in smaller cities and rural areas with attendant increases in crime, domestic violence, child abuse and neglect, and myriad health and dental problems (meth mouth) among users. Presently, over 80 percent of the methamphetamine consumed in the United States is produced in superlabs. The traffickers standardized their production methods to the extent that when two geographically distant superlabs were busted in 2004, it was found they both used the same high-thread-count Martha Stewart sheets for filtration.

The simple (but not safe) production method allowed even the most amateur chemist to set up a "mom and pop" lab, which was most often located in rural areas to avoid detection. Meth labs generate noxious fumes and leave behind many highly toxic chemicals used in the production process which can include: ether or acetone, red phosphorous, hydrogen chloride, iodine, caustic soda, lithium, and Freon.

The fumes and chemical byproducts make the labs easily identifiable in populous areas which is why they are generally located far from major or even mid-sized urban centers.

Because the chemicals used in the production process are volatile and combustible, fiery explosions are often the beacons that lead law enforcement authorities to local meth labs. The quote that provides the title for this section is from a meth lab operator whose explosive mishap resulted in severe facial and bodily burns. Home meth lab proprietors, addicts themselves, often disregard their safety and the safety of others. It is not uncommon for child protection authorities to discover children playing near the labs, inhaling the toxic fumes and at risk for severe chemical burns or worse. By the late 1990s, national surveys of local law enforcement agencies indicated methamphetamine had become their biggest drug problem far surpassing cocaine, heroin, and marijuana even though national surveys suggested there were relatively few methamphetamine users overall. The discrepancy highlights a limitation of national surveys, which exclude people living in institutions, truants, prisoners, and the homeless and as a result, despite sophisticated sampling techniques, might under-represent rural populations.

Another group was also affected by methamphetamine use. Gay and bisexual men living mainly in large urban centers began using the drug to enhance sexual activity. The 1990s were a time of transition for gays and bisexuals. New drugs for effectively treating HIV/AIDS were being discovered at a rapid rate and incorporated into drug cocktails as part of a treatment regimen called Highly Active Anti-Retroviral Treatment (HAART). The new treatments could reduce the HIV level in the bloodstream to undetectable and made HIV infection a chronic but treatable disease. This led to the notion that HIV was not as big a concern after all ("treatment optimism").

Unshackled from AIDS as a death sentence, younger gay men coming of age in the 1990s who were spared seeing many of their friends wither and die from AIDS and older gay men who were tired of condom use and years of practicing safe sex to avoid HIV infection ("safe sex fatigue") stopped using condoms and began having unprotected sex with multiple partners. Anonymous sexual encounters at large, weekend long-parties held in alternating cities and called circuit parties were fueled by the use of drugs such as methamphetamine, club drugs (ketamine, GHB, amyl nitrite or "poppers"), and drugs for treating erectile dysfunction such as Viagra. Gay and bisexual men, including those who were HIV positive, began using Internet sites to advertise for sexual partners. Advertisements with the acronym "PnP" for "party and play" meant an expectation that drugs—particularly methamphetamine—would be used during sex. A highly pure, smokable form of methamphetamine called *Tina* in the gay community but more commonly known as *ice* because of its crystalline appearance has been a favored form of the drug for such encounters.

The uptick in unsafe sex fostered by the use of methamphetamine and other drugs led to an increase in the rates of sexually transmitted infections among gay men, including an increase in HIV infections, after a decade of declines and stability. To date, gay and bisexual men are the only group(s) at high risk of HIV infection for whom infection rates continue to increase (see sidebar on HIV/AIDS in the United States, 2011). Black gay men in their early 20s are at especially high risk.

The Combat Methamphetamine Act of 2005 was not the first time federal legislators attempted to restrict access to precursor drugs. In each case, up to and including the 2005 legislation, there was a temporary disruption in the production and use of methamphetamine followed by a rebound as producers found ways to circumvent the laws:

- In 1988, the "Chemical Diversion and Trafficking Act" restricted access to and required record keeping for ephedrine and pseudoephedrine obtained in bulk. However, intense lobbying by the pharmaceutical industry, which makes billions on the sale of over-the-counter cold and decongestant remedies that contain ephedrine and pseudoephedrine, resulted in a loophole that exempted over-the-counter sales from the new restrictions. The decline in methamphetamine production and use was short-lived as home-cooks began getting the precursor drugs by shopping at the local pharmacy.
- In 1993, the "Domestic Chemical and Diversion Act" eliminated the loophole for over-the-counter products that contained ephedrine but not pseudoephedrine. Meth producers switched to using pseudoephedrine. Pseudoephedrine in pill form requires an extra processing step that involves the use of flammable chemicals. As a result, meth labs go from being toxic to being toxic and combustible.
- In 1996, the "Comprehensive Methamphetamine Control Act" closed the loophole for pseudoephedrine but exempted over-the-counter medications that contained pseudoephedrine as long as they were sold in *blister packs*. It was thought this form of packaging would make processing the pills more difficult and discourage meth producers. It didn't. The superlabs continued to get their precursor drugs through Mexico, where bulk purchases of ephedrine and pseudoephedrine. U.S.-based producers could also get the precursor drugs from Canada, where regulations were also lax.

And the effects of the 2005 legislation? Forty states followed suit and enacted laws that, to varying degrees, required medications containing pseudoephedrine be kept behind the counter at pharmacies to further restrict access and established a centralized computer database of all such purchases to discourage "smurfing," the act of driving from store to store to purchase as much of the drugs as legally allowable at each store. Two states, Oregon and Mississippi passed laws that made products containing pseudoephedrine available only by prescription. These states have seen the sharpest declines in methamphetamine use, but the pharmaceutical industry continues to lobby heavily against making these drugs prescription-only and favors the idea of a centralized database. Mexico, declaring war on drugs in 2006, finally banned importation of pseudoephedrine in 2009.

Home lab producers adjusted by adopting a new, simpler method of producing methamphetamine called "shake-and-bake" or "one pot" whereby a much smaller amount of pseudoephedrine is needed. The process is simpler and accomplished in a single step but still involves the use of toxic and combustible chemicals that can result in fiery explosions. Superlab producers have adjusted by finding new sources of bulk ephedrine and pseudoephedrine and smuggling the drugs by rerouting them through other countries before importation into the United States and Mexico. Interestingly, they have also begun using the precursor drug originally used by biker gangs in the 1970s, phenyl-2-propanone.

After declines in methamphetamine use, lab seizures, and treatment admissions between 2006 and 2008 shortly after the Combat Methamphetamine Act went into effect, all increased again in 2009. Moreover, based on the DEA's *National Drug Threat Assessment* for 2011, production continues apace:

> High levels of production in Mexico along with an increase in the number of domestic manufacturing operations have combined to make methamphetamine readily available throughout the United States. Methamphetamine production in Mexico is robust and stable, as evidenced by recent law enforcement reporting, laboratory seizure data, an increasing flow from Mexico, and a sustained upward trend in Mexican methamphetamine availability in U.S. markets. . . .
>
> Rates of domestic methamphetamine production, particularly in small-scale laboratories, will remain high in 2011, even as availability of Mexico-produced methamphetamine increases.

As for biker gangs, it appears they did not completely abandon the methamphetamine trade either. In September 2011, an arrest warrant was issued for a Cal State San Bernardino Associate Professor in Kinesiology, Dr. Stephen J Kinzey, who is also a member of the "Devils Diciples [*sic*] Outlaws" biker gang. A police raid on Dr. Kinzey's home after a months-long investigation yielded more than a pound of methamphetamine. Prior to turning himself in, "Skinz," as he referred to himself in biker circles, thoughtfully phoned the police to inquire about his bond amount.

FURTHER READING

Centers for Disease Control and Prevention (2005, April 15). Acute public health consequences of methamphetamine laboratories—16 states, January 2000–June 2004. *Morbidity and Mortality Weekly*, 356–359.

Cimino, K. (2005). *The politics of crystal meth: Gay men share stories of addiction and recovery*. Boca Raton, FL: Universal Publishers.

Congressional Subcommittee on Criminal Justice, Drug Policy, and Human Resources. (2005, June 27). *Fighting meth in America's heartland: Assessing federal, state, and local efforts*. Washington, DC: U.S. Government Printing Office.

Cunningham, J. K., Borjoquez, I., Campollo, O., Liu, L-M., & Maxwell, J.C. (2010). Mexico's methamphetamine precursor *chemical* interventions: Impacts on drug treatment admissions. *Addiction, 105*, 1973–1983.

Cunningham, J. K., & Lon-Miu, L. (2009). Impact of US and Canadian precursor regulation on methamphetamine purity in the United States. *Addiction, 104*, 441–453.

Egan, T. (2002, February 6). Meth building its hell's kitchen in rural America. *The New York Times*, A14.

Gonzales, R., Mooney, L., & Rawson, R. A. (2010). The methamphetamine problem in the United States. *Annual Review of Public Health, 31*, 385–398.

DRUG "EPIDEMICS" AND THE MEDIA

> We call it an epidemic now. That means white folks are doing it.
>
> –Richard Pryor

When considering the history of drug policy in the United States, it is important to keep in mind that there has often been a good deal of hysteria and overstatement accompanying what have been called drug "epidemics" but what are really more accurately characterized in epidemiological terms as modest increases in the incidence (i.e., number of new users) of use of a particular drug. Most often use of a drug during these so-called epidemics has remained relegated to a small percentage of the population and to a largely segmented group of users (e.g., inner cities in the case of the 1970s heroin epidemics; scattered rural counties and southwestern states in the case of the more recent methamphetamine epidemic). This is not to downplay the consequences of the increases in drug use that have occurred at different times or the effects they have had on the areas and populations hardest hit. The intent is to suggest that press coverage of drug use trends has often lacked perspective

(continued)

DRUG "EPIDEMICS" AND THE MEDIA

(continued)

on the cultural, historical, and epidemiological contexts as well as on the absolute numbers of people affected.

Exaggerations of the extent and consequences of drug use by the press and politicians alike have often fostered a "sky is falling" perception each time use of a particular drug has increased. In many instances, when a new drug has come into vogue or re-emerged, it has been termed the "most dangerous substance on earth" (e.g., marijuana, LSD, cocaine, crack, heroin, ice, methamphetamine) or some equivalent designation. In some cases, as in the 1930s when Hearst publications grossly exaggerated the consequences of marijuana use, the intent to distort was deliberate and racially motivated amounting to a smear campaign targeted at Mexicans. Harry Anslinger effectively used the national press to portray marijuana as a dangerous drug through penning widely published essays built on distortion and outright falsehoods such as *The Assassin of Youth*.

Less politically advertent but resulting in considerable exaggeration of the extent of the drug problem nonetheless was the press coverage of the increase in methamphetamine use in the 1990s. Most accounts failed to mention that national surveys consistently have indicated that less than 1 percent of the adult U.S. household population reported using methamphetamine in the past year. When viewing a television show, magazine, newspaper, or Internet-based article on the inevitable next "most dangerous substance on earth," it is important to weigh the broader social and historical contexts and to understand the overall incidence of use before the severity of the problem can be fully and accurately assessed. Distorted information and perceptions too often lead to fear and fear leads to bad policy decisions.

Halkitis, P.N., Parsons, J.T., & Stirratt, M.J. (2001). A double epidemic: Crystal methamphetamine drug use in relation to HIV transmission among gay men. *Journal of Homosexuality, 41*, 17–35.

Jacobs, A. (2006, February 21). Battling HIV where sex meets crystal meth. *New York Times*.

Maxwell, J.C., & Rutkowski, B.A. (2008). The prevalence of methamphetamine and amphetamine abuse in North America: A review of indicators, 1992–2007. *Drug & Alcohol Review, 27*, 229–235.

Nieves, E. (2001, May 13). Drug labs in valley hideouts feed nation's habit. *New York Times*, A1.

Office of National Drug Control Policy. (2010). *Methamphetamine trends in the United States: Fact Sheet.* Washington, DC: Author. Available at: http://www.whitehousedrugpolicy.gov/publications/html/pseudoephedrine.html.

Sheff, N. (2009). *Tweak: Growing up on methamphetamines*. New York: Atheneum Books.

Rowaniak, S. (2009). Safe sex fatigue, treatment optimism, and serosorting: New challenges to HIV prevention among men who have sex with men. *Journal of the Association of Nurses in AIDS Care, 20*, 31–38.

Weisheit, R., & White, W.L. (2009). *Methamphetamine: Its history, pharmacology, and treatment*. Center City, MN: Hazeldon.

On the Internet

An Associated Press story on the new, "shake-and-bake" method of producing methamphetamine is available at: http://www.msnbc.msn.com/id/32542373/ns/us_news-crime_and_courts/t/new-meth-formula-avoids-anti-drug-laws/#.Tme9nE9LeS4.

The federal government maintains a website with information on methamphetamine prevention and treatment programs and policy at: http://methresources.gov.

Information on the Combat Methamphetamine Act of 2005 including the full text of the act as well as explanatory information about the act's provisions is available at the DEA website at: http://www.deadiversion.usdoj.gov/meth/index.html.

Lifelube is a website devoted to promoting health among gay and bisexual men. It includes information on HIV prevention as well as substance use and abuse in the LGBT community in the context of a holistic framework. Information and resources related specifically to crystal meth use among gay men are available at: http://www.lifelube.org/crystal.php.

The Montana Meth Project is a somewhat controversial campaign to prevent teenagers from using methamphetamine through the use of very graphic and disturbing images showing the drug's effects. Ads featured in the campaign as well as information on methamphetamine are available at their website: http://www.montanameth.org/

The PBS series *Frontline* did an episode titled "The Meth Epidemic" that can be viewed in its entirety along with supporting information on methamphetamine at: http://www.pbs.org/wgbh/pages/frontline/meth/

"It's All Rather Irrelevant"

- ***Document:*** War on Drugs: Report of the Global Commission on Drug Policy
- ***Date:*** June 2011
- ***Where:*** The world but mainly the United States
- ***Significance:*** The "War on Drugs" was first officially declared in June 1971 by President Richard Nixon. Befitting its status as the world's sole superpower, the United States has been influential in how that war has been waged internationally. The effort has been marked by a heavy reliance on the criminal justice system, tough legal sanctions, interdiction at the borders, and crop eradication in source countries. To a far lesser extent, there has been support for treatment, prevention, and rehabilitation. European countries have mostly followed the lead of the United States but have been more liberal with respect to their implementation of harm reduction measures such as needle exchange programs, supervised injection sites, prescription heroin, and the decriminalization of marijuana.

The following report issued by the Global Commission on Drug Policy on the anniversary of Nixon's declaration is highly critical of U.S. and international policies. It cites a number of statistics to support its contention that the punitive emphasis of drug policy has been a failure, causing more harm than good and recommends policy changes. Through the Office of National Drug Control Policy (ONDCP), the U.S. issued a terse press release to rebut the report's findings. The following excerpt is from the Executive Summary of the Commission's report. The ONDCP rebuttal is considered in the analysis.

DOCUMENT

Executive Summary

The global war on drugs has failed, with devastating consequences for individuals and societies around the world. Fifty years later the initiation of the UN Single Convention on Narcotic Drugs, and 40 years after President Nixon launched the US government's war on drugs, fundamental reforms in national and global drug control policies are urgently needed.

Vast expenditures on criminalization and repressive measures directed at producers, traffickers and consumers of illegal drugs have clearly failed to effectively curtail supply or consumption. Apparent victories in eliminating one source or trafficking organization are negated almost instantly by the emergence of other sources and traffickers. Repressive efforts directed at consumers impede public health measures to reduce HIV/AIDS, overdose fatalities and other harmful consequences of drug use. Government expenditures on futile supply reduction strategies and incarceration displace more cost-effective and evidence-based investments in demand and harm reduction.

Our principles and recommendations can be summarized as follows:

End the criminalization, marginalization, and stigmatization of people who use drugs but who do no harm to others. Challenge rather than reinforce common misconceptions about drug markets, drug use and drug dependence.

Encourage experimentation by governments with models of legal regulation of drugs to undermine the power of organized crime and safeguard the health and security of their citizens. This recommendation applies especially to cannabis, but we also encourage other experiments in decriminalization and legal regulation that can accomplish these objectives and provide models for others.

Offer health and treatment services to those in need. Ensure that a variety of treatment modalities are available, including not just methadone and buprenorphine treatment but also the

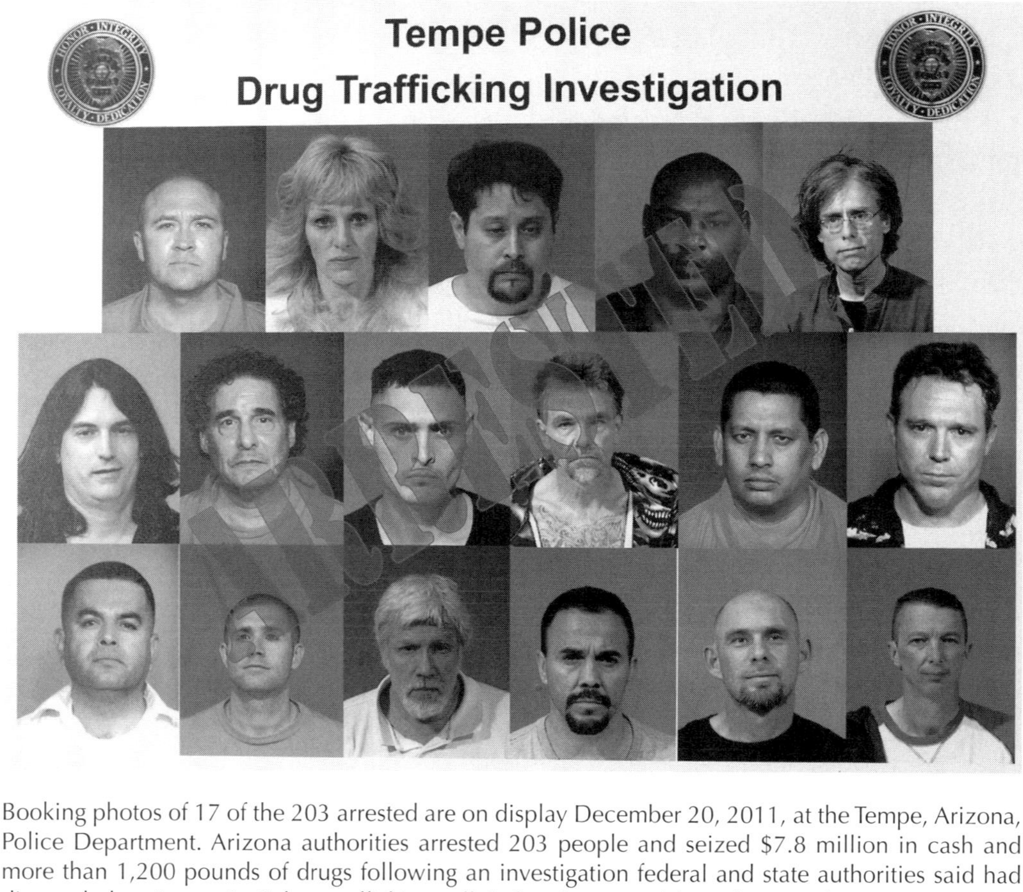

Booking photos of 17 of the 203 arrested are on display December 20, 2011, at the Tempe, Arizona, Police Department. Arizona authorities arrested 203 people and seized $7.8 million in cash and more than 1,200 pounds of drugs following an investigation federal and state authorities said had dismantled an "extensive" drug-trafficking cell tied to the powerful Sinaloa cartel. However, as with similar high-profile raids conducted almost routinely since the 1930s and with similar fanfare, such efforts have done little to stem the massive flow of drugs into the United States. (AP/Wide World Photos)

heroin-assisted treatment programs that have proven successful in many European countries and Canada. Implement syringe access and other harm reduction measures that have proven effective in reducing transmission of HIV and other blood-borne infections as well as fatal overdoses. Respect the human rights of people who use drugs. Abolish abusive practices carried out in the name of treatment—such as forced detention, forced labor, and physical or psychological abuse—that contravene human rights standards and norms or that remove the right to self-determination.

Apply much the same principles and policies stated above to people involved in the lower ends of illegal drug markets, such as farmers, couriers and petty sellers. Many are themselves victims of violence and intimidation or are drug dependent. Arresting and incarcerating tens of millions of these people in recent decades has filled prisons and destroyed lives and families without reducing the availability of illicit drugs or the power of criminal organizations. There appears to be almost no limit to the number of people willing to engage in such activities to better their lives, provide for their families, or otherwise escape poverty. Drug control resources are better directed elsewhere.

Invest in activities that can both prevent young people from taking drugs in the first place and also prevent those who do use drugs from developing more serious problems. Eschew simplistic "just say no" messages and "zero tolerance" policies in favor of educational efforts grounded in credible information and prevention programs that focus on social skills and peer influences. The most successful prevention efforts may be those targeted at specific at-risk groups.

Focus repressive actions on violent criminal organizations, but do so in ways that undermine their power and reach while prioritizing the reduction of violence and intimidation. Law enforcement efforts should focus not on reducing drug markets per se but rather on reducing their harms to individuals, communities and national security.

Begin the transformation of the global drug prohibition regime. Replace drug policies and strategies driven by ideology and political convenience with fiscally responsible policies and strategies grounded in science, health, security and human rights—and adopt appropriate criteria for their evaluation. Review the scheduling of drugs that has resulted in obvious anomalies like the flawed categorization of cannabis, coca leaf and MDMA. Ensure that the international conventions are interpreted and/or revised to accommodate robust experimentation with harm reduction, decriminalization and legal regulatory policies.

Break the taboo on debate and reform. The time for action is now.

SOURCE: War on Drugs: Report of the Global Commission on Drug Policy. Rio de Janeiro: Global Commission on Drug Policy. June 2011. Available at http://www.globalcommissionondrugs.org/Report.

ANALYSIS

Prohibitions are always enacted by US to govern the conduct of THEM.

—Charles H. Whitebread II

Nixon probably never anticipated that his proclamation of a war on drugs would be among the most lasting legacies of his presidency. In what has become something of an annual ritual, opponents of America's drug policies—and there are many both domestically and internationally—use the anniversary to proclaim that the policy has been a failure. Although Nixon's proclamation may have made the emphasis of drug policy on enforcement explicit, that emphasis has been the norm for far longer than 40 years and dates back to at least 1914 with the passage of the Harrison Stamp Tax. Thus, America's drug war whereby drug use has been treated more as a criminal matter rather than a public health problem—excepting a very brief period in the 1960s and 1970s—is arguably nearing its 100-year anniversary. No one is breaking out the champagne just yet.

The excerpted report of the Global Commission on Drug Policy is but one of many critiques of current policy that could have been cited. Numerous books have been devoted to the topic and the list is growing. Those who oppose America's current policy recommend changes that run the gamut from the outright legalization of drugs to the more measured recommendations contained in the Global Commission Report such as greater flexibility to experiment with new treatment and harm reduction approaches and a de-emphasis though not complete abandonment of law enforcement and interdiction.

Proponents of the current policies—and there are many of those as well—argue that moving away from law enforcement will lead to increases in supply and demand and to corresponding surges in use and crime for any drug that is decriminalized or depenalized. They support treatment and prevention but not at the expense of law enforcement. For them, expansion of treatment within the criminal justice system for those already arrested and convicted represents an acceptable compromise. But those same proponents, in defending the status quo, have to walk a delicate balance between arguing that current policies are working to suppress use while at the same time making the case for renewed or additional funding because drugs remain plentiful or portraying the next horrendous drug threat is imminent despite current efforts.

This is the same balancing act Harry Anslinger successfully maintained during his 30 years in office as the first drug czar. He had to argue that on the one hand, his federal agency were doing a wonderful job reducing crime and preventing America's youth from falling prey to unscrupulous and unsavory characters (i.e., most often drug-using racial and ethnic minorities) with designs on seducing the young (and women) into drug use and all manner of other depravities. On the other hand, in order to continue this good work, Congress must appropriate more money because drug use is again on the rise despite our best efforts and unless we get more resources we could experience a new drug epidemic the likes of which we have not seen before.

This politically effective but logically inconsistent strategy—we're doing so well that we need more money to stop all the bad things that are nonetheless happening from spinning further out of control—worked then and continues to work now. Anslinger had the benefit of controlling the statistics on drug use so the data presented (to the extent any data were presented) supported whatever side of the case he needed to make. But selective use of data to emphasize either the success of current policy or the need for additional funding to deal with a looming crisis has been honed to a fine art in the present day. A case in point is the ONDCP's immediate response to the Global Commission's Report via a relatively brief press release. Excerpts of the main points of the response follow and are italicized. They are followed by comments and analysis to show how the response to the Global Commissions critique selectively uses data to support its rebuttal:

Overall drug use in the United States has dropped substantially over the past 30 years, with the number of Americans using illicit drugs today at half the rate it was in the late 70s.

As described in the sections above that cover the 1970s, drug use had broad cultural acceptance at the time. The long decline in use that began in 1979–1980 started well before the punitive legal sanctions that frame current drug policy (1986) were put into place and had more to do with a cultural shift in perceptions of drugs than with policy change. Measured against the point in time at which drug use peaked in the modern era, any other subsequent point shows a decline. Moreover, using overall illicit drug use, which is predominantly driven by marijuana use, masks the fact that use of other illicit drugs has waxed and waned and that there was a significant rebound in the use of most illicit drugs including marijuana beginning in the 1990s despite the huge number of arrests and incarcerations. The response makes it seem as if it has been a smooth sustained decline maintained by current policy. The emphasis on illicit drugs also fails to account for the current surge in the illegal use of prescription drugs.

According to the latest UN World Drug Report (2010) "Demand for cocaine in the U.S. has been in long-term decline."

This is true but the supply of cocaine remains plentiful despite drops in production in Colombia and decreased demand in the United States. In fact, part of the decline in cocaine use in the United States is due to Colombian traffickers giving greater emphasis to European markets, which were more lucrative because of the higher monetary value of the Euro. The entitling quote for this section is from a government employee asked to estimate the number of hectares (i.e., about 1 hectare equals 2.5 acres) of cocaine crops eliminated by current eradication efforts. Declining to give a precise response, he noted that it was "it's all irrelevant anyway" because there was so much cocaine available that even with the significant reduction in crops, the remaining supply was more than enough to meet United States and world demand.

Drugs go in and out of popularity, as has been the case with cocaine, which virtually disappeared between the 1930s and 1970s. The changes in popularity usually have little to do with official policy and more with cultural trends and the public's perception of a drug. History suggests cocaine or another stimulant will rebound in popularity again and be in demand.

Note too that the ONDCP response focuses on one drug, cocaine, but is mute about all others and for good reason. The demand for and availability of other illicit drugs in the United States remain high. Per the DEA's 2011 threat assessment: "The overall availability of illicit drugs in the United States is increasing." The 2010 National Survey on Drug Use and Health found that 22.6 million Americans (8.9% of the population) had used an illicit drug in the past month, higher than the rates from 2002 through 2008. These more comprehensive statistics are hardly a ringing endorsement of the effectiveness of current policies and it is clear the administration chose to emphasize the one illegal drug where there has been a recent decline and to ignore other drugs. The ONDCP is certainly aware of these statistics but chose not to represent them in its response.

The President's inaugural Drug Control Strategy—released one year ago—is a marked departure from previous approaches to drug policy. The Strategy focuses on both the public health and public safety aspects of drug abuse and addiction. It focuses on addiction as a disease and on the importance of preventing drug use, as well as providing treatment to those who need it, including those who are involved in the criminal justice system. For the *first time, it emphasizes support for millions of individuals who are in recovery from drug addiction. The President's Budget, dedicates over $10 billion in Federal funds for reducing drug consumption in the United States.*

The 2011 and 2012 ONDCP budgets request an allocation of 60 percent for enforcement and interdiction and 40 percent for treatment and prevention. This is slightly more balanced than 70 percent/30 percent splits in the past but the emphasis is still on enforcement/interdiction despite the language that supports treatment and prevention. Virtually every administration, regardless of the emphasis on supply reduction, has publicly supported demand reduction. It's just that the money has not followed the public pronouncements. It still doesn't. The 2012 budget request increases funding for enforcement while maintaining treatment and prevention dollars at 2011 levels.

Legalization remains a non-starter in the Obama Administration because research shows that illegal drug use is associated with voluntary treatment admissions, fatal drugged driving accidents, mental illness, and emergency room admissions.

This response makes it appear as if the Global Commission Report suggests outright legalization is the only way to change current policy. Decriminalization can mean a lessening of criminal sanctions (depenalization is the more accurate term) short of full legalization. But the report also suggests other measures that can be taken such as making a variety of treatment programs more available and being open to at least studying options such as heroin-assisted treatment and syringe exchange programs. The ONDCP response ignores these other recommendations, perhaps in an attempt to marginalize the report by making its recommendations seem more extreme than they are.

An independent 2010 study from RAND concluded that "legalizing marijuana in California will not dramatically reduce the drug revenues collected by Mexican drug trafficking organizations from sales to the United States," We also know that these groups produce and traffic methamphetamine and heroin, continue to move significant amounts of cocaine, and conduct an array of criminal activities including kidnapping, extortion, and human trafficking . . . illicit "product lines" will not result in their disbanding their criminal organizations.

This point references California's 2010 attempt to fully legalize marijuana via a ballot initiative known as Proposition 19. More than 60 percent of the voters voted down the initiative. The RAND study might be correct regarding the effects of full legalization of marijuana on the profits of the Mexican cartels. But rescheduling marijuana to allow for research into its potential medical benefits is not the same as full legalization. The main argument for medical marijuana is not to put the Mexican cartels out of business. It is to make available a drug that might have legitimate medical benefits to people who need it. The report is ambiguous in its language and the ONDCP response exploited that ambiguity by only considering the consequences of full legalization and failing to address the consequences of the less extreme step of medical marijuana. The response is also curious for the fact that it tacitly admits to the continuing success of Mexican traffickers in light of current policy.

The United States has been clear that we cannot arrest our way out of the drug problem. In August 2010, the President signed the fair sentencing act which reduces the disparity in the amounts of powder cocaine and crack cocaine required for the imposition of mandatory minimum sentences and eliminates the mandatory minimum sentence for simple possession of crack cocaine.

The fair sentencing act reduced but did not eliminate sentencing disparities and maintained long mandatory minimum sentences for many illicit drugs including marijuana. While the change in the law may reduce the racial disparities in the incarceration rates for drug violations of federal law, it will do little to reduce the overall number of such incarcerations in federal prisons. It is heartening, however, to see ONDCP acknowledge that we cannot arrest our way out of the drug problem. Simple numbers support that. There are about 2 million people in jails and prisons in the United States. Given the data from the just cited NSDUH report that 22.6 million people used an illicit drug in the past year, even arresting half of them would mean increasing the number of prisons five-fold. The ONDCP response should have gone further, however, to state that we cannot arrest, incarcerate, eradicate, or interdict our way out of the problem. Until we can reduce the demand for drugs, they will continue to flow into the country and people will continue to use them.

Unfortunately, it does not appear we can treat our way out of the problem either. Treatment and prevention are not panaceas, at least not as currently practiced. Prevention efforts have only had marginal, short-lived effects at best. Popular programs such as DARE have been repeatedly assessed as having almost no effect and yet continue to receive funding because they are politically popular. Treatment can be effective for some, but it is still not very effective for many despite advances in evidence-based practices. Whereas addiction has been recognized as a chronic, relapsing disease, programs continue to provide treatment only for the short term. There has been recent research on providing long-term, ongoing case management and other treatment services but in an environment where even minimal treatment is scarce, the likelihood of programs that include such long-term care happening any time soon is very low.

One estimate suggests that if we could provide treatment on demand, given current effectiveness levels, it would cut the number of drug users by well less than half (see the paper by Reuter and Pollack in Further Reading). Even so, this would be a large improvement over the current situation. Treatment is less expensive and more effective than incarceration and criminal sanctions for reducing both crime and drug use for which there is little evidence of effectiveness beyond incapacitation. The inflexibility of present policy—one of the points in the Global Commission Report ignored by ONDCP—insures the continued underutilization of less mainstream but potentially effective harm-reduction treatments such as methadone and buprenorphine. The recent lifting of the ban on syringe exchange programs provides a glimmer of hope that such programs will be more fully funded and expanded in the near future. But heroin-substitution treatment or supervised injection sites will not be implemented any time soon in the United States as is being done in some European countries and Canada.

Treatment in the United States is grossly underfunded and far less available than the demand. Many who would benefit from treatment simply do not have access. This is true even accounting for the high numbers of people addicted to drugs that do not think they have a problem and who would not enter treatment even if it were available and accessible. Another consequence of the underfunding is that the treatment that does exist is often poorly implemented. Underpaid, undertrained, and underqualified staff churns in and out of programs making it hard to provide or maintain quality services. Programs pay lip service to providing the latest, scientifically based treatment model such as cognitive-behavioral therapy but what happens in reality due to staffing and supervisory problems is far from the prescribed model. Many programs continue to operate as therapeutic procrustean beds; one size fits all regardless of the clinical presentation or personal preferences of the clients.

There has been and continues to be a glaring lack of continuity for people moving from one phase of treatment to another such as from a residential program or halfway house to outpatient treatment. People returning to the community who receive treatment while in prison (the fortunate few) are challenged to find housing, training, and employment as they face *invisible sanctions* that continue to work against them on release. They return to communities with few employment options and high levels of drug use and availability making relapse and re-incarceration all but certain. Opponents of current policy argue all of these impediments are direct consequences of the punitive, law enforcement emphasis.

Programs are not held fully accountable for outcomes, which are poorly monitored and not tied to funding, making improvement difficult for lack of an incentive and no yardstick against which to measure progress. Still, treatment advocates are constantly being asked to demonstrate their programs are effective while criminal justice advocates almost never are. This double standard has worked against treatment improvement as well because advocates are rightly concerned that publicly admitting problems, ineffectiveness, and areas for improvement could easily be used as arguments for defunding treatment.

Instead, in place of a public, honest, dialog about the limitations of treatment and how these should best be addressed or consideration of new strategies, professional conferences of treatment providers intended for the exchange of scientific information and best practices too often take on the tenor of an Amway rally. Speeches by successful entrepreneurs, exhortations to sell more product, and promises of imminent wealth are replaced by emotion-laden speeches from carefully selected successful treatment clients who are now counselors, self-congratulatory reminders that *treatment works*, and whooping cheers by the audience all in the interest of maintaining the *esprit de corps* in what otherwise has been a very dispiriting time. Who can blame them for wanting some positive news? They've been defending the castle walls for more than 60 years (see the sidebar on Alfred Lindesmith).

Without the resources to fund research and to provide better education and staffing to treatment programs and without the ability to have an open dialog for fear of political reprisal, there is little reason for optimism that substantial improvements in treatment effectiveness can be achieved. The current lingering recession whereby states have begun cutting social safety net programs such as Medicaid, which funds at least minimal treatment, and with the conversation in Washington turning to *how* not *if* there should be additional cuts in other safety net programs there is even less likelihood the drug treatment system will be maintained at present levels let alone expanded and improved.

Cementing the whole system in place is the fact that there is little upside and considerable downside for politicians to reduce or eliminate criminal sanctions, the recent decrease in sentencing disparities being a rare counter-example. Fear and indignation are more potent motivators at election time than feel-good gestures such as proposing more treatment for people with addictions. This is especially true when many in the general public are losing their jobs and along with them their health insurance coverage. The most politically expedient solution to a perceived new drug threat continues to be proposing tough new sanctions and stepped up interdiction. In a 1995 speech to the California Judge's Association on the history of the non-medical use of drugs in the United States, Charles Whitebread summed it up about right:

> . . . we love this idea of prohibitions, we can't live without them. They are our very favorite thing because we know how to solve difficult, social, economic, and medical problems—a new criminal law with harsher penalties in every category for everybody.

If the history of drug policy teaches us anything, however, it should be that law enforcement has never been and never will be either an effective or efficient solution for controlling drug use. Criminal sanctions may suppress use by the ambivalent to an extent but they do not deter determined users no matter how tough the laws. If they did, New York State would have been drug free following passage of the Rockefeller Drug Laws. It wasn't. Not even close. Americans would have been blissfully dry and working hard following Prohibition. They weren't. Although overall alcohol consumption was down, many Americans continued to flock to the rapidly proliferating speakeasies. And with a few brief exceptions, interdiction has done little to reduce the flow of drugs into the country. There will always be new fields to plant to replace the ones that have been eradicated. Sealing the U.S. border is simply impossible. Make one precursor drug illegal, a good chemist will find a new process that uses a different one.

Forty years into the declared war on drugs and nearly 100 years into the unofficial war on drugs, virtually anyone in America who wants any drug and has cash on hand can get it with relative ease. High-tech surveillance methods, crop eradication, stepped-up interdiction, and jails and prisons filled with drug users and dealers have not changed this simple fact. Mention of the continuing ample supply of illicit drugs was notably absent from ONDCP's response to the Global Commission's Report but is clearly present in the 2011 DEA Threat Assessment Report. The bottom line appears to be that as long as people want to use drugs to feel good, to relax, to forget, to feel more attractive, to withdraw, to enhance sex, to join with friends who do drugs, or to at least feel a little less bad—as they always have—there will be people with the chutzpah, know-how, and willingness to enrich themselves by

SYNTHETIC CANNABIS ("K2/SPICE") AND "BATH SALTS"

Within the past few years, in an effort to circumvent existing laws, a number of new drugs packaged as harmless household products have hit the market via the Internet or sold in "head shops." One such drug, known as K2 or Spice, consists of dried leaves of various plants that have been sprayed with synthetic designer cannabinoids. The synthetics are chemically dissimilar enough to the main active ingredient in marijuana that existing law did not cover them. The synthetic cannabinoids consist of an alphabet soup of different drugs, any and all of which might be in a single packet of K2/Spice: HU-210, HU-211, JWH-018, and JWH-073. Sometimes marketed as fake weed, the product is sold in small packages carefully labeled to caution against human consumption. The labeling is simply a ploy to get around existing drug laws, which do not regulate nonconsumable products. But the drugs are indeed consumed by humans and have effects similar to marijuana. Because of the varying composition, K2/Spice can cause unpredictable results such as paranoia, panic attacks, and hallucinations. On March 1, 2011, the DEA used emergency provisions of the Controlled Substances Act to place the most common synthetic cannabinoids in K2/Spice on Schedule I, making their use illegal for 12 months thereafter with the provision to extend the ban for an additional 6 months.

Bath salts are synthetic stimulants derived from cathinone, the active chemical and a mild stimulant found in khat, a flowering plant that grows in East Africa and the Arabian Peninsula. Cathinone is a Schedule I drug in the United States but is legal in some other countries. The DEA reports the most common synthetics found in products marketed as bath salts are Mephedrone and MDPV and believes that the drugs are manufactured in India and China. Bath salts are also sold in small foil packets and are also labeled as not being for human consumption. Humans consume these drugs too and bath salts can be snorted, smoked, or injected. They have effects similar to cocaine or amphetamine but again, because these drugs are unregulated, the composition can vary and there are reports in the press of users showing up with symptoms of violent agitation and paranoia, similar to an amphetamine or PCP-induced psychosis. Mephedrone is an analog of cathinone and as such, is a Schedule I drug with use prohibited in the United States. But MDPV is currently not scheduled. To date, the DEA has not moved to temporarily ban MDPV. Presently, 28 states have banned baths salts.

supplying drugs. The list is long and growing. It includes a rogues gallery, some of whom have been discussed in this book: Al Capone, Lucky Luciano, Max Jacobson, Griselda Blanco, Carlos Lehder, and Pablo Escobar. And should the illicit drug traffickers falter for one reason or another or be defeated, causing a temporary disruption in supply, a compensatory supply of well-advertised, aggressively marketed, and readily diverted pharmaceuticals are available to fill the void.

AMY WINEHOUSE—"DIVA WITH DEMONS"

Amy Jade Winehouse, whose well-publicized struggles with drug and alcohol addiction brought her considerable notoriety to go along with her rapid rise to fame, is the most recent inductee to the "27 Club"; a group of influential musicians who all happened to die at age 27. She joins, among others, Jimi Hendrix, Jim Morrison, Janis Joplin, Brian Jones, and Kurt Cobain. A recent tribute article in *Rolling Stone* describes Winehouse as a "diva with demons" noting both her considerable musical talent as well as her penchant for self-destructive behavior that centered on alcoholism and drug abuse over the course of her short adult life.

Blending the music of the 1960s with both jazz and hip-hop influences, Winehouse achieved her greatest success with the album *Back to Black,* released in the UK in 2006. The album brought her international fame and multiple Grammy Awards in 2008 including Best Female Pop Vocal Performance, Record of the Year, and Song of the Year for her hit single, "Rehab." The lyrics of "Rehab," now redolent with irony given her ensuing battles with alcohol and drugs, describe her resistance to going into treatment for alcoholism as reflected in the refrain: "They tried to make me go to rehab and I said 'no, no, no'."

Her relationship with, marriage to, separation from, reconciliation with, divorce from, and continuing contact with Blake Fielder-Civil, a high-school dropout, a sometime music video production assistant, a sometime petty crook, and a full-time drug addict, contributed heavily to her self-destructive tendencies. Their very public *folie à deux* included protestations of their sincere love for one another, domestic violence, incidents of violent behavior towards others, and lots of drugs. Fielder-Civil introduced her to hard drugs including ecstasy, crack cocaine, ketamine, and heroin. Through it all heavy drinking was a near constant in Winehouse's life.

The nadir came on June 18, 2011, in Belgrade, Serbia, the first date of a European tour scheduled for 12 dates. Drunk and unable to perform, Winehouse was booed

(continued)

FURTHER READING

Babor, T., Caulkins, J., Edwards, G. et al. (2010). *Drug policy and the public good.* New York: Oxford University Press.

Bayer, R. (1991). The great drug policy debate—What means this thing called decriminalization? *The Milbank Quarterly,* 69, 341–363.

Bull, S. (2011, July 26). Amy Winehouse, 27, found dead at her London flat after suspected "drug overdose." *Mail Online.* http://www.dailymail.co.uk/tvshowbiz/article-2018020/Amy-Winehouse-dead-London-flat-drug-overdose.html.

Dermota, K. (2007, July/August). Snow fall. *The Atlantic Monthly.* http://www.theatlantic.com/magazine/archive/2007/07/snow-fall/5966/

Eliscu, J. (,)2007 June. Amy Winehouse. *Rolling Stone* (1028), 44–47.

Kleiman, M.A.R., Caulkins, J. P., & Hawken, A. (2011). *Drugs and drug policy: What everyone needs to know.* New York: Oxford University Press.

Kristof, N. (2009, June 13). Drugs won the war. *The New York Times,* Available at: http://www.nytimes.com/2009/06/14/opinion/14kristof.html.

MacCoun, R. J. (1993). Drugs and the law: A psychological analysis of drug prohibition. *Psychological Bulletin, 113,* 497–512.

MacCoun, R. J., & Reuter, P. (2001). *Drug war heresies: Learning from other vices, times, & places.* New York: Cambridge University Press.

McLellan A. T. (2006). What we need is a system: Creating a responsive and effective substance abuse treatment system. In: Miller, W.R., & Carroll, K.M. (Eds.) *Rethinking substance abuse: What the science shows, and what we should do about it* (pp. 275–292). New York: Guilford Press.

Reuter, P., & Pollack, H. (2006). How much can treatment reduce national drug problems. *Addiction, 101,* 341–347.

Room, R. (2003). Rethinking alcohol, tobacco and other drug control. *Addiction,* 98, 713–716.

Zimring, F. E., & Hawkins, G. (1995). *The search for rational drug control.* New York: Cambridge University Press.

Weatherburn, D. (2009). Dilemmas in harm minimization. *Addiction,104,* 335–339.

On the Internet

A copy of the full report of the Global Commission on Drugs as well as more information about the organization is available at: http://www.globalcommissionondrugs.org.

Text of the rebuttal of the Office of National Drug Control Policy Director's response to the Global Commission's report is available at: http://ofsubstance.gov/blogs/pushing_back/archive/2011/06/02/51896.aspx.

A copy of the full report *New Information on Counternarcotics in South America* by the United States Senate Committee on Homeland Security & Governmental Affairs Subcommittee on Contracting Oversight is available at: http://mccaskill.senate.gov/files/documents/pdf/CNReportFINAL.pdf.

The U.S. Department of Justice's National Drug Intelligence Center National Drug Threat Assessment Report for 2010 is available at: http://www.justice.gov/ndic/pubs38/38661/index.htm.

AMY WINEHOUSE— "DIVA WITH DEMONS"

(continued)

off the stage but not before she managed to throw a shoe at the audience. When a video of the disastrous performance hit the Internet and went viral, the rest of the tour was suddenly canceled.

A little over one month later, Winehouse was found dead in her apartment. Her adamant refusals in the song "Rehab" to the contrary, she did enter alcohol and drug treatment programs on several occasions and had reportedly stopped using all drugs—except for alcohol—for some time. A final autopsy report issued in October 2011 gave the cause of death as acute alcohol poisoning brought on when, after a sustained period of abstinence, Winehouse suddenly resumed drinking heavily.

BIBLIOGRAPHY

Acker, C. J. *Creating the American junkie: Addiction research in the classic era.* Baltimore, MD: Johns Hopkins University Press, 2002.

Acker, C. J. The early years of the PHS narcotic hospital at Lexington, Kentucky. *Public Health Reports, 112,* 245–247, 1997.

Adler, W. M. *One family's quest for the American dream in the age of crack.* New York: Penguin Group, 1996.

Allen, F. L. *Only yesterday: An informal history of the 1920s.* New York: Harper Collins, 2000.

Altmam, L. K. New homosexual disorder worries health officials. *The New York Times,* C1, May 11, 1982.

Angell, M. *The truth about the drug companies: How they deceive us and what to do about it.* New York: Random House, 2006.

Anslinger, H. J., & Ousler, W. *The murderers: The shocking story of the narcotics gangs.* New York: Farrar, Strauss, and Dudahy, 1963.

Anthony, G. *The summer of love: Haight-Ashbury at its highest.* San Francisco, CA: Last Gasp, 1995.

Antonowicz, A. Woman with the golden gun; America's evil drugs godmother . . . true-life face of the film *Traffic. The Mirror, Section 1,* 24–25, January 30, 2001.

Asbridge, M., & Weerasignhe, S. Homicide in Chicago from 1890 to 1930: Prohibition and its impact on alcohol and non-alcohol-related homicides. *Addiction, 104,* 355–364, 2009.

Auerbach, D. M., Darrow, W. W., Jaffe, H. W., & Curran, J. W. Cluster of cases of the acquired immunodeficiency syndrome. Patients linked by sexual contact. *American Journal of Medicine, 76,* 487–492, 2009.

Babor, T., Caulkins, J., Edwards, G., et al. *Drug policy and the public good.* New York: Oxford University Press, 2010.

Ball, J. C., Thompson, W. O., Allen, D. M. Readmission rates at Lexington Hospital for 43,215 narcotic drug addicts. *Public Health Reports,* 85, 610–616, 1970.

Baum, D. *Smoke and mirrors: The war on drugs and the politics of failure, 1st edition.* New York: Little, Brown, and Company, 1996.

Bayer, R. The great drug policy debate—What means this thing called decriminalization? *The Milbank Quarterly*, 69, 341–363, 1991.

Beaver, A. L. Getting a fix on cocaine sentencing policy: Reforming the sentencing scheme of the Anti-Drug Abuse Act of 1986. *Fordham Law Review, 78*, 2531–2575, 2010.

Beck, J. 100 years of "Just Say No" versus "Just Say Know": Reevaluating drug education goals for the coming century. *Evaluation Review, 22*, 15–45, 1998.

Belair, F. Drug drive opens at Mexico border. *The New York Times*, A1, p. 39, September 22, 1969.

Berger, M. Tea for a viper. *The New Yorker*, 36–48, March 12, 1969.

Bergreen, L. *Capone: The man and the era*. New York: Simon & Schuster, 1994.

Blocker, J. S. Did prohibition really work? Alcohol prohibition as a public health innovation. *American Journal of Public Health*, 96, 233–243, 2006.

Bonnie, R. J., & Whitebread, C. H. The forbidden fruit and the tree of knowledge: An inquiry into the legal history of American marijuana prohibition. *Virginia Law Review*, 56, 1052–1063, 1970.

Bonnie, R. J. & Whitebread, C. H. *The marihuana conviction: A history of marihuana prohibition in the United States*. Charlottesville, VA: University Press of Virginia, 1974.

Boodman, S. G. HHS AIDS brochure: Frank, explicit, and ready to be mailed. *The Washington Post*, A21, May 5, 1988.

Bourgois, P. *In search of respect: Selling crack in El Barrio*. New York: Cambridge University Press, 2003.

Bowden, M. *Doctor dealer: The rise and fall of an All-American boy and his multimillion-dollar cocaine empire*. New York: Grove Press, 2001.

Breyer, C., Malinowska-Sempruch, K., Kamarulzaman, A., & Strathdee, S. A. 12Myths about HIV/AIDS and people who use drugs. *Lancet*, *376*, 208–210, 2010.

Bromberg, W. Marihuana intoxication: A clinical study of Cannabis Sativa intoxication. *American Journal of Psychiatry*, *91*, 303–330, 1934.

Brown, C. *Manchild in the promised land*. New York: Simon & Shuster, 1999.

Bull, S. Amy Winehouse, 27, found dead at her London flat after suspected "drug overdose." *Mail Online*. Retrieved from http://www.dailymail.co.uk/tvshowbiz/article-2018020/Amy-Winehouse-dead-London-flat-drug-overdose.html, July 26, 2011.

Burns, E. *Spirits of America: A social history of alcohol*. Philadelphia, PA: Temple University Press, 2004.

Burroughs, W. S. *Junky: The definitive text of "junk," 50th Anniversary Edition*. New York: Penguin Books, 2003.

Burroughs, W. S. *Naked lunch*. New York: Grove Press, 1990.

Byck, R. (Ed.). *Cocaine papers: Sigmund Freud*. New York: Stonehill Publishing Co., 1974.

Campbell, H. *Drug war zone: Frontline dispatches from the streets of El Paso and Juárez*. Austin, TX: University of Texas Press, 2009.

Campbell, N. D. A "new deal" for the drug addict: The addiction research center, Lexington, Kentucky. *Journal of the History of Behavioral Sciences*, *42*, 135–157, 2006.

Campbell, N. D., Olsen, J. P., & Walden, L. *The narcotic farm: The rise and fall of America's first prison for drug addicts*. New York: Abrams, 2008.

Carroll, R. The Narcotic Control Act triggers the great nondebate: Treatment loses to punishment. In: J. Erlen & J. E. Spillane (Eds.) *Federal drug control* (pp. 101–144). Binghamton, NY: Haworth Press, 2004.

Caulkins, J. P., Kilmer, B., Maccoun, R. J., Pacula, R. L., & Reuter, P. Design considerations for legalizing cannabis: Lessons inspired by analysis of California's Proposition 19. *Addiction* [Epub ahead of print], 2011.

Caulkins, J. P., Reuter, P., & Coulson, C. Basing drug scheduling decisions on scientific ranking of harmfulness: False promises from false premises. *Addiction, 106, 1886-1890*, 2011.

Centers for Disease Control. Syringe exchange programs—United States, 2008. *Morbidity and Mortality Weekly Report, 59*, 1488–1451, November 9, 2010.

Centers for Disease Control and Prevention. Acute public health consequences of methamphetamine laboratories—16 states, January 2000–June 2004. *Morbidity and Mortality Weekly, 54*, 356–359, April 15, 2005.

Chalk, P. *The Latin American drug trade: Scope, dimensions, impact, and response*. Santa Monica, CA: Rand Corporation, 2011.

Charters, A. *Beat down to your soul. What was the beat generation?* New York: Penguin Group, 2001.

Ciccarone, D. Heroin in brown, black and white: Structural factors and medical consequences in the US heroin market. *International Drug Policy, 20*, 277–282, 2009.

Cimino, K. *The politics of crystal meth: Gay men share stories of addiction and recovery.* Boca Raton, FL: Universal Publishers, 2005.

Claiborne, W.N.Y. drug crackdown called a failure. *Washington Post,* A3, June 21, 1977.

Clines, F. X., & Meier, B. Cancer painkillers pose new abuse threat. *The New York Times*, A1, February 9, 2001.

Cohen, P. J. Medical marijuana 2010: It's time to fix the regulatory vacuum. *Journal of Law, Medicine, & Ethics, 38*, 654–666, 2011.

Collins, T. R. Invasion of the pill mills in South Florida. *Time Magazine*, April 13, 2010. Retrieved from http://www.time.com/time/nation/article/0,8599,1981582,00.html.

Compton, W. M., & Volkow, N. D. Major increases in opioid analgesic abuse in the United States: Concerns and strategies. *Drug and Alcohol Dependence, 81*, 103–107, 2006.

Conant, E. Pot and the GOP. Is the party of "Just Say No" morphing into the part of "Just Say Grow"? *Newsweek Magazine*, p. 30, November 1, 2010.

Congressional Subcommittee on Criminal Justice, Drug Policy, and Human Resources. *Fighting meth in America's heartland: Assessing federal, state, and local efforts*. Washington, DC: U.S. Government Printing Office, June 27, 2005.

Cook, C. *Mexico's drug cartels: CRS report for Congress*. Washington, DC: Congressional Research Service, October 16, 2007.

Courtwright, D. T. *Dark paradise: A history of opiate addiction in America*. Cambridge, MA: Harvard University Press, 2001.

Courtwright, D. T. The Controlled Substances Act: How a "big tent" reform became a punitive drug law. *Drug and Alcohol Dependence, 76*, 9–15, 2004.

Courtwright, D. T. The roads to H: The emergence of the American heroin complex, 1898–1956. In: D. F. Musto (Ed.) *One hundred years of heroin* (pp. 43–54). Westport, CT: Greenwood Press, 2002.

Crittenden, A., & Ruby, M. Cocaine: The champagne of drugs. *The New York Times Magazine*, pp. 14–17, September 1, 1974.

Cunningham, J.K., Borjoquez, I., Campollo, O., Liu, L-M., & Maxwell, J.C. Mexico's methamphetamine precursor chemical interventions: Impacts on drug treatment admissions. *Addiction, 105*, 1973–1983, 2010.

Cunningham, J.K., & Lon-Miu, L. Impact of US and Canadian precursor regulation on methamphetamine purity in the United States. *Addiction, 104*, 441–453, 2009.

Dallek, R. *An unfinished life: Kennedy, 1917–1963*. New York: Back Bay Books, 2004.

Das, G. Cocaine abuse in North America. *Journal of Clinical Pharmacology, 33*, 296–301, 1993.

Degenhardt, L., Mathers, B., Vickerman, P., Rhodes, T., Latkin, C., & Hickman, M. Prevention of HIV infection for people who inject drugs: Why individual, structural, and combination approaches are needed. *Lancet, 376*, 285–301, 2010.

DeGrandpre, R. *The cult of pharmacology: How America became the world's most troubled drug nation*. Durham, NC: Duke University Press, 2006.

Dermota, K. Snow fall. *The Atlantic Monthly*. Retrieved from http://www.theatlantic.com/magazine/archive/2007/07/snow-fall/5966/, July/August, 2007.

Dole, V.P., & Nyswander, M.E. Heroin addiction—a metabolic disease. *Archives of Internal Medicine, 120*, 19–24, 1967.

Domoslawski, A. *Drug policy in Portugal: The benefits of decriminalizing drug use*. Warsaw, Poland: Open Society Foundation. Retrieved from http://www.soros.org/initiatives/drugpolicy, June 2011.

Dos Reis Jr., A. Sigmund Freud (1856–1939) and Karl Koller (1857–1944) and the discovery of local anesthesia. *Revista Brasilear de Anestesiologia, 59*, 244–257, 2009.

Dupont, R.L. Heroin addiction in the nation's capital, 1966–1973. In: D.F. Musto (Ed.) *One hundred years of heroin* (pp. 67–90). Westport, CT: Greenwood Publishing, 2002.

Duster, T. Pattern, purpose, and race in the drug war. In: C. Reinarman & H.G. Levine (Eds.) *Crack in America: Demon drugs and social justice* (pp. 260–287). Berkeley, CA: University of California Press, 1997.

Earlywine, M. *Understanding marijuana: A new look at the scientific evidence*. New York: Oxford University Press, 2005.

Eddy, P., Sabogal, H., & Walden, S. *The cocaine wars*. New York: Bantam Books, 1989.

Editorial: Marijuana Problems. *Journal of the American Medical Association, 127*, 1129, 1945.

Edwards, G. Seeing America—diary of a drug-focused study tour made in 1967. *Addiction, 105*, 984–990, 2010.

Edwards, J. Who signed off on Purdue's misleading OxyContin Chart? Judge may want answers. *CBS Interactive Network*. Retrieved from http://www.bnet.com/blog/drug-business/who-signed-off-on-purdues-misleading-oxycontin-chart-judge-may-want-answers/3832, January 7, 2010.

Egan, T. Meth building its hell's kitchen in rural America. *The New York Times*, A14, February 6, 2002.

Eliscu, J. Amy Winehouse. *Rolling Stone*, 44–47, August 18, 2011.

Engel, J. *The epidemic: A global history of AIDS*. Harper Collins e-book, 2006.

Feiling, T. *Cocaine nation: How the white trade took over the world*. New York: Pegasus Books, 2009.

Fergusson, D. M., Boden, J. M., & Horwood, J. Cannabis use and other illicit drug use: Testing the cannabis gateway hypothesis. *Addiction, 101*, 556–559, 2006.

Finnegan, W. Silver or lead; the drug cartel La Familia gives local officials a choice: Take a bribe or a bullet. *New Yorker Magazine*, May 31, 2010.

Fitzgerald, F. S. *The great Gatsby, reissue edition*. New York: Scribner, 2004.

Frank, G. *Judy*. New York: Da Capo Press, 1999.

Freud, S. Classics revisited: Über coca. *Journal of Substance Abuse Treatment, 1*, 205–217, 1984.

Friend, L. Heroes and heroin. *RIP Magazine*, July 1992.

Furek, M. *The death proclamation of Generation X: A self-fulfilling prophecy of goth, grunge, and heroin*. Bloomington, IN: iUniverse, 2008.

Galbis-Reig, D. Sigmund Freud and Carl Koller: The controversy surrounding the discovery of local anesthesia. *International Congress Series, 1242*, 571–575, 2003.

Galliher, J. F., Keys, D. P., & Elsner, M. Lindesmith v. Anslinger: An early government victory in the failed war on drugs. *Journal of Criminal Law and Criminology*, 88, 661–682, Winter, 1998.

Galliher, J. F., & Walker, A. "The puzzle of the social origins of the Marihuana Tax Act of 1937," *Journal of Social Problems, 24*, 367-376, 1977.

Gibler, J. *To die in Mexico: Dispatches from inside the drug war*. San Francisco, CA: City Lights Books, 2011.

Ginsberg, A. *Howl and other poems*. San Francisco, CA: City Light Pocket Poets, 2001.

Gitler, I. *Swing to bop: An oral history of the transition in jazz in the 1940s*. New York: Oxford University Press, 1987.

Glasser, I., & Siegel, L. "When Constitutional rights seem too extravagant to endure": The crack scare's impact on civil rights and liberties. In: C. Reinarman & H. G. Levine (Eds.) *Crack in America: Demon drugs and social justice* (pp. 229–248). Berkeley, CA: University of California Press, 1997.

Goldstein, P. The drugs/violence nexus: A tripartite conceptual framework. *Journal of Drug Issues, 39*, 143–174. Retrieved from http://www.drugpolicy.org/docUploads/nexus.pdf, 1985.

Gonzales, R., Mooney, L., & Rawson, R. A. The methamphetamine problem in the United States. *Annual Review of Public Health, 31*, 385–398, 2010.

Goodnough, A., & Zezima, K. An alarming new stimulant, legal in many states. *The New York Times*, July 16, 2011.

Grace, F. *Carry A. Nation: Retelling the life (Religion in North America)*. Bloomington, IN: Indiana University Press, 2001.

Grayson, G. W. *Mexico: Narco-violence and a failed state*. Piscataway, NJ: Transaction Publishers, 2009.

Greenwald, G. *Drug decriminalization in Portugal; lessons for creating fair and successful drug policies*. Washington, DC: The Cato Institute. Retrieved from http://www.cato.org/pub_display.php?pub_id = 10080, 2009.

Grim, R. *This is your country on drugs: The secret history of getting high in America*. Hoboken, NJ: John Wiley & Sons, 2009.

Gugliotta, G., & Leen, J. *Kings of cocaine: Inside the Medellin cartel—an astonishing true story of murder, money, and international corruption*. New York: Simon and Schuster, 1989.

Guralnick, P. *Careless love: The unmaking of Elvis Presley*. New York: Little, Brown, and Company, 1999.

Halberstam, D. *The fifties*. New York: Ballentine Books, 1994.

Halkitis, P.N., Parsons, J.T., & Stirratt, M.J. A double epidemic: Crystal methamphetamine drug use in relation to HIV transmission among gay men. *Journal of Homosexuality, 41*, 17–35, 2001.

Hall, W. What are the policy lessons of national alcohol prohibition in the United States, 1920–1933? *Addiction, 105*, 1164–1173, 2010.

Hall, W., & Lynskey, M. The challenges in developing a rational cannabis policy. *Current Opinion in Psychiatry, 22*, 258–262, 2009.

Hawley, C. On the border, a crisis escalates: Mexican cartels wage a war of unprecedented violence that's spreading into the USA. *USA Today*, 1A, February, 2009.

Herzberg, D. *Happy pills in America: From Miltown to Prozac*. Baltimore, MD: Johns Hopkins University Press, 2007.

Hodgson, B. *In the arms of Morpheus: The tragic history of laudanum, morphine, and patent medicines*. Buffalo, NY: Firefly Books Inc., 2001.

Hodgson, B. *Opium: A portrait of the heavenly demon*. Vancouver, BC: Greystone Books, 1999.

Hoffmann, D.E., & Weber, E. Medical marijuana and the law. *New England Journal of Medicine, 362*, 1453–1457, 2010.

Hollister, L.E. Criminal laws and the control of drugs of abuse: An historical view of the law (or, it's the lawyer's fault). *Journal of Clinical Pharmacology, 9*, 345–348, 1969.

Howell, J.C., & Decker, S.H. *The youth gangs, drugs, and violence connection*. U.S. Department of Justice, Office of Justice Programs, Office of Juvenile Justice and Delinquency Prevention (NCJ 171152). Washington, DC: Author, January 1999.

Huber, C. Needle Park: What can we learn from the Zürich experience? *Addiction, 89*, 513–516, 1994.

Inciardi, J. *The war on drugs IV: The continuing saga of the mysteries and miseries of intoxication, addiction, crime, and public policy, 4th edition*. Boston, MA: Allyn and Bacon, 2007.

Inciardi, J.A. Beyond cocaine: Basuco, crack, and other coca products. *Contemporary Drug Problems, 14*, 461–492, 1987.

Isikoff, M. Bennett's anti-drug initiative making little headway in D.C. *Washington Post*, A1, October 17, 1989.

Isikoff, M. Drug buy set up for Bush speech; DEA lured seller to Lafayette Park. *The Washington Post*, A1, September 22, 1989.

Jacobs, A. Battling HIV where sex meets crystal meth. *The New York Times*, February 21, 2006.

Jaffe, J.H. One bite of the apple: Establishing the Special Action Office for Drug Abuse Prevention. In D.F. Musto (Ed.) *One hundred years of heroin* (pp. 43–54). Westport, CT: Greenwood Publishing, 2002.

Jaffe, J.H. A follow-up of Vietnam drug users: Origins and context of Lee Robins classic study. *American Journal on Addictions, 19*, 212–214, 2010.

Johnson, N. (2010). *Boardwalk empire: The birth, high times, and corruption of Atlantic City*. Medford, NJ: Plexus Publishing.

Johnston, L.D., O'Malley, P.M., Bachman, J.G., & Schulenberg, J.E. *Monitoring the Future: National survey results on drug use, 1975–2010, Volume 1*. Ann Arbor, MI: Institute for Social Research, University of Michigan. Retrieved from http://www.monitoringthefuture.org/pubs.html#reports, 2011.

Jonnes, J. *Hep-cats, narcs, and pipe dreams: A history of America's romance with illegal drugs*. New York: Scribner, 1996.

Jonsson, P. US prisoners sentenced under strict crack cocaine laws get relief. *The Christian Science Monitor*. Retrieved from http://www.csmonitor.com/USA/Justice/2011/0630/US-prisoners-sentenced-under-strict-crack-cocaine-laws-get-relief, June 30, 2011.

Joplin, J. *Love, Janis*. New York: Harper, 2005.

Kahn, G., & Hirschfield, A. *The speakeasies of 1932: Over 400 drawings, paintings, and photos*. New York: Glenn Young Books/Applause, 2005.

Kandel, D.B. *Stages and pathways of drug involvement: Examining the Gate-way hypothesis*. Cambridge, MA: Cambridge University Press, 2002.

Kantor, A.F. Upton Sinclair and the Pure Food and Drugs Act of 1906: "I aimed at the public's heart and by accident I hit it in the stomach." *American Journal of Public Health*, *66*, 1202–1205, 1976.

Karch, S.B. *A brief history of cocaine, 2nd edition*. New York: CRC, 2006.

Kefauver, E. *Crime in America*. Westport, CT: Greenwood Press, 1969.

Kerouac, J. *On the road*. New York: Penguin Books, 1976.

Kerr, P. Anatomy of the drug issue: How, after years, it erupted. *The New York Times*, A1, November 17, 1986.

Kerr, P. Cocaine glut pulls New York market into drug rings' tug-of-war. *The New York Times*, B1, August 24, 1988.

Kerr, P. From center of cocaine trade to a Florida jail. *The New York Times*, A1, February 13, 1987.

Kinder, D.C., & Walker, W.O. Stable force in a storm: Harry J. Anslinger and United States narcotic foreign policy, 1930–1962. *Journal of American History*, *72*, 908–927, 1986.

Kleber, H. Methadone maintenance 4 decades later: Thousands of lives saved but still controversial. *Journal of the American Medical Association*, *300*, 2303–2305, 2008.

Kleiman, M. Neither prohibition nor legalization: Grudging toleration in drug control policy. *Daedalus*, *121*, 53–83, 1992.

Kleiman, M.A.R., Caulkins, J.P., & Hawken, A. *Drugs and drug policy: What everyone needs to know*. New York: Oxford University Press, 2011.

Kohler-Hausmann, J. "The Attila the Hun law": New York's Rockefeller drug laws and the making of a punitive state. *Journal of Social History*, *44*, 71–95, 2010.

Kolb, L., & Ossenfort, W.F. The treatment of addicts at the Lexington Hospital. *Southern Medical Journal*, *31*, 914–920, 1938.

Kornblum, W. Drug legalization and the minority poor. *The Millbank Quarterly*, 69, 415–435, 1991.

Kristof, N. Drugs won the war. *The New York Times*. Retrieved from http://www.nytimes.com/2009/06/14/opinion/14kristof.html, June 13, 2009.

Krogh, E. Heroin politics and policy under President Nixon. In: D.F. Musto (Ed.) *One hundred years of heroin* (pp. 39–42). Westport, CT: Greenwood Publishing, 2002.

Kyvig, D.E. *Repealing national prohibition*. Kent, OH: Kent State University Press, 2000.

Lansky, A., Brooks, J.T., DiNenno, E., Heffelfinger, J., Hall, H.I., & Mermin, J. Epidemiology of HIV in the United States. *Journal of Acquired Immunodeficiency Syndromes, 15*(Suppl 2), S64–S68, 2010.

Lattin, D. *The Harvard psychedelic club: How Timothy Leary, Ram Dass, Huston Smith, and Andrew Weil killed the fifties and ushered in a new age for America*. New York: HarperCollins, 2011.

Leary, T. *Turn on, tune in, drop out*. Oakland, CA: Ronin Publishing, 1999.

Lee, M.A., & Shlain, B. *Acid dreams. The complete social history of LSD: The CIA, the sixties, and beyond*. New York: Grove Press, 1992.

Leshner, A. Science based views of drug addiction and its treatment. *Journal of the American Medical Association, 282*, 1314–1316, 1999.

Levine, H.G., & Reinarman, C. From Prohibition to regulation: Lessons from alcohol policy for drug policy. *The Milbank Quarterly, 69*, 461–494, 1991.

Lindesmith, A.R. A sociological theory of drug addiction. *American Journal of Sociology, 43*, 593–613, 1938.

Lindesmith, A.R. Can chimpanzees become morphine addicts? *Journal of Comparative Psychology, 39*, 109–117, 1946.

Llana, S.M. Mexico drug war death toll up 60 percent in 2010. Why? *The Christian Science Monitor,* January 13, 2011.

Longmire, S. *Cartel: The invasion of Mexico's drug wars*. New York: Palgrave Macmillan, 2011.

Lowry, R. Our hero, heroin. *National Review*, October 28, 1996.

Lytle Mark, H. *America's uncivil wars: The sixties era: From Elvis to the fall of Richard Nixon*. New York: Oxford University Press, 2006.

MacCoun, R.J. Drugs and the law: A psychological analysis of drug prohibition. *Psychological Bulletin, 113*, 497–512, 1993.

MacCoun, R.J. Toward a psychology of harm reduction. *American Psychologist, 53*, 1199–1208, 1998.

MacCoun, R.J. What can we learn from the Dutch cannabis coffeeshop system? *Addiction, 105*, 1899–1910, 2011.

MacCoun, R.J., & Reuter, P. *Drug war heresies: Learning from other vices, times, & places*. New York: Cambridge University Press, 2001.

Macleod, J., & Hickman, M. How ideology shapes the evidence and the policy: What do we know about cannabis use and what should we do? *Addiction, 105*, 1326–1330, 2010.

Manchikanti, L. National drug control policy and prescription drug abuse: Facts and fallacies. *Pain Physician, 10*, 399–404, 2007.

Markel, H. *An anatomy of addiction: Sigmund Freud, William Halsted, and the miracle drug cocaine*. New York: Pantheon Books, 2011.

Marlatt, G.A., & Witkiewitz, K. Update on harm-reduction policy and intervention research. *Annual Review of Clinical Psychology, 6*, 591–606, 2010.

Massing, M. The two William Bennetts. *The New York Review of Books*, March 1, 1990.

Massing, M. The war on cocaine. *The New York Review of Books*, December 22, 1988.

Massing, M. Crime and drugs: The new myths. *The New York Review of Books*, February 1, 1996.

Massing, M. *The fix*. New York: Simon & Shuster, 1998.

Massing, M. The narco-state? *The New York Review of Books*, June 15, 2002.

Massing, M. What ever happened to the war on drugs? *The New York Review of Books*, June 11, 1992.

Maxwell, J.C., & Rutkowski, B.A. The prevalence of methamphetamine and amphetamine abuse in North America: A review of indicators, 1992–2007. *Drug & Alcohol Review, 27*, 229–235, 2008.

Mayor's Committee on Marihuana. *The Marihuana problem in the City of New York: Sociological, medical, psychological and pharmacological studies*. Metuchen, NJ: Scarecrow Reprint Co., 1973.

McAdams, L. *Birth of the cool: Beat, bebop, and the American avant-garde*. New York: The Free Press, 2001.

McAuliffe, W.E., & Gordon, R.A. A test of Lindesmith's theory of addiction: The frequency of euphoria among long-term addicts. *American Journal of Sociology, 79*, 795–840, 1974.

McCoy, A.W. *The politics of heroin: CIA complicity in the global drug trade, 1st edition*. Brooklyn, NY: Lawrence Hill Books, 1991.

McKinley, J. California pulling back on medical marijuana. *The International Herald Tribune*, p. 2, June 10, 2008.

McLellan, A.T. What we need is a system: Creating a responsive and effective substance abuse treatment system. In: W.R. Miller & K.M. Carroll (Eds.) *Rethinking substance abuse: What the science shows, and what we should do about it* (pp. 275–92). New York: Guilford Press, 2006.

McNally, D. *Desolate angel: Jack Kerouac, the beat generation and America.* Cambridge, MA: DeCapo Press, 2003.

McWilliams, J.C. *The protectors: Harry J. Anslinger and the Federal Bureau of Narcotics*. Newark, DE: University of Delaware Press, 1989.

McWilliams, J.C. (1989). Unsung partner against crime: Harry J. Anslinger and the Federal Bureau of Narcotics, 1930–1962. *Pennsylvania Magazine of History and Biography, 113*, 207–236, 1989.

Mendelson, J., Flower, K., Pletcher, M.J., & Galloway, G.P. Addiction to prescription opioids: Characteristics of the emerging epidemic and treatment with buprenorphine. *Experimental and Clinical Psychopharmacology, 16*, 435–441, 2008.

Mezzerow, M., & Wolfe, B. *Really the blues*. New York: Citadel Press, 1946.

Miller, B. Narcotics "expert" said to be fraud: Witness to D.C. criminal's cases is charged with perjury. *Washington Post*, B8, February 4, 2000.

Miron, J.A. Violence and the U.S. prohibitions of drug and alcohol, *American Law and Economics Review, 1*, 78–114, 1999.

Montagnier, L. 25 years after HIV discovery: Prospects for cure and vaccine. *Virology, 20*, 248–254, 2010.

Moore William, H. The Kefauver Committee and the politics of crime. Columbia, MO: University of Missouri Press, 1974.

Morganthau, T., Greenberg, N.H., Murr, A., Miller, M., & Raine, G. Crack and crime. *Newsweek Magazine*, National Affairs, p. 16, June 16, 1986.

Musto, D. A study in cocaine: Sherlock Holmes and Sigmund Freud. *Journal of the American Medical Association, 204*, 27–32, 1968.

Musto, D. America's first cocaine epidemic. *Wilson Quarterly, 13*, 59–64, 1989.

Musto, D. *The American disease: Origins of narcotics control, 3rd edition*. New York: Oxford University Press, 1999.

Musto, D. F., & Korsmeyer, P. *The quest for drug control: Politics and federal policy in a period of increasing substance abuse (1963–1981)*. New Haven, CT: Yale University Press, 2002.

Nieves, E. Drug labs in valley hideouts feed nation's habit. *The New York Times*, A1, May 13, 2001.

Nurco, D. N., Ball, J. C., Shaffer, J. W., & Hanlon, T. E. The criminality of narcotic addicts. *Journal of Nervous and Mental Disease, 173*, 94–102, 1985.

Nutt, D. J., King, L. A., & Phillips, L. D. Drug harms in the UK: A multicriteria decision analysis. *Lancet, 376*, 1558–1565, 2010.

Office of National Drug Control Policy Methamphetamine trends in the United States: Fact Sheet. Washington, DC.: Author. Retrieved from http://www.whitehousedrugpolicy.gov/publications/html/pseudoephedrine.html, 2010.

Okrent, D. *Last call: The rise and fall of prohibition*. New York: Scribner, 2010.

Okrent, D., & Wayne B. Wheeler: The man who turned off the taps. *Smithsonian Magazine*, May, 2010.

Oshinsky, D. M. *A conspiracy so immense: The world of Joe McCarthy*. New York: Oxford University Press, 2005.

Ostrow, D. Substance abuse and HIV infection. *Psychiatric Clinics of North America, 17*, 69–89, 1994.

Palmateer, N., Kimber, J., Hickman, M., Hutchinson, S., Rhodes, T., & Goldberg, D. Evidence for the effectiveness of sterile injecting equipment provision in preventing hepatitis C and human immunodeficiency virus transmission among injecting drug users: A review of reviews. *Addiction, 105*, 844–859, 2010.

Pearson, G. *Drug-control policies in Britain. Crime and Justice, 14*, 167–177, 1991.

Peck, G. *The Prohibition hangover: Alcohol in America from demon rum to cult cabernet*. New Brunswick, NJ: Rutgers University Press, 2009.

Pegram, T. R. *Battling demon rum: The struggle for a dry America, 1800–1933 (The American Ways Series)*. Landham, MD: Ivan R. Dee, 1999.

Perez-Reverte, A. *The queen of the south*. New York: G. P. Putnam's Sons, 2004.

Perry, C. *The Haight-Ashbury: A history, 1st Edition*. New York: Wenner Media, 2005.

Podhoretz, N. The know-nothing bohemians. Reprinted in *The Norman Podhoretz reader: A selection of his writings from the 1950s through the 1990s* (pp. 29–40). Simon & Schuster: New York, NY, 2004.

Prato, G. *Grunge is dead: The oral history of Seattle rock music*. Toronto, ON: ECW Press, 2009.

President's advisory commission on narcotic and drug abuse—final report. Washington, DC: Government Printing Office, 1963.

Provine, D. M. *Unequal under the law: Race in the war on drugs*. Chicago, IL: The University of Chicago Press, 2007.

Public Law 78–797 (Opium Poppy Control Act), December 11, 1942.

Quinones, M. A. Drug abuse during the Civil War (1861–1865). *International Journal of the Addictions, 10*, 1007–1020, 1975.

Raffa, R. B., & Pergolizzi, J. V. Opioid formulations designed to resist deter abuse. *Drugs, 70*, 1657–1675, 2010.

Rasmussen, N. *On speed: The many lives of amphetamine*. New York: New York University Press, 2009.

Reinarman, C., & Levine, H. G. The crack attack: Politics and media in the crack scare. In: C. Reinarman & H. G. Levine (Eds.) *Crack in America: Demon drugs and social justice* (pp. 18–52). Berkeley, CA: University of California Press, 1997.

Reinarman, C., Waldordf, D., Murphy, S. B., & Levine, H. G. The contingent call of the pipe: Bingeing and addiction among heavy cocaine smokers. In: C. Reinarman & H. G. Levine (Eds.) *Crack in America: Demon drugs and social justice* (pp. 77–97). Berkeley, CA: University of California Press, 1997.

Rensenberger, B. Amphetamines used by a physician to lift moods of famous patients. *The New York Times, 1*, 34–35, December 4, 1972.

Reuter, P. Hawks ascendant: The punitive trend of American drug policy. *Daedalus, 121*, 15–52, Summer, 1992.

Reuter, P. Why can't we make prohibition work better? Some consequences of ignoring the unattractive. *Proceedings of the American Philosophical Society, 141*, 262–275, 1997.

Reuter, P. Why has research had so little impact on drug policy? *Addiction*, 96, 373–376, 2001.

Reuter, P., & Kleiman, M. Risks and prices: An economic analysis of drug enforcement. *Crime and Justice, 7*, 289–340, 1986.

Reuter, P., & Pollack, H. How much can treatment reduce national drug problems? *Addiction, 101*, 341–347, 2006.

Rinfret, M. Cocaine price, purity, and trafficking trends. In: S. Schober & C. Schade (Eds.) *The epidemiology of cocaine use and abuse* (pp. 297–303). NIDA Research Monograph Series 110 (ADM 91–1787). Rockville, MD: U.S. Department of Health and Human Services, 1991.

Robins, L. N., Helzer, J. E., Hesselbrock, M., & Wish, E. Vietnam veterans three years after Vietnam: How our study changed our view of heroin. *The American Journal on Addictions, 19*, 203–211, 2010.

Room, R., Fischer, B., Hall, W., Lenton, S., & Reuter, P. *Cannabis policy: Moving beyond the stalemate*. New York: Oxford University Press, 2010.

Room, R. Rethinking alcohol, tobacco and other drug control. *Addiction*, 98, 713–716, 2003.

Rosenberg, D. How one town got hooked. *Newsweek*, Society, 48, April 9, 2001.

Ross, M. W., & Williams, M. L. Sexual behavior and illicit drug use. *Annual Review of Sex Research, 12*, 290–310, 2001.

Rouse, B. Trends in cocaine use in the general population. In: S. Schober & C. Schade (Eds.) *The epidemiology of cocaine use and abuse* (pp. 5–18). NIDA Research Monograph Series 110 (ADM 91–1787). Rockville, MD: U.S. Department of Health and Human Services, 1991.

Rowaniak, S. Safe sex fatigue, treatment optimism, and serosorting: New challenges to HIV prevention among men who have sex with men. *Journal of the Association of Nurses in AIDS Care, 20*, 31–38, 2009.

Rush, B. *An inquiry into the effects of ardent spirits upon the human body and mind, with an account of the means of preventing, and of the remedies for curing them* (1785), reprinted in *Medical Inquiries and Observations*. New York: Arno, 1972.

Russell, R. *Bird lives! The high life and hard times of Charlie (Yardbird) Parker*. New York: Charterhouse, 1973.

Samuels, D. How medical marijuana is transforming the pot industry. *The New Yorker, 84*, 49, July 28, 2008.

Schneider, E. C. *Smack: Heroin and the American city*. Philadelphia, PA: University of Pennsylvania Press, 2008.

Schou, N. Kill the messenger: *How the CIA's crack-cocaine controversy destroyed journalist Gary Webb*. New York: Nation Books, 2006.

Schuckit, M. A. *Drug and alcohol abuse*. New York: Springer, 2010.

Seelke, C. R., & Finklea, K. M. *The U.S.-Mexican security cooperation: The Mérida Initiative and beyond: CRS report for Congress*. Washington, DC: Congressional Research Service, August 15, 2011.

Server, L. *Robert Mitchum: Baby, I don't care*. New York: St. Martin's Press, 2001.

Shah, S. Living with HIV in the shadow of the White House. *Lancet, 376*, 223–224, 2010.

Shapiro, B. The corruption of Col. James Hiett. *Salon Magazine*. Retrieved from http://www.salon.com/news/feature/2000/07/05/hiett/index.html, July 5, 2000.

Shattock, R. J., Warren, M., McCormack, S., & Hankins, C. A. Turning the tide against HIV. *Science, 333*, 42–43, July 1, 2011.

Sheff, N. *Tweak: Growing up on methamphetamines*. New York: Atheneum Books, 2009.

Shenk, J. W. Hooked on dogma; U.S. drug warriors ignore Switzerland's success. *Washington Post*, C1, December 21, 1997.

Shilts, R. *And the band played on: Politics, people, and the AIDS Epidemic, 20th Anniversary Edition*. New York: St. Martin's Griffin, 2007.

Siegel, R. K. Cocaine smoking: Nature and extent of coca paste and cocaine free-base abuse. In: A. M. Washton & M. S. Gold (Eds.) *Cocaine: A clinician's handbook* (pp. 175–191). New York: Guilford Press, 1987.

Siegel, R. K. Repeating cycles of cocaine use and abuse. In: D. R. Gerstein & H. J. Harwood (Eds.) *Treating drug problems—Volume 2* (pp. 289–316). Washington, DC: National Academy Press, 1992.

Sloman, L. R. *Reefer madness: A history of marijuana*. New York: St. Martins Griffin Edition, 1998.

Sneader, W. The discovery of heroin. *Lancet, 352*, 1697–1699, 1998.

Speaker, S. From "Happiness Pills" to "National Nightmare": Changing cultural assessment of minor tranquilizers in America, 1955–1980. *Journal of the History of Medicine and Allied Sciences, 52*, 338–376, 1997.

Special to The New York Times: Belushi's death attributed to heroin and cocaine. *The New York Times*, A22, March 10, 1982.

Spillane, J. F. Debating the controlled substances act. *Drug and Alcohol Dependence, 76*, 17–29, 2004.

Spindler, A. M. A death tarnishes fashion's "heroin look." *The New York Times*, A1, May 20, 1997.

Steuart, J. *Wayne wheeler, dry boss: An uncensored biography of Wayne B. Wheeler*. Santa Barbara, CA: Greenwood Press, 1971.

Stimson, G. V., & Oppenheimer, O. *Heroin addiction: Treatment and control in Britain*. London: Tavistock, 1982.

Strang, J. Ruben, S., Farrell, M. et al. The history of prescribing heroin and other injectable drugs as addiction treatment in the UK. In: J. Strang and M. Gossop (Eds.) *Heroin addiction and the British system: Treatment and policy responses, volume 2* (pp. 1–16). New York: Routledge, 2005.

Subcommittee on Criminal Justice, Drug Policy, and Human Resources. *Committee on Government Reform House of Pros and cons of drug legalization, decriminalization, and harm reduction* (Serial No. 106–99). Washington, DC: U.S. Government Printing Office, Representatives June 16, 1999.

Swift, W., Coffey, C., Degenhardt, L., et al. Cannabis and progression to other substance use in young adults: Findings from a 13-year prospective population-based study. *Journal of Epidemiology and Community Health*, eprint, 2011.

Tarabar, A. F., & Nelson, L. S. The resurgence and abuse of heroin by children in the United States. *Current Opinion in Pediatrics*, *15*, 210–215, 2003.

Taxation of Marijuana, Hearings before the Committee on Ways and Means, U.S. House of Representatives, 75th Cong., Ist Sess., on H.R. 6385, April 27–30 and May 4, 1937. Washington D.C.: U.S, Government Printing Office, 1937.

Taxman, F. S., & Bouffard, J. Treatment inside the drug treatment court: The who, what, where, and how of treatment services. *Substance Use and Misuse*, *37*, 1665–1688, 2002.

Terry, C. E., & Pellens, M. *The opium problem* (Bureau of Social Hygiene, reprint from 1928). Montclair, NJ: Patterson Smith Publishing, 1970.

38 Slain in Four Years of Inter-gang Warfare. *Chicago Daily Tribune*, 2. February 15, 1929.

Thomas, E. "I am addicted to prescription pain medication." *Newsweek Magazine*, Society, p. 42, October 20, 2003.

Tone, A. *The age of anxiety: America's turbulent affair with tranquilizers*. New York: Basic Books, 2009.

Trafford, A., & Thompson, L. The muddled state of AIDS policy. *The Washington Post*, T16, August 23, 1988.

Treaster, J. B. Echoes of prohibition: 20 years of war on drugs, and no victory yet. *The New York Times*, Section 4, p. 7, June 14, 1992.

Treaster, J. B. The 1992 campaign: Candidates' records; four years of Bush's drug war: New funds but an old strategy. *The New York Times*, A1, July 28, 1992.

Trebach, A. S. Lessons from needle park. *Washington Post*, A17, March 17, 1992.

Uchtenhagen, A. A. Heroin maintenance treatment: From idea to research to practice. *Drug and Alcohol Review*. *30*, 130–137, 2011.

Van de Water, F. *The real* McCoy. Mystic, CT: Flat Hammock Press, 2007.

Van Gundy, K., & Rebellon, C. J. A life-course perspective on the "Gateway Hypothesis." *Addiction*, *51*, 244–259, 2010.

Vaughn, M. G., Perron, B. E., & Howard, M. O. Is crack cocaine use associated with greater violence than powdered cocaine use? Results from a national sample. *The American Journal of Drug and Alcohol Abuse*, *36*, 181–186, 2010.

Veilleux, J. C., Colvin, P. J., Anderson, J., York, C., & Heinz, A. J. A review of opioid dependence treatment: Pharmacological and psychological interventions to treat opioid addiction. *Clinical Psychology Review*, *30*, 155–166, 2010.

Warner-Smith, M., Darke, S., Lynskey, M., & Hall, W. Heroin overdose: Causes and consequences. *Addiction*, *96*, 1113–1125, 2001.

Weatherburn, D. Dilemmas in harm minimization. *Addiction, 104*, 335–339, 2009.

Webb, G. *Dark alliance: The CIA, the contras, and the crack cocaine explosion*. New York: Seven Stories Press:, 1999.

Weisheit, R., & White, W.L. *Methamphetamine: Its history, pharmacology, and treatment*. Center City, MN: Hazeldon, 2009.

Werb, D., Rowell, G., Guyatt, G., Kerr, T. et al. Effect of drug law enforcement on drug market violence: A systematic review. *International Journal of Drug Policy, 22*, 87–94, 2011.

Western, B., & Pettit, B. Incarceration and social inequality. *Daedalus, 139*, 8–19, 2010.

White, H.R., & Gorman, D.M. Dynamics of the drug-crime relationship. In: G. LaFree (Ed.) *Criminal justice 2000, volume I the nature of crime: Continuity and change* (pp. 151–218). Washington, DC: U.S. Department of Justice, 2000.

White, W. *Slaying the dragon*. Bloomington, IL: Chestnut Health Systems, 1998.

Wilson, J.Q., & Kelling, G. Broken windows: The police and neighborhood safety. *The Atlantic Monthly, 249*, 29–38, 1982.

Woestendiek, J. An old killer strikes teens/Heroin? In the affluent suburbs? *The Philadelphia Inquirer*, A01, February 15, 1998.

Wolfe, T. *The electric kool-aid acid test*. New York: Oxford University Press, 1999.

Woodman, Z., & Williamson, C. HIV molecular epidemiology: Transmission and adaptation to human populations. *Current Opinion in HIV and AIDS, 4*, 247–252, 2009.

Wren, C.S. Clinton calls fashion ads' "heroin chic" deplorable. *The New York Times*, May 22, 1997.

Yardley, W. New federal crackdown confounds states that allow medical marijuana. *The New York Times*, A13, May 8, 2011.

Zimring, F. How New York City beat crime. *Scientific American, 305*, 74–79, 2011.

Zimring, F.E., & Hawkins, G. *The search for rational drug control*. New York: Cambridge University Press, 1995.

INDEX

About the Author

James A. Swartz, PhD, is an associate professor in the Jane Addams College of Social Work at the University of Illinois at Chicago where he has taught on mental health policy including drug policy, research and statistics, and program evaluation for the past 10 years. He earned his doctorate in clinical psychology in 1990 from the Northwestern University Medical School, Department of Psychiatry and Medical Sciences. His research interests and the subjects of his more recent peer-reviewed publications include: co-occurring health conditions, substance use disorders, and mental illnesses; screening and diagnosis; HIV/AIDS prevention and intervention for high-risk populations; and the use of technology to improve the delivery of behavioral health care and prevention services.